Data Analytics in Cognitive Linguistics

Applications of Cognitive Linguistics

Editors
Gitte Kristiansen
Francisco J. Ruiz de Mendoza Ibáñez

Honorary editor
René Dirven

Volume 41

Data Analytics in Cognitive Linguistics

Methods and Insights

Edited by
Dennis Tay
Molly Xie Pan

ISBN 978-3-11-135346-3
e-ISBN (PDF) 978-3-11-068727-9
e-ISBN (EPUB) 978-3-11-068734-7
ISSN 1861-4078

Library of Congress Control Number: 2022935004

Bibliographic information published by the Deutsche Nationalbibliothek
The Deutsche Nationalbibliothek lists this publication in the Deutsche Nationalbibliografie;
detailed bibliographic data are available on the Internet at http://dnb.dnb.de.

Chapter "Lectal variation in Chinese analytic causative constructions: What trees can and
cannot tell us" © Xiaoyu Tian, Weiwei Zhang and Dirk Speelman

© 2023 Walter de Gruyter GmbH, Berlin/Boston
This volume is text- and page-identical with the hardback published in 2022.
Typesetting: Integra Software Services Pvt. Ltd.
Printing and binding: CPI books GmbH, Leck

www.degruyter.com

Contents

Dennis Tay, Molly Xie Pan
Data analytics in cognitive linguistics —— 1

Bodo Winter
Mapping the landscape of exploratory and confirmatory data analysis in linguistics —— 13

Dennis Tay
Time series analysis with python —— 49

Matteo Fuoli
Structural equation modeling in R: A practical introduction for linguists —— 75

Mariana Montes, Kris Heylen
Visualizing distributional semantics —— 103

Xiaoyu Tian, Weiwei Zhang, Dirk Speelman
Lectal variation in Chinese analytic causative constructions: What trees can and cannot tell us —— 137

Molly Xie Pan
Personification metaphors in Chinese video ads: Insights from data analytics —— 169

Han Qiu, Dennis Tay
The interaction between metaphor use and psychological states: A mix-method analysis of trauma talk in the Chinese context —— 197

Jane Dilkes
Prospecting for metaphors in a large text corpus: Combining unsupervised and supervised machine learning approaches —— 229

Jonathan Dunn
Cognitive linguistics meets computational linguistics: Construction grammar, dialectology, and linguistic diversity —— 273

Karlien Franco
What Cognitive Linguistics can learn from dialectology (and vice versa) —— 309

Index —— 345

Dennis Tay, Molly Xie Pan
Data analytics in cognitive linguistics

1 Is data analytics just another name for statistical analysis?

Data analytics is commonly defined as the "processing and analysis of data to extract information for enhancing knowledge and decision-making", with minor differences among definitions. Although large amounts of data are collected non-stop around the clock, people still describe today's world with the old phrase "data rich but information poor" (Peters and Waterman 1982). The process of turning data into useful information is like finding "a small set of precious nuggets from a great deal of raw material" (Han et al. 2000: 5–6), and would indeed seem like a daunting task to the unacquainted. On the other hand, those who have received some training in general data analysis, including many linguists, might see data analytics as little more than an attempt to refashion applied statistics and quantitative methods in a more marketable way. The gist of it still appears to be making sense of data in numerical rather than verbal or qualitative forms, and popular techniques like clustering and regression still bear the same name as when they were taught in traditional statistics courses. There is some merit to this cynicism given that we live in a world where it seems to be important to put a new spin on old things all the time. However, we would be remiss to overlook some nuanced but important differences between the two. The first difference is that while most data analytic techniques are indeed based on quantitative and statistical methods, there is a strong emphasis on the importance of *substantive expertise* (Conway 2010) or *domain knowledge* in order to maximize their potential for insight. This follows from the fact that just about any type of data from historical archives to complex multimodal artifacts can be viewed from the lenses of data analytic techniques as long as there are good theoretical or practical reasons for doing so. It also means that general statistical methods like classification and regression are continuously adopted to meet the specific needs

---

Acknowledgement: The editorial work involved in this volume was partly supported by the HKSAR Research Grants Council (Project number: 15601019).

Dennis Tay, Department of English and Communication, The Hong Kong Polytechnic University, e-mail: dennis.tay@polyu.edu.hk
Molly Xie Pan, College of Foreign Languages and Literatures, Fudan University, e-mail: mollyxiaoxie@foxmail.com

https://doi.org/10.1515/9783110687279-001

of different domains like business (Chen et al. 2012) and healthcare (Raghupathi and Raghupathi 2014), with ever expanding functions, applications, and specialized interpretations of models and results. The second difference pertains to a perceived difference in scope between the two. There is a tendency among many novice and experienced researchers alike to view statistical analysis as a set of standard 'tests' that are applied to measurements collected under some strictly controlled guidelines in order to determine whether some hypothesis is 'correct' or otherwise. This seems to be especially true in the field of applied linguistics where testing, assessment, and other forms of measurement are commonplace. The typical question *which test should I use?* is often answered by convenient heuristical tools like flow charts, abundantly available on the internet, that attempt to link stock scenarios like 'comparing the means of two groups' or 'comparing the means of three or more groups' to the t-test, one-way ANOVA, and so on. While this approach of 'choosing the correct test to use' might be convenient and helpful for learners, it reinforces the narrow view that statistical analysis is all about trying to prove or disprove a hypothesis at a specific stage of the research process. This in turn makes it easy to see statistical analysis as an independent set of procedures that apply to all types of, and are hence divorced from, specific subject matter knowledge. Data analytics, on the other hand, is more in line with the broader notion of *statistical thinking* that has been gaining traction in modern statistics education. There are many different definitions of statistical thinking but they all focus on cultivating a "more global view" (Chance 2002) in learners right from the start. For researchers, this means learning to see data analysis as holistic and contextual, rather than linear and procedural. Some concrete steps to do so include exploring and visualizing data in new and creative ways, understanding why a certain analytical procedure is used rather than what or how to use it, reflecting constantly on alternative approaches to think about the data and situation at hand, appreciating how subject matter and contextual knowledge can potentially shape analytic decisions, and learning how to interpret conclusions in non-statistical terms. Compared to the traditional conception of statistical analysis described above, we can therefore describe data analytics as encompassing a more exploratory spirit, being 'messier' in a positive sense, and even as a means to inspire emergent research questions rather than a resolution of existing ones. At the same time, data analytics can also be described as being very context-specific and purpose driven, and thus potentially more engaging for focused learners than what the traditional 'decontextualized' view of statistics presents. Tools for the actual implementation of data analytic techniques on increasingly large volumes of data have also become more available today. Powerful open-source programming languages like *R* and *Python* are continuously developed and freely available to personal users, which can be a great relief for many learners relying on expensive commercial statistical software packages like *SPSS*, *Stata*, *MATLAB* etc.

Data analytics can be classified as four subtypes(Evans and Lindner 2012) in order of increasing complexity and value-addedness (Figure 1). Originally conceived for business contexts where complexity and value are measured in relatively concrete financial terms, these notions also have meaningful interpretations for researchers. We may understand the four subtypes as representing progressive phases of inquiry into a certain dataset. Descriptive analytics is roughly synonymous with the classic notion of descriptive statistics. It involves summarizing and depicting data in intuitive and accessible ways, often to prepare for later phases of analysis. A simple example is to depict the central tendency and distribution of a dataset with box plots or histograms. With an increasing premium placed on visual aesthetics and user engagement, however, data visualization has become a growing field in itself, with increasingly sophisticated and interactive forms of visualization driving the development of contemporary descriptive analytics. The next subtype or phase known as diagnostic analytics involves discovering relationships in the data using various statistical techniques. It is deemed more complex and valuable than descriptive analytics because the connections between different aspects of our data help us infer potential causes underlying observed effects, addressing the *why* behind the *what*. In an applied linguistics context, for example, the descriptive step of uncovering significant differences in the mean scores of student groups might motivate a broader correlational study of scores and demographics to diagnose potential sociocultural factors that explain this difference. Following that, if we see diagnostic analytics as revealing why something might have happened in the past, the next phase known as predictive analytics is aimed at telling us what might happen in the future. This involves predicting the values of future data points using present and historical data points, supported by core techniques like regression, classification, and time series analysis. It should be clear why predictive analytics represents a quantum leap in value for businesses that are inherently forward looking. To a lesser extent perhaps, the same applies for linguistics research that aims to predictively categorize new texts, speakers, and varieties, or forecast language assessment scores, based on existing data. As ever-increasing volumes of data become available, both diagnostic and predictive analytics are turning towards machine learning – the use of artificial intelligence to quickly identify patterns, build models, and make decisions with little or no human intervention. Applications in computational linguistics and natural language processing (NLP) best reflect these advances in the field of linguistics research. Lastly, prescriptive analytics fill the gap between knowing and doing by translating the above insights into concrete courses of action. It goes beyond knowing what is likely to happen based on predictive analytics, which may or may not be ideal, to suggest what needs to be done to optimize outcomes. Examples that require split-second decisions to everchanging information and conditions include the optimization of airline prices, staffing in large organizations, and the modern self-driving car. While linguistics is not likely to involve this level of challenge, prescriptive analytics still interfaces with the ubiquitous notion of applied or *appliable* research, which ultimately boils down to the growing need to demonstrate how our findings positively inform personal and social action.

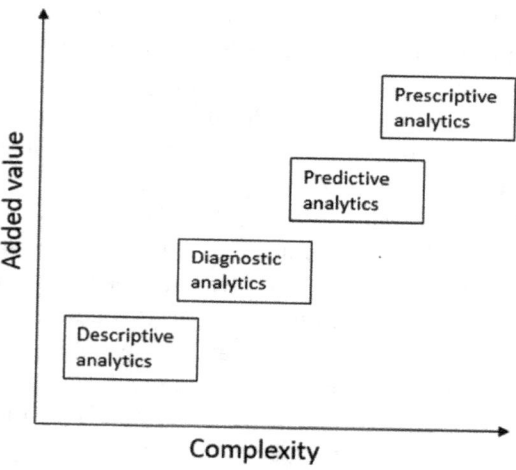

Figure 1: Four subtypes of data analytics.

2 Data analytics in cognitive linguistics

Cognitive linguistics has undergone remarkable development since its inception. Luminaries of the field like George Lakoff, Leonard Talmy, Ronald Langacker, Charles Fillmore, and Gilles Fauconnier established some of the most influential theories about the interfaces between linguistic meaning, structure, and cognition, basing much of their introspective analyses on made-up examples. This mode of inquiry has however come to be criticized on both philosophical and methodological grounds over the years. Philosophically, reliance on introspection reduces "cognition" to psychological reality and neglects its neurobiological underpinnings (Lamb 1999). This is often reflected in the common use of the terminology "mind/brain" to conflate the two for analytic convenience.

The use of introspective examples has also been susceptible to charges of argumentative circularity, like in the case of conceptual metaphor theory where invented utterances are taken as both evidence and product of conceptual mappings (Kertész and Rákosi 2009). More generally, there are obvious limitations to our ability as humans to accurately introspect upon many of our cognitive processes (Gibbs 2006). The concern motivating the present volume is more methodological in nature. The past decades have witnessed steady growth in the (combined) use of empirical methods like corpora, surveys, and experimentation in humanities research in general and cognitive linguistics in particular (Gibbs 2007, 2010; Kertész et al. 2012). A key argument for empirical over introspective methods in cognitive linguistics is their compatibility with the basic tenet that linguistic structure and meaning emerge from *multiple usage contexts*. These are inherently beyond the introspective ambit of individuals, and we therefore need transparent methods that can deal with measures and their variability on larger scales. This 'empirical turn' has at the same time dovetailed with the call for cognitive linguistics to demonstrate its applications in real world activities, including but not limited to the traditional areas of language acquisition and education. Many examples in the Applications of Cognitive Linguistics book series have powerfully illustrated this point.

The above conditions imply that cognitive linguistics – as a specialized knowledge domain aspiring to be truly "applied" – presents a fertile but underexplored ground for data analytics. While not all empirical methods are quantitative in nature, the majority used by cognitive linguists including corpora, surveys, and experiments do involve different extents of quantification and statistical analysis. There is certainly no lack of advocacy, pedagogy, and application of quantitative and statistical methods by cognitive linguists interested in different topics ranging from metaphor and metonymy to constructions and lexical semantics (Glynn and Robinson 2014; Gonzalez-Marquez et al. 2007; Janda 2013; Tay 2017; Winter 2019; Zhang 2016). A cursory review of articles in specialized journals like *Cognitive Linguistics*, *Review of Cognitive Linguistics* and *Cognitive Linguistic Studies* quickly shows that there is an increasing use of quantitative methods in theoretical and empirical work alike. We are fortunate to already have many examples of textbooks, introductory overviews, step-by-step guides, as well as more advanced applications of a wide variety of statistical methods to analyze linguistic data. However, with respect to the distinct features of data analytics outlined above, two aspects remain critically underexplored in the cognitive linguistics literature. Firstly, existing work has made ample use of *descriptive analytics* to account for data, *diagnostic analytics* to investigate hypotheses, and *predictive analytics* to make inferences about patterns of language use. It nevertheless stops short at *prescriptive analytics*; i.e. suggesting concrete courses of action, which is crucial if cognitive linguistics wishes to be truly "applied". This goes beyond the traditional ambit of language acquisition and pedagogy (Achard and Niemeier 2008; Littlemore 2009) to other contexts like advertising (Littlemore et al. 2018), design (Hurtienne et al. 2015), and aspects of healthcare where language plays a key role (Demjén et al. 2019; Tay 2013). As mentioned earlier, while linguistic research is not likely (yet) to require the most sophisticated prescriptive analytics, it is time to consider how the "practical implications" of our work could be more intimately informed by prior analytical steps and articulated as such.

The second underexplored aspect is the aforementioned holistic guiding role of data analytics throughout the research trajectory – from data description to hypothesis setting, testing, and the eventual interpretation and application of findings. This contrasts in important ways with the widely held belief that statistical and quantitative methods only apply to "top-down" investigation of experimental hypotheses determined in advance. It is in fact the case that many "bottom-up" designs across different cognitive linguistic topics – ranging from corpus-driven studies to (conceptual) metaphors in discourse – can be critically informed by various data analytic techniques. A dedicated space is required to demonstrate the different possibilities with reference to diverse areas in current cognitive linguistics research. From a pedagogical point of view, researchers new to data analytics could be made more aware that even a working familiarity with basic skills, including programming languages like *R* and *Python*, can go a long way towards the formulation and refinement of different research objectives.

3 This volume as a first step

This volume is a modest first step towards the aforementioned goals. It features ten contributions from established and up-and-coming researchers working on different aspects of cognitive linguistics. As far as practicable, the contributions vary in terms of their aims, featured languages and linguistic phenomena, the social domains in which these phenomena are embedded, the types of data analytic techniques used, and the tools with which they are implemented. Some chapters are conceptual discussions on the relationships between cognitive linguistic research and data analytics, some take a more pedagogical approach to demonstrate the application of established as well as underexplored data analytic techniques, while others elaborate these applications in with full independent case studies. Examples from multiple languages and their varieties like English, Mandarin Chinese, Dutch, French, and German will be discussed. Phenomena and constructs to be analyzed include verbal and visual metaphors, constructions, language variation, polysemy, psychological states, and prototypicality. The case studies address relevant issues in different social domains like business, advertising, politics, and mental healthcare, further underlining the applied dimensions of cognitive linguistics. The featured data analytic techniques span across descriptive, to the threshold of prescriptive analytics as described above. These include innovative ways of data visualization, machine learning and computational techniques like topic modeling, vector space models, and regression, underexplored applications in (cognitive) linguistics like time series analysis and structural equation modeling, and initial forays into prescriptive analytics in the mentioned social domains. The contributions also showcase a diverse range of implementation tools from traditional statistical software packages like *SPSS* to programming languages like *Javascript, R,* and *Python,* with code and datasets made available either in print, via external links, or upon request by contributors.

The volume starts with Chapter 1 where **Bodo Winter** provides an excellent overview of the landscape of statistical analysis in cognitive as well as general linguistics research. Framing data analysis as a process of modeling the data with respect to domain and contextual knowledge rather than the ritualistic application of statistical tests, he communicates the central message of this volume and discusses how a modeling approach could address perceived issues of replicability and reproducibility in cognitive linguistics research. This overview is followed by two tutorial-style chapters aimed at introducing useful data analytic techniques that are likely to be less familiar to cognitive linguists. In Chapter 2, **Dennis Tay** discusses the underexplored relevance of time series data – consecutive observations of a random variable in orderly chronological sequence – in cognitive linguistics research. Key steps of the widely used Box-Jenkins method, which applies a family of mathematical models called ARIMA models to express values at the present time period in terms of past periods, are explained with reference to a guiding example of metaphors across psychotherapy sessions. Sample code from the *Python* programming language is provided to encourage readers to attempt and implement the method to their own datasets. **Matteo Fuoli**'s Chapter 3 follows closely with an introduction of structural equation modelling. This is a technique for testing complex causal models among multiple related variables, and has much underexplored potential in cognitive linguistics work. Experimental data on the psychological effects of stance verbs (e.g. *know, want, believe*) in persuasive business discourse comprise the guiding example, this time using the *R* programming language for implementation. Learners might also find in these two chapters an opportunity to compare *Python* and *R* code for themselves.

The volume then transits into a series of four case studies that, as mentioned above, feature a diverse range of phenomena, settings, and data analytic techniques. In Chapter 4, **Mariana Montes** and **Kris Heylen** highlight the importance and increasing sophistication of data visualization techniques, and how they interface with processes of statistical data analysis. They argue that the process of visualization helps researchers recognize, interpret, and reason about otherwise abstract statistical patterns in more intuitive ways. The crucial role played by interactive visual analytics is then demonstrated by a corpus-based case study of Dutch, where distributional semantic models are used to analyze structural properties of word meaning like polysemy and prototypicality as they emerge from contextual usage patterns. Chapter 5 by **Xiaoyu Tian, Weiwei Zhang,** and **Dirk Speelman** is a case study of lectal variation in analytic causative constructions across three varieties of Chinese used in Mainland China, Taiwan, and Singapore. The authors are interested in how features of the cause and the effected predicate might influence the choice of near-synonymous causative markers *shi, ling,* and *rang* in these varieties. They demonstrate how a combination of data analytic techniques – conditional random forests and inference trees, complemented by logistic regression models, can enhance the explanatory power and insight offered by tree-based methods alone. We remain in the Chinese-speaking context in Chapter 6 by **Molly Xie Pan**, turning our attention to the use of personification metaphors in Chinese video advertisements. Besides showing how these metaphors are constructed and distributed across product types, with prescriptive implications for advertisers, another important objective of this chapter is to underline how data analytic techniques like log-linear and multiple correspondence analysis can guide researchers to explore larger datasets with multiple categorical variables, as a starting point to inspire subsequent research questions. Chapter 7 moves from the social domain of advertising to mental health and politics. Working with interview and psychometric data from affected individuals in the recent social unrest in Hong Kong where protestors occupied a university and disrupted its operation, **Han Qiu** and **Dennis Tay** apply multiple linear regression to analyze the interaction between metaphor usage profiles and measures of psychological trauma, interpreting the results and implications in a contextually specific way. As a step towards predictive analytics, they show how aspects of metaphor use (e.g. targets, sources, conventionality, emotional valence) at the level of individuals could reasonably predict performance in the Stanford Acute Stress Reaction Questionnaire, which in turn suggests concrete courses of actions by healthcare professionals.

The final three chapters showcase innovations in the application of data analytics, both in terms of refining methodology in established research areas as well as tilling new grounds for collaborative cross-disciplinary work. In

Chapter 8, **Jane Dilkes** discusses metaphor identification, a foundational step in metaphor research that is well known for its (over)reliance on manual human judgement. She shows how a combination of supervised and unsupervised machine learning techniques in natural language processing can be harnessed to prospect for "community metaphor themes" in an extensive online English cancer-related forum. This in turn paves the way for investigating associations between metaphor use and other measures of language style. Chapters 9 and 10 by **Jonathan Dunn** and **Karlien Franco** respectively argue for closer collaboration between cognitive linguistics and the neighboring fields of computational linguistics and dialectology. In Chapter 9, the growing area of computational cognitive linguistics is showcased as a truly usage-based approach operating on a large enough scale to capture meaningful generalizations about actual usage. Computational methods are used to model language learning and variation from respective theoretical perspectives of construction grammar and dialectology, featuring a vast dataset that covers seven languages (English, French, German, Spanish, Portuguese, Russian, Arabic) and their 79 distinct national dialects. In Chapter 10, potential synergies between cognitive linguistics and dialectology are further explored with three case studies that offer a cognitive linguistic take on sociolinguistic principles like transmission, diffusion, and communicative need. To operationalize this cross-fertilization of theoretical ideas, generalized additive models, as extensions of generalized linear models that flexibly accommodate parametric and non-parametric relationships between (in)dependent variables, are combined with other correlational analyses to investigate dialectal lexical variation in Dutch.

In this way, the volume is divided into three natural and overlapping sections. Chapters 1 to 3 are more conceptually and pedagogically oriented by presenting a broad overview followed by tutorial-style contributions aimed at learners. Chapters 4 to 7 feature specific case studies with a range of data analytic techniques, phenomena, and social contexts, and Chapters 8 to 10 conclude the volume by offering glimpses of promising future directions for data analytics in cognitive linguistics. While the target audience are cognitive linguists, the techniques underpinning the theoretical issues and examples are readily applicable to other areas of social and linguistic research with appropriate reconceptualization of the design and variables. We believe that the volume will be most beneficial to researchers who have some foundational knowledge in statistics and data analytics, and want to further understand how a range of underexplored as well as established techniques could operate in actual research contexts.

References

Achard, Michel & Susanne Niemeier. 2008. *Cognitive linguistics, second language acquisition, and foreign language teaching.* Berlin: Walter de Gruyter.

Chance, Beth L. 2002. Components of statistical thinking and implications for instruction and assessment. *Journal of Statistics Education* 10(3).

Chen, Hsinchun, Roger HL Chiang & Veda C Storey. 2012. Business intelligence and analytics: From big data to big impact. *MIS quarterly.* 1165–1188.

Conway, Drew. 2010. The Data Science Venn Diagram. *blog.revolutionanalytics.com.*

Demjén, Zsófia, Agnes Marszalek, Elena Semino & Filippo Varese. 2019. Metaphor framing and distress in lived-experience accounts of voice-hearing. *Psychosis* 11(1). 16–27.

Evans, James R & Carl H Lindner. 2012. Business analytics: The next frontier for decision sciences. *Decision Line* 43(2). 4–6.

Gibbs, Raymond W. 2006. Introspection and cognitive linguistics. *Annual Review of Cognitive Linguistics* 4. 131–151.

Gibbs, Raymond W. 2007. Why cognitive linguists should care more about empirical methods. In Monica Gonzale-Marquez, Irene Mittelberg, Seana Coulson & J. Michael Spivey (eds.), *Methods in cognitive linguistics,* 2–18. Amsterdam: John Benjamins.

Gibbs, Raymond W. 2010. The wonderful, chaotic, creative, heroic, challenging world of researching and applying metaphor. In Graham Low, Zazie Todd, Alice Deignan & Lynne Cameron (eds.), *Researching and applying metaphor in the real world,* 1–18. Amsterdam: John Benjamins.

Glynn, Dylan & Justyna Robinson (eds.). 2014. *Corpus methods for semantics: Quantitative studies in polysemy and synonymy.* Amsterdam: John Benjamins.

Gonzalez-Marquez, Monica, Irene Mittelberg, Seana Coulson & J. Michael Spivey (eds.). 2007. *Methods in cognitive linguistics.* Amsterdam: John Benjamins.

Han, Jiawei, Micheline Kamber & Jian Pei. 2000. *Data mining concepts and techniques* 3rd edn. San Francisco, CA: Morgan Kaufmann.

Hurtienne, Jörn, Kerstin Klöckner, Sarah Diefenbach, Claudia Nass & Andreas Maier. 2015. Designing with image schemas: Resolving the tension between innovation, inclusion and intuitive use. *Interacting with Computers* 27(3). 235–255.

Janda, Laura A. 2013. *Cognitive linguistics: The quantitative turn.* Berlin & New York: Walter de Gruyter.

Kertész, András & Csilla Rákosi. 2009. Cyclic vs. circular argumentation in the Conceptual Metaphor Theory. *Cognitive Linguistics* 20(4). 703–732.

Kertész, András, Csilla Rákosi & Péter Csatár. 2012. Data, problems, heuristics and results in cognitive metaphor research. *Language Sciences* 34(6). 715–727.

Lamb, Sydney M. 1999. *Pathways of the brain: The neurocognitive basis of language.* Amsterdam: John Benjamins Publishing.

Littlemore, Jeannette. 2009. *Applying cognitive linguistics to second language learning and teaching.* Basingstoke/New York: Palgrave Macmillan.

Littlemore, Jeannette, Paula Pérez Sobrino, David Houghton, Jinfang Shi & Bodo Winter. 2018. What makes a good metaphor? A cross-cultural study of computer-generated metaphor appreciation. *Metaphor and Symbol* 33(2). 101–122.

Peters, Thomas J & Robert H Waterman. 1982. *In search of excellence: Lessons from America's best-run companies.* New York: Harper Collins Business.

Raghupathi, Wullianallur & Viju Raghupathi. 2014. Big data analytics in healthcare: Promise and potential. *Health information science and systems* 2(1). 1–10.
Tay, Dennis. 2013. *Metaphor in psychotherapy: A descriptive and prescriptive analysis*. John Benjamins Publishing.
Tay, Dennis. 2017. Time series analysis of discourse: A case study of metaphor in psychotherapy sessions. *Discourse Studies* 19(6). 694–710.
Winter, Bodo. 2019. *Statistics for linguists: An introduction using R*. New York: Routledge.
Zhang, Weiwei. 2016. *Variation in metonymy: Cross-linguistic, historical and lectal perspectives*. Berlin, Germany: Walter de Gruyter.

Bodo Winter
Mapping the landscape of exploratory and confirmatory data analysis in linguistics

1 The data gold rush

Linguistics has and still is undergoing a quantitative revolution (Kortmann 2021; Levshina 2015; Sampson 2005; Winter 2019a). Over the last few decades in particular, methodological change has arguably taken up speed. For example, many researchers have criticized the over-reliance on introspective data in generative linguistics (Gibson and Fedorenko 2010; Pullum 2007; Schütze 1996) and cognitive linguistics (Dąbrowska 2016a; Dąbrowska 2016b; Gibbs 2007). This critique of introspection was one of the driving forces spurring an increased adoption of quantitative methods. Other factors that have spurred the quantitative revolution in our field include the ever-increasing ease with which data can be extracted from corpora, or crowdsourced via platforms such as Amazon Mechanical Turk and Prolific (Bohannon 2011; Paolacci, Chandler and Ipeirotis 2010; Peer, Vosgerau and Acquisti 2014; Sprouse 2011). In addition, it is becoming increasingly easy to access freely available web data, such as the results of large-scale word rating studies (Winter 2021).

In the cognitive sciences, Griffiths (2015) speaks of the 'big data' computational revolution. Buyalskaya and colleagues (2021) speak of 'the golden age of social science.' This new era, in which we are inundated by a large amount of freely available or easily obtainable datasets, means that data analytics is increasingly becoming an essential part of linguistic training. However, even though some linguistics departments offer excellent statistical education, many others still struggle with incorporating this into their curricula. Many linguistics students (and sometimes their supervisors!) feel overwhelmed by the sheer number of different approaches available to them, as well as the many different choices they have to make for any one approach.

Acknowledgement: Bodo Winter was supported by the UKRI Future Leaders Fellowship MR/T040505/1.

Bodo Winter, Dept. of English Language and Linguistics, University of Birmingham, e-mail: B.Winter@bham.ac.uk

https://doi.org/10.1515/9783110687279-002

To readers who are new to the field, the landscape of statistical methodology may look very cluttered. To begin one's journey through this landscape, there is no way around reading at least one book-length introductory text on statistical methods, of which there are by now many for linguists (e.g., Baayen, 2008; Larson-Hall, 2015), cognitive linguists (e.g., Levshina, 2015; Winter, 2019b), and corpus linguists (Desagulier 2017; Gries 2009). We simply cannot expect to learn all relevant aspects of data analysis from a short paper, online tutorial, or workshop. Statistical education needs more attention than that, and reading book-length statistical introductions should be a mandatory part of contemporary linguistic training.

The available books are often focused on teaching the details of particular statistical procedures and their implementation in the R statistical programming language. These books generally cover a lot of ground – many different approaches are introduced – but they are often less focused on giving a big picture overview. This chapter complements these introductions by taking a different approach: without going into the details of any one particular method, I will try to map out a path through the landscape of statistics. My goal is not to give the reader a set of instructions that they can blindly follow. Instead, I will focus on giving a bird's eye overview of the landscape of statistics, hoping to reduce the clutter.

This chapter is written decidedly with the intention of being accessible to novice analysts. However, the chapter should also be useful for more experienced researchers, as well as supervisors and statistics educators who are in need for high-level introductions. Even expert analysts may find the way I frame data analytics useful for their own thinking and practice. Moreover, I want to chart the map of statistics in light of the modern debate surrounding the replication crisis and reproducible research methods (§2), using this chapter as an opportunity to further positive change in our field.

Our journey through the landscape of statistics starts with a characterization of data analysis as a cognitive activity, a process of sensemaking (§3). There are two main sub-activities via which we can make sense of data, corresponding to exploratory and confirmatory data analysis. Some have (rightfully) criticized the distinction between exploration and confirmation in statistics (Gelman 2004; Hullman and Gelman 2021), as it often breaks down in practice. Regardless of these critiques, the exploration-confirmation divide will serve as useful goal posts for framing this introduction, as a means for us to split the landscape of statistics into two halves, each with their own set of approaches that are particularly suited for either confirmation or exploration. And it is fitting for this volume, which includes chapters that are relatively more focused on confirmatory statistics (e.g., Tay; Fuoli, this volume), as well as chapters that are relatively more focused on exploratory statistics (e.g., Dilkes; Tian and Zhang; Pan, this volume).

Within the confirmatory part of the statistical landscape, a critique of the significance testing framework (§4) motivates a discussion of linear models (§5–6) and their extensions (§7), including logistic regression, Poisson regression, mixed models, and structural equation models, among others. My goal in these sections is to focus on the data analysis process from the perspective of the following guiding question: How can we express our theories in the form of statistical models? Following this, I will briefly sketch a path through the landscape of exploratory statistics by looking at Principal Components Analysis, Exploratory Factor Analysis, and cluster analysis to showcase how exploration differs from confirmation (§8.1). Section §8.2 briefly mentions other techniques that could be seen as exploratory, such as classification and regression trees (CART), random forests, and NLP-based techniques such as topic modeling.

2 The replication crisis and reproducible research

We start our journey by considering how statistical considerations are intrinsically connected to the open science movement and the 'replication crisis' that has been unfolding over the last decade. No introduction to statistics is complete without considering the important topic of open and reproducible research. Any statistical analysis is pointless if it is not reproducible, and we cannot, and should not, trust results that do not meet modern standards of open science. Given how essential reproducibility and transparency are for the success of linguistics as a science, not including discussions of open science and reproducibility into the statistics curriculum is doing our field a disservice.

Large-scale efforts in psychology have shown that the replicability of study results is much lower than people hoped for, with one study obtaining only 36 successful replications out of 100 studies from three major psychological journals (Open Science Collaboration, 2015; see also Camerer et al., 2018). Linguistics is not safe from this "replication crisis," as evidenced by the fact that some high-profile findings relating to language have failed to replicate, such as the idea that bilingualism translates into advantages in cognitive processing (e.g., de Bruin et al., 2015; Paap and Greenberg, 2013).

Cognitive linguists in particular should be particularly wary of the replication crisis, as a number of the results that have failed to replicate relate to one of the core tenets of cognitive linguistics, the idea that the mind is embodied (see Evans, 2012; Gibbs, 2013; Lakoff and Johnson, 1999). Embodied cognition results that have failed to replicate include, among others, the finding that reading age-related words makes people walk more slowly (Doyen et al. 2012), that experiencing warm physical temperatures promotes social warmth (Chabris et al. 2018), that reading immoral stories makes people more likely to clean their hands (Gámez, Díaz and Marrero 2011), and that reading action-related sentences facilitates congruent movements (Papesh 2015). In fact, embodied cognition research may be one of the most non-replicable areas of cognitive psychology (see discussion in Lakens, 2014). Thus, linguists, and especially cognitive linguists, need to take the replication crisis very seriously. A recent special issue in the journal *Linguistics* (de Gruyter) includes several papers focused on discussing the relevance of the replication crisis for linguistics (Grieve 2021; Roettger 2021; Sönning and Werner 2021; Winter and Grice 2021).

The reasons for failures to replicate are manifold and cannot be pinned down to just one cause. This also means that a variegated set of solutions is required (e.g., Asendorpf et al., 2013; Finkel et al., 2017), including replicating existing studies, performing meta-analyses of existing studies, preregistering one's planned methodology ahead of time, increasing the sample size of studies where possible, placing more emphasis on effect sizes in one's analysis, being more rigorous about the application of statistical methodology, as well as making all materials, data, and analysis code publicly available. The latter factor – open data and open code – is particularly relevant for us here. In linguistics, including cognitive linguistics, it is still not required for publications to make everything that can be shared available, although this situation is changing rapidly (see, e.g., Berez-Kroeker et al., 2018; Roettger et al., 2019). Two of the flagship cognitive linguistics journals (*Cognitive Linguistics*, de Gruyter; *Language and Cognition*, Cambridge University Press) now require data to be shared on publicly available repositories.

In Winter (2019b), I explicitly discussed the issue of replicability in the context of cognitive linguistic research, focusing on "reproducibility" rather than replication. Reproducibility is defined as the ability of another analyst to take the existing data of a study and reproduce each and every published value (see e.g., Gentleman and Temple Lang, 2007; Munafò et al., 2017; Peng, 2011; Weissgerber et al., 2016). In many ways, reproducibility is an even more basic requirement than replicability. Replication involves the repetition of a study with a new dataset; reproducibility includes that even for the very same data, another person should be able to trace each and every step, ultimately being able to re-create all figures and statistical results on one's own machine.

Lakoff (1990) proposed that the subfield of cognitive linguistics can be characterized by three "commitments": the cognitive reality commitment, the convergent evidence commitment, and the generalization and comprehensiveness commitment. The details of each of these commitments is irrelevant for our purposes, but taken together, they ground cognitive linguistics in the empirical sciences (see also Gibbs, 2007), including the incorporation of research from the wider cognitive sciences. However, if the cognitive science results that cognitive linguists use to ground their theories in empirical research turn out to be non-reproducible, all commitment to empirical work is vacuous. Therefore, in analogy to Lakoff's foundational commitments, I have argued that cognitive linguists should add the "reproducibility commitment" to their canon of commitments, repeated here as follows:

> The Reproducibility Commitment: "An adequate theory of linguistics needs to be supported by evidence that can be reproduced by other linguists who did not conduct the original study." (Winter 2019b: 126)

When focused on data analysis, this commitment, at a bare minimum, compels us to make all data and code available.[1]

From this reproducibility commitment, we can get an easy question out of the way that some beginning data analysts may have: What statistical software package should be used? On what software should a novice analyst focus their efforts on? The Reproducibility Commitment rules out any statistical software that is proprietary, i.e., that costs money and is not open source (SPSS, SAS, STATA, Matlab, Mplus etc.). Instead, efforts have to be directed to freely available open-source software (such as R and Python). Reproducibility commits us to use software that can be accessed and understood by everyone in the community without the need to acquire expensive licenses. Clearly, software does not make one a statistician, and many software packages other than R and Python are very powerful, but if we want to follow open science principles, we should not be using software that restricts access to certain members of the linguistic community. Especially the R programming environment (R Core Team 2019) is by now the de facto standard in linguistics, one could even say the 'lingua franca' of our field (Mizumoto and Plonsky 2016). A common objection against R (and other programming languages such as Python) is the belief that they may be harder to learn than software with graphical user interfaces such as SPSS. However, there simply is no empirical evidence to support this claim, and the few studies that have actually looked at students' reactions to different software packages suggest claims about R being substantially harder may be overstated (Rode and Ringel 2019). But even if R were harder than software such as SPSS, teaching the latter is simply put unethical given how incompatible the use of proprietary software is with the core principles of open and reproducible research.

---

1 For a response to common objections to data and code sharing, see Winter (2019b, Ch. 2).

With the fundamental topics of reproducibility and the question as to what software we should use out of the way, we can now begin charting a map of the landscape of statistics.

3 Data analysis as a cognitive process: Confirmatory and exploratory sensemaking

Data analysis is fruitfully seen as a cognitive process, one that involves making sense of data. As stated by Grolemund and Wickham (2014: 189):

> "Data analysis is a sensemaking task. It has the same goals as sensemaking: to create reliable ideas of reality from observed data. It is performed by the same agents: human beings equipped with the cognitive mechanisms of the human mind. It uses the same methods."

Any sensemaking process is an interaction between the external world and the sensemaker's preexisting beliefs. The same way, data analysis is shaped not only by what's in the data, but also by the state of the cognizer. Psychologists distinguish between bottom-up perception (the input, that what directly comes from the world around us) and top-down perception (influence from our preexisting beliefs). Visual perception is both bottom-up and top-down, and so is data analysis. However, in contrast to visual perception, which is generally automatic, the researcher performing a data analysis has a choice to make about *how much* they want to be bottom-up or top-down. A data analyst should think about whether they are primarily looking into the data to discover new patterns – with relatively fewer existing beliefs intervening – or whether they are looking to the data to either confirm or disconfirm their existing beliefs. If we are in a maximally confirmatory mode, all hypotheses are specified a priori; in exploratory statistics, much fewer hypotheses are specified a priori, and the data itself is allowed to suggest new patterns, including some that the researcher may not have thought of. Very informally, we can think of exploratory statistics as answering the question: What does my data have to offer? In turn, confirmatory statistics can be thought of as answering the question: Is my theory consistent with the data?

Ultimately, there is a continuum between confirmation and exploration because every method will always take something from the data, and every method will always come with some set of assumptions. The distinction between confirmatory and exploratory statistics is therefore one that comes in degrees, depending on how much a given statistical methodology requires specifying structures in advance. And of course, the distinction between confirmatory and exploratory statistics pertains to the difference in the purpose of an analysis. Generally speaking, the same method can be used for both confirmation and exploration, depending on the analyst's goals. That said, within the field of linguistics, some methods are more aligned with exploratory versus confirmatory purposes. Because of this, the following sections will proceed from confirmatory statistics (§4-6) to exploratory statistics (§7) to frame this introduction. Moreover, even though the exploration-confirmation distinction may break down in practice, it is important not to frame the results of exploratory analysis in terms of confirmatory analysis, as if they had been predicted in advance (Roettger, Winter and Baayen 2019).

The majority of the remainder of this chapter is devoted to confirmatory statistics as opposed to exploratory statistics not because the latter is less important, but because confirmatory statistics has recently undergone massive changes in our field, away from significance tests towards statistical models and parameter estimation. Because this approach is still new in some subfields and new textbooks do not necessarily teach the full scope of this framework, the emphasis will be on confirmatory statistical models.

4 Why cognitive linguistics needs to move away from significance tests

We start the journey of confirmatory statistics with what is still the status quo in many subfields of linguistics. To this day, the notion of 'statistics' is synonymous with 'null hypothesis significance testing' (NHST) to many researchers. Undergraduate statistics courses still emphasize the use of such NHST procedures as t-tests, ANOVAs, Chi-Square tests etc. This includes many existing introductions in cognitive and corpus linguistics (Brezina 2018; Gries 2009; Levshina 2015; Núñez 2007; Wallis 2021). All significance tests have a primary goal, which is to yield a p-value. Informally, this statistic measures the incompatibility of a given dataset with the null hypothesis. If a p-value reaches a certain threshold, the ritual of NHST involves that the null hypothesis is rejected, and the researcher claims to have obtained a "significant" result. The true meaning of the p-value, however, is so counter-intuitive that even most statistics textbooks (Cassidy et al. 2019) and statistics teachers fail to discuss it accurately (Gigerenzer 2004; Haller and Krauss 2002; Lecoutre, Poitevineau and Lecoutre 2003; Vidgen and Yasseri 2016). By itself, the p-value alone does not tell us very much (Spence and Stanley 2018), and is only a very weak indicator of whether a study will replicate, or is strong, or "reliable."

The over-reliance on significance tests in the behavioral and cognitive sciences, including linguistics, has been widely criticized in the statistical and psychological literature for now nearly a century (Kline 2004). In fact, many now believe that the 'statistical rituals' (Gigerenzer 2004) encouraged by the use of significance tests may be one of the key factors that have contributed to the replication crisis in the first place. But data analysis is so much more than subjecting the data to a prefab hypothesis testing procedure, which is why the field of linguistics has undergone a dedicated shift away from these methods towards the more theory-guided process of statistical modeling and parameter estimation (Baayen, Davidson and Bates 2008; Jaeger 2008; Jaeger et al. 2011; Tagliamonte and Baayen 2012; Wieling et al. 2014). This change from statistical testing to statistical modeling is also happening in cognitive linguistics (e.g., Gries, 2015a; Levshina, 2016, 2018; Winter, 2019b). To be clear: significance testing can also be done with statistical models, but a key difference is that the emphasis shifts from subjecting the data to an off-the-shelf procedure such as a t-test or a Chi-square test, towards considering the estimation of parameters in the form of multifactorial statistical models (Gries 2015b; Gries 2018). The latter approach is less limiting and allows for a more theory-guided approach to statistical analysis.

Most importantly for our purposes, significance tests make for a very bad way of decluttering the landscape of statistics. Each significance test is a highly specific tool that can be applied only in extremely limited circumstances. Recommendations about statistical methodology then often take the form of decision trees and statements like "if you have this hypothesis and this data, use test X, otherwise use test Y". However, rather than worrying about picking the right test, we should channel our energy into theory-driven reasoning about data. In contrast to significance testing as a conceptual framework, statistical modeling encourages thinking about how our preexisting beliefs (= linguistic domain knowledge / theories / hypotheses / assumptions) relate to a dataset at hand in a more principled fashion. This is ultimately much more intellectually engaging than picking a test from a decision tree of different pre-classified options, and it encourages thinking more deeply about how one's theory relates to the data at hand.

Luckily, the world of statistical modeling also turns out to be much easier to navigate than the world of significance testing. In fact, there is just one tool that will cover most of the use cases that commonly arise in linguistics. This tool is the linear model, an approach that can be flexibly extended to deal with all sorts of different theoretical proposals and data structures. The linear model framework makes it possible to represent the same data structures that significance tests are used for, which renders it unnecessary to teach significance tests in this day and age.

5 Using linear models to express beliefs in the form of statistical models

The statistical models we will discuss here are all versions of what is called the 'linear model,' or sometimes 'general linear model,' also discussed under the banner of '(multiple) regression analysis.' It is potentially confusing to novices that the different models bear different names that may sound like they are entirely different approaches. For example, consider this long list of terms:

> generalized linear models, linear mixed effects models, multilevel models, generalized additive models, structural equation models, path analysis, mediation analysis, moderation analysis, Poisson regression, logistic regression, hierarchical regression, growth curve analysis, . . .

This array of terms may seem daunting at first, but we should take comfort in the fact all of it is built on the same foundations. In fact, they are all versions or extensions of a particular approach that, in its essence, is easy to grasp. This is one of the key conceptual advantages of the linear model framework, which is that it leads to a very unified and coherent picture of the landscape of statistics, regardless of the apparent diversity of terms suggested by the list above.

Any of the linear models or regression models we will consider here have the same structure: One singular response or 'outcome' variable is described as varying by a set of predictor variables. An alternative terminology is to say that the dependent variable is modeled as a function of one or more independent variables. Thus, this form of statistical model is focused on describing how one singular quantity of interest (such as ratings, response times, accuracies, performance scores, word frequencies etc.) is influenced by one or more predictors. The analyst then focuses on thinking about which predictors they think would influence the response, thereby implementing their assumptions about the relations in the data into a statistical model.

To give a concrete example of a linear model, consider the observation that in English, many words related to taste are positive (such as *sweet, delicious, juicy, tasty, peachy*), whereas on average, words related to smell are relatively more negative (such as *rancid, pungent, stinky, odorous*) (Winter 2016; Winter 2019b). To test this generalization, we can use existing perceptual ratings for words (Lynott and Connell 2009) in combination with 'emotional valence' ratings, which describe the degree to which a word is good or bad (Warriner, Kuperman and Brysbaert 2013). Figure 1.1a visualizes the correlation between these two quantities (taste-relatedness and emotional valence). As can be seen, words that are relatively more strongly related to taste are on average more positive than words that are less strongly related to taste, although this is obviously a very weak relationship given the large scatter seen in Figure 1.1 a.

The superimposed line shows the corresponding linear or 'regression' model. This model describes the average emotional valence (whether a word is good or bad, on the y-axis) as a function of how much a word relates to taste (on the x-axis). The beauty of the linear model framework is that the underlying mathematics of lines can easily be extended to incorporate predictors that are categorical, such as seen in Figure 1.1b. This works by pretending that the corresponding categories (in this case, the binary distinction between 'taste words' and 'smell words') are positioned on a coordinate system (Winter, 2019b, Ch. 7).

The two models corresponding to Figure 1.1a and Figure 1.1b can be expressed in R as follows, with the first line (dark grey) representing the user input command, and the following lines (light grey) showing the output. The reader interested in the details of the implementation within R should consult Winter (2019a), a book-length introduction to the basics of linear models. Here, only a brief overview of the overall logic of the approach is presented.

```
lm(valence ~ taste_relatedness)
Coefficients:
        (Intercept)         taste
             3.2476        0.4514


lm(valence ~ taste_vs_smell)
Coefficients:
        (Intercept)    taste_vs_smellSmell
             5.3538               -0.9902
```

The R function lm() is named this way because it fits linear models. The tilde in the formula specifies that the term on the left-hand side (in this case, emotional valence) is 'described by', 'predicted by', 'conditioned on', or 'modeled as a function of' the term on the right-hand side. All input to linear models takes this general form, with the response on the left, and the predictor(s) on the right: 'response ~ predictors'. Each of the terms in the model, such as in this case valence, taste_relatedness, and taste_vs_smell, corresponds to a column in the spreadsheet that is loaded into R.

To understand the above output and interpret the model, we need to remind ourselves that a line can be described by two numbers: an intercept, and a slope. The intercept is the point where the line crosses the y-axis (which is

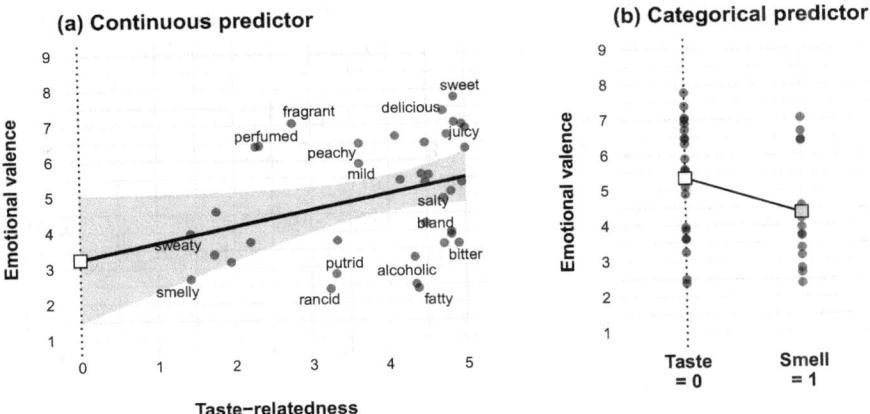

Figure 1.1: a) Emotional valence as a function of how much a word relates to smell; b) emotional valence as a function of the categorical taste versus smell difference.

conventionally positioned at x = 0). Informally, we can think of the intercept as corresponding to the 'height' of the regression line (higher intercepts mean that the line is overall shifted upwards). The slope describes the degree to which y depends on x, with Figure 1.1a giving an example of a positive slope and Figure 1.1b giving an example of a negative slope.

Taken together, the intercept and slope are called 'coefficients.'[2] In any actual data analysis, a considerable amount of time should be spent on *interpreting* the coefficients to understand what exactly it is that a model predicts. For the continuous model above, the output value of the intercept, 3.2476, corresponds to the white square in Figure 1.1a, where the line crosses the y-axis. This is the predicted value for a word with zero taste rating. The intercept is often not particularly interesting, but it is necessary to 'fix' the line along the y-axis. Oftentimes we are more interested in the slopes, as each slope expresses the relationship between the response and a given predictor. In the output above, the slope value of 0.4514 has the following interpretation: increasing the taste-relatedness by one rating unit leads to a positive increment in emotional valence ratings by this value. Our model of this data, then, corresponds to the equation of a line: y = 3.25 + 0.45 * taste (rounded). We can use this equation to make predictions: For example, we can plug in a taste rating of '3' to assess what emotional valence rating this model predicts for this specific taste rating: 3.25 + 0.45 * 3 = 4.6 (rounded).

---

[2] Some textbooks use the term 'coefficient' only for the slope.

This basic picture does not look markedly different for the case of a categorical predictor, except that the corresponding slope has to be interpreted as a categorical difference between two groups. In the output above, the number −0.9902 represents the difference in emotional valence between taste and smell words. Thinking in terms of lines, this difference can be conceptualized as moving from the taste words at $x = 0$ (the intercept) down to the smell words at $x = 1$. It is this mathematical trick – positioning categories within a coordinate system – that allows linear models to easily incorporate continuous predictors (Figure 1.1a) as well as categorical predictors (Figure 1.1b).

The basic idea of expressing the relation between y and x in terms of coefficients can be extended to the case of 'multiple regression,' which involves adding more predictors to the model, each one associated with its own coefficient that describes how that particular predictor is related to the response variable. This is exemplified in the following schematic R function call:

```
lm(response ~ predictor1 + predictor2 + predictor3)
Coefficients:
        (Intercept)   predictor1   predictor2   predictor3
             ?            ?            ?            ?
```

The function call (dark grey) can be thought of as a more technical way of expressing our hypotheses in the form of an equation. This particular formula notation can be paraphrased as "I want to assess whether the response is influenced jointly by predictor1, predictor2, and predictor3." The linear model will then *estimate* the corresponding coefficients – one slope for each predictor. Each slope expresses the relationship between the response and that specific predictor while holding all the other predictors constant. For example, the slope of predictor1 corresponds to how much predictor1 is statistically associated with the response while controlling for the influence of the other predictors. If the slope is positive, increases in predictor1 result in an increase of the response. If the slope is negative, increases in predictor1 result in a decrease of the response.

We can think of the coefficients as placeholders specified by the user, which the linear model in turn will 'fill' with estimates based on the data. In the schematic function call above, this placeholder nature is represented by the question marks. This highlights how fitting a linear model essentially corresponds to a set of questions (what is the slope of each of these terms?) that the model will try to answer. Given a model specification and given a particular dataset, the model actually fills the question marks with the *best-fitting* coefficient estimates, those values that ensure that the predictions are closest to all data points. However, the linear model only performs optimally with respect to the set of instructions that the data analyst has specified. If the user has missed important predictors, the model cannot know this. It can only answer the questions it has been asked to answer, which is why researchers should spend a lot of time thinking about the linear model equation – ideally prior to collecting the data.

If one uses linear models in a confirmatory fashion, the inclusion of each predictor into the model should be theoretically motivated. It is therefore good practice to specify a linear model in advance – before loading the data into any statistical software. Or, even more in line with a fully confirmatory approach, a researcher can pre-register one's analysis in a publicly accessible repository prior to collecting the data (Roettger 2021). The two cognitive linguistics-oriented journals *Language and Cognition* and *Cognitive Linguistics* have a special article category called 'Registered Reports' that requires pre-specifying an analysis plan prior to collecting the data. In my experience teaching statistics, novice analysts generally make their life harder by jumping into a statistical software package too quickly. Everything becomes much easier if considerable time is spent on determining which predictors should or should not be included in advance, based on theory, literature, and domain knowledge.

There are procedures for changing the model in response to the data (e.g., "model selection" techniques such as LASSO) that will not be discussed here. Moreover, in Bayesian statistics, several researchers recommend expanding models based on how well they can generate novel data in line with existing data (Gelman and Shalizi 2013; Kruschke 2013). However, despite the existence of such approaches, it is still useful and recommended to think as much as possible about a model in advance of performing an analysis or collecting the data.

The next section discusses how linear models can be expanded to assess more complex theoretical ideas involving interactions.

6 Linear models with interactions

Linear models can be expanded to include interaction terms. These are best explained by example. Here, I will draw from Winter and Duffy (2020), an experimental study on gesture and time metaphors in which interactions were of key theoretical interest. This experiment follows up on the famous "Next Wednesday" question that has been used extensively to probe people's metaphorical conceptualization of time (Boroditsky and Ramscar 2002; McGlone and Harding 1998). When asked the following question . . .

"Next Wednesday's meeting has been moved forward two days – what day is the meeting on now?"

... about half of all English speakers respond 'Friday,' and half respond 'Monday' (Stickles and Lewis 2018). This is because there are two ways of conceptualizing time in English, one with an agent moving forward through time (reflected in such expressions as *We are approaching Christmas*), another one with the agent being stationary and time moving towards the agent (reflected in such expressions as *Christmas is coming*). Jamalian and Tversky (2012) and subsequently Lewis and Stickles (2017) showed that certain gestures can change whether people respond Monday or Friday. If the question asker moves the gesturing hands forwards (away from their torso), an ego-moving perspective is primed, which implies a shift from Wednesday towards Friday. If the question asker moves the gesturing hand backwards (from an extended position towards their torso), a time-moving perspective is primed, thus implying a shift from Wednesday to Monday.

In our follow-up study to these experiments, we wanted to know to what extent gesture *interacts* with the concomitant language. That is, how much do language and gesture *co-depend* on each other in determining time concepts? For example, can forwards/backwards movement in gesture alone push people forwards/backwards along the mental time line, even if the corresponding language does not use any spatial language at all? Or is spatial language needed in order to make people pay attention to the direction of the gesture? In one of our experiments (Winter and Duffy, 2020, Experiment 4), we manipulated two factors, each one of which is a categorical predictor in the corresponding linear model: The first factor is gestural movement, whether the hands move forwards or backwards. The second factor is whether the language was spatial (*moved* by two days) or not (*changed* by two days). The corresponding model that we used had the following basic structure:

```
glm(response ~ gesture * language, . . .)
Coefficients:
          (Intercept)   gesture   language   gesture:language
              ?            ?          ?              ?
```

The use of `glm()` as opposed to `lm()` is irrelevant for the present discussion and will be explained in the next section (§7). What matters here is the fact that the above function call combines predictors with the multiplication symbol '*' rather than using the plus symbol '+', as in the last section. This difference in notation instructs the statistical model to not only estimate the effects of gesture and language, but also the effects of unique combinations of both predictors. Another way of thinking about this interaction is to say that one predictor has a different effect for *specific values of the other predictor*. For example, the forwards/backwards effect could be nullified if the language is non-spatial, which is indeed what we found (Winter and Duffy 2020). In the output, the interaction appears as a third term in the model, gesture:language. The size of this coefficient corresponds to the strength of the interaction. The larger this coefficient is (both positive or negative), the more do the gesture and language predictors co-depend on each other in changing the response.

In linguistics, many statistical models include such interactions. One issue that arises, however, is that once two predictors are 'interlocked' by virtue of participating in an interaction, each predictor's influence has to be interpreted with respect to the specific values of the other predictor. In the presence of an interaction, what influence a predictor has on the response variable will depend on the specific level of the other predictor, and so there is no easy-to-interpret 'across the board' effect for the individual predictors anymore. As a result, interactions generally make models harder to interpret. Thus, while interactions are often theoretically interesting and need to be included if a hypothesis actually specifies that one predictor's influence on the response depends on another predictor, including interaction terms also comes at the epistemological cost of making models harder to interpret. The question whether an interaction should or should not be included depends on theory. In the case of Winter and Duffy (2020), the interaction was the primary effect of theoretical interest and therefore had to be included into the model. As it is easy to misinterpret the output of statistical models that contain interactions, the reader is advised to consult a statistics textbook on this material. Winter (2019a) has a full chapter focused on the interpretation of interactions.

7 Becoming a more flexible data analyst via extensions of linear models

7.1 Generalized linear models

In the first regression example we discussed above (§5), the response was continuous. Each word was represented by an average rating where words are more or less good, in a scalar manner (Warriner, Kuperman and Brysbaert 2013). The Monday/Friday response in the second example (§6) was discrete. As discussed above, predictors in linear models can be continuous or categorical. However, to incorporate discrete *responses*, a more substantive change to the model is required. Generalized linear models (GLMs) are an extension of linear models that allow incorporating different assumptions about the nature of the response variable. The generalized linear model framework subsumes the linear models we discussed so far. That is, the multiple regression models we discussed above (§5-6) are specific cases of the generalized linear model. Table 1.1 gives an overview of the three 'canonical' generalized linear models that cover a lot of common use cases in linguistics.

Table 1.1: Three of the most common types of response variables and the most canonical generalized linear models that correspond to them.

Response variable	Generalized linear model
continuous	multiple regression
discrete: binary (fixed *N*)	logistic regression
discrete: count (no fixed *N*)	Poisson regression

In linguistics, logistic regression is generally used when the response variable is binary, such as was the case with the Monday/Friday responses in the example above. Other response variables that are binary include things such as the English dative alternation (Bresnan et al. 2007), the usage of *was* versus *were* (Tagliamonte and Baayen 2012), or the presence/absence of a metaphor (Winter 2019b). Any case where the response involves only two categories is amenable to logistic regression, and in the form of multinomial logistic regression, the approach can be extended to include response variables with more than two categories.

Poisson regression is another type of generalized linear model that is incredibly useful for linguistics because it is the canonical model type to deal with count variables that have no known or fixed upper limit. Example applications include showing that visual words are more frequent than non-visual words (Winter, Perlman and Majid 2018), or modeling the rate of particular fillers and discourse markers as a function of whether a speaker speaks politely or informally (Winter and Grawunder 2012). Given that linguists frequently count the frequency of discrete events, Poisson regression should be a natural part of the linguistic toolkit (Winter and Bürkner 2021).

Conceptually, the core ideas discussed in relation to multiple regression (§4) carry over to the case of generalized linear models. Just as before, fitting a generalized linear model to a dataset yields estimates of slopes, with each slope representing how much a binary variable (logistic regression) or unbounded count variable

(Poisson regression) depends on the predictor(s) of interest. However, a key difference to the more basic case of multiple regression is that the slopes will appear in a different metric. In the case of Poisson regression for unbounded count data, the coefficients will appear as logged values; in the case of logistic regression for binary data, the coefficients will appear as log odds. The reader is advised to read an introductory text on generalized linear models to aid the interpretation of the exact numerical values of the coefficients (Winter 2019a; Winter and Bürkner 2021).

7.2 Mixed models / multilevel models

All generalized linear models, including standard multiple regression, assume that data points are independent. For linguistics, this means that an 'individual' can only contribute one data point to the whole data set. What counts as 'individual' in linguistics depends on the type of study and how it is designed (Winter and Grice 2021): In many contexts, the 'individual' is an actual person. This is often the case in such subfields as psycholinguistics, phonetics, sociolinguistics, or experimental syntax where repeated measures designs are common, which leads to experiments that include multiple data points from each person. However, the term 'individual' as used here has a broader meaning, essentially incorporating any grouping factor. For example, if a corpus analysis included multiple data points from the same text, then 'text' could be an individual unit of observation. If the same corpus analysis included multiple data points from the same author, 'author' would be another grouping factor.

Ignoring the fact that data contains multiple data points from the same individual or group has dire consequences for the outcomes of a statistical analysis. These problems are discussed under the banner of the "independence assumption" of statistical tests, and they are also discussed under the banner of 'pseudoreplication', which is a term used in certain fields, such as ecology, to refer to erroneously treating statistically dependent observations as independent. For a classic introduction to the notion of "pseudoreplication", see Hurlbert (1984). For a more general discussion of the independence assumption in statistical modeling and consequences for different subfields of linguistics, including corpus linguistics, see Winter and Grice (2021). It is now standard in many different subfields of linguistics to include individual or grouping factors into the modeling process to statistically account for the fact that data points from the same individual or group are dependent (see e.g., Baayen et al., 2008; Tagliamonte and Baayen, 2012; Winter, 2019b, Ch. 13). In fact, the ability to account for multiple grouping data structures in a principled manner is one of the major reasons why the field has moved away from significance tests (Winter and Grice 2021), which make it hard and sometimes impossible to account for multiple nested or crossed dependencies in the data.

The way to deal with non-independent clusters of observations within a generalized linear model framework is to incorporate *random effects* into the model. The *mixing* of the regular predictors we have dealt with in the last few sections (now called 'fixed effects' in this framework) and what are called 'random effect' predictors is what gives mixed models their name. Mixed models are also called multilevel models, linear mixed effects models, or multilevel regression, and specific instances of these models are also discussed under the banner of hierarchical linear regressions. Gries (2015a) calls mixed models "the most under-used statistical method in corpus linguistics." McElreath (2020: 400) states that such "multilevel regression deserves to be the default approach." Clearly, there is no point in using mixed models if a particular application does not call for it. However, because data sets in linguistics will almost always include repeated data points from the same 'individual' (person, word, language family, text etc.), mixed models are almost always needed (Winter and Grice 2021).

A random effect can be any categorical variable that identifies subgroups in the data, clusters of observations that are associated with each other by virtue of coming from the same individual. The word 'random' throws some novices off because differences between grouping factors are clearly not 'random', i.e., a specific participant may systematically respond differently from another participant in a study. It therefore helps to think of 'randomness' in terms of 'ignorance': by fitting a specific grouping variable as a random effect, we are effectively saying that prior to the study, we are ignorant about the unique contribution of each individual. Random effects then estimate the variation across individuals.

It is entirely possible (and indeed, often required) to have random effects for participants in the same model in which there are also fixed effects that are tied to the same individuals. For example, we may hypothesize that gender and age systematically affect our response variable, and we want our mixed model to include these two variables as fixed effects. In addition, the same model can, and indeed probably should, also contain a random effect for participant. Whereas the fixed effects capture the systematic variation that an individual is responsible for (e.g., for an increase in x years of age, the response changes by y); the random effects capture the idiosyncratic contribution of that individual. Thus, including fixed effects tied to specific individuals does not preclude the inclusion of additional individual-specific random effects.

Importantly, the incorporation of random effects into the modeling process is key to avoiding violations of the independence assumption. Ignoring important random effects can lead to grossly misleading results, as has been extensively discussed in linguistics and elsewhere (Barr 2013; Barr et al. 2013; Matuschek et al. 2017; Schielzeth and Forstmeier 2008; Winter 2019a; Winter and Grice 2021). The reason for this is that fixed effects, such as condition effects, have to be evaluated against random effect variation. If the random effect variation is not actively estimated in the modeling process, fixed effects estimates can be severely overconfident, leading to a much higher rate of spuriously significant results. Because of this, it is of utmost importance that the researcher spends a lot of time thinking about whether there are non-independent clusters in their data set that need to be accounted for.

The perspective so far has focused on the perspective of including random effects to make sure that the fixed effects in the same model are estimated accurately. However, it is important to emphasize that random effect variation itself may actually be the primary thing that is of theoretical interest in some studies (for examples, see Baumann and Winter, 2018; Drager and Hay, 2012; Idemaru et al., 2019; Mirman et al., 2008). Some analyses may also require models that have more random effects than fixed effects (e.g., Ćwiek et al., 2021). It is important to think about random effect variation as theoretically interesting in its own right, and to interpret the random effect output of one's models. For a basic introduction to mixed models, see Winter (2019a).

7.3 Example models within cognitive linguistics

The trajectory of this chapter so far has been an expansion of the statistical modeling repertoire. This is not, like in the case of significance tests, adding new, fundamentally distinct tools to our toolkit. Instead, we take the very same tool (focused on the relation of a response and a predictor in terms of lines) and expand this tool to binary and count data (generalized linear models: logistic regression and Poisson regression), as well as to cases where there are multiple data points for the same grouping factor (mixed models). Table 1.2 shows some different types of models applied to test cognitive linguistic theories. Plain text descriptions of the corresponding R formula notation should help the reader get a better grasp of the extent of the linear model framework, and how this translates into actual data analyses conducted in cognitive linguistics. While the models have different names ("multiple regression", "logistic regression" etc.), it has to be borne in mind that they are built on the same foundations.

Table 1.2: Examples of linear model formulas in cognitive linguistic work.

Littlemore et al. (2018)
`lm(metaphor_goodness ~ frequency + concreteness + emotional_valence)`

Multiple regression: This model describes the extent to which a continuous measure of metaphor goodness depends on the frequency, concreteness, and emotional valence of a metaphor.

Winter (2019a, Ch. 17)
`lm(metaphoricity ~ iconicity + valence)`

Multiple regression: This study operationalized metaphoricity in a continuous fashion using a corpus-based measure; the research question was whether iconicity (e.g., the words *bang* and *beep* are iconic) and the emotional quality of words determine the likelihood with which the words are used as source domains in metaphor.

Winter, Perlman, and Majid (2018)
`glm(word_frequency ~ sensory_modality, family = poisson)`

Poisson regression: The token frequency of words in a corpus (a categorical count variable) was conditioned on which sensory modality (touch, taste, smell, sight, sound) the word belongs to; of interest here is whether visual words are more frequent than non-visual words.

Hassemer and Winter (2016)
`glm(height_versus_shape ~ pinkie finger curl * index curve, family = binomial)`

Logistic regression: In this experimental study, participants had to indicate whether a gesture depicted the height or the shape of an object; the above model formula expresses the belief that this binary categorical response depends on two predictors that we experimentally manipulated: either the index finger was more or less curved, or the pinkie finger was more or less curled in. Additionally, we were interested in the interaction of these two hand configuration predictors (it is plausible that specific combinations of pinkie curl and index curve values have a unique effect on the choice variable).

Winter, Duffy and Littlemore (2020), simplified
`lmer(RT ~ participant_gender * profession_term_gender * verticality)`
(additional random effects for participant and item not shown)

Linear mixed effects regression: In this reaction time experiment, we were interested in replicating the finding that people automatically think of power in terms of vertical space because of the conceptual metaphor POWER IS UP. The basic idea is that seeing a word pair such as "doctor ~ nurse" with the word "doctor" shown on top of a screen and the word "nurse" shown at the bottom of the screen will be faster than the reverse mapping (with the less powerful position on top). In addition, we manipulated the gender of the profession terms (e.g., "male doctor" or "female doctor") and we also wanted to assess whether responses differed as a function of the participant's gender. Our results provided evidence for a three-way interaction between the participant's gender, the gender of the profession term, and whether the vertical arrangement was in line with POWER IS UP or not: male participants responded much more quickly when the vertical alignment was consistent with the metaphor *and* the male profession term was shown on top.

7.4 Further extensions of the framework

Further extensions of the linear model framework are possible, and specific data sets and theoretical assumptions may require a move towards more complex model types. One set of extensions is in the direction of structural equation models (SEM), which involve extending the linear model framework either by adding what are called 'latent variables' (variables that cannot be directly observed), or by adding complex causal paths between predictors, such as when one predictor influences the responses indirectly, mediated by another predictor. Fuoli, this volume, discusses these concepts in more detail.

An additional extension of linear models are generalized additive models, or GAMs. These models are increasingly gaining traction within linguistics (Wieling et al. 2014; Winter and Wieling 2016), especially psycholinguistics (Baayen et al. 2017) and phonetics (Wieling 2018). GAMs are (generalized) linear models that involve the addition of 'smooth terms,' which are predictors that are broken up into a number of smaller functions. This allows the inclusion of nonlinearities into one's modelling process. Such nonlinearities are useful when dealing with spatial data, such as in dialectology, sociolinguistics, or typology, but they are also useful for dealing with temporal data, such as in time series analysis (compare Tay, this volume). This means that GAMs could be used, for example, for modeling such diverse aspects of linguistic data as pitch trajectories, mouse movements in a mouse-tracking study, gesture movements on a continuous scale, or language evolution over time.

Both SEMs and GAMs can also incorporate random effects, in which case they would be mixed SEMs or mixed GAMs. Moreover, since all of these are extensions of the same generalized linear model framework, each one of these approaches can also be logistic regression models (binary data) or Poisson regression models (unbounded count data), just with additional paths or latent variables (SEM) or with additional smooth terms (GAM). In fact, all of these different extensions of linear models are mutually compatible. For example, a GAM can also include random effects or latent variables. Figure 1.2 gives one overview of how the different classes of models can be conceptualized.

At this stage in this overview, the reader may get the impression that we are back to some sort of decision tree where we have to choose the right model, just what I have argued is a conceptual disadvantage of the significance testing framework. However, the picture painted here is fundamentally different to the case of significance tests. In the case of the linear model framework, the analysis process involves reasoning about one's model and building all the things that are hypothesized to matter into a singular model. For example, if there are multiple observations from the same individual in a dataset, random effects need to

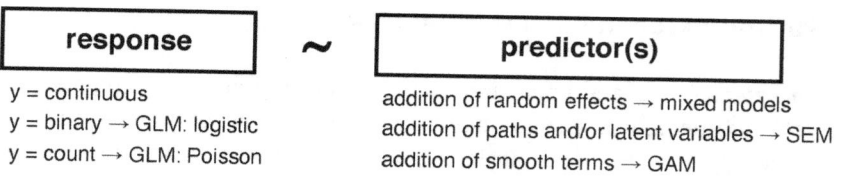

Figure 1.2: Snapshot of a portion of the generalized linear model framework and some common extensions.

be added. If there are also hypothesized nonlinear effects, smooth terms need to be added, and so on. What type of model is needed, then, follows from theoretical considerations and one's domain knowledge about the dataset at hand.

The reader should not put the question "What model should I choose?" first, but instead focus on the guiding question: "What are my assumptions about this data?" Or, more informally, "What do I know about this data that my model needs to know?" There simply is no default way of answering these questions, as this depends on the knowledge, assumptions, and theoretical leaning of the data analyst. Therefore, different researchers come up with different statistical analyses for the same research questions (Botvinik-Nezer et al. 2020; Silberzahn et al. 2018), and this subjectivity of statistical modeling should be endorsed, rather than eschewed (McElreath 2020). We should stay away from any default recipes and instead focus on the thinking part in statistical modeling, arguably that what makes data analysis fun and inspiring.

8 Exploratory statistics: A very brief overview of some select approaches

8.1 General overview

As mentioned above, exploratory data analysis is one of the two key ways that we engage with data, it is one of the two 'sensemaking modes' of data analysis. Within statistics, one of the names that is most commonly associated with exploratory data analysis is John Tukey, who characterizes the process of exploratory data analysis as "detective work" (Tukey 1977: 1). It is arguably the case that exploratory data analysis has historically been more important for linguists (Grieve 2021), given that the field is founded on detailed and genuinely exploratory "detective work", such as the early historical linguistics in the 19th century, the rich tradition of descriptive and field linguistics throughout the 20th century, and the rich tradition of observational research conducted under the banner of corpus linguistics since the middle of the 20th century. It is important that exploratory statistics are not viewed as theory-neutral or inferior to confirmatory statistics (Roettger, Winter and Baayen 2019).

One form of exploratory data analysis is data visualization, and indeed, this was a primary focus of Tukey's work on this topic. In fact, all descriptive statistics (summarizing data) and visualization can be conducted in a genuinely exploratory fashion, looking to see what the data has to offer. For an excellent practical introduction to data visualization with R, see Healy (2019). However, here I want to focus on two approaches that are not only particularly useful for cognitive linguists, but that have also been widely used within the language sciences, especially in corpus linguistics. These approaches can be split up into two broad categories, shown in Table 1.3. Other approaches, with different goals, will be discussed below.

Table 1.3: Two common goals in exploratory data analysis and corresponding approaches.

Goal	Example techniques
grouping variables	Exploratory Factor Analysis, (Multiple) Correspondence Analysis, ...
grouping data points	*k*-means, hierarchical cluster analysis, Gaussian mixture models, ...

Each row in this table corresponds to a specific analysis goal: Is the target of one's investigation to look at relationships between lots of variables, grouping them together into a smaller set of underlying factors? Or is the target of one's investigation to find subgroups of data points ('clusters')? The approaches that are used to answer these two questions differ from the above-mentioned linear model framework in a fundamental fashion in that they are genuinely *multivariate*. This means that in contrast to regression modeling, there is no one primary response variable. Instead, these approaches deal with multiple outcome variables at the same time. For the approaches listed in Table 1.3, there is no asymmetry between 'predictor' and 'response'. All variables are on equal terms.

8.2 Grouping variables with exploratory factor analysis

To exemplify both approaches, we can follow an analysis presented in Winter (2019b), which uses the perceptual ratings for adjectives from Lynott and Connell (2009). The input data has the following structure, with each column corresponding to ratings on one sensory modality, and each row corresponding to a particular adjective. The word *abrasive*, for example, has a relatively high touch rating and much lower taste and smell ratings. In contrast, the word *acidic* is much more strongly related to taste and smell.

```
             sight      touch     sound       taste       smell
abrasive   2.894737   3.684211  1.6842105  0.57894737  0.57894737
absorbent  4.142857   3.142857  0.7142857  0.47619048  0.47619048
aching     2.047619   3.666667  0.6666667  0.04761905  0.09523809
acidic     2.190476   1.142857  0.4761905  4.19047619  2.90476190
```

With Exploratory Factor Analysis (EFA), we focus on relationships between the columns. The entire correlation structure between all variables is investigated in a simultaneous fashion, looking to see whether particular variables can be re-expressed in terms of being part of a single underlying factor. Running an EFA on this 'word by modality' matrix suggests that there may be two underlying factors in this set of variables. The following summary of 'loadings' allows looking at how the original variables relate to the new set of factors. A loading expresses how strongly an individual variable latches onto a factor, with the sign of the loading expressing whether there is a positive association or negative association, which can be thought of as being analogous to a positive correlation (more of X gives more of Y) or a negative correlation (more of X gives less of Y). Two loadings for factor 2 are missing in the output below because they do not exceed the threshold taken to be a strong-enough loading by the base R function `factanal()` used to compute these results.

```
Loadings:
        Factor1  Factor2
sight   -0.228    0.674
touch   -0.177    0.496
sound   -0.445   -0.654
taste    0.824
smell    0.945
```

A crucial part of doing an Exploratory Factor Analysis is *interpreting* what the new factors mean. It is not guaranteed that an EFA will yield a theoretically interpretable solution. In this case, however, clear patterns emerge: The positive values for taste and smell, as opposed to the negative values for all other modalities, suggest that the first factor represents how much a word is related to taste and smell. The fact that these two variables load heavily onto the same factor is theoretically interesting given that prior psychological research suggests that taste and smell are perceptually and neurally highly coupled (e.g., Auvray and Spence, 2008; De Araujo et al., 2003). Sight and touch load heavily onto the second factor, with a strong negative loading for sound, suggesting that this factor represents how much things can be touched and seen as opposed to heard.

Theoretically, this factor solution can be thought of as an alternative, more parsimonious, way of representing the perceptual structure of the sensory lexicon of English. There are two underlying factors that allow capturing most of the ways words differ from each other in terms of their sensory characteristics. In this case, these two factors together account for 60% of the variance in the overall ratings. The insight here is that a larger set of variables can be compressed into a much smaller set of factors without losing too much information. This general principle is called dimensionality reduction and can be likened to looking at the night sky, which is a two-dimensional projection of three-dimensional space. Other dimensionality reduction techniques include Principal Components Analysis and (Multiple) Correspondence Analysis. Multidimensional Scaling is a conceptually similar approach that is aimed at finding the underlying structure of similarity or dissimilarity data.

8.3 Grouping data points with cluster analysis

The above Exploratory Factor Analysis answers the question: Are there any groups of *variables*? We can use the same data to answer the question: Are there any groups of *data points*? For this, we use the same 'word by rating' matrix, but our focus will be on grouping the words (rows) rather than the columns (variables). 'Cluster analysis' – itself a vast field of statistics – is the approach that allows answering this question. There are many different specific algorithms that realize this goal, with *k*-means and various forms of hierarchical cluster analysis being common in corpus linguistics. For a conceptual introduction to cluster analysis in cognitive linguistics, see Divjak and Fieller (2014).

In the case of the sensory modality data, I opted to use the specific clustering technique of Gaussian mixture models (Winter 2019b). In contrast to such approaches as *k*-means and hierarchical cluster analysis, Gaussian mixture modeling is a clustering technique that has the key theoretical advantage of allowing for fuzzy overlap between clusters, with some words being more and others being less certain members of each cluster. Moreover, Gaussian mixture models actually yield a genuine *model* of clusters (with parameter estimates), rather than merely a heuristic partitioning of the data. Either way, applying this method to the sensory modality rating dataset yielded 12 clusters (various model fit criteria can be used to find the best cluster solution). The same way that there is no guarantee that Exploratory Factor Analysis produces interpretable factors, there is no guarantee that any cluster analysis method produces interpretable clusters. To *interpret* whether the cluster solution produces sensible results that can be meaningfully related to existing linguistic proposals, we can look at the most certain words for each cluster, shown in Table 1.4.

Table 1.4: Two common goals in exploratory data analysis and corresponding approaches.

Clusters	Proposed name	Adjectives ordered in terms of certainty
1	pure sight	*gray, red, brunette, brown, blonde, reddish, yellow, . . .*
2	shape and extent	*triangular, conical, circular, curved, little, bent, . . .*
3	gross surface properties	*crinkled, bristly, prickly, big, sharp, bumpy, wiry, . . .*
4	motion, touch, and gravity	*craggy, ticklish, low, swinging, branching, scratchy, . . .*
5	skin and temperature	*tingly, lukewarm, tepid, cool, warm, clammy, chilly, . . .*
6	chemical sense	*acrid, bitter, tangy, sour, salty, antiseptic, tasteless, . . .*
7	taste	*cheesy, chocolatey, bland, unpalatable, alcoholic, . . .*
8	smell	*odorous, whiffy, perfumed, reeking, smelly, stinky, . . .*
9	sound 1	*noisy, deafening, bleeping, silent, whistling, . . .*
10	sound 2	*sonorous, squeaking, melodious, muffled, creaking, . . .*
11	impression-related	*stormy, cute, crowded, crackling, clear, lilting, . . .*
12	multisensory	*beautiful, burning, gorgeous, sweaty, clean, strange, . . .*

In Winter (2019b), I discussed these different clusters and their relation to the existing literature on sensory words in detail. The words in some clusters form clearly semantically coherent groups, such as the 'purse sight' cluster, which contains color words. Other clusters, however, are less semantically coherent, such as the 'multisensory' and 'impression-related' categories. Just like EFA, cluster analysis is a purely statistical procedure, and it is up to the analyst to use this procedure within their sensemaking process.

8.4 Other statistical techniques commonly used for exploratory data analysis

The examples discussed so far should clarify how EFA and cluster analysis are very different from the linear models discussed in the previous sections. In contrast to linear models, the exploratory approaches discussed so far consider all variables together without an asymmetric relation between response and predictor. There are, however, approaches that allow dealing with this asymmetric relationship in a genuinely exploratory fashion, such as classification and regression trees (CART, for a conceptual introduction for linguists, see Gries, 2019). Such trees use a method called binary recursive partitioning to split the data into a representation that essentially looks like a decision tree, with discrete split points for different variables in an analysis (see Strobl et al., 2009 for an introduction). For example, a split point for the data shown in Figure 1.1a above could be a taste rating of <2.3, below which most values are very negative. The process of recursively splitting the data into smaller groups can also incorporate multiple different variables, so that, for example, within the set of words with <2.3 taste rating, we may consider a new split along a different variable. Resulting from this recursive splitting procedure is a tree-like representation of the complex relations of how different predictors influence a singular response. The type of data that one can use classification and regression trees for is similar to the type of data one would use regression for, in that it involves multiple predictors and just one response variable. However, in contrast to regression, CART approaches are generally used when there are no clear expectations about how the predictors relate to the response, and which predictors should or should not be included.

Random forests are a further extension of CART, involving an ensemble of different classification or regression trees. Tian and Zhang (this volume) discuss random forests in more detail, but a brief introduction is given here nonetheless: With random forests, each tree is fit on a random subset of data as well as a random subset of variables. This ensures that whatever CART algorithm is used does not learn too much from the specific data at hand (what is called 'overfitting'). This facilitates generalization to novel, unseen data, rather than honing in on the idiosyncratic characteristics of a specific dataset at hand. Among other things, random forests provide a simple measure that tells the analyst which variables in a study are most influential. For an application of random forests to sound symbolism research, see Winter and Perlman (2021).

However, CART and random forests also care about the independence assumption mentioned above in section §7.2 above. The results ascertained via these approaches are just as much biased in the presence of multiple dependent data points as other approaches. As almost all data in linguistics has nested or crossed dependencies (Winter and Grice 2021), standard CART and random forest models can very rarely be applied to linguistic data. In the case of the random forest analysis in Winter and Perlman (2021), we had to exclude etymologically related forms to ensure that the random forest results are not biased due to etymological relatedness. There are, however, approaches to random forests that allow the incorporation of dependencies (Hajjem, Bellavance and Larocque 2014; Karpievitch et al. 2009; Stephan, Stegle and Beyer 2015). Another important issue that is not often discussed in the linguistic literature is that random forests should generally not be used without tuning the hyperparameters (the settings used by the algorithms) to a specific dataset (Probst, Wright and Boulesteix 2019).

Finally, it should be noted that the set of exploratory techniques covered here is by no means exhaustive. Levshina (2015) in particular discusses many useful exploratory techniques not covered here. Within corpus linguistics in particular, exploratory techniques can also be seen as encompassing such techniques as keyword analysis or topic modeling, and more generally, the class of approaches covered under the banner of "distributional semantics" (Günther, Rinaldi and Marelli 2019). The reader is encouraged to learn more about these techniques and how they are implemented in R.

9 The landscape of statistics: Minefield or playground?

This chapter introduced readers to the landscape of statistical analysis in linguistics, focusing on confirmatory approaches within the domain of linear models, as well as a select group of exploratory approaches. To some novel analysts, statistics may appear like a minefield, with a bewildering array of different approaches, each one of which has many different ways in which it can be misapplied. Others may see statistics as a playground, with so many different toys to play with. Both of these extreme views are dangerous. The minefield perspective is stifling; the playground perspective invites an attitude of 'anything goes' and 'whatever yields the desired effects.' But the statistical landscape is neither a minefield nor a playground. We can chart a clear path through this landscape by being clear about our analysis goals. The task of data analysis becomes substantially easier when we put our research questions first, and to be clear about whether we are in a primarily confirmatory or a primarily exploratory mode of data analysis. I have found that oftentimes, lack of clarity about statistics is not genuinely rooted in lack of knowledge about statistics, but in being unclear about one's goals and hypotheses.

The German physicist Werner Heisenberg once said that "What we observe is not nature in itself but nature exposed to our method of questioning." This statement is equally true of linguistics: What we observe is not language itself, but language exposed to our method of questioning. This chapter discussed methods that expand the repertoire of questions we can ask when engaging in data analysis. Knowing what is "out there" puts the analyst in the best position to traverse the landscape of statistics. But ultimately, it is the research questions that chart the path, not the statistical methods that hinge on those questions.

References

Asendorpf, Jens B., Mark Conner, Filip De Fruyt, Jan De Houwer, Jaap JA Denissen, Klaus Fiedler, Susann Fiedler, David C. Funder, Reinhold Kliegl and Brian A. Nosek. 2013. Recommendations for increasing replicability in psychology. *European Journal of Personality*. Wiley Online Library 27(2). 108–119. https://doi.org/10.1002/per.1919.

Auvray, Malika and Charles Spence. 2008. The multisensory perception of flavor. *Consciousness and Cognition*. Elsevier 17(3). 1016–1031. https://doi.org/10.1016/j.concog.2007.06.005.

Baayen, Harald. 2008. *Analyzing linguistic data: A practical introduction to statistics using R*. Cambridge, UK: Cambridge University Press.

Baayen, Harald, Douglas J. Davidson and Douglas M. Bates. 2008. Mixed-effects modeling with crossed random effects for subjects and items. *Journal of Memory and Language* 59(4). 390–412.

Baayen, Harald, Shravan Vasishth, Reinhold Kliegl and Douglas Bates. 2017. The cave of shadows: Addressing the human factor with generalized additive mixed models. *Journal of Memory and Language*. Elsevier 94. 206–234.

Barr, Dale J. 2013. Random effects structure for testing interactions in linear mixed-effects models. *Frontiers in Psychology* 4. 328.

Barr, Dale J., Roger Levy, Christoph Scheepers and Harry J. Tily. 2013. Random effects structure for confirmatory hypothesis testing: Keep it maximal. *Journal of Memory and Language* 68(3). 255–278.

Baumann, Stefan and Bodo Winter. 2018. What makes a word prominent? Predicting untrained German listeners' perceptual judgments. *Journal of Phonetics* 70. 20–38. https://doi.org/10.1016/j.wocn.2018.05.004.

Berez-Kroeker, Andrea L., Lauren Gawne, Susan Smythe Kung, Barbara F. Kelly, Tyler Heston, Gary Holton, Peter Pulsifer, et al. 2018. Reproducible research in linguistics: A position statement on data citation and attribution in our field. *Linguistics* 56(1). 1–18. https://doi.org/10.1515/ling-2017-0032.

Bohannon, John. 2011. Social science for pennies. *Science* 334(6054). 307.

Boroditsky, Lera and Michael Ramscar. 2002. The roles of body and mind in abstract thought. *Psychological Science* 13(2). 185–189.

Botvinik-Nezer, Rotem, Felix Holzmeister, Colin F. Camerer, Anna Dreber, Juergen Huber, Magnus Johannesson, Michael Kirchler, Roni Iwanir, Jeanette A. Mumford and R. Alison Adcock. 2020. Variability in the analysis of a single neuroimaging dataset by many teams. *Nature*. Nature Publishing Group 582(7810). 84–88. https://doi.org/10.1038/s41586-020-2314-9.

Bresnan, Joan, Anna Cueni, Tatiana Nikitina and Harald Baayen. 2007. Predicting the dative alternation. In *Cognitive foundations of interpretation*, 69–94. KNAW.

Brezina, Vaclav. 2018. *Statistics in corpus linguistics: A practical guide.* Cambridge, UK: Cambridge University Press.

Bruin, Angela de, Barbara Treccani and Sergio Della Sala. 2015. Cognitive advantage in bilingualism: An example of publication bias? *Psychological Science*. Sage Publications Sage CA: Los Angeles, CA 26(1). 99–107. https://doi.org/10.1177/0956797614557866.

Buyalskaya, Anastasia, Marcos Gallo and Colin F. Camerer. 2021. The golden age of social science. *Proceedings of the National Academy of Sciences*. National Academy of Sciences 118(5). https://doi.org/10.1073/pnas.2002923118.https://www.pnas.org/content/118/5/e2002923118 (26 September, 2021).

Camerer, Colin F., Anna Dreber, Felix Holzmeister, Teck-Hua Ho, Jürgen Huber, Magnus Johannesson, Michael Kirchler, Gideon Nave, Brian A. Nosek and Thomas Pfeiffer. 2018. Evaluating the replicability of social science experiments in Nature and Science between 2010 and 2015. *Nature Human Behaviour*. Nature Publishing Group 2(9). 637–644. https://doi.org/10.1038/s41562-018-0399-z.

Cassidy, Scott A., Ralitza Dimova, Benjamin Giguère, Jeffrey R. Spence and David J. Stanley. 2019. Failing grade: 89% of introduction-to-psychology textbooks that define or explain statistical significance do so incorrectly. *Advances in Methods and Practices in Psychological Science*. Sage Publications Sage CA: Los Angeles, CA 2(3). 233–239. https://doi.org/10.1177/2515245919858072.

Chabris, Christopher F., Patrick R. Heck, Jaclyn Mandart, Daniel J. Benjamin and Daniel J. Simons. 2018. No evidence that experiencing physical warmth promotes interpersonal warmth. *Social Psychology*. Hogrefe Publishing. https://doi.org/10.1027/1864-9335/a000361.

Ćwiek, Aleksandra, Susanne Fuchs, Christoph Draxler, Eva Liina Asu, Dan Dediu, Katri Hiovain, Shigeto Kawahara, et al. 2021. Novel vocalizations are understood across cultures. *Scientific Reports*. Nature Publishing Group 11(1). 10108. https://doi.org/10.1038/s41598-021-89445-4.

Dąbrowska, Ewa. 2016a. Looking into introspection. In Grzegorz Drożdż (ed.), *Studies in Lexicogrammar: Theory and applications*, 55–74. Amsterdam: John Benjamins.

Dąbrowska, Ewa. 2016b. Cognitive Linguistics' seven deadly sins. *Cognitive Linguistics* 27(4). 479–491. https://doi.org/10.1515/cog-2016-0059.

De Araujo, Ivan ET, Edmund T. Rolls, Morten L. Kringelbach, Francis McGlone and Nicola Phillips. 2003. Taste-olfactory convergence, and the representation of the pleasantness of flavour, in the human brain. *European Journal of Neuroscience*. Wiley Online Library 18(7). 2059–2068. https://doi.org/10.1046/j.1460-9568.2003.02915.x.

Desagulier, Guillaume. 2017. *Corpus linguistics and statistics with R: Introduction to quantitative methods in linguistics.* Berlin: Springer.

Divjak, Dagmar and Nick Fieller. 2014. Finding structure in linguistic data. In Dylan Glynn and Justyna Robinson (eds.), *Corpus methods for semantics: Quantitative studies in polysemy and synonymy*, 405–441. Amsterdam: John Benjamins.

Doyen, Stéphane, Olivier Klein, Cora-Lise Pichon and Axel Cleeremans. 2012. Behavioral priming: It's all in the mind, but whose mind? *PloS One*. Public Library of Science 7(1). e29081. https://doi.org/10.1371/journal.pone.0029081.

Drager, Katie and Jennifer Hay. 2012. Exploiting random intercepts: Two case studies in sociophonetics. *Language Variation and Change* 24(1). 59–78. https://doi.org/10.1017/S0954394512000014.

Evans, Vyvyan. 2012. Cognitive linguistics. *Wiley Interdisciplinary Reviews: Cognitive Science*. Wiley Online Library 3(2). 129–141. https://doi.org/10.1002/wcs.1163.

Finkel, Eli J., Paul W. Eastwick and Harry T. Reis. 2017. Replicability and other features of a high-quality science: Toward a balanced and empirical approach. *Journal of Personality and Social Psychology*. American Psychological Association 113(2). 244. https://doi.org/10.1037/pspi0000075.

Gámez, Elena, José M. Díaz and Hipólito Marrero. 2011. The uncertain universality of the Macbeth effect with a Spanish sample. *Spanish Journal of Psychology* 14(1). 156–162.

Gelman, Andrew. 2004. Exploratory data analysis for complex models. *Journal of Computational and Graphical Statistics*. Taylor and Francis 13(4). 755–779. https://doi.org/10.1198/106186004X11435.

Gelman, Andrew and Cosma Rohilla Shalizi. 2013. Philosophy and the practice of Bayesian statistics. *British Journal of Mathematical and Statistical Psychology* 66(1). 8–38. https://doi.org/10.1111/j.2044-8317.2011.02037.x.

Gentleman, Robert and Duncan Temple Lang. 2007. Statistical analyses and reproducible research. *Journal of Computational and Graphical Statistics*. Taylor and Francis 16(1). 1–23. https://doi.org/10.1198/106186007X178663.

Gibbs, Raymond W. 2007. Why cognitive linguists should care more about empirical methods. In Monica Gonzalez-Marquez, Irene Mittelberg, Seana Coulson and Michael Spivey (eds.), *Methods in Cognitive Linguistics*, 2–18. Amsterdam: John Benjamins.

Gibbs, Raymond W. 2013. Walking the walk while thinking about the talk: Embodied interpretation of metaphorical narratives. *Journal of Psycholinguistic Research*. Springer 42(4). 363–378. https://doi.org/10.1007/s10936-012-9222-6.

Gibson, Edward and Evelina Fedorenko. 2010. Weak quantitative standards in linguistics research. *Trends in Cognitive Sciences* 14(6). 233. https://doi.org/10.1016/j.tics.2010.03.005.

Gigerenzer, Gerd. 2004. Mindless statistics. *The Journal of Socio-Economics*. Elsevier 33(5). 587–606. https://doi.org/10.1016/j.socec.2004.09.033.

Gries, Stefan. 2009. *Quantitative corpus linguistics with R: A practical introduction*. New York: Routledge.

Gries, Stefan. 2015a. The most under-used statistical method in corpus linguistics: Multi-level (and mixed-effects) models. *Corpora* 10(1). 95–125. https://doi.org/10.3366/cor.2015.0068.

Gries, Stefan. 2015b. Some current quantitative problems in corpus linguistics and a sketch of some solutions. *Language and Linguistics*. SAGE Publications Sage UK: London, England 16(1). 93–117. https://doi.org/10.1177/1606822X14556606.

Gries, Stefan. 2018. On over-and underuse in learner corpus research and multifactoriality in corpus linguistics more generally. *Journal of Second Language Studies*. John Benjamins 1(2). 276–308. https://doi.org/10.1075/jsls.00005.gri.

Gries, Stefan. 2019. On classification trees and random forests in corpus linguistics: Some words of caution and suggestions for improvement. *Corpus Linguistics and Linguistic Theory*. De Gruyter Mouton 16(3). 617–647. https://doi.org/10.1515/cllt-2018-0078.

Grieve, Jack. 2021. Observation, experimentation, and replication in linguistics. *Linguistics*. De Gruyter Mouton 59(5). 1343–1356. https://doi.org/10.1515/ling-2021-0094.

Griffiths, Thomas L. 2015. Manifesto for a new (computational) cognitive revolution. *Cognition*. Elsevier 135. 21–23. https://doi.org/10.1016/j.cognition.2014.11.026.

Grolemund, Garrett and Hadley Wickham. 2014. A cognitive interpretation of data analysis. *International Statistical Review*. Wiley Online Library 82(2). 184–204. https://doi.org/10.1111/insr.12028.

Günther, Fritz, Luca Rinaldi and Marco Marelli. 2019. Vector-space models of semantic representation from a cognitive perspective: A discussion of common misconceptions. *Perspectives on Psychological Science*. Sage Publications Sage CA: Los Angeles, CA 14(6). 1006–1033. https://doi.org/10.1177/1745691619861372.

Hajjem, Ahlem, François Bellavance and Denis Larocque. 2014. Mixed-effects random forest for clustered data. *Journal of Statistical Computation and Simulation*. Taylor and Francis 84(6). 1313–1328. https://doi.org/10.1080/00949655.2012.741599.

Haller, Heiko and Stefan Krauss. 2002. Misinterpretations of significance: A problem students share with their teachers. *Methods of Psychological Research* 7(1). 1–20.

Hassemer, Julius and Bodo Winter. 2016. Producing and perceiving gestures conveying height or shape. *Gesture* 15(3). 404–424.

Healy, Kieran. 2019. *Data Visualization: A Practical Introduction*. Princeton, NJ: Princeton University Press.

Hullman, Jessica and Andrew Gelman. 2021. Designing for interactive exploratory data analysis requires theories of graphical inference. *Harvard Data Science Review*. PubPub.

Hurlbert, Stuart H. 1984. Pseudoreplication and the design of ecological field experiments. *Ecological Monographs* 54(2). 187–211. https://doi.org/10.2307/1942661.

Idemaru, Kaori, Bodo Winter, Lucien Brown and Grace Eunhae Oh. 2020. Loudness trumps pitch in politeness judgments: Evidence from Korean deferential speech. *Language and Speech* 63(1). 123–148. https://doi.org/10.1177/0023830918824344.

Jaeger, T. Florian. 2008. Categorical data analysis: Away from ANOVAs (transformation or not) and towards logit mixed models. *Journal of Memory and Language* 59(4). 434–446.

Jaeger, T. Florian, Peter Graff, William Croft and Daniel Pontillo. 2011. Mixed effect models for genetic and areal dependencies in linguistic typology. *Linguistic Typology* 15(2). 281–319. https://doi.org/10.1515/lity.2011.021.

Jamalian, Azadeh and Barbara Tversky. 2012. Gestures alter thinking about time. In *Proceedings of the Annual Meeting of the Cognitive Science Society*, vol. 34.

Karpievitch, Yuliya V., Elizabeth G. Hill, Anthony P. Leclerc, Alan R. Dabney and Jonas S. Almeida. 2009. An introspective comparison of random forest-based classifiers for the analysis of cluster-correlated data by way of RF++. *PloS One*. Public Library of Science 4(9). e7087. https://doi.org/10.1371/journal.pone.0007087.

Kline, Rex B. 2004. *Beyond significance testing: Reforming data analysis methods in behavioral research*. Washington, DC: American Psychological Association.

Kortmann, Bernd. 2021. Reflecting on the quantitative turn in linguistics. *Linguistics*. De Gruyter Mouton 59(5). 1207–1226. https://doi.org/10.1515/ling-2019-0046.

Kruschke, John K. 2013. Posterior predictive checks can and should be Bayesian: Comment on Gelman and Shalizi, 'Philosophy and the practice of Bayesian statistics.' *British Journal of Mathematical and Statistical Psychology* 66(1). 45–56. https://doi.org/10.1111/j.2044-8317.2012.02063.x.

Lakens, Daniel. 2014. Grounding social embodiment. *Social Cognition*. Guilford Press 32 (Supplement). 168–183.

Lakoff, George. 1990. The invariance hypothesis. *Cognitive Linguistics* 1(1).

Lakoff, George and Mark Johnson. 1999. *Philosophy in the flesh: The embodied mind and its challenge to western thought.* New York: Basic Books.

Larson-Hall, Jenifer. 2015. *A guide to doing statistics in second language research using SPSS and R.* New York, NY: Routledge.

Lecoutre, Marie-Paule, Jacques Poitevineau and Bruno Lecoutre. 2003. Even statisticians are not immune to misinterpretations of Null Hypothesis Significance Tests. *International Journal of Psychology*. Wiley Online Library 38(1). 37–45. https://doi.org/10.1080/00207590244000250.

Levshina, Natalia. 2015. *How to do linguistics with R: Data exploration and statistical analysis.* Amsterdam: John Benjamins.

Levshina, Natalia. 2016. When variables align: A Bayesian multinomial mixed-effects model of English permissive constructions. *Cognitive Linguistics*. De Gruyter Mouton 27(2). 235–268. https://doi.org/10.1515/cog-2015-0054.

Levshina, Natalia. 2018. Probabilistic grammar and constructional predictability: Bayesian generalized additive models of help. *Glossa: A Journal of General Linguistics* 3(1). https://doi.org/10.5334/gjgl.294.

Lewis, Tasha N. and Elise Stickles. 2017. Gestural modality and addressee perspective influence how we reason about time. *Cognitive Linguistics* 28(1). 45–76. https://doi.org/10.1515/cog-2015-0137.

Littlemore, Jeannette, Paula Pérez Sobrino, David Houghton, Jinfang Shi and Bodo Winter. 2018. What makes a good metaphor? A cross-cultural study of computer-generated metaphor appreciation. *Metaphor and Symbol* 33(2). 101–122. https://doi.org/10.1080/10926488.2018.1434944.

Lynott, Dermot and Louise Connell. 2009. Modality exclusivity norms for 423 object properties. *Behavior Research Methods* 41(2). 558–564.

Matuschek, Hannes, Reinhold Kliegl, Shravan Vasishth, Harald Baayen and Douglas Bates. 2017. Balancing Type I error and power in linear mixed models. *Journal of Memory and Language* 94. 305–315.

McElreath, Richard. 2020. *Statistical rethinking: A Bayesian course with examples in R and Stan.* 2nd edn. New York: CRC press.

McGlone, Matthew S. and Jennifer L. Harding. 1998. Back (or forward?) to the future: The role of perspective in temporal language comprehension. *Journal of Experimental Psychology: Learning, Memory, and Cognition* 24(5). 1211–1223. https://doi.org/10.1037/0278-7393.24.5.1211.

Mirman, Daniel, James A. Dixon and James S. Magnuson. 2008. Statistical and computational models of the visual world paradigm: Growth curves and individual differences. *Journal of Memory and Language*. Elsevier 59(4). 475–494. https://doi.org/10.1016/j.jml.2007.11.006.

Mizumoto, Atsushi and Luke Plonsky. 2016. R as a lingua franca: Advantages of using R for quantitative research in applied linguistics. *Applied Linguistics* 37(2). 284–291. https://doi.org/10.1093/applin/amv025.

Munafò, Marcus R., Brian A. Nosek, Dorothy VM Bishop, Katherine S. Button, Christopher D. Chambers, Nathalie Percie Du Sert, Uri Simonsohn, Eric-Jan Wagenmakers, Jennifer J. Ware and John PA Ioannidis. 2017. A manifesto for reproducible science. *Nature human behaviour*. Nature Publishing Group 1(1). 1–9.

Núñez, Rafael. 2007. Inferential statistics in the context of empirical cognitive linguistics. In Raymond W. Gibbs, Monica Gonzalez-Marquez, Irene Mittelberg, Seana Coulson and Michael Spivey (eds.), *Methods in cognitive linguistics*, 87–118. Amsterdam: John Benjamins.

Open Science Collaboration. 2015. Estimating the reproducibility of psychological science. *Science*. American Association for the Advancement of Science 349(6251). aac4716. https://doi.org/10.1126/science.aac4716.

Paap, Kenneth R. and Zachary I. Greenberg. 2013. There is no coherent evidence for a bilingual advantage in executive processing. *Cognitive Psychology*. Elsevier 66(2). 232–258. https://doi.org/10.1016/j.cogpsych.2012.12.002.

Paolacci, Gabriele, Jesse Chandler and Panagiotis G. Ipeirotis. 2010. Running experiments on Amazon Mechanical Turk. *Judgment and Decision Making* 5(5). 411–419.

Papesh, Megan H. 2015. Just out of reach: On the reliability of the action-sentence compatibility effect. *Journal of Experimental Psychology: General*. American Psychological Association 144(6). e116. https://doi.org/10.1037/xge0000125.

Peer, Eyal, Joachim Vosgerau and Alessandro Acquisti. 2014. Reputation as a sufficient condition for data quality on Amazon Mechanical Turk. *Behavior Research Methods* 46(4). 1023–1031.

Peng, Roger D. 2011. Reproducible research in computational science. *Science*. American Association for the Advancement of Science 334(6060). 1226–1227. https://doi.org/10.1126/science.1213847.

Probst, Philipp, Marvin N. Wright and Anne-Laure Boulesteix. 2019. Hyperparameters and tuning strategies for random forest. *Wiley Interdisciplinary Reviews: Data Mining and Knowledge Discovery*. Wiley Online Library 9(3). e1301. https://doi.org/10.1002/widm.1301.

Pullum, Geoffrey K. 2007. Ungrammaticality, rarity, and corpus use. *Corpus Linguistics and Linguistic Theory*. De Gruyter Mouton 3 (1).33–47.

R Core Team. 2019. *R: A language and environment for statistical computing*. Vienna: R Foundation for Statistical Computing.

Rode, Jacob B. and Megan M. Ringel. 2019. Statistical software output in the classroom: A comparison of R and SPSS. *Teaching of Psychology*. Sage Publications Sage CA: Los Angeles, CA 46(4). 319–327. https://doi.org/10.1177/0098628319872605.

Roettger, Timo B. 2021. Preregistration in experimental linguistics: Applications, challenges, and limitations. *Linguistics*. De Gruyter Mouton 59(5). 1227–1249. https://doi.org/10.1515/ling-2019-0048.

Roettger, Timo B., Bodo Winter and Harald Baayen. 2019. Emergent data analysis in phonetic sciences: Towards pluralism and reproducibility. *Journal of Phonetics*. Elsevier 73. 1–7. https://doi.org/10.1016/j.wocn.2018.12.001.

Sampson, Geoffrey. 2005. Quantifying the shift towards empirical methods. *International Journal of Corpus Linguistics*. John Benjamins 10(1). 15–36. https://doi.org/10.1075/ijcl.10.1.02sam.

Schielzeth, Holger and Wolfgang Forstmeier. 2008. Conclusions beyond support: Overconfident estimates in mixed models. *Behavioral Ecology* 20(2). 416–420. https://doi.org/10.1093/beheco/arn145.

Schütze, Carson T. 1996. *The empirical base of linguistics: Grammaticality judgments and linguistic methodology*. Chicago, IL: University of Chicago Press.

Silberzahn, Raphael, Eric L. Uhlmann, Daniel P. Martin, Pasquale Anselmi, Frederik Aust, Eli Awtrey, Štěpán Bahník, Feng Bai, Colin Bannard and Evelina Bonnier. 2018. Many analysts, one data set: Making transparent how variations in analytic choices affect results. *Advances in Methods and Practices in Psychological Science*. Sage Publications Sage CA: Los Angeles, CA 1(3). 337–356. https://doi.org/10.1177/2515245917747646.

Sönning, Lukas and Valentin Werner. 2021. The replication crisis, scientific revolutions, and linguistics. *Linguistics*. De Gruyter Mouton 59(5). 1179–1206. https://doi.org/10.1515/ling-2019-0045.

Spence, Jeffrey R. and David J. Stanley. 2018. Concise, simple, and not wrong: In search of a short-hand interpretation of statistical significance. *Frontiers in Psychology* 9. 2185. https://doi.org/10.3389/fpsyg.2018.02185.

Sprouse, Jon. 2011. A validation of Amazon Mechanical Turk for the collection of acceptability judgments in linguistic theory. *Behavior Research Methods* 43(1). 155–167.

Stephan, Johannes, Oliver Stegle and Andreas Beyer. 2015. A random forest approach to capture genetic effects in the presence of population structure. *Nature Communications*. Nature Publishing Group 6(1). 1–10. https://doi.org/10.1038/ncomms8432.

Stickles, Elise and Tasha N. Lewis. 2018. Wednesday's meeting really is on Friday: A meta-analysis and evaluation of ambiguous spatiotemporal language. *Cognitive Science* 42(3). 1015–1025. https://doi.org/doi.org/10.1111/cogs.12559.

Strobl, Carolin, James Malley and Gerhard Tutz. 2009. An introduction to recursive partitioning: Rationale, application, and characteristics of classification and regression trees, bagging, and random forests. *Psychological Methods* 14(4). 323. https://doi.org/10.1037/a0016973.

Tagliamonte, Sali A. and Harald Baayen. 2012. Models, forests, and trees of York English: Was/were variation as a case study for statistical practice. *Language Variation and Change* 24(2). 135–178.

Tukey, John W. 1977. *Exploratory data analysis*. Vol. 2. Reading, Mass.: Addison-Wesley.

Vidgen, Bertie and Taha Yasseri. 2016. P-values: Misunderstood and misused. *Frontiers in Physics*. Frontiers 4. 6. https://doi.org/10.3389/fphy.2016.00006.

Wallis, Sean. 2021. *Statistics in Corpus Linguistics Research: A New Approach*. New York, NY: Routledge.

Warriner, Amy Beth, Victor Kuperman and Marc Brysbaert. 2013. Norms of valence, arousal, and dominance for 13,915 English lemmas. *Behavior research methods* 45(4). 1191–1207.

Weissgerber, Tracey L., Vesna D. Garovic, Stacey J. Winham, Natasa M. Milic and Eric M. Prager. 2016. Transparent reporting for reproducible science. *Journal of Neuroscience Research* 94(10). 859–864. https://doi.org/10.1002/jnr.23785.

Wieling, Martijn. 2018. Analyzing dynamic phonetic data using generalized additive mixed modeling: A tutorial focusing on articulatory differences between L1 and L2 speakers of

English. *Journal of Phonetics*. Elsevier 70. 86–116. https://doi.org/10.1016/j.wocn.2018.03.002.

Wieling, Martijn, Simonetta Montemagni, John Nerbonne and Harald Baayen. 2014. Lexical differences between Tuscan dialects and standard Italian: Accounting for geographic and sociodemographic variation using generalized additive mixed modeling. *Language* 90(3). 669–692.

Winter, Bodo. 2016. Taste and smell words form an affectively loaded and emotionally flexible part of the English lexicon. *Language, Cognition and Neuroscience* 31(8). 975–988.

Winter, Bodo. 2019a. *Statistics for linguists: An introduction using R*. New York, NY: Routledge.

Winter, Bodo. 2019b. *Sensory linguistics: Language, perception, and metaphor*. Amsterdam: John Benjamins.

Winter, Bodo. 2021. Managing semantic norms for cognitive linguistics, corpus linguistics, and lexicon studies. In Andrea L. Berez-Kroeker, Bradley McDonnell, Eve Koller and Lauren B. Collister (eds.), *The open handbook of linguistic data management*. Cambridge, MA: MIT Press.

Winter, Bodo and Paul-Christian Bürkner. 2021. Poisson regression for linguists: A tutorial introduction to modeling count data with brms. *Language and Linguistics Compass*. https://doi.org/10.1111/lnc3.12439.

Winter, Bodo and Sarah E. Duffy. 2020. Can co-speech gestures alone carry the mental timeline? *Journal of Experimental Psychology: Learning, Memory, and Cognition* 46(9). 1768–1781. https://doi.org/10.1037/xlm0000836.

Winter, Bodo, Sarah E. Duffy and Jeannette Littlemore. 2020. Power, gender, and individual differences in spatial metaphor: The role of perceptual stereotypes and language statistics. *Metaphor and Symbol*. Taylor and Francis 35(3). 188–205. https://doi.org/10.1080/10926488.2020.1794319.

Winter, Bodo and Sven Grawunder. 2012. The phonetic profile of Korean formal and informal speech registers. *Journal of Phonetics* 40(6). 808–815. https://doi.org/10.1016/j.wocn.2012.08.006.

Winter, Bodo and Martine Grice. 2021. Independence and generalizability in linguistics. *Linguistics* 59(5). 1251–1277. https://doi.org/10.1515/ling-2019-0049.

Winter, Bodo and Marcus Perlman. 2021. Size sound symbolism in the English lexicon. *Glossa: A journal of general linguistics*. Open Library of Humanities 6(1). 1–13. https://doi.org/10.5334/gjgl.1646.

Winter, Bodo, Marcus Perlman and Asifa Majid. 2018. Vision dominates in perceptual language: English sensory vocabulary is optimized for usage. *Cognition* (179). 213–220.

Winter, Bodo and Martijn Wieling. 2016. How to analyze linguistic change using mixed models, Growth Curve Analysis and Generalized Additive Modeling. *Journal of Language Evolution*. Oxford University Press 1(1). 7–18. https://doi.org/10.1093/jole/lzv003.

Dennis Tay
Time series analysis with python

1 Introduction

A time series is a set of consecutive measurements of a random variable usually made at equal time intervals. Examples of important time series in the social and physical world include stock prices, heartbeat, rainfall, and birth/death rates. Figure 2.1 is a plot of a randomly generated series over 100 intervals. The fluctuations are a key visual trait of time series data that should look familiar to many people.

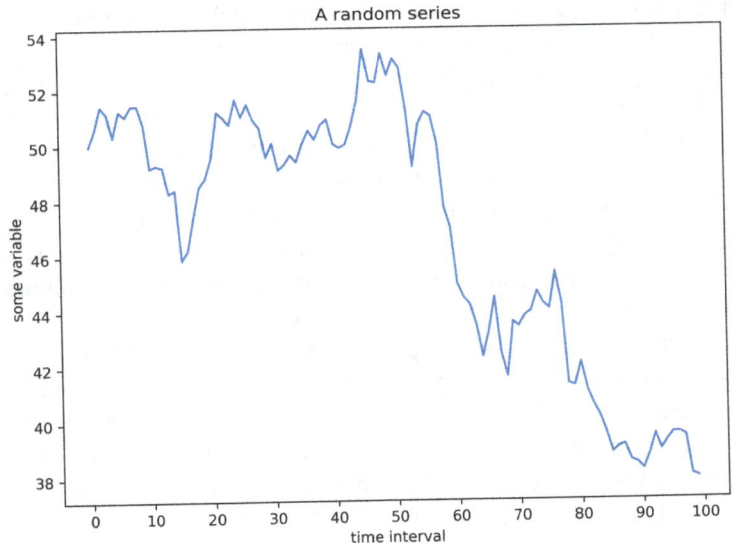

Figure 2.1: A randomly generated time series.

Acknowledgement: This work was supported by the HKSAR Research Grants Council (Project number: 15601019).

Dennis Tay, Department of English and Communication, The Hong Kong Polytechnic University, e-mail: dennis.tay@polyu.edu.hk

https://doi.org/10.1515/9783110687279-003

Examples like stock prices and birth/death rates are different phenomena that unfold over time intervals ranging from seconds to decades. However, those who analyze them share common objectives like discovering possible regularities underlying the fluctuations and forecasting future values. There are two broad information sources that support these objectives. In cases where the phenomenon and its contributing factors are well understood and measurable, we can use the latter as predictor variables and build various types of regression models. A country's life expectancy may for example be predictable from income, education, and/or healthcare levels. If on the other hand we are dealing with a "messier" phenomenon, then the observed past values of the series become the most reliable information source instead. More specifically, if past values are correlated with one another (i.e. autocorrelation or serial correlation), a mathematical model or equation can be derived to express present/future values in terms of past values. The parameters and coefficients of this model can then be interpreted to understand structural regularities underlying the series.

That is essentially what Time Series Analysis (TSA) is about. This chapter introduces and demonstrates the widely used Box-Jenkins methodology for TSA (Box et al. 2015) and its potential application in a cognitive linguistics setting. It assumes basic knowledge of statistical terminology especially with regard to regression. I begin with a brief survey of contexts in which time series data is of potential interest to cognitive linguists, and what insights TSA may reveal. I then illustrate the methodology with a focused example of the use of metaphors across 60 psychotherapy sessions. This chapter draws from Chapter 2 of Tay (2019), a book-length account introducing TSA to discourse researchers. However, it differs substantially in its emphases in accordance with the central points of the present volume: that data analytics i) blend automated statistical analysis with domain-specific knowledge and experience, and ii) induce analytic possibilities from relatively unstructured datasets where few assumptions are initially made. Equations will be used only when necessary to elaborate concepts. The methodology is implemented in Python 3.7. Annotated code is provided at the end of this chapter.

2 Time series data in cognitive linguistic contexts

Time series data is obviously not exclusive to cognitive linguistics. There are however many examples where time is an underexplored variable of interest to cognitive linguists. Various linguistic and related phenomena can be patterned

across time in ways that have not always been explicitly accounted for. A cursory list of examples includes
- Corpora for the study of grammaticalization, inter- and intra-speaker variation, and so on (Neels 2020)
- Experimental data; e.g. psychophysiological response markers to linguistic stimuli (Tay 2020)
- Discourse and interactional analyses under a cognitive sociolinguistic framework (Geeraerts et al. 2010; Kristiansen and Dirven 2008)

As this volume shows, compared to fixing independent and dependent variables for statistical analysis in (cognitive) linguistics, data analytics aim to explore relatively unstructured datasets and induce emergent research questions. Such a bottom-up approach squares with the *black box* philosophy of the Box-Jenkins TSA method (Keating and Wilson 2019). Compare, for example, a standard regression model with a TSA model. Both seem to be conceptually similar in expressing an outcome variable of interest as a (linear) combination of other variables. However, the former involves pre-specifying and measuring predictor variables to test their 'fit' with the outcome variable. We will see that TSA starts instead with *only* the observed series itself. It is a process of extracting patterns from the series until pure randomness or, in statistical parlance, *white noise* remains. Only then are the patterns interpreted, with respect to domain-specific knowledge (i.e. linguistic theory), as potential explanations of why the series turned out the way it did. This dovetails with two key assumptions underpinning our guiding example of discourse analysis; i) the data-generating processes behind discourse are not easily modeled with preconceived variables, and ii) emergent patterns and phenomena are often expected and interpreted *a posteriori*.

As a further illustration of the above, imagine an outcome variable y measured over 30 intervals. A standard linear regression model is fitted to test for a relationship between y and the passing of time. Figure 2.2 shows i) the plot of y against time t with the estimated regression line and ii) the plot of residuals; i.e. the difference between the observed and predicted value at each time point. They suggest a good overall fit as the observed values are close to the regression line, and the residuals are equally distributed around zero in either direction. Both the intercept and coefficient are statistically significant ($p < 0.0001$). The translucent band around the regression line indicating 95% confidence intervals is reasonably thin, and $R^2 = 0.857$ is considered high. The model ($y_t = 0.812t + 14.274$) could thus be considered good for general purposes.

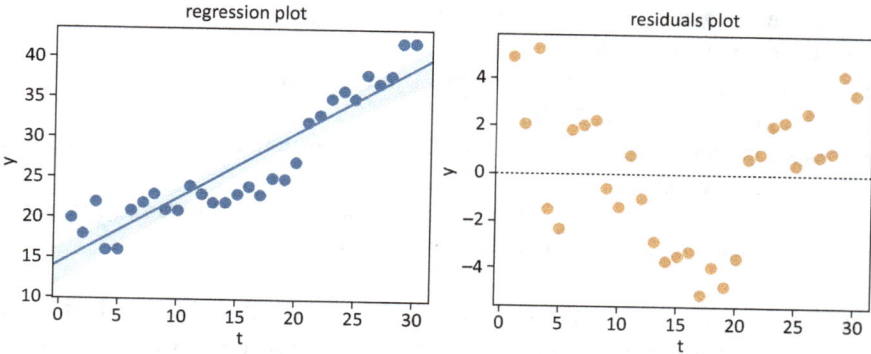

Figure 2.2: A hypothetical standard regression and residuals plot.

However, a closer look reveals that the residuals, or prediction errors, tend to persist in the same direction over many consecutive intervals. The values for intervals 20–30 are all predicted to be lower than what they actually are, with visual clues of a growing upward deviation. If the objective of this model is to forecast the 31st interval and beyond, we will be making a forecast error in the wrong direction. In other words, the overall "fit" conceals localized upward and downward movements that may be revealing context-specific implications such as a growing/falling momentum in the use of some discourse feature. TSA models, in contrast, account for these movements because they are based on the fundamental property of *autocorrelation* in the series; i.e. how successive values in time are correlated with one another. In other words, they are intended to capture not just the way things are, but the way things move (Hyndman and Athanasopoulos 2018).

3 Autocorrelation in time series

Autocorrelation or serial correlation is the correlation between values within a series separated by a given number of intervals. We can see it as the correlation between the series and a "lagged" version of itself. Table 2.1 illustrates this concept by reproducing the data from Figure 2.2 above.

Figure 2.2 was generated by correlating the 30 paired values of t and y_t as per standard linear regression. This imposes a general fit on the data and assumes independence among the 30 y values. The lag 1 and lag 2 columns in Table 2.1, on the other hand, juxtapose each y_t value with the value one and two intervals later respectively (i.e. y_{t+1} and y_{t+2}). We can then calculate the

Table 2.1: Autocorrelation at lags 1 and 2.

t	Lag 0 (original series) y_t	Lag 1 y_{t+1}	Lag 2 y_{t+2}
1	20	18	22
2	18	22	16
3	22	16	16
4	16	16	21
5	16	21	22
6	21	22	23
7	22	23	21
8	23	21	21
9	21	21	24
10	21	24	23
11	24	23	22
12	23	22	22
13	22	22	23
14	22	23	24
15	23	24	23
16	24	23	25
17	23	25	25
18	25	25	27
19	25	27	32
20	27	32	33
21	32	33	35
22	33	35	36
23	35	36	35
24	36	35	38
25	35	38	37
26	38	37	38

Table 2.1 (continued)

Lag 0 (original series)	Lag 1	Lag 2
27	37	38	42
28	38	42	42
29	42	42	–
30	42	–	–

(Pearson's) correlation between the 29 paired values of y_t and y_{t+1}, as well as the 28 paired values of y_t and y_{t+2}, and so on, to derive the "lag 1 autocorrelation" and "lag 2 autocorrelation" – or more generally, the "lag k autocorrelation". The longer the time series, the greater number of lagged autocorrelations we can calculate, but each higher lag will have one pair of values less. The original series in the first column is thus called "lag 0", and the lag 0 autocorrelation is always +1 because it is simply the correlation of the series with itself. Autocorrelations explicitly measure the degree of interdependence within the series as the values are sequenced in time.

Like any other correlation coefficient, a lag k autocorrelation ranges from −1 to +1. A statistically significant positive lag k autocorrelation means that values at time t and $t+k$ tend to move in the same direction up/downwards. A significant negative lag k autocorrelation means that values at time t and $t+k$ tend to move in opposite directions. Therefore, a series of up/downward movements over consecutive intervals imply a strong autocorrelation at low lags since neighboring values are moving in the same direction. As we will see, the TSA process involves calculating all autocorrelations up to a specified k (usually at least 10) to yield the overall autocorrelation function (ACF) of the series. The ACF is sometimes called the *sample* autocorrelation as opposed to the *theoretical* autocorrelation. This is because each set of time series data is considered a sample instantiation of an idealized underlying theoretical series.

Closely related to and as important as the autocorrelation function is the *partial* autocorrelation function (PACF). The lag k partial autocorrelation is simply the correlation between values at time t and $t+k$ with the effects of the intervening time periods (from $t+1$ to $t+k-1$) controlled for. As we will see, the ACF and PACF of a time series often exhibit contrasting behavior, which provide clues or "signatures" that are crucial in helping the analyst decide on candidate models. Like the ACF, the PACF is sometimes called the *sample* partial autocorrelation as opposed to the *theoretical* partial autocorrelation.

4 Components of time series data

Before moving on to illustrate Box-Jenkins TSA step by step, Figure 2.3 shows the various structural components of a typical time series. The concept of autocorrelation will now help us understand TSA as a process of "filtering out" or extracting patterns from these components until the series becomes purely random.

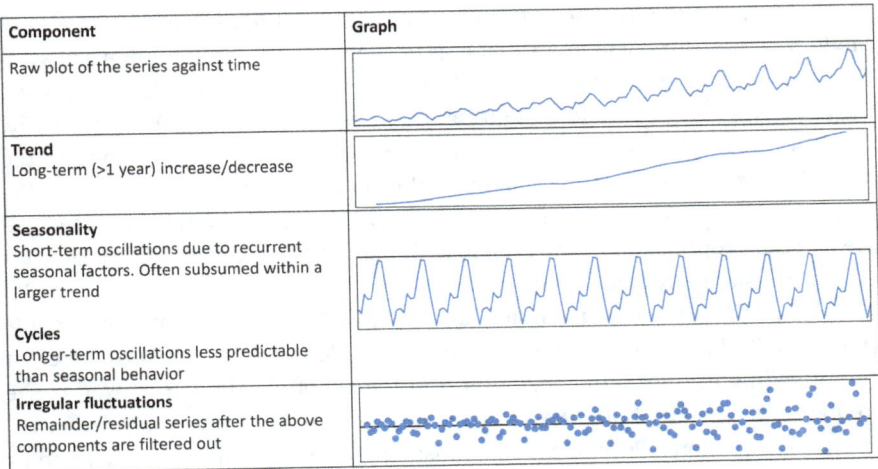

Component	Graph
Raw plot of the series against time	
Trend Long-term (>1 year) increase/decrease	
Seasonality Short-term oscillations due to recurrent seasonal factors. Often subsumed within a larger trend	
Cycles Longer-term oscillations less predictable than seasonal behavior	
Irregular fluctuations Remainder/residual series after the above components are filtered out	

Figure 2.3: Components of time series data.

The raw plot is like Figure 2.1, a simple initial plot of the series against time. Many naturally occurring series (e.g. Gross Domestic Product) are in fact decomposable into the components of trends, seasons, cycles, and irregular fluctuations. Trends are gradual increases or decreases over a long-term period which is usually defined as more than one year. Our example shows a steady increase that will be marked by strong autocorrelations that may persist into many lags (i.e. a high k), since values at time t and $t+k$ move in the same direction. In the GDP context, this would be likely due to general economic growth that persists in the background despite potential occasional drops (e.g. due to the recent COVID-19). Note that if the autocorrelation is negative, e.g. at lag 1, we will see a zig-zagging pattern instead since values at time t and $t+1$ move in opposite directions.

Seasonality or seasons refers to short-term oscillations due to stable recurrent factors like increases in sales during annual holidays. Because of their predictability, they are often subsumed under larger trends. They are likewise marked by a strong positive autocorrelation at lag *k* where *k* is some multiple that defines the season. If we are tracking monthly sales data of Christmas gifts over several years, then we would expect a strong autocorrelation at lag 12 because the pattern recurs every 12 months (e.g. gradual rise into December followed by a gradual dip). Cycles, on the other hand, are less predictable longer-term oscillations such as five to seven-year business cycles of expansion and recession. They can be misinterpreted as trends if the observed series is not long enough.

The remainder after the above components are "filtered out" is a series of random or irregular fluctuations that are conceptually similar to residuals in standard regression models. It should be clear by now that TSA crucially depends on the autocorrelational structure of the series, as elaborated below. Very generally, the TSA process follows either an additive or multiplicative approach where the series is modeled as either the sum or product of trends, seasons, and cycles. We will illustrate only the additive approach here. In general, multiplicative models are more appropriate only when the magnitude of trends, cycles, and/or seasons change substantially across time.

Many TSA textbooks use financial examples to explain these components (Box et al. 2015; Chatfield 1989; Vandaele 1983). Here is where we introduce our cognitive linguistic example for the rest of the chapter – the normalized usage frequencies of metaphors in a consecutive series of 60 weekly psychological counseling sessions. Psychological counseling (or psychotherapy) is defined as a mental healthcare activity where therapists use clinical methods and interpersonal stances to modify behaviors, cognitions, and/or emotions in clients (Norcross 1990). Metaphors are frequently used to conceptualize and express things that are otherwise hard to describe (McMullen 2008; Tay 2013), but relevant research has tended to focus on isolated examples and their therapeutic functions and overlook usage patterns across the span of treatment (Tay 2017).

In order to focus on explaining the methodology, the observed variable is simply the number of metaphorically used words per 100 words in each session transcript without further classification into source and target domains. A trend in this case would mean a stable increase or decrease in overall metaphor use as the sessions progress, while a season or cycle would imply an interesting and underexplored periodicity in usage. We will see that TSA allows the analyst to capture specific details of such regularities where they exist, critically relate them to contextual and theoretical aspects underpinning the data, and conduct comparative analyses across contexts if desired.

5 Steps of the Box-Jenkins TSA methodology

The rest of the chapter will illustrate the six steps of the Box-Jenkins TSA methodology as shown in Figure 2.4.

Step 1
Inspect and transform series if necessary

Step 2
Calculate (partial) autocorrelations

Step 3
Identify candidate models

Step 4
Estimate parameters   *inadequate*

Step 5
Evaluate goodness-of-fit, residual diagnostics

Step 6   *adequate*
Forecasting and other uses

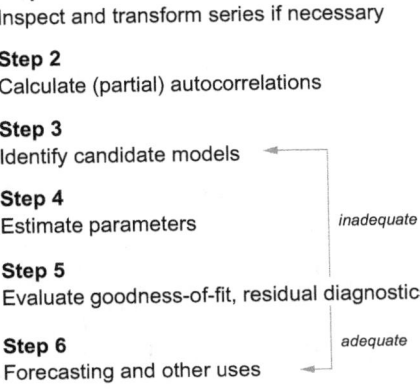

Figure 2.4: Steps of the Box-Jenkins TSA methodology.

We will see that the method combines computation with informed manual judgement and is thus rightly described as much of a skill as a procedure. In Steps 1, 3, 5 and 6, the analyst needs to make manual judgements on software-computed results for key tasks like candidate model selection and interpretation of the final model. Steps 2 and 4 are more purely computational and do not involve manual judgment. Step 5 also reflects the iterative nature of the method – if the selected model is deemed inadequate, the process returns to Step 3 where an alternative model is selected and tested.

5.1 Step 1: Inspect and transform series if necessary

We saw how inspecting the series can reveal clues about trends, seasons, and cycles. A more important reason for doing so is that TSA involves estimating properties of an abstract underlying process (e.g. usage patterns of metaphor in psychotherapy) based on just one realization of it (i.e. the actual dataset at hand). It is intuitively clear in contexts like financial data that only one realization is possible because we cannot go back in time to collect another "sample" of the same naturally occurring series. For valid statistical inferencing, we must therefore ensure that key properties of our "single-sample" series like mean and variance do not change across different sections of time. Such a series is known as "stationary", meeting the condition of stationarity. If a series is non-stationary, it needs to be transformed before proceeding to Step 2.

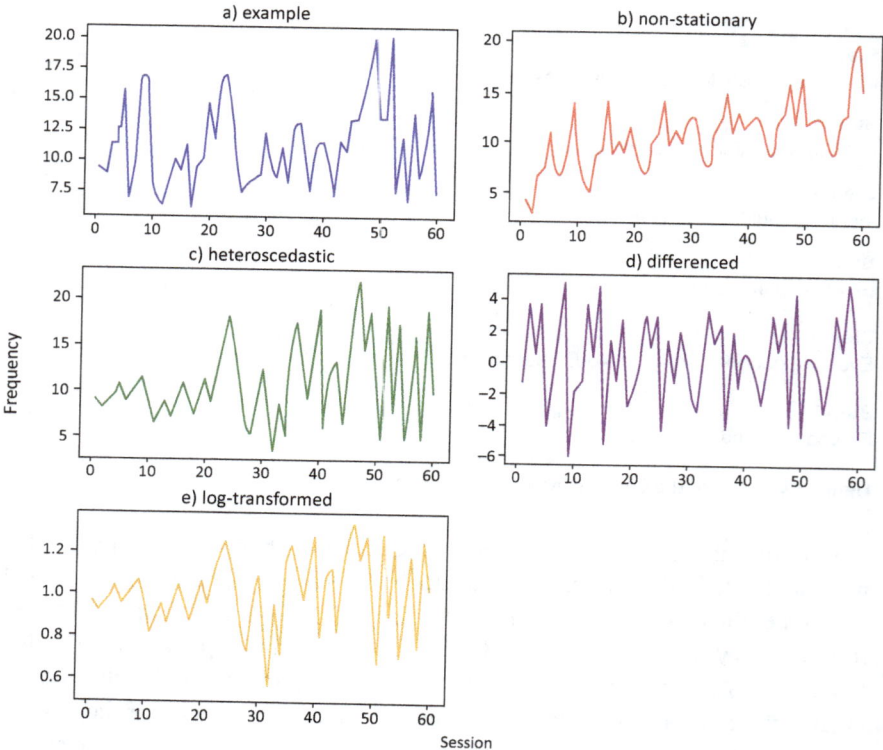

Figure 2.5: Examples of (non-)stationary series.

Figure 2.5 shows various examples of stationary series, non-stationary series, and outcomes of transformation procedures. Plot a) is our example metaphor series. By visual inspection, the mean of the series appears to be constant over time as the plot fluctuates consistently around a midpoint along the y-axis. We can verify this formally using the Durbin-Watson or Augmented Dickey-Fuller (ADF) test where H_0 = the series is non-stationary. The variance of the series also appears to be constant over time since the dispersion around the mean is not obviously changing. Such a series is known as "homoscedastic", meeting the condition of homoscedasticity. Generally, a stationary series is also homoscedastic but not vice-versa. Homoscedasticity can be verified with the Breusch-Pagan test or White test, where H_0 = the series is homoscedastic, but these are more often used on the variance of residuals from cross-sectional regression models.

Our example series in a) can therefore proceed to Step 2. Before that, let us consider some problematic cases. Plot b) is an example of a non-stationary series where the mean can be observed to rise steadily and is therefore not constant over time. To deal with this, we transform the series with a technique known as *differencing*. First-order differencing means to subtract the values of adjacent observations to derive a new series z_t (i.e. $z_t = y_t - y_{t-1}$). The outcome of differencing plot b) is shown in plot d), the mean of which is now constant over time. This is why some values in plot d) are negative. If the differenced series is still non-stationary, we can perform a further second-order differencing; i.e. difference the first-differenced series one more time ($z_t - z_{t-1}$). Most non-stationary time series will become stationary after at most two orders of differencing. Note that with every order of differencing, we "lose" one observed value. The recommended minimum number of observations for accurate TSA is 50 (McCleary et al. 1980).

Plot c) is an example of a heteroscedastic series with the dispersion around the mean visibly increasing over time. There are several options to deal with this. The first is to perform a log-transformation by converting each value y_t to $\log(y_t)$, the result of which is shown in plot e). This is known as variance stabilization – although the shape of the series remains the same, the scale of the y-axis is now reduced. Another option is to model the changing variance explicitly by using a different set of (G)ARCH (Generalized Autoregressive Conditional Heteroskedasticity) models (Bollerslev 1986). These are beyond the present scope, and as we will see, are much harder to interpret for our discourse analytic purposes compared to ARIMA models. This is because ARIMA models directly represent how the observed variable changes in time, while the modeled variances in (G)ARCH models have no obvious discourse analytic import. This is also why I would claim that the ARIMA approach to TSA is more suited to the modeling of language/discourse, because it is less easy to intuit an discourse analytic interpretation from models in other established approaches like exponential smoothing (Gardner 1985).

In some cases, the raw series may need to undergo both differencing and variance stabilization. If both procedures are required, variance stabilization should be performed first. Note that most TSA software will eventually convert transformed series back into their original forms when presenting forecasting results.

5.2 Step 2: Calculate (P)ACF

Once the series is stationary, we move on to calculate the (P)ACF in Step 2. The calculations are automatically performed in most software but subsequent interpretation of statistically significant autocorrelations, crucial for identifying candidate models, requires manual judgement. The (P)ACF are often presented in the form of correlograms (Figure 2.6), typically up to at least lag 10. Correlograms provide a useful visual aid for identifying candidate models in Step 3.

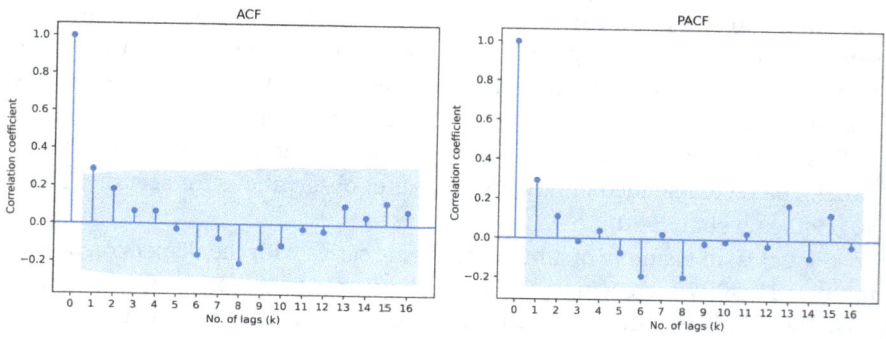

Figure 2.6: (P)ACF of example series.

For both ACF and PACF, the y-axis shows the correlation coefficient at the lag indicated by the x-axis. Notice that the value is always 1.0 at lag 0. The shaded boundaries are 95% confidence bands, beyond which the correlation is statistically significant at $\alpha=0.05$. Significant lag k autocorrelations will thus appear as "spikes" or vertical bars that extend beyond the confidence bands. In Figure 2.6, both the ACF and PACF clearly extend beyond the bands at lag 1 (only). Also notice that there is no seasonal behavior in our series as there are no spikes at higher seasonal lags. In unclear cases where the (P)ACF are very close to the bands, most software will calculate its t statistic (i.e. the correlation coefficient at that lag divided by its standard error) to determine if a spike exists. At $\alpha=0.05$, the absolute value of the t statistic should exceed 1.6 at low lags ($k<3$) and exceed 2.0 at higher lags.

Notice that while both ACF and PACF are significant at lag 1 in our example, the former tapers off or "dies down" gradually into later lags while the latter "cuts off" more abruptly. In some cases, the converse occurs, while in others both ACF and PACF die down or cut off in similar fashion. As mentioned earlier, the relative behavior of (P)ACF provides clues that help us select candidate models in Step 3.

5.3 Step 3: Identify candidate models

Candidate models in the Box-Jenkins TSA methodology are known as ARIMA (Autoregressive Integrated Moving Average) models. In Step 3, we decide which of the major ARIMA model types best describes our data based on the relative behavior of (P)ACF: an autoregressive (AR) model, a moving average (MA) model, or a combination of both (ARMA/ARIMA). Mathematically, AR models express the current value of the time series as a function of its past values, MA models express it as a function of irregular fluctuations in past intervals, while ARMA models combine both. The difference between ARMA and ARIMA is the letter I for "integrated". The latter is basically used in cases where differencing was performed to achieve stationarity in Step 1. We will soon discuss what these imply or "mean" in a discourse context.

For now, Table 2.2 offers key guidelines for candidate model selection based on the five most common behavior patterns of (P)ACF.

Table 2.2: Basic guidelines for model selection.

Behavior pattern	Candidate model
ACF has spikes up to lag k and cuts off after lag k PACF dies down	MA model of order k; i.e. MA(k) model
PACF has spikes up to lag k and cuts off after lag k ACF dies down	AR model of order k; i.e. AR(k) model
Both ACF and PACF have spikes up to lag k and cuts off after lag k	If ACF cuts off more abruptly, use MA(k) model If PACF cuts off more abruptly, use AR(k) model If both appear to cut off equally abruptly, try both models to see which fits better
Both ACF and PACF die down	ARMA model of order k; i.e. both MA(k) and AR(k) model
Both ACF and PACF have no spikes at all lags	No suitable model since autocorrelations are absent

The constant k for each model corresponds to the number of lags for which the (P)ACF is significant. The general form of an MA(k) model is $y_t = \mu - a_t - \theta_1 a_{t-1} \ldots - \theta_k a_{t-k}$ where
- y_t is the present value in the series
- μ is the mean of the series
- a_t is the residual (i.e. observed – predicted value) at time t

- $a_{t-1} \ldots a_{t-k}$ are past residuals from time *t-1* to *t-k*
- $\theta_1 \ldots \theta_k$ are coefficients also known as MA(k) operators

An MA(k) model is thus described as an MA model of order k. Likewise, the general form of an AR(k) model is $y_t = (1 - \Phi_1 - \ldots \Phi_k)\mu + a_t + \Phi_1 y_{t-1} \ldots + \Phi_k y_{t-k}$ where
- y_t is the present value in the series
- μ is the mean of the series
- a_t is the residual (i.e. observed − predicted value) at time *t*
- $y_{t-1} \ldots y_{t-k}$ are past series values from time *t-1* to *t-k*
- $\Phi_1 \ldots \Phi_k$ are coefficients also known as AR(k) operators
- $(1 - \Phi_1 - \ldots \Phi_k)\mu$ is known as the constant term of the model

An AR(k) model is thus described as an AR model of order k. ARMA models, by definition, simply combined AR/MA(k) models additively and therefore share the characteristics of both. It is not necessary to fully understand the above general forms, and they will be explained in context when we discuss our example later.

Applying the guidelines in Table 2.2 to the (P)ACF correlograms of our example series (Figure 2.6), where ACF has spikes up to lag 1 and dies down/PACF has spikes up to lag 1 and cuts off, we determine an AR(1) model to be the candidate model. Another common way to denote an ARIMA model is by ARIMA(p,d,q) where p=the number of AR operators, q=the number of MA operators and d=how many orders of differencing were performed. Our example AR(1) model can therefore also be expressed as an ARIMA(1,0,0) model. Even more generally, we have SARIMA or seasonal ARIMA models which capture seasonal phenomena in the data. This is beyond the present introductory scope, and seasonality is in any case seldom seen in spontaneous discourse contexts. Having determined a candidate model, we now move on to the standard statistical modeling procedures of estimating its parameters and determining the goodness-of-fit.

5.4 Step 4: Estimate parameters

Following common practice in data analytics, it is advisable to exclude the last few observations in a time series from the parameter estimation process, and later compare the predictions of the fitted model with these observations as an indication of its predictive quality. If the predictive quality and other aspects of goodness-of-fit are deemed acceptable, these observations can then be re-incorporated to re-estimate the model parameters and make further forecasts into the future. In TSA, this is known as "out-of-time validation" using a training (i.e. the series minus the last few observations) and validation dataset (the last few observations).

There is no hard and fast rule about the required size of the validation dataset, with recommendations ranging from 20% of the training dataset to being at least as large as the number of forecasting intervals eventually required. Many analysts further distinguish the validation dataset from a test dataset which will not be elaborated here (Ripley 1996: 354).

Figure 2.7 illustrates the relationship between the training and validation dataset. The first twelve observations are used to fit the model, and the final four are to be used as a comparison against the four-interval-ahead predictions of the fitted model. As per the second recommendation just described, four observations were used because the eventual purpose is to use the model to forecast four intervals into the (unobserved) future; i.e. on the dotted line.

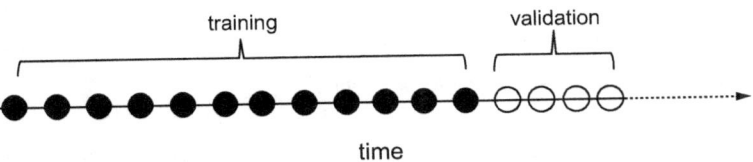

Figure 2.7: Training vs. validation data.

In general, a larger training dataset increases model precision because there are more samples from which to induce patterns. On the other hand, a larger validation dataset gives a better indication of how well these patterns predict actual data that has not been "seen" by the model. For our present example, we will withhold the final three observed values and use the first 57 values to estimate the model parameters.

Recall that the general form of an ARIMA model resembles that of a simple linear regression model $y = \beta_0 + \beta_1 x_1 \ldots + \beta_k x_k \ldots + e_t$. The intercept β_0 corresponds to the constant term $(1 - \Phi_1 - \ldots \Phi_k)\mu$ in AR models, and to μ in MA models. The independent variables $x_1 \ldots x_k$ correspond to past values $y_{t-1} \ldots y_{t-k}$ in AR models, and to past residuals $a_{t-1} \ldots a_{t-k}$ in MA models. The coefficients $\beta_1 \ldots \beta_k$ correspond to the AR and MA operators. Lastly, the error term e_t is conceptuaish equivalent to a_t. Therefore, the main parameters to be estimated in an ARIMA model are
– the intercept
– the AR/MA operators, or coefficients

Figure 2.8 shows the output of estimating the parameters of our AR(1) model using the SARIMAX class in *statsmodels*, a popular Python module.

```
Dep. Variable:                        y       No. Observations:              57
Model:               SARIMAX(1, 0, 0)         Log Likelihood           −148.192
Date:                Wed, 03 Jun 2020         AIC                       302.385
Time:                        11:05:48         BIC                       308.514
Sample:                             0         HQIC                      304.767
                                 - 57
Covariance Type:                  op8
------------------------------------------------------------------------------
                  coef    std err          z      P>|z|      [0.025      0.975]
------------------------------------------------------------------------------
intercept       7.4269      1.640      4.529      0.000       4.213      10.641
ar.L1           0.3295      0.120      2.743      0.006       0.094       0.565
sigma2         10.5892      2.245      4.718      0.000       6.190      14.988
==============================================================================
Ljung-Box (Q) :                 39.88    Jarque-Bera (JB):             1.08
Prob (Q) :                       0.48    Prob(JB):                     0.58
Heteroskedasticity (H) :         1.52    Skew:                         0.30
Prob (H) (two-sided) :           0.37    Kurtosis:                     2.68
------------------------------------------------------------------------------
```

Figure 2.8: Parameter estimation using SARIMAX in Python.

Among other details, the top panel shows the model being estimated (1,0,0), the number of observations (57), and different model fit statistics such as AIC and BIC. The bottom panel also includes model fit and residual diagnostics like the Ljung-Box Q and its associated p-value. These will be discussed in the next step. The middle panel shows the main estimated parameters and coefficients (coef), standard errors (std err) and z-scores (z; i.e. number of standard deviations away from 0), whether they are statistically significantly different from zero (P>|z|), and 95% confidence intervals of the estimates [0.025 0.975]. Our intercept is 7.4369 and AR(1) operator is 0.3295, both of which are significantly different from zero. The sigma2 estimates the variance of the error term a_t, which essentially quantifies how well the model predicts observed values and also affects the standard errors of the coefficients. In sum, our AR(1) model takes the form of y_t = 7.4269 + 0.3295$_1 y_{t-1}$ + a_t. Note that 7.4269 = (1− Φ_1 − ... Φ_k)μ or (1−0.3295)μ. We can verify the mean of the series μ in this way. It should be mentioned that different statistical software may produce slightly different results because of alternative computations of some of the above. For example, sigma2 estimates can be "biased" on "unbiased" depending on whether the number of model parameters is taken into account (Brockwell and Davis 2016). These differences are usually of little practical consequence, and as before, it is not necessary to fully understand all the technical details involved in order to perform basic TSA.

We are almost ready to interpret what this model reveals about metaphor frequencies across our psychotherapy sessions. Before doing that, we need the final step of evaluating the goodness-of-fit and performing residual diagnostics on this model.

5.5 Step 5: Evaluate goodness-of-fit, residual diagnostics

Evaluating the model practically consists of two sub-steps: how well it "fits" the data (goodness-of-fit), and whether it has captured all available patterns from the data (residual diagnostics). We first consider goodness-of-fit.

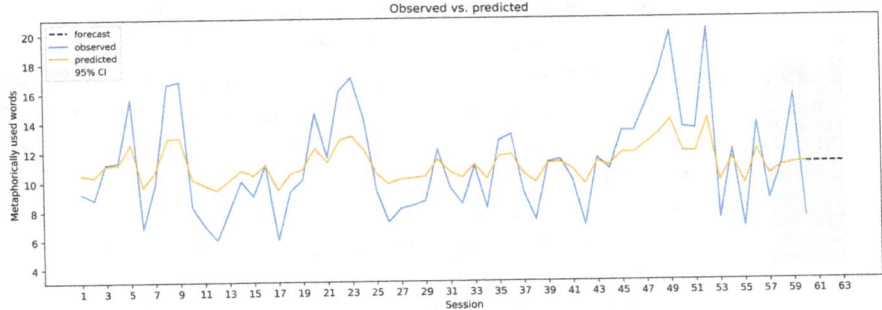

Figure 2.9: Observed vs. predicted plot.

Figure 2.9 superimposes the plot of the observed series with predicted values generated from our model ($y_t = 7.4269 + 0.3295y_{t-1} + a_t$), as well as forecasted values of future sessions 61 and 63 (dotted). Recall that our training dataset used only Session 1 to 57, so the disparity between the lines from session 58 to 60 provides an indication of predictive quality using data that was not "seen" by the model. The gray boundary from session 58 onwards indicates 95% confidence intervals of each prediction/forecast. Many analysts also calculate prediction intervals, which we will briefly discuss later.

Goodness-of-fit can be subjectively evaluated by visual inspection of Figure 2.9 and supported by more objective measures of model fit and forecast errors. We see from Figure 2.9 that the model seems better at capturing the "shape" of the series than its magnitude. The predicted values plot accurately depicts the vacillation of the series but is clearly more "compressed" than it. It also correctly predicts the increase from session 57 to 58, but not the decrease afterwards. Because the model is AR(1), the forecasts of future sessions will be "bootstrapped" onto the prior session, so any forecast beyond the final observed value will move in the same direction.

In terms of objective measures, we can first consider the Akaike Information Criterion (AIC) or Bayesian Information Criterion (BIC), two common measures of out-of-sample prediction error (Chakrabarti and Ghosh 2011). A lower value indicates higher predictive accuracy. Our values are 302.285 and 308.514

respectively as shown in the upper right corner of Figure 2.8. However, AIC/BIC are relative measures used to decide between more than one candidate model; e.g. cases where the third (P)ACF behavior pattern in Table 2.2 is seen. In our example, only one model was explicitly identified, so there is no reference point for our AIC/BIC values. We therefore use other ways to directly quantify the error magnitude. One option is the mean absolute error (MAE) which simply sums the absolute error (predicted − observed, positive values only) for all observations and divides this by the number of observations. Similar to this is the root mean squared error (RMSE) which first squares each error and then takes the square root of the mean of squared errors, analogous to the calculation of variance and standard deviation. MAE and RMSE are easy to interpret because they reflect the error directly in terms of the unit of the series involved. In our example, RMSE=2.383, which roughly means our model is off by 2.383 metaphors per session on average. They are thus described as scale-dependent measures. However, if we want to compare modeling results across different phenomena with different units, scale-independent measures that calculate errors as percentages are preferred. The most common among these is the mean absolute percentage error (MAPE), which sums the percentage error ([predicted − observed] / observed * 100%) for all observations and divides this by the number of observations. The biggest disadvantage with MAPE is when observed values are 0 or close to 0, leading to undefined or extreme MAPE values. Another less obvious disadvantage is when the unit is not a ratio variable and has an arbitrary zero point (e.g. temperature), rendering percentage errors meaningless. In our example of metaphors in therapy, MAPE=19.326. This is quite high compared to non-linguistic time series (e.g. finance data) and time series of other linguistic phenomena I have observed (e.g. personal pronouns), but should be interpreted in light of what we expect from the nature of both the phenomenon and context at hand. It is also advisable to evaluate the predictive accuracy of the model at hand with the outcomes of more simplistic models that often perform surprisingly well. These include the "mean model" where the next forecasted value is simply the mean value of all observations, and the "naïve model" where the next forecasted value is simply the most recently observed value. The latter in particular is widely believed to reflect the "random walk" nature of finance data where the past often provides no reliable insight on future prices. As per Occam's razor, if the fitted ARIMA model does not substantially outperform these simple alternatives, there is little reason to use it.

We then move on to consider whether the model has extracted all available patterns from the data using a set of procedures called residual diagnostics. Residual diagnostics are important for almost all types of statistical modeling. In TSA, it means "diagnosing" if the modeling process has really transformed the original series into irregular fluctuations (Figure 2.3). We do this by treating the residuals itself as a time series, lining up each residual (predicted value − observed value) from Session 1 to 60 and checking whether this series contains any patterns across time.

The first thing is to check for autocorrelation in the residual series, just like Step 2 of our main process. Absence of spikes in (P)ACF at all lags implies that there is no more information left in the residuals. Spikes would suggest that the residuals are still patterned across time, which needs to be addressed either by modeling the residual series and adding it to the original model, or going back to Step 3 to choose another candidate model. The second thing is to check that the residual series has a mean value close to zero, which suggests that positive and negative errors cancel one another out. A non-zero mean would lead to biased forecasts in either direction, which is often addressed by simply adjusting forecasts by an amount equivalent to the mean. In addition to these two conditions, it is ideal (but not necessary) for the residuals to be normally distributed and heteroscedastic for easier calculation of forecast prediction intervals. For example, the 95% prediction intervals for a one-step-ahead forecast would simply be the forecasted value ± 1.96 standard deviations of the normally distributed residual series. More complex bootstrapping methods might be required otherwise.

Figure 2.10 is a convenient "package" of plots related to the diagnostics described above. The correlograms show that there are no spikes in (P)ACF in the residuals. This reflects the result of the Ljung-Box Q test (Q=39.88, p=0.48) shown at the bottom left of Figure 2.8, where H_0 = the series is independently distributed and has zero autocorrelation. Our p=0.48 thus suggests that our residuals are likely to be sampled from such a series. The density plot shows that the mean of the residual series is near zero, and the histogram further suggests it to be normally distributed. This is again supported by a Shapiro-Wilk test of normality (W=0.988, p=0.853) where, H_0 = the series is normally distributed.

It is now time to consider all the above information and decide if our AR(1) model is adequate. Recall from earlier that Step 5 involves both computation and manual judgment. While goodness-of-fit and residual diagnostic statistics are automatically computed, the final decision may depend on other factors like knowledge of the modeled phenomenon and the specific objectives of modeling. It is well known that discourse is "messy" in content and structure alike (Eubanks 1999). Therefore, although we may indeed find meaningful time series patterns in metaphors in a spontaneous interactional context like psychotherapy, we should not expect the same extent of structural regularity as, for example, sales data of a common product. We can further consider if our focus is to understand the "shape" of the series or to make reliable forecasts.

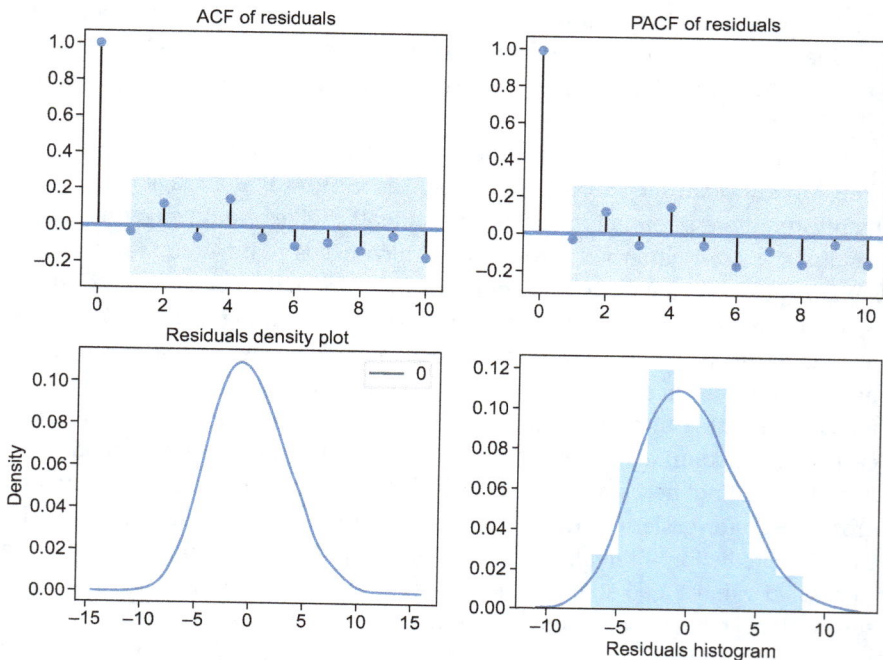

Figure 2.10: Residual diagnostics.

Understanding the shape of the series is likely to be more pertinent than forecasting in most discourse analytic contexts. Given these considerations, we would thus pay more attention to the fact that i) the model parameters are statistically significant, ii) the shape of the observed and predicted plot are similar, and iii) the residuals are not autocorrelated and have a near-zero mean. We would be more inclined to overlook high AIC/BIC, poor predictive accuracy (e.g. MAPE), non-normally distributed residuals, and/or large prediction intervals of forecasts. We can therefore conclude that our AR(1) model is adequate, and proceed to the final step of forecasting and other uses. If we instead conclude that the model is inadequate, the process reverts to Step 3 where another candidate model is chosen.

5.6 Step 6: Forecasting and other uses

Forecasting is an essential aspect in contexts where there is a practical need to predict future values. Recall that our final AR(1) model is formally expressed as $y_t = 7.4269 + 0.3295 y_{t-1} + a_t$. To forecast one interval ahead, we simply substitute the most recent value of y_t into the equation. For example, if today's value is 10, tomorrow's value is forecasted as **7.4269 + 0.3295(10) + a_t** or **10.7219 + a_t** where a_t is the error term that will only be known when tomorrow's actual value is observed. We may be able to provide a reasonable forecast of this error term if, for example, the already observed error terms (or residuals) follow a well-understood distribution like the normal distribution as mentioned above.

We can refer back to Figure 2.9 where each value of the orange line and the dotted line thereafter is predicted based on our model. Note that if a longer forecasting horizon is required beyond the present interval, each successive forecast will itself be based upon a forecasted value. Prediction intervals take this into account and thus always become longer as the horizon increases. Confidence intervals, on the other hand, estimate the uncertainty of each predicted value only at that point in time. The difference between them is nonetheless not always insisted upon (Granger and Newbold 1986).

In most cognitive linguistic contexts, however, forecasting is probably not the primary objective of the descriptivist linguist. Our example of metaphor use in psychotherapy might be an exception – therapists might for instance want to anticipate clients' future uses of different types of metaphor, in order to plan or adjust their interaction styles if deemed necessary (Tay 2017). This is broadly analogous to using time series models for statistical process control (Alwan and Roberts 1988) in manufacturing and other industries. Statistical forecasting techniques that rely entirely on data and probability principles should nevertheless be seen as just one of many tools for the analyst/practitioner. Judgmental or qualitative forecasts that rely more on knowledge and experience could be just as important in research and practice (Hyndman and Athanasopoulos 2018).

Going back to our example from a discourse analytic point of view, it would be more interesting to use the model for a structural interpretation of the regularities underlying the existing data. This is done by examining the parameters and coefficients of the model $y_t = 7.4269 + 0.3295_1 y_{t-1} + a_t$.

Recall that y_t is the number of metaphorically used words per 100 words in session t of 60 psychological counseling transcripts. The model informs us that
- the estimated mean number of metaphorically used words is 11.1 per 100; i.e. the metaphor density is 11.1% (7.4269 = $(1- \Phi_1)\mu$)
- an increase of 1 unit of metaphor use in the previous session is linked to a 0.3295 unit increase in the present session

The first point can be discussed with respect to relevant literature on the expected frequencies of metaphor use in psychotherapy and other discourse contexts. The second point suggests that metaphor use across the sessions is characterized by a short-term continuity. Since we have an AR(1) model, past sessions exert a (non-causal) influence across a relatively short one-session span. Also, because the AR(1) coefficient 0.3295 is positive, consecutive sessions tend to move in the same direction, maintaining either a local rise or fall. The analyst can then return to the transcripts and look for potential explanations for this continuity. A possible scenario is that the dyad has chanced upon a particularly insightful metaphor (See Ferrara 1994) and spontaneously make a *short term* commitment to engage with and elaborate on it. The converse scenario of a short-term continuous decrease is also not uncommon, as an initially interesting metaphor gradually fades away. The variable at hand could of course be far more nuanced than the present example, for example the frequencies of specific sources and targets of theoretical interest.

At an even more general level, the very initial step of whether the variable at hand is "modelable" can also be discussed (Tay 2021). A modelable series is simply one for which a well-defined model can be found to fit adequately, like our example. Conversely, a non-modelable series randomly fluctuates over time, such that (P)ACF have no spikes at all lags (Table 2.2). In other words, the series is equivalent to white noise right from the start. Recall that a modelable series means we can predict with varying degrees of accuracy the value at any interval. In a discourse analytic context, we could then explore which of the following is more likely

- the predictability of the discourse variable stems from corresponding predictability of the background event; i.e. the discourse passively "reflects" the event, an example being the stable four-yearly increase in the phrase "olympic games" in newspapers
- the predictability of the discourse variable exists *despite* unpredictable background events; i.e. the discourse might in some way be construing the event

It should be clear that the latter resonates better with constructivist or cognitive linguistic notions of "construal"; i.e. how language is used to construct understandings of the social world (Taylor and MacLaury 1995). It is also likely to be the better explanation for our metaphor in therapy example, since most therapeutic dyads are by nature unpredictable. On the other hand, a non-modelable series implies that regardless of whether the background event is predictable, the use of that linguistic/discursive variable does not evidence noteworthy patterning across time. An analogous reasoning process can be applied to other types of cognitive linguistic data, such as experimental data, for deeper insights.

6 Conclusion

This chapter demonstrated how time series analysis with the Box-Jenkins approach can inform cognitive linguistics research, with the central example of metaphor use in psychotherapy sessions. The six basic steps involved were explained in detail, and should provide an adequate introduction for interested readers to perform a similar analysis on their own data. Interpretation of time series models could be made at two levels depending on the objectives at hand: i) more generally, whether a series is modelable can shed light on the relationship between the data and its generating context. For discourse analyses this is directly relevant to the notion of construal; ii) each specific model can also be interpreted in detail with reference to its parameters and coefficients, for deeper understanding of the precise nature of its structural regularities across time.

Appendix: Python 3.7 code

```
#import relevant packages and libraries
import seaborn as sns
import numpy as np
import pandas as pd
import statsmodels.api as sm
import matplotlib.pyplot as plt
from pandas import read_csv
from pandas import Series
from pandas import DataFrame
from scipy import stats
from statsmodels.graphics.tsaplots import plot_acf
from statsmodels.graphics.tsaplots import plot_pacf
from statsmodels.graphics.gofplots import qqplot
from statsmodels.tsa.arima_model import ARIMA
from statsmodels.tsa import seasonal
from statsmodels.tsa.stattools import adfuller
from statsmodels.stats.diagnostic import het_breuschpagan

#import data and plot raw/differenced series as required
series = pd.read_csv(data.csv', header=0, index_col='Time')
series.plot()
series.diff(periods=1).plot()
```

```
#remove final few observations to form training dataset. duplicate series
('originalseries') for later comparison of observations and predictions
series=series.iloc[0:len(series)-3]
originalseries = series

#plot (P)ACF
plot_acf(series.Tone, lags=16)
plot_pacf(series.Au, lags=16)

# Augmented Dickey-Fuller (ADF) test for stationarity
result=adfuller(series, autolag='AIC')
print('ADF statistic: %f' % result[0])
print('p-value: %f' % result[1])
print('Critical Values:')
for key, value in result[4].items():
    print('\t%s: %.3f' % (key, value))
if result[1]>0.05:
    print ('Series is not stationary')
else:
    print ('Series is stationary')

#fit non-seasonal model (p,d,q)
model=sm.tsa.SARIMAX(series.Tone, order=(0,0,0),trend='c')
model_fit=model.fit()
print(model_fit.summary())

#use fitted model to predict and forecast values
predict=(model_fit.get_prediction(start=1,end=3+len(series)))
predictinfo=predict.summary_frame()
forecast=(model_fit.get_forecast(steps=6))
forecastinfo=forecast.summary_frame()

#plot predicted and observed values ('originalseries')
fig, ax = plt.subplots(figsize=(15, 5))
forecastinfo['mean'].plot(ax=ax, style='k--',label="forecast")
plt.plot(originalseries, label="observed",color='blue')
plt.plot(predict.predicted_mean, label="predicted",color='orange')
ax.fill_between(forecastinfo.index, forecastinfo['mean_ci_lower'],
forecastinfo['mean_ci_upper'], color='k', alpha=0.05, label="95% CI")
ax.set_ylabel('Score')
```

```
ax.set_xlabel('Interval')
ax.set_title('Observed vs. predicted')
plt.legend(loc='upper right',fontsize=9)
plt.setp(ax, xticks=np.arange(1, 115, step=4))
ax.tick_params(axis ='x', rotation = 0)

#residual diagnostics
residuals = DataFrame(model_fit.resid)
fig,axes=plt.subplots(2,2)
fig.tight_layout(pad=2.0)
fig.suptitle('Residual diagnostics',fontsize=14,y=1.05)
plot_acf(residuals, ax=axes[0,0], alpha=0.05, title='ACF of residuals',
lags=10)
plot_pacf(residuals, ax=axes[0,1], alpha=0.05, title='PACF of
residuals', lags=10)
residuals.plot(kind='kde',ax=axes[1,0], title='Residuals density
plot')
sns.distplot(residuals,kde=True, color='blue', axlabel='Residuals
histogram',ax=axes[1,1])

#calculate MAPE
predicted=(predict.predicted_mean)
observed=originalseries
APE=0
for i in range(1, len(originalseries)):
    PE=100*abs(predicted.iloc[i]-observed.iloc[i]) / observed.iloc[i]
    APE=PE+APE
MAPE=APE/(len(series))
print('MAPE: %f' % MAPE)
```

References

Alwan, Layth C. & Harry V. Roberts. 1988. Time-series modeling for statistical process control. *Journal of Business & Economic Statistics* 6(1). 87–95.

Bollerslev, Tim. 1986. Generalized autoregressive conditional heteroskedasticity. *Journal of Econometrics* 31(3). 307–327.

Box, George E.P., Gwilym M. Jenkins, Gregory C. Reinsel & Greta M. Ljung. 2015. *Time series analysis: Forecasting and control*, 5th edn. Hoboken, New Jersey: John Wiley & Sons.

Brockwell, Peter J. & Richard A. Davis. 2016. *Introduction to time series and forecasting*. Switzerland: Springer.

Chakrabarti, Arijit & Jayanta K. Ghosh. 2011. AIC, BIC and recent advances in model selection. *Philosophy of Statistics 7*. 583–605.

Chatfield, Christopher. 1989. *The analysis of time series: An introduction*, 4th edn. London: Chapman and hall.

Eubanks, Philip. 1999. Conceptual metaphor as rhetorical response: A reconsideration of metaphor. *Written Communication* 16(2). 171–199.

Ferrara, Kathleen Warden. 1994. *Therapeutic ways with words*. New York: Oxford University Press.

Gardner, Everette S. 1985. Exponential smoothing: The state of the art. *Journal of Forecasting* 4(1). 1–28.

Geeraerts, Dirk, Gitte Kristiansen & Yves Peirsman. 2010. *Advances in cognitive sociolinguistics*. Berlin: Mouton de Gruyter.

Granger, Clive William John & Paul Newbold. 1986. *Forecasting economic time series*, 2nd edn. New York: Academic Press.

Hyndman, Rob J. & George Athanasopoulos. 2018. *Forecasting: Principles and practice*. An online textbook.

Keating, Barry & J. Holton Wilson. 2019. *Forecasting and Predictive Analytics: WithForecastX*, 7th edn. New York: McGraw-Hill Education.

Kristiansen, Gitte & René Dirven. 2008. *Cognitive sociolinguistics: Language variation, cultural models, social systems*. Berlin: Mouton de Gruyter.

McCleary, Richard, Richard Hay, Errol E. Meidinger & David McDowall. 1980. *Applied time series analysis for the social sciences*. Beverly Hills, Calif: Sage Publications.

McMullen, Linda M. 2008. Putting it in context: Metaphor and psychotherapy. In Raymond W. Gibbs (ed.), *The Cambridge Handbook of Metaphor and Thought* 397–411. Cambridge: Cambridge University Press.

Neels, Jakob. 2020. Lifespan change in grammaticalisation as frequency-sensitive automation: William Faulkner and the let alone construction. *Cognitive Linguistics* 31(2). 339–365.

Norcross, John C. 1990. An eclectic definition of psychotherapy. In Jeffrey K. Zeig & Michael W. Munion (eds.), *What is psychotherapy? Contemporary Perspectives*, 218–220. San Francisco: Jossey-Bass.

Ripley, Brian D. 1996. *Pattern recognition and neural networks*. Cambridge: Cambridge university press.

Tay, Dennis. 2013. *Metaphor in psychotherapy: A descriptive and prescriptive analysis*. John Benjamins Publishing.

Tay, Dennis. 2017. Time series analysis of discourse: A case study of metaphor in psychotherapy sessions. *Discourse Studies* 19(6). 694–710.

Tay, Dennis. 2019. *Time Series Analysis of Discourse: Method and Case Studies* London and New York: Routledge.

Tay, Dennis. 2020. Affective engagement in metaphorical versus literal communication styles in counseling. *Discourse Processes* 57(4). 360–375.

Tay, Dennis. 2021. Modelability across time as a signature of identity construction on YouTube. *Journal of Pragmatics 182*. 1–15.

Taylor, John R. & Robert E. MacLaury. 1995. *Language and the Cognitive Construal of the World*. Berlin: Mouton de Gruyter.

Vandaele, Walter. 1983. *Applied time series and Box-Jenkins models*. New York: Academic Press.

Matteo Fuoli
Structural equation modeling in R: A practical introduction for linguists

1 Introduction

This chapter provides a hands-on introduction to structural equation modeling (SEM), a powerful statistical technique that allows researchers to test complex causal models involving multiple interconnected variables. SEM is widely used in the social and behavioral sciences. Within linguistics, its application has been largely confined to the areas of second language acquisition and language testing (e.g. Koizumi and In'nami 2020; Zhang 2017). Work in Cognitive Linguistics has yet to harness the potential of this approach. In this chapter, I aim to show that SEM can be a useful tool to uncover the psychological effects of linguistic choices in discourse and advance our understanding of the cognitive underpinnings of language.

The main purpose of the chapter is to describe the key steps involved in performing a SEM analysis using the open source statistical programming language R (R Core Team 2016). The dataset I will use to illustrate this technique comes from an experimental study which investigated the effects of the use of *stance* verbs such as *know, want, believe* in a persuasive genre of business discourse (Fuoli and Hart 2018). Specifically, the study investigated how the use of these linguistic devices influences the recipient's trust in the company who produced the text. The complete R code as well as the data used in the analysis are available on the Open Science Framework: bit.ly/3Lbv7oh.

I will begin by reviewing the basics of SEM and by outlining the fundamental steps of this method. Next, I will briefly summarize the case study and introduce the data. I will then demonstrate how to carry out the analysis in R. As the chapter is intended as a hands-on introduction to SEM, I will not go into the details of the mathematical principles behind this technique. Instead, I will explain how SEM works at a conceptual level and provide practical guidance on how to perform the analysis and interpret the results. Readers who are interested in a more in-depth discussion of this technique can refer to one of the many excellent books dedicated to it, such as Byrne (2010), Rex B Kline (2016) or Schumacker and Lomax (2016).

Matteo Fuoli, University of Birmingham, e-mail: m.fuoli@bham.ac.uk

https://doi.org/10.1515/9783110687279-004

2 Basic concepts and principles of structural equation modeling

SEM is a theory-driven multivariate technique that combines aspects of regression and factor analysis to examine causal relationships between variables. SEM is primarily conceived as a confirmatory approach (Byrne 2010: 3). Within this paradigm, researchers first develop a hypothetical model of the relationships between the variables of interest based on theory and/or previous empirical research, and then test the model against sample data to assess how well it explains the patterns observed. If the model fits the data well and the theoretical principles underlying it are robust, it can be accepted as a plausible explanation for the phenomenon under study.

Causal relationships in a SEM model are typically represented graphically by means of path diagrams, such as the one shown in Figure 3.1. This diagram represents some of the key hypotheses tested in an experimental study by Flusberg et al. (2017), which investigates how the metaphors used to talk about climate change influence people's attitudes towards this problem. While the authors themselves do not use SEM in their analysis, the study lends itself well to this approach and offers a good illustration of how SEM may be applied in the context of a cognitive linguistic study. Flusberg et al. (2017) hypothesized that the type of metaphorical framing used to describe efforts to mitigate climate change – whether responding to climate change is referred to as a *war* or a *race* – will have an effect on individuals' perceptions of the urgency of the problem, their perceptions of the risks associated with it and their willingness to change their behavior.[1] In path diagrams, causal effects of this kind are represented as single-headed arrows linking independent and dependent variables. In addition to the choice of metaphorical framing, Flusberg et al. (2017) also considered two non-linguistic control variables, political ideology and belief in global warming, to account for the potential influence of participants' prior beliefs on their attitudes towards climate change. The authors found these

---

[1] In the interest of space and clarity, I am presenting here a simplified version of Flusberg et al.'s (2017) study. In addition to the war and metaphor framings, the original study also included a baseline condition in which the issue of climate change was presented in non-metaphorical terms. In addition, the time frame for a set of proposed measures to mitigate climate change was manipulated in the experimental stimuli. The survey also included a "yes or no" question about the feasibility of the proposed measures. Due to space constraints, SEM analysis involving categorical dependent variables is not discussed in this chapter. A complete overview of how categorical data is approached in a SEM framework is given in Hoyle (2012: Chapter 12).

two variables to be correlated with one another. That is, participants who identified as politically conservative tended to express a weaker belief in global warming. In path diagrams, correlations between pairs of variables are represented using double-headed arrows.

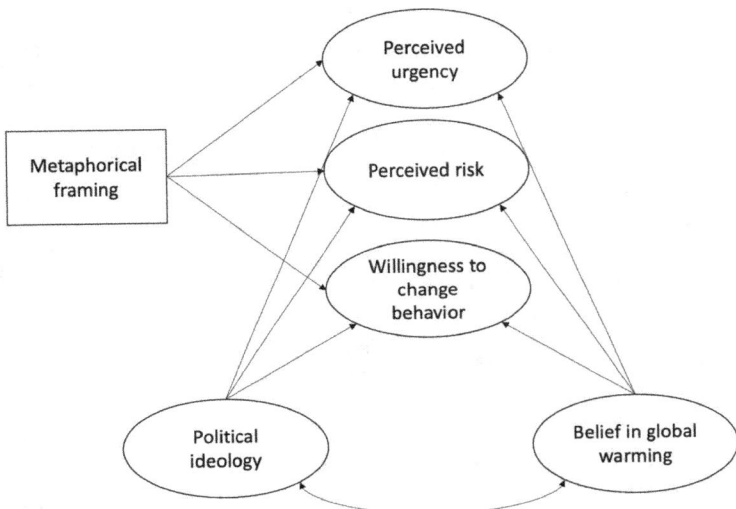

Figure 3.1: Path diagram representing an adapted version of the hypothetical model tested by Flusberg et al. (2017).

One of the main advantages of SEM compared to traditional statistical technique such as multiple regression is that it can flexibly accommodate both *observed* and *latent* variables. The former are variables that can be measured directly, such as age, income or nationality. Latent variables, on the other hand, can only be measured indirectly, via for example rating scales. By convention, latent factors are represented in path diagrams using ovals. Observed and experimentally manipulated variables are indicated with rectangles. Latent variables often capture psychological or attitudinal constructs that are by nature unobservable. All the dependent variables considered by Flusberg et al. (2017) are latent. Each of them is measured by the participants' scores on one or more questionnaire items, as shown in Figure 3.2. Participants' willingness to change their behavior, for example, was measured with six questions, each focusing on one specific behavior that is known to have negative consequences on the environment. The scores themselves are treated as observed variables and are assumed to be directly influenced by the latent variable they are intended to measure. This is why the arrows linking the latent factor and the questionnaire items point towards the latter. The latent factor is hypothesized to be the "cause" of the item scores (De-Vellis 2012: 19). The model representing the links between the latent variables and their respective observed measures is referred to as the *measurement model*. The model depicting relationships between the latent variables themselves and any other experimental or observed variable is called the *structural model* (Figure 3.1).

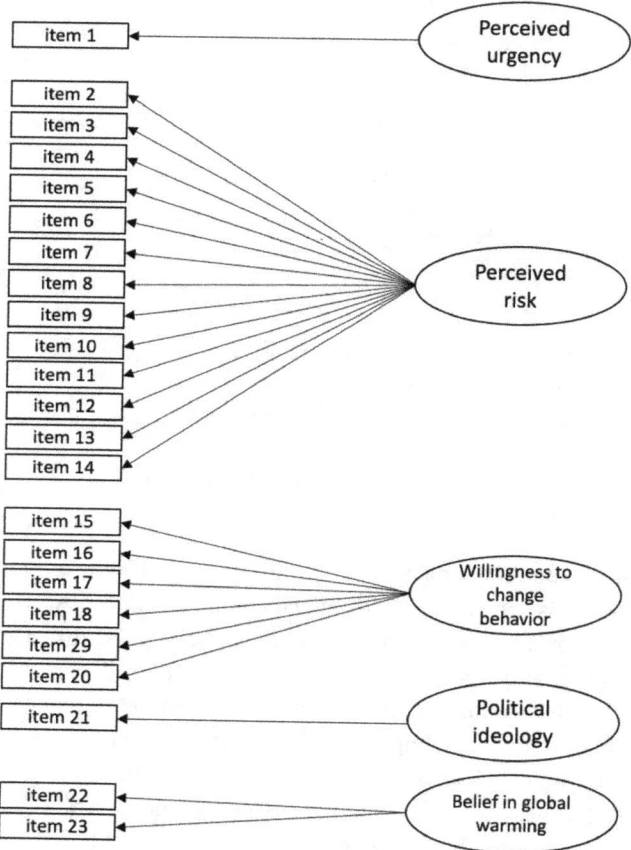

Figure 3.2: Measurement model adapted from Flusberg et al. (2017).

Another strength of SEM is that it allows researchers to test *indirect effects* between variables in a single analysis. This is possible because any variable in a SEM model may simultaneously be affected by, and have an effect on, other variables. Variables that are influenced by at least another variable in the system are called *endogenous*. Variables that are not affected by any other variables in the model are termed *exogenous*. Crucially, endogenous variables may simultaneously act as dependent and independent variables in different equations within a SEM model. In the case of Flusberg et al.'s (2017) study, for example, we could hypothesize that metaphorical framing does not affect individuals' willingness to change their behavior directly, but does so indirectly by altering their perceptions of the urgency and risks posed by climate change. In other words, we could recast perceptions of urgency and risk as psychological antecedents to willingness to change one's behavior. This hypothesis is in line with previous empirical studies showing that beliefs and attitudes around climate change are a key driver of behavioral change (Haden et al. 2012; A. Mayer and Smith 2019; O'Connor et al. 1999). This indirect effect is shown in the revised hypothetical model in Figure 3.3, where perceived urgency and perceived risk intervene between metaphorical framing and willingness to change.

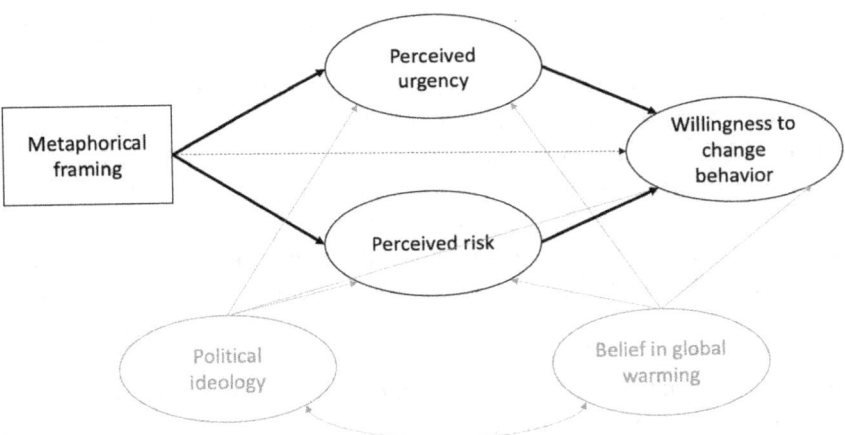

Figure 3.3: Revised hypothetical model based on Flusberg et al. (2017).

SEM analysis typically involves two main phases (Anderson and Gerbing 1988). The first step consists in assessing the validity of the measurement model which, as noted above, specifies the relationship between the latent variables and their corresponding observed indicators (Figure 3.2). The aim of this step is to verify that the latent variables have been correctly operationalized, which is a necessary prerequisite for establishing causal links between them reliably (Hair et al. 2014: 600). The validity of the measurement model is assessed by means of *confirmatory factor analysis* (CFA). The second step involves analyzing the structural model. This is where the hypotheses proposed in the study are tested. First, the validity of the model as a whole is evaluated. Next, each regression path is inspected in order to assess the strength of the causal relationships among variables.

The validity of both the measurement and the structural model is established by means of a global test that assesses how well the hypothesized model *as a whole* fits the sample data. The test works by comparing the *observed covariance matrix*, which describes pairwise relationships among variables computed directly from the sample data, and the *estimated covariance matrix*, which contains the predicted values for each pairwise relationship resulting from the direct and indirect paths specified in the hypothesized model (Hair et al. 2014: 561–565). If the difference between estimated and observed covariances is small, the model is accepted as a valid representation of the relationships among the variables in the system. A chi-square test is used to compare the matrices and assess the statistical probability that they are actually equal in the population (Hair et al. 2014: 577). Thus, unlike other scenarios where the chi-square test is used, in SEM the desired outcome is a χ^2 value that is close to zero and non-significant, as this would indicate that the difference between covariances predicted on the basis of the hypothesized model and covariances observed in the sample is negligible from a statistical point of view (Schumaker and Lomax 2016: 79). The chi-square test, however, is influenced by both sample size and by the number of observed variables (Hair et al. 2014: 78). For these reasons, researchers have proposed a number of alternative *goodness-of-fit indices* that can be used in conjunction with the chi-square test to provide a more robust assessment of the validity of a SEM model. Table 3.1 reports some of the most commonly used indices and their corresponding cut-off values.[2] These indices are part of the standard output produced by most SEM programs, including SEM packages in R. From a practical perspective, then, evaluating the validity of a model ultimately boils down to comparing the scores obtained from the analysis output with these well-established benchmarks. It is best practice in SEM to consider and report multiple fit indices when evaluating the goodness-of-fit of a model, rather than focusing on single parameter (Hu and Bentler 1999).

When the analysis is based on questionnaire data, an additional step in evaluating the measurement model consists in testing the *convergent* and *discriminant* validity of the rating scales used to measure the latent variables. Convergent validity concerns the extent to which items intended to measure the

---

[2] A detailed discussion of these criteria is beyond the scope of this chapter. Comprehensive overviews are given in Hair et al. (2014: 576–582) and Schumaker and Lomax (2016: 112–117).

Table 3.1: Commonly-used goodness-of-fit indices and corresponding recommended cut-off values.

Goodness-of-fit index	Recommended cut-off value
p value for the global χ^2 test	> .05
Comparative Fit Index (CFI)	> .95
Goodness-of-Fit Index (GFI)	> .95
Adjusted Goodness-of-Fit Index (AGFI)	> .90
Root Mean Square Error of Approximation (RMSEA)	< .06

same latent variable share a high proportion of variance (Hair et al. 2014: 618). Discriminant validity, by contrast, is the extent to which different constructs are truly distinct from one another (Hair et al. 2014: 619). In the case of the measurement model shown in Figure 3.2, for example, we would expect scores from items 2–14 to be strongly related to one another (convergent validity) but less strongly related to items 15–20, which measure a different construct (discriminant validity).

There are three measures that are commonly used to assess convergent validity: standardized factor loadings, Average Variance Extracted (AVE), and construct reliability coefficients. Factor loadings reflect the strength of the relationship between individual questionnaire items and the latent variable they are intended to measure. Standardized estimates higher than .70 are indicative of a strong relationship (Hair et al. 2014: 618). AVE measures the amount of variance that is explained by the latent factor in relation to the amount of variance due to random measurement error (Fornell and Larcker 1981). An AVE of .50 or higher is considered acceptable (Hair et al. 2014: 619). Finally, construct reliability measures the internal consistency of a scale, with values higher than .70 interpreted as indicating good reliability (Hair et al. 2014: 619). Discriminant validity can be assessed in two ways. First, the hypothesized model is compared with alternative, more parsimonious models by means of chi-square difference tests (Bagozzi and Phillips 1982). For example, the model in Figure 3.2 could be compared with a more parsimonious model in which perceived urgency and perceived risk are conflated into a single factor, and with a unidimensional model where all items are loaded onto one single factor. If the hypothesized model is shown to outperform these alternative models, we may conclude that it exhibits good discriminant validity. An alternative method for evaluating discriminant validity consists in comparing the AVE values for each pair of latent variables with the square of their correlation (Fornell & Larcker 1981). Positive evidence of discriminant validity is obtained when the AVE value is greater than the squared correlation estimates, as this shows that the latent factor explains more of the variance in the indicator items than it shares with another factor (Hair et al. 2014: 620).

Once the validity of the measurement model has been established, the full structural model, which specifies the hypothesized causal relationships between variables, can be assessed. The first step in this phase of the analysis involves conducting a global goodness-of-fit test to evaluate whether the structural model as a whole represents a plausible explanation for the empirical data under scrutiny. Next, the causal paths linking the variables in the model are examined and each individual hypothesis is tested. This part of the analysis is conceptually similar to performing several regression analyses, each focusing on one node in the SEM network. However, unlike with multiple regression, all the equations in a SEM model are computed at once, and thus each path is estimated taking into account all the other relationships specified in the model (Hair et al. 2014: 562). The program will return unstandardized and standardized estimates, standard errors, p-values, R squared values etc. for each exogenous variable in the model. From these values, researchers can infer the strength and probability of each causal relationship specified in the model, and verify whether their hypotheses hold.

As noted above, SEM is conceived as a confirmatory technique. This does not, however, preclude the possibility of revising a model and testing it again should the analysis reveal poor fit with the data. In fact, in most situations, researchers initially specify a tentative model and then proceed to iteratively modify it until a version of the model which is theoretically sound, reasonably parsimonious and sufficiently consistent with the sample data is identified (Kline 2016, Jöreskog 1993). A strictly confirmatory approach, where one single model is tested and either retained or discarded based on goodness-of-fit measures is rarely followed (Byrne 2010: 8). Crucially, however, modifications to the initial model need to be theoretically justified to ensure that the final model is not just statistically sound but also substantively meaningful (Byrne 2010, Chou and Huh 2012, Kline 2016). Theoretical considerations should always guide model (re-)specification, as in any scenario there can be multiple alternative models that, from a purely statistical perspective, would fit the data equally well (Chou and Huh 2012: 232). SEM, as Kline (2016: 466) puts it, "is about testing theories, not just models". A common strategy for identifying areas where the model can be improved consists in examining *modification indices*. Modification indices suggest paths that could be added to the model to obtain better fit (Schumacker and Lomax 2016: 99). Modification indices are an incredibly useful aid in the process of refining the model. Any changes made on the basis of them, however, needs to make theoretical sense.

Like other statistical techniques, SEM makes certain distributional assumptions about the data that need to be met for reliable results. An important assumption is that the sample data conforms to a *multivariate normal* distribution, meaning that each variable is normally distributed and that the linear combination of the variables is also normally distributed (Hair et al. 2014: 686, Kline 2012: 74). A common way of testing this assumption is by means of Mardia's (1970) multivariate normality test, which is based on measures of multivariate skewness and kurtosis. A well-established strategy for dealing with non-normal data is *bootstrapping* (for an accessible overview of this method, see Byrne 2010: Chapter 12). With bootstrapping, multiple sub-samples are drawn at random from the data *with replacement*, which means that each observation may be selected more than once in any given iteration. Estimates obtained from each sub-sample are then averaged to obtain more reliable p values for the chi-square test of model fit as well as for the path coefficients.

In this section, I have outlined the fundamentals of SEM and the key steps involved in conducting the analysis. The remainder of this chapter will be devoted to showing how to execute this technique with R. The next section introduces the case study I will use as the basis for the tutorial.

3 The case study

The data we will explore was collected as part of an experimental study which investigated the effects of a set of persuasive strategies commonly used by large corporations in their social and environmental communications (Fuoli and Hart 2018). Specifically, we focused on strategies involving the use of stance verbs expressing belief and volition, such as *believe* and *want*, and verbs indicating shared perspective, such as *understand* and *recognize*. These linguistic devices are often used by companies in their public discourse to highlight their commitment to business ethics and project a caring and sympathetic corporate image (Fuoli 2017), as illustrated in the examples below.

(1) We believe business should play a greater role in meeting social, economic and environmental challenges.
(2) We understand and recognize the many barriers and obstacles there are on the path to better health and we are committed to finding new and innovative ways of overcoming them.

The study examined the extent to which statements such as these would influence readers' trust in a company accused of misconduct. Based on Sperber et al.'s (2010) model of *epistemic vigilance*, we hypothesized that these persuasive strategies would improve individuals' perceptions of the company's trustworthiness and, as a result, would make them more inclined to believe the company's rebuttal of the allegations. The study is situated within Critical Discourse Analysis (e.g. Fairclough 2013; Hart 2014; Wodak and Meyer 2015) and, as such, it ultimately aims to shed light on mechanisms of discursive legitimation and power.

Participants in the experiment read a fabricated news article about a lawsuit brought against a fictitious multinational pharmaceutical company named Avita. The article reported that a whistle-blower had accused a group of company executives of paying illegal kickbacks to doctors to induce them to prescribe the company's drugs instead of cheaper alternatives. The article also reported that the whistle-blower was sacked, allegedly in retaliation for exposing the fraudulent scheme. The company, however, firmly denied the accusations, dismissing them as a baseless attack from a disgruntled former employee. In this scenario, then, trust is a key factor as both the company's and the employee's account may be seen as plausible.

Before reading the news article, half of the participants were asked to read an extract from the company's "about us" webpage which contained the persuasive linguistic devices described above. Our expectation was that participants who were exposed to this text would develop a more positive image of the company and would therefore be more inclined to believe its denial compared to those who did not read the text. An additional factor that we hypothesized would influence subjects' judgment of the trustworthiness of the company was the strength of the evidence supporting the allegations. Accordingly, we created two versions of the news text, one in which the evidence against Avita was presented as compelling and one in which it was presented as weak. Participants were randomly assigned to one of the experimental conditions. Our hypothesis was that participants in the strong evidence condition would display comparatively lower levels of trust. In addition to these two experimentally manipulated variables, we also considered the influence of pre-existing beliefs that we expected to be relevant in this scenario, namely people's attitudes towards pharmaceutical corporations in general and their political orientation. We anticipated that individuals who tend to distrust corporations in general and who have liberal political views would be less prone to trust Avita. A detailed discussion of these hypotheses is beyond the scope of this chapter, but can be found in the original article.

The variables considered in the experiment and their hypothesized relationships are represented in the path model in Figure 3.4. As discussed above, we hypothesized that exposure to the company's webpage would enhance participants' perceptions of its trustworthiness. Based on previous work on trust (e.g. Mayer et al. 1995; see Fuoli and Hart 2018 and Fuoli and Paradis 2014 for details), we separated the construct of trustworthiness into two major components: benevolence and integrity. Benevolence concerns someone's perceived care and goodwill. Integrity relates to their character and ethical principles. We hypothesized that participants' impressions of the company's benevolence and integrity would, in turn, feed into their assessment of the credibility of the company's denial. Thus, the persuasive devices contained in the webpage will have an indirect positive effect on perceptions of the company's culpability and help the organization protect itself from reputational damage. In line with our hypotheses, evidence of the company's guilt will negatively affect both perceived trustworthiness and credibility of the company's denial. As a whole, then, the model describes the role of discourse in a situation where trust in a powerful organization is at stake and accounts for the complex interplay of linguistic and extra-linguistic factors.

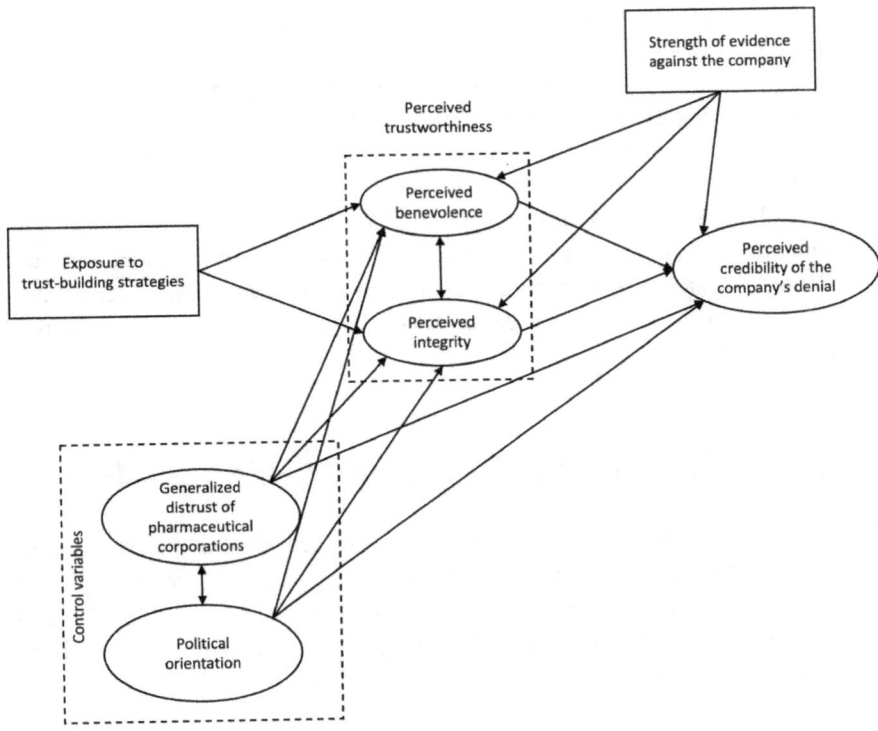

Figure 3.4: Hypothetical model tested in Fuoli and Hart (2018).

After reading the stimulus texts, participants completed a questionnaire designed to measure the five endogenous latent variables included in the model. The questionnaire included a set of psychometric scales adapted from previous studies. Perceived benevolence and integrity, for example, were each measured using three items drawn from Mayer and Davis (1999), as shown below.

> Perceived benevolence (from 1 *strongly disagree* to 7 *strongly agree*)
> Avita seems very concerned about the welfare of people like me.
> The needs and desires of people like me seem to be very important to Avita.
> Avita seems to really look out for what is important to people like me.
>
> Perceived integrity (from 1 *strongly disagree* to 7 *strongly agree*)
> Avita seems to have a strong sense of justice.
> Avita appears to try hard in being fair to others.
> Sound moral principles seem to guide Avita's behavior.

Adapting measurement scales from previous studies, where this is a viable option, offers two main advantages compared to developing new scales from the ground up. First, it is significantly less time and resource consuming as developing new measurement instruments typically involves a number of iterative steps and rounds of empirical testing (DeVellis 2012). Second, as the scales have already been assessed by other researchers they are more likely to be reliable and valid.

A total of 297 subjects took part in the study. They were recruited from staff and student populations at several universities in the United Kingdom and Sweden. More information about the participants and the experimental design is given in Fuoli and Hart (2018). In the next section, we will apply SEM to the results of the experiment using R.

4 Conducting SEM in R: A step-by-step guide

This section illustrates, step by step, how to perform SEM in R. The analysis will follow the procedure described in Section 2. Accordingly, we will first validate the measurement model and then assess the full structural model. The R markdown file and data set used in the analysis can be downloaded from OSF at the link provided in the introduction.

4.1 Preliminaries: Loading packages and data

Before we begin the analysis, we load the necessary R packages. The main package we will use is lavaan (Rosseel 2012), which provides a comprehensive suite of tools for SEM. In addition, we will use the package MVN (Korkmaz et al. 2014) for assessing the multivariate normality of our data and the package semTools (Jorgensen et al. 2020) for computing measures of convergent validity.

```
library(lavaan) # Comprehensive package for SEM
library(MVN) # Package for assessing multivariate normality
library(semTools) # Suite of additional tools for SEM
```

Next, we load the data set we will be working with.

```
SEM_data=read.csv("dataset for SEM.txt", header=T, sep="\t") # load data
```

As shown below, the data frame is made up of 297 rows and 23 columns. Each row corresponds to data from one participant. The first two columns, "about_us" and "evidence" refer to the two variables that were manipulated in the experiment, namely exposure to the Avita's webpage containing the discursive strategies of interest, and strength of the evidence against the company. These variables are dummy coded, which means that factor levels are represented as numbers. In the case of the "exposure" variable, 1 stands for the condition where participants read the company's webpage prior to reading the news article, and 0 stands for the condition where they did not. With strength of evidence, 0 indicates that evidence against Avita was weak and 1 that it was strong. Columns 3 to 15 contain the participants' responses to the rating scales in the questionnaire. These are grouped according to the construct they are intended to measure. For example, items ben_1, ben_2 and ben_3 belong to the "perceived benevolence" scale. Items belonging to the "dist" scale measure one of our two control variables: generalized distrust of pharmaceutical corporations. Columns 16 to 23 include demographic information about the participants and measures for the second control variable, political orientation.

```
str(SEM_data) # show structure of data frame

## 'data.frame':    297 obs. of  23 variables:
```

```
##  $ about_us     : int  0 0 0 1 1 0 1 1 0 0 ...
##  $ evidence     : int  0 1 0 0 1 0 1 0 0 0 ...
##  $ ben_1        : int  1 4 4 6 2 2 5 1 2 2 ...
##  $ ben_2        : int  1 3 4 6 2 2 4 1 2 4 ...
##  $ ben_3        : int  1 3 4 6 2 2 4 1 2 2 ...
##  $ int_1        : int  2 4 4 4 2 3 5 2 1 2 ...
##  $ int_2        : int  2 3 4 5 2 3 6 1 1 2 ...
##  $ int_3        : int  2 3 4 5 2 3 5 1 1 2 ...
##  $ cred_1       : int  3 4 5 2 3 4 5 1 2 2 ...
##  $ cred_2       : int  5 4 5 4 3 4 2 1 2 3 ...
##  $ cred_3       : int  5 3 5 4 3 4 3 1 2 3 ...
##  $ dist_1       : int  5 4 5 6 5 5 5 7 5 2 ...
##  $ dist_2       : int  5 3 2 5 5 5 2 4 3 2 ...
##  $ dist_3       : num  4 4 3 5 5 4 5 6 4 2 ...
##  $ dist_4       : int  5 5 4 7 6 5 5 7 6 4 ...
##  $ gender       : Factor w/ 3 levels "female","male",..: 1 1 2 2 2 2 1 2 1 1 ...
##  $ age          : int  27 20 21 19 26 23 21 32 26 26 ...
##  $ nationality  : Factor w/ 48 levels "","American",..: 1 7 8 7 44 44 44 22 12 44 ...
##  $ occupation   : Factor w/ 3 levels "other","student",..: 1 2 2 2 3 2 2 2 2 2 ...
##  $ pol_orient   : int  3 3 6 1 2 3 2 2 4 1 ...
##  $ education    : Factor w/ 6 levels "a.levels","bachelors",..: 5 1 4 1 2 1 4 5 2 1 ...
##  $ english      : Factor w/ 2 levels "no","yes": 1 2 2 2 1 1 1 1 1 1 ...
##  $ proficiency  : int  9 NA NA NA 10 10 9 10 9 9 ...
```

4.2 Evaluating the measurement model

As explained above, the first step in SEM consists in validating the measurement model via confirmatory factor analysis (CFA). Before we can proceed with the analysis, however, we need to check whether our data meets the multivariate normality assumption. To test this assumption, we use Mardia's test of multivariate normality, which is available in the MVN package. As shown below, the output of this test indicates that our data deviates significantly from a multivariate normal distribution (MVN Result = NO). This means that the results of the chi-square test for the model as a whole as well as the significance tests for the path coefficients may be unreliable. To address this problem and obtain more reliable estimates, we will use bootstrapping throughout all stages of the analysis.

```
multi <- mvn(SEM_data[,3:15], mvnTest = "mardia") # apply mvn() function
to scores from questionnaire items
multi$multivariateNormality # display results of multivariate normality test

##              Test     Statistic                 p value Result
## 1 Mardia Skewness 1345.14280966542 8.60019610253535e-89     NO
## 2 Mardia Kurtosis 24.8071531529422                    0     NO
## 3             MVN              <NA>                <NA>    NO
```

After checking the multivariate normality assumption, we are ready to perform the CFA. We will use the R package lavaan to do this. The first step in the analysis consists in specifying our measurement model. Lavaan uses three operators to specify relationships between variables in the model:
- =~ translates to "is measured by" and is used to define latent variables
- ~ means "is regressed on" and is used to specify regression paths in the analysis of full structural models
- ~~ stands for "is correlated with" and is used to postulate correlations between variables

The goal of CFA is to verify that latent variables have been adequately operationalized and measured. Accordingly, the analysis will focus on our questionnaire items. We postulate a relationship between the items and the four latent variables they are assumed to reflect. The syntax for doing so is presented below. We create a model object named "CFA_model". The model specification is enclosed in single quotation marks and maps out which items belong to which latent construct. The first line, for example, indicates that the latent construct "benevolence" is measured by the questionnaire items ben_1, ben_2 and ben_3.

```
# STEP 1: specify the hypothetical measurement model
CFA_model <- '
  benevolence =~ ben_1 + ben_2 + ben_3
  integrity =~ int_1 + int_2 + int_3
```

```
  credibility =~ cred_1 + cred_2 + cred_3
  distrust =~ dist_1 + dist_2 + dist_3 + dist_4
```

After we have specified our hypothetical measurement model, we fit it to the observational data from our study. We use the lavaan function cfa() to accomplish that, using our theoretical model and data as arguments. Because, as seen above, our data violates the multivariate normality assumption, we need to use bootstrapping. Accordingly, we include in our code the estimator option *test = "bootstrap"* to compute a bootstrap-corrected p value for the chi-square test of model fit and the estimator option *se = "bootstrap"* to generate bias-corrected parameter estimates for all path coefficients in the model. We set the number of random bootstrap samples at 2000.

```
# STEP 2: fit the model to the data
CFA_model_fit <- cfa(CFA_model, data = SEM_data, test = "bootstrap", se = "bootstrap", bootstrap = 2000)
```

Now we are ready to explore the results of the CFA. First, we inspect the results of the chi-square test comparing the observed and estimated covariance matrices. The output includes the total number of observations, the estimation method used, which in our case is the widely used "maximum likelihood", degrees of freedom and two p-values. The second p-value is the one we should consider, as this is the boostrap-corrected p-value. Recall that in SEM, the desired outcome is a χ^2 value that is as small as possible and non-significant. Our boostrap-adjusted p-value abundantly exceeds the conventional 0.05 threshold for statistical significance. This is a positive result, as it indicates that the difference between our hypothesized model and the observed relationships among variables in our data is statistically negligible.

```
# STEP 3: evaluate goodness of fit
CFA_model_fit

## lavaan (0.5-23.1097) converged normally after  37 iterations
##
##   Number of observations                            297
```

```
## 
## Estimator                                          ML
## Minimum Function Test Statistic               77.252
## Degrees of freedom                                59
## P-value (Chi-square)                           0.056
## P-value (Bollen-Stine Bootstrap)               0.413
```

Next, we inspect goodness-of-fit indices. We use the code below to extract four commonly used indices from our CFA model object. The results show that all of these coefficients are within the recommended cut-offs (see Table 3.1). Based on the combined results of the chi-square test and the goodness-of-fit indices we conclude that our model fits our observational data very well.

```
# STEP 3: evaluate goodness of fit
fitMeasures(CFA_model_fit, c("cfi", "gfi", "agfi", "rmsea"))

##   cfi   gfi  agfi rmsea
## 0.992 0.961 0.940 0.032
```

The next step in validating the measurement model consists in assessing the convergent and discriminant validity of the scales we used to measure our latent variables. To assess the former, we first of all inspect standardized factor loadings. Recall that factor loadings higher than .70 are indicative of a strong relationship between an item and the latent construct it is used to measure. As we can see in the output below, all the loadings are comfortably above this threshold.

```
inspect(CFA_model_fit, what="std")$lambda # extract standardized factor
loadings from cfa model

##        bnvlnc intgrt crdblt dstrst
## ben_1  0.860  0.000  0.000  0.000
## ben_2  0.819  0.000  0.000  0.000
## ben_3  0.897  0.000  0.000  0.000
## int_1  0.000  0.843  0.000  0.000
## int_2  0.000  0.869  0.000  0.000
## int_3  0.000  0.894  0.000  0.000
## cred_1 0.000  0.000  0.829  0.000
```

```
## cred_2 0.000   0.000   0.822   0.000
## cred_3 0.000   0.000   0.882   0.000
## dist_1 0.000   0.000   0.000   0.726
## dist_2 0.000   0.000   0.000   0.779
## dist_3 0.000   0.000   0.000   0.753
## dist_4 0.000   0.000   0.000   0.708
```

The other two measures of convergent validity that are commonly used in SEM are Average Variance Extracted (AVE) and construct reliability. These measures can be obtained using the reliability() function from the package semTools. When applied to a lavaan model object, this function returns a series of reliability indices, including AVE. The first and last rows are of interest here. The former reports Chronbach's alpha values for each latent construct as well as a comprehensive value for the entire set of items. All of these values are well above the 0.70 recommended threshold, indicating that the scales used are reliable. The last row reports individual and aggregate AVE values. These too meet the recommended cutoff (0.50), providing further positive evidence of convergent validity.

```
reliability(CFA_model_fit) # compute AVE and construct reliability
```

```
##          benevolence integrity credibility distrust    total
## alpha    0.8926995   0.9017395 0.8798974   0.8288456   0.7815639
## omega    0.8932148   0.9019332 0.8820399   0.8316498   0.9107113
## omega2   0.8932148   0.9019332 0.8820399   0.8316498   0.9107113
## omega3   0.8936226   0.9021339 0.8839174   0.8315039   0.9099784
## avevar   0.7361259   0.7540655 0.7140527   0.5551378   0.6797174
```

As explained above, one strategy for assessing discriminant validity consists in comparing the hypothesized model with alternative, more parsimonious models by means of chi-square difference tests. In the code below, we fit and compare two alternative models. Mod1 is our original hypothesized model. Mod2 is an alternative model where the variables benevolence and integrity have been merged into one single factor. By comparing these two models, we can ascertain whether benevolence and integrity are two truly independent constructs or whether, in fact, they measure the same thing. We use the function anova() to perform a chi-square different test comparing the two models. Next, we compare goodness-of-fit indices to see whether the alternative, more parsimonious model provides a better explanation of our data. The results show that there is a significant difference between these two models, with the alternative model exhibiting a higher χ² value. Goodness-of-fit indices show that our original model fits our data better than the alternative one. Based on these results, we conclude that our original model has better discriminant validity than the alternative one because it draws a distinction between benevolence and integrity which is both theoretically and empirically supported.

```
# specify hypothesized model
mod1 <- '
  benevolence =~ ben_1 + ben_2 + ben_3
  integrity =~ int_1 + int_2 + int_3
  credibility =~ cred_1 + cred_2 + cred_3
  distrust =~ dist_1 + dist_2 + dist_3 + dist_4
'
# specify alternative model
mod2 <- '
  trustworthiness =~ ben_1 + ben_2 + ben_3 + int_1 + int_2 + int_3
  credibility =~ cred_1 + cred_2 + cred_3
  distrust =~ dist_1 + dist_2 + dist_3 + dist_4
'
# fit models
fit1 <- cfa(mod1, data = SEM_data)
fit2 <- cfa(mod2, data = SEM_data)
# compare models with chi-square different test
anova(fit1, fit2)

## Chi Square Difference Test
##
##      Df    AIC   BIC  Chisq Chisq diff Df diff Pr(>Chisq)
## fit1 59 10634 10752  77.252
## fit2 62 10873 10980 322.130     244.88       3  < 2.2e-16 ***
## ---
## Signif. codes:  0 '***' 0.001 '**' 0.01 '*' 0.05 '.' 0.1 ' ' 1

# compare goodness-of-fit indices
fitMeasures(fit1, c("cfi", "gfi", "agfi", "rmsea"))
```

```
##   cfi   gfi  agfi rmsea
## 0.992 0.961 0.940 0.032
```

fitMeasures(fit2, **c**("cfi", "gfi", "agfi", "rmsea"))

```
##   cfi   gfi  agfi rmsea
## 0.888 0.828 0.748 0.119
```

Taken together, the results above provide robust evidence for the validity of our measurement model. This means that the four latent factors we considered in our study were appropriately operationalized and measured. Having establish the validity of the measurement model, we may now turn to the analysis of the full structural model.

4.3 Evaluating the full structural model

The procedure for evaluating the full structural model is very similar to the one shown above for assessing the measurement model. The main difference is that in a full SEM we not only specify relationships between observed measures and latent factors, but also the causal relationships between all the variables in the model. The syntax for specifying the full structural model is presented below. We create a model object named full_SEM. In the first section of the model specification code, we define our latent variables in the exact same way as we did in the CFA. In the second section, we use the ~ operator to set the regression paths connecting our variables. These correspond to the causal links postulated in our hypothetical SEM model (see Figure 3.3). Next, we use the ~~ operator to postulate a correlation between benevolence and integrity and between generalized distrust of pharmaceutical corporations and political orientation, in line with our model. Finally, we constrain covariance between our experimental variables to 0. This step is necessary to prevent our dummy coded experimental factors to be treated as exogenous latent variables and to be automatically correlated with the other latent variables as a result.

```
# STEP 1: specify the full structural model
full_SEM <- '
# define latent variables
```

```
  benevolence =~ ben_1 + ben_2 + ben_3
  integrity =~ int_1 + int_2 + int_3
  credibility =~ cred_1 + cred_2 + cred_3
  distrust =~ dist_1 + dist_2 + dist_3 + dist_4
# establish regression paths
  benevolence ~ about_us + evidence + distrust + pol_orient
  integrity ~ about_us + evidence + distrust + pol_orient
  credibility ~ benevolence + integrity + evidence + distrust + pol_orient
# variable correlations
  benevolence ~~ integrity
  distrust ~~ pol_orient
# fix covariance between experimental variables to 0
  about_us ~~ 0*evidence '
```

After specifying the hypothetical model, we fit it to our observational data, adding bootstrapping options to our code.

```
# STEP 2: fit the model to the data
SEM_model_fit <- sem(full_SEM, data = SEM_data, test = "bootstrap", se = "bootstrap", bootstrap = 2000)
```

Finally, we are ready to evaluate our model. First, as in the case of the CFA, we look at the results of the χ^2 test for the model as a whole. As shown below, the boostrap-corrected p-value is insignificant, which we interpret as positive evidence of model fit.

```
# STEP 3: evaluate goodness of fit
SEM_model_fit

## lavaan (0.5-23.1097) converged normally after  40 iterations
##
##   Number of observations                           297
##
##   Estimator                                         ML
##   Minimum Function Test Statistic              113.437
##   Degrees of freedom                                92
```

```
## P-value (Chi-square)                    0.064
## P-value (Bollen-Stine Bootstrap)        0.406
```

Next, we inspect commonly-used goodness-of-fit indices. All of these values meet recommended cutoffs, providing further evidence of adequate model fit. Based on these results, we conclude that our hypothetical model offers a plausible explanation for the relationships among variables observed in our data.

```
# STEP 3: evaluate goodness of fit
fitMeasures(SEM_model_fit, c("cfi", "gfi", "agfi", "rmsea"))

##   cfi   gfi  agfi rmsea
## 0.991 0.954 0.932 0.028
```

Having validated the model as a whole, we now turn to exploring each individual regression path in order to test our hypotheses about causal relationships between our variables. The lavaan function standardizedSolution() returns standardized estimates for all the parameters in the model. The section of the output that is of interest to us here is within lines 14 and 26, where the estimates for the regressions paths are given. When we compare these against our hypothesized regression paths, we can see that the vast majority of our hypotheses are supported. There are only four non-significant causal paths out of thirteen. Strength of the evidence against Avita did not have a significant effect on perceptions of the company's benevolence (line 15). Similarly, perceptions of the company's benevolence did not show a reliable effect on credibility of the company's denial. We offer a detailed explanation for why this may be the case in the original paper (Fuoli and Hart 2018). The other two non-significant paths relate to one of our two control variables: political orientation. This variable only had a significant effect on perceived benevolence, such that the more conservative the political orientation of the participant, the more benevolent the company was seen as being.

```
# STEP 4: assess individual regression paths
std_estimates <- standardizedSolution(SEM_model_fit)
std_estimates[std_estimates$op == "~",] # display regression
coefficients only

##         lhs op      rhs est.std      se         z pvalue
```

```
## 14 benevolence  ~   about_us    0.309  0.053   5.806  0.000
## 15 benevolence  ~   evidence   -0.065  0.055  -1.179  0.238
## 16 benevolence  ~   distrust   -0.211  0.060  -3.498  0.000
## 17 benevolence  ~ pol_orient    0.171  0.058   2.945  0.003
## 18   integrity  ~   about_us    0.148  0.060   2.479  0.013
## 19   integrity  ~   evidence   -0.218  0.055  -3.983  0.000
## 20   integrity  ~   distrust   -0.186  0.065  -2.886  0.004
## 21   integrity  ~ pol_orient    0.088  0.056   1.564  0.118
## 22 credibility  ~ benevolence   0.143  0.093   1.537  0.124
## 23 credibility  ~  integrity    0.491  0.088   5.564  0.000
## 24 credibility  ~   evidence   -0.149  0.047  -3.189  0.001
## 25 credibility  ~   distrust   -0.194  0.062  -3.137  0.002
## 26 credibility  ~ pol_orient    0.070  0.057   1.219  0.223
```

This final hypothesis-testing step concludes our SEM analysis. Overall, the results indicate that our hypothetical model adequately explains the causal relationships among variables in our data and, with minor exceptions, provides support for our hypothesis. As the model presented above is firmly grounded in theory, as discussed in the original paper (Fuoli and Hart 2018), we may accept it as valid and stop here. However, for illustrative purposes, in the next section we will explore modification indices in order to see how, if at all, our model may be improved.

4.4 Modification indices

In situations where the analysis demonstrates poor model fit, the researcher may explore ways of improving the model by adding, removing or altering parameters. Modification indices show how model fit would improve by adding new paths and can therefore be of great help in this process. Recall, however, that model re-specification should always be guided by theory and any change made to the model should have a sound theoretical basis. The lavaan function modindices() can be used to explore modification indices. As shown below, the function prints out a list of additional parameters that could be added to the model together with their corresponding modification index (mi). This value represents the improvement in χ^2 which would be obtained if a particular path was added to the model. Typically, we would start by considering parameters with the largest mi value. We would proceed by adding to our model those parameters that make good theoretical sense, one at a time, re-fit the model and explore the results to check whether it has improved. Looking at the table below, none of the suggested parameters seems to be theoretically justifiable. Many of them postulate additional correlations between questionnaire items and different latent variables from the ones they were originally designed to measure. Since none of these parameters has a clear theoretical rationale and given that our analysis demonstrated excellent model fit, it would be perfectly reasonable to ignore modification indices and accept the model as originally specified.

```
SEM_model_fit_nobtsp <- sem(full_SEM, data = SEM_data) # modindices seems
incompatible with bootstrapped models. Therefore, we refit the model
omitting the boostrapping estimator options
modind <- modindices(SEM_model_fit_nobtsp, sort. = TRUE)
head(modind, 15)
```

```
##                lhs op        rhs    mi    epc sepc.lv sepc.all sepc.nox
## 190         cred_2 ~~   about_us 6.524 -0.054  -0.054   -0.096   -0.096
## 184         cred_1 ~~ pol_orient 5.976  0.154   0.154    0.092    0.092
## 179         cred_1 ~~     dist_2 5.522 -0.102  -0.102   -0.063   -0.063
## 137          ben_3 ~~     dist_2 5.075  0.095   0.095    0.053    0.053
## 168          int_3 ~~     cred_3 5.025 -0.065  -0.065   -0.042   -0.042
## 116          ben_2 ~~      ben_3 5.021  0.137   0.137    0.074    0.074
## 183         cred_1 ~~   evidence 4.898  0.053   0.053    0.088    0.088
## 91         distrust =~      ben_3 4.826  0.133   0.116    0.087    0.087
## 76      credibility =~      ben_1 4.818  0.153   0.152    0.109    0.109
## 199         cred_3 ~~ pol_orient 4.712 -0.126  -0.126   -0.079   -0.079
## 89         distrust =~      ben_1 4.698 -0.142  -0.123   -0.088   -0.088
## 180         cred_1 ~~     dist_3 4.300  0.097   0.097    0.057    0.057
## 204         dist_1 ~~   evidence 4.187  0.055   0.055    0.091    0.091
## 198         cred_3 ~~   evidence 4.168 -0.045  -0.045   -0.078   -0.078
## 176         cred_1 ~~     cred_2 4.160 -0.096  -0.096   -0.071   -0.071
```

To illustrate the potential usefulness of modification indices, let us imagine a scenario where our initial hypothetical model contained fewer parameters than the model we tested above. Specifically, let us omit both control variables from the regression equations as well as the correlation between them.

```
# speficy simpler SEM model
simple_SEM <- '
# latent variable definitions
  benevolence =~ ben_1 + ben_2 + ben_3
  integrity =~ int_1 + int_2 + int_3
  credibility =~ cred_1 + cred_2 + cred_3
  distrust =~ dist_1 + dist_2 + dist_3 + dist_4
# regressions
  benevolence ~ about_us + evidence
  integrity ~ about_us + evidence
  credibility ~ benevolence + integrity + evidence
# variable correlations
  benevolence ~~ integrity
# fix experimental variable covariance to 0
  about_us ~~ 0*evidence
'
# fit simpler SEM model
simple_SEM_model_fit <- sem(simple_SEM, data = SEM_data)
```

If we inspect the resulting modification indices table, we can see that some of the omitted relations are among the suggested parameters exhibiting the largest mi values. Lavaan suggests adding a correlation between credibility and distrust (line 197) and a correlation between benevolence and distrust (line 194). Note that the algorithm is not suggesting that we add distrust as a predictor of benevolence and credibility (indicated by the ~ symbol), as we postulate in the model we developed and tested above. This highlights the importance of theory in informing our model specification decisions. It is based on theoretical considerations that we postulate distrust of pharmaceutical corporations to have a causal effect on benevolence and credibility of the company's denial, rather than to be simply correlated with them. Modification indices should thus be interpreted in light of theory, rather than implemented blindly to simply boost model fit.

```
modind <- modindices(simple_SEM_model_fit, sort. = TRUE)
head(modind, 15)

##             lhs op    rhs      mi     epc sepc.lv sepc.all sepc.nox
```

```
## 197 credibility  ~~ distrust  15.099 -0.175 -0.203 -0.203 -0.203
## 161       cred_1 ~~   dist_2   7.453 -0.121 -0.121 -0.074 -0.074
## 171       cred_2 ~~ about_us   7.225 -0.056 -0.056 -0.101 -0.101
## 78      distrust =~    ben_1   5.680 -0.143 -0.125 -0.090 -0.090
## 59     integrity =~   cred_3   5.328 -0.146 -0.168 -0.146 -0.146
## 194 benevolence  ~~ distrust   5.266 -0.118 -0.113 -0.113 -0.113
## 169       cred_2 ~~   dist_3   4.836 -0.097 -0.097 -0.061 -0.061
## 66   credibility =~    ben_1   4.834  0.154  0.151  0.109  0.109
## 151        int_3 ~~   cred_3   4.707 -0.062 -0.062 -0.041 -0.041
## 61     integrity =~   dist_2   4.705 -0.113 -0.130 -0.096 -0.096
## 123        ben_3 ~~   dist_2   4.639  0.091  0.091  0.051  0.051
## 165       cred_1 ~~ evidence   4.594  0.051  0.051  0.086  0.086
## 84      distrust =~   cred_1   4.550 -0.119 -0.104 -0.087 -0.087
## 73   credibility =~   dist_2   4.436 -0.130 -0.128 -0.094 -0.094
## 95         ben_1 ~~   cred_2   4.405  0.072  0.072  0.046  0.046
```

5 Conclusion

This chapter has presented a hands-on introduction to Structural Equation Modeling and has shown how this technique can be applied to the analysis of data from a linguistic experiment. One of the aims of the chapter was to illustrate some of the advantages of SEM compared to more popular multivariate methods such as multiple regression. As I have argued above, the main strengths of a SEM approach lie in the fact that it can handle complex models comprising both observed and latent variables and that it makes it easy to estimate indirect effects between variables. SEM can therefore help linguists develop and test sophisticated theoretical models of the psychological and cognitive mechanisms underpinning language. As discussed above, SEM takes a confirmatory approach to the analysis of empirical data. This does not mean that hypothetical models are either accepted "as is" or discarded, but rather that theory plays a prominent role in the analysis process and should guide our thinking and decisions as we build and revise our models. As the example of Flusberg et al. (2017) above shows, SEM offers promising possibilities for experimental research within a cognitive linguistic framework and could help us achieve a more nuanced understanding of how language influences thought. But SEM is not only applicable to experimental studies. In fact, this technique has been mainly used in non-experimental research (Kline 2016: 10).

Thus, SEM could be employed in observational studies from a cognitive linguistic perspective to shed new light on the latent forces that shape language use. I hope this chapter will encourage more linguists to take up this underused yet powerful and versatile statistical technique.

References

Anderson, James C and Gerbing, David W (1988), Structural equation modeling in practice: A review and recommended two-step approach, *Psychological Bulletin 103* (3). 411.

Bagozzi, Richard P and Phillips, Lynn W (1982), Representing and testing organizational theories: A holistic construal, *Administrative Science Quarterly*. 459–89.

Byrne, Barbara M (2010), *Structural equation modeling with AMOS: Basic concepts, applications, and programming (Second Edition)* (Second edn., New York: Routledge, 396) 7384.

Chou, Chih-Ping and Huh, Jimi (2012), Model Modification in Structural Equation Modeling, in Rick H. Hoyle (ed.), *Handbook of Structural Equation Modeling* (New York and London: The Guilford Press), 232–46.

DeVellis, Robert F (2012), *Scale development: Theory and applications (3rd edition)* (Thousand Oaks, CA: Sage publications).

Fairclough, Norman (2013), *Critical discourse analysis: The critical study of language* (Routledge).

Flusberg, Stephen J, Matlock, Teenie, and Thibodeau, Paul H (2017), Metaphors for the war (or race) against climate change, *Environmental Communication 11* (6).769–83.

Fornell, Claes and Larcker, David F (1981), Evaluating structural equation models with unobservable variables and measurement error, *Journal of Marketing Research*, 39–50.

Fuoli, Matteo (2017), 'Building a trustworthy corporate identity: A corpus-based analysis of stance in annual and corporate social responsibility reports', *Applied Linguistics*.

Fuoli, Matteo and Paradis, Carita (2014), 'A model of trust-repair discourse', *Journal of Pragmatics*, *74*, 52–69.

Fuoli, Matteo and Hart, Christopher (2018), 'Trust-building strategies in corporate discourse: An experimental study', *Discourse & Society*, *29* (5), 514–52.

Haden, Van R, et al. (2012), Global and local concerns: What attitudes and beliefs motivate farmers to mitigate and adapt to climate change?, *PloS One 7* (12). e52882.

Hair, Joseph F, et al. (2014), *Multivariate data analysis (7th edition)* (7; Harlow: Pearson).

Hart, Christopher (2014), *Discourse, grammar and ideology: Functional and cognitive perspectives* (Bloomsbury Publishing).

Hoyle, Rick H. (ed.), (2012), *Handbook of Structural Equation Modeling* (New York and London: The Guilford Press).

Hu, Li-tze and Bentler, Peter M (1999), Cutoff criteria for fit indexes in covariance structure analysis: Conventional criteria versus new alternatives, *Structural Equation Modeling: A Multidisciplinary Journal 6* (1). 1–55.

Jorgensen, T. D., et al. (2020), semTools: Useful tools for structural equation modeling. R package version 0.5-3. Retrieved from https://CRAN.R-project.org/package=semTools'.

Jöreskog, Karl Gustav (1993), Testing structural equation models, in Kenneth A. Bollen and J. Scott Long (eds.), Testing structural equation models (Newbury Park, CA: Sage), 294–316.

Kline, Rex B (2016), *Principles and practice of structural equation modeling* (Fourth edn.: New York: The Guildford Press).

Kline, Rex B. (2012), Assumptions in Structural Equation Modeling, in Rick H. Hoyle (ed.), *Handbook of Structural Equation Modeling* (New York and London: The Guilford Press), 111–25.

Koizumi, Rie and In'nami, Yo (2020), Structural equation modeling of vocabulary size and depth using conventional and Bayesian methods, *Frontiers in Psychology 11*. 618.

Korkmaz, Selcuk, Goksuluk, Dincer, and Zararsiz, Gokmen (2014), MVN: An R package for assessing multivariate normality, *The R Journal 6* (2). 151–62.

Mardia, Kanti V (1970), Measures of multivariate skewness and kurtosis with applications, *Biometrika*. 519–30.

Mayer, Adam and Smith, E Keith (2019), Unstoppable climate change? The influence of fatalistic beliefs about climate change on behavioural change and willingness to pay cross-nationally, *Climate Policy 19* (4). 511–23.

Mayer, Roger C and Davis, James H (1999), The effect of the performance appraisal system on trust for management: A field quasi-experiment, *Journal of Applied Psychology 84* (1). 123.

Mayer, Roger C, Davis, James H, and Schoorman, F David (1995), An integrative model of organizational trust, *Academy of Management Review 20* (3). 709–34.

O'Connor, Robert E, Bard, Richard J, and Fisher, Ann (1999), Risk perceptions, general environmental beliefs, and willingness to address climate change, *Risk Analysis 19* (3). 461–71.

Rosseel, Yves (2012), Lavaan: An R package for structural equation modeling and more. Version 0.5–12 (BETA), *Journal of Statistical Software 48* (2). 1–36.

Schumacker, Randall E and Lomax, Richard G (2016), *A beginner's guide to structural equation modeling* (Fourth edn.: New York: Routledge).

Sperber, Dan, et al. (2010), Epistemic vigilance, *Mind & Language 25* (4). 359–93.

Team, R Core (2016), *R: A Language and Environment for Statistical Computing, R Foundation for Statistical Computing*, Vienna, Austria. https://www.R-project.org/.

Wodak, Ruth and Meyer, Michael (2015), *Methods of critical discourse studies* (Sage).

Zhang, Dongbo (2017), Derivational morphology in reading comprehension of Chinese-speaking learners of English: A longitudinal structural equation modeling study, *Applied Linguistics 38* (6). 871–95.

Mariana Montes, Kris Heylen
Visualizing distributional semantics

1 Introduction

In this chapter, we present a visual analytics approach to the corpus-based study of lexical semantics. The approach combines distributional semantic modelling of word tokens with an interactive visualization to analyze how structural properties of word meaning, like polysemy and prototypicality, emerge from contextual usage patterns. We will argue that different distributional models highlight different semantic aspects of contextual usage and we advocate exploring and analyzing these differences through a visual interaction with the models. As an illustration, we look at a polysemous verb in Dutch and we interpret the results within a Cognitive Linguistics framework. In the following paragraphs, we situate our approach within the tradition of quantitative, corpus-based analyses of lexical semantics and polysemy in Cognitive Linguistics and we introduce our illustrative case study.

1.1 Cognitive linguistics and distributional semantics

Cognitive linguistics understands meaning as categorization, without assuming definitions based on necessary and sufficient conditions. These categories, meanings or senses, are not necessarily discrete (Geeraerts 1993; Glynn 2014a, 2014b) nor homogeneous: they exhibit different kinds of prototypicality effects, from central and peripheral members to fuzzy boundaries (Geeraerts 2000).

Prototypicality can be observed on different levels. On the one hand, we can distinguish between an intensional level and an extensional level. The former refers to the prototypical structure of the features that characterize a category, while the latter refers to the relationship between the exemplars of the category, e.g. corpus occurrences of a lexeme. On the other hand, prototypicality

---

Acknowledgement: This research was carried out within the research project *Nephological Semantics: Using token clouds for meaning detection in variation linguistics* financed by KU Leuven project grant 3H150305.

Mariana Montes, QLVL – KU Leuven, e-mail: mariana.montes@kuleuven.be
Kris Heylen, QLVL – KU Leuven, Dutch Language Institute – Leiden,
e-mail: kris.heylen@kuleuven.be

can be identified at both the level of the lexeme and the level of its senses. At the level of the lexeme, we can devise a network of senses, some of which are more central and from which the other senses derive through various mechanisms. At the level of the sense itself, we find that certain features (at the intensional level) or instances (at the extensional level) can be more prominent or more characteristic.[1]

In corpus-based approaches to lexical semantics, prototypicality effects may be studied by using frequency as a proxy for salience; it is an imperfect tool (Arppe et al. 2010), but a useful operationalization (Glynn 2014a). Understanding meaning as emergent from use, usage patterns as found in corpus data can be used to describe the semasiological structure of a lexical item: we don't just describe how a given form can be used, but also how often in the language sample under investigation. Glynn argues that quantitative corpus-driven methods, in particular collocation and multifactorial analysis (aka behavioral profiles) are a natural progression of the radial network and prototypicality studies:

> [T]he results of multifactorial analysis and collocation analysis are, in fact, structured as fuzzy-bounded prototype categories. Since the results are based upon relative frequency, they are, therefore, necessarily "prototype" structured (at least if we accept a frequency-based operationalisation of prototypicality) and are not discrete. Moreover, multifactorial feature analysis identifies "meanings" as tendencies, where a tendency is a multidimensional pattern of use. This, quite literally, produces networks of different uses – a frequency-based and complex multidimensional network of sense relations. The radial network analysis produced prototype maps of meaning upon one "semantic" dimension where the "nodes" were discrete reified senses. Today, multifactorial feature analysis produces multidimensional networks of usage patterns that can be interpreted as emergent language structure. The difference between the two is a natural progression, not a methodological schism. (2014a: 27)

As we will discuss in Section 2.1, distributional semantics are a technological extension of these methods. Vector space models rely on co-occurrence frequency of features and represent how similar different linguistic items are to each other based on these distributional profiles. Their quantitative, probabilistic nature makes them ideal to show relationships between items without forcing discrete, reified categories. While they are also suited for studies with an onomasiological approach (i.e. studying the forms that can be used to express a meaning), in this case we will focus on a semasiological perspective (i.e. describing the meanings that a form can express). By modelling individual instances or

---

[1] Prototypicality can also be identified from an onomasiological perspective, with different word forms being preferred for certain concepts or in certain situations (Geeraerts 2016), but this approach goes beyond the scope of this chapter.

concordance lines, token-based vector space models represent the semasiological structure of the item under study as relative distances between these occurrences. Internal categories, such as senses or, rather, usage patterns, can be identified as clusters of occurrences in similar contexts. Clustering algorithms can define them as discrete entities, but they need not be represented as such. Instead, via dimensionality reduction it is possible to map these distances on a low-dimensional space and visualize them as scatterplots. An interactive exploration of these plots can show fuzzy boundaries between categories and denser cores may point to prototypical patterns.

1.2 Illustrative case study: Dutch *heffen*

The Dutch verb *heffen* has two main senses: a concrete one meaning 'to lift/raise', such as *de handen heffen* 'to lift your hands', and an abstract, financial meaning 'to levy (taxes, interests)' – not 'to increase'. Examples are given in (1) and (2) respectively, where *heffen* is highlighted in boldface.

(1) *De heer des huizes **hief** afgelopen zondagmiddag zijn handen ten hemel.*
'The lord of the house **rose** his hands to the heavens last Sunday noon.'

(2) *De overheid mag nooit tol **heffen** op wegen die geheel met belastinggeld zijn betaald.*
'The government may never **levy** a toll on roads that were fully paid with taxes.'

These basic two senses can be found in a concise dictionary like the *Van Dale groot woordenboek hedendaags Nederlands* 'Great Van Dale Dictionary of Current Dutch' (Van Sterkenburg, Verhoeven & Parqui 2006), although other dictionaries report finer grained distinction (e.g. den Boon & Geeraerts 2007; den Boon & Hendrickx 2017). Note that this lemma is in competition with the derived form *opheffen* for the meaning 'to lift', and as a result it has a restricted set of applications in this sense.[2]

---

[2] This is precisely the kind of behavior that vector space models are good at representing, and the reason why this is a good illustrative example. Other words with more varied distributional behavior result in less clear visual representations, which do not necessarily imply a bad modelling, but rather a more complex underlying picture. However, such an example would require a more detailed discussion on the methods involved, which would deviate us from the purpose of this chapter, namely to talk about visualization.

We extracted a random selection of 240 occurrences of the verb *heffen* from a corpus of Dutch and Flemish newspapers[3] published between 1999 and 2004. This is a lectally balanced corpus with 520 million tokens (for a more detailed description, see De Pascale 2019: 30). The concordance was annotated by undergraduate students of Linguistics at a Flemish university, who assigned one of these two senses or "none of the above", and we ruled on the disagreements.[4]

Almost 10% of the occurrences were removed because of parsing errors: they were either typos or instances of separable compound verbs with *heffen* as root.[5] Of the rest, 78 correspond to the concrete, physical sense ('to lift') and 140 to the financial sense ('to levy'). During the annotation, we could already identify relatively fixed patterns related to the physical sense: *de handen ten hemel heffen* 'to raise your hands to the heavens', *het glas heffen* 'to raise the glass' and *een vinger(tje) heffen* 'to raise a (small) finger'. These patterns refer to expressive gestures with different meanings, such as 'to toast' for *het glas heffen* 'lit. to raise the glass' and 'to reprimand someone' for *een vinger(tje) heffen* 'lit. to raise a finger', and can be easily used metonymically. The few 'to lift' instances that don't match these idiomatic expressions are normally variations on the first one, e.g. with arms instead of hands or without explicit mention of the heavens.

From dictionaries, introspective native knowledge and manual annotation, we already have an idea of the main senses of Dutch *heffen*, their relative frequencies in a certain corpus and some prototypical patterns of usage. Later we will look at distributional models of the manually annotated concordance of *heffen* and discuss what their visual representations can tell us about its behavior in corpus. Could we find internal categories even without manual annotation? How is prototypicality rendered in a vector space model? We won't just generate one model but hundreds. With the visualization, we will look at the different perspectives that a variety of models can offer, and how they enrich our understanding of the case study.

---

3 *Algemeen Dagblad, Het Parool, NRC Handelsblad, De Volkskrant, Het Laatste Nieuws, Het Niewsblad, De Standaard* and *De Morgen*.
4 The occurrences were split in 6 batches of 40 instances with 15 words to the left and right of the key word, and 3 annotators annotated each batch independently. The agreement was very high: Fleiss' κ was of 0.627 in one of the batches and ranged from 0.905 to 1 in the rest, always with p-value < 0.001.
5 Dutch verbs can consist of a root and a prefix, and some of them can be split in certain situations. In such cases, verbs with *heffen* as root, such as *opheffen*, can be mistakenly parsed as the verb *heffen* and the preposition *op*.

The chapter presents two more sections, followed by a conclusion. In Section 2 we introduce distributional semantic models and how they relate to other corpus-based approaches in lexical semantics. We give a brief overview of the many different approaches to token-level modelling and situate the models that we will be using in our case study. In Section 3 we present the Visual Analytics tool developed within the QLVL research group at KU Leuven for the exploration of token-level vector space models (Montes & Wielfaert 2021). As we describe the most relevant features, we will illustrate their utility with the case of *heffen*.

2 Quantitative and usage-based methods in cognitive linguistics

In this section we will first introduce a number of corpus-based approaches to studying polysemy, distinguished by whether the identification of features and/or the detection of patterns are performed manually or statistically. Afterwards we will focus on distributional semantics in particular and discuss the different approaches to vector space modelling.

2.1 Corpus-based approaches

A corpus-based approach to semantics implies, first, the identification of contextual features and, second, the detection of usage patterns and senses; either step can be performed manually or statistically.

In the first place, approaches that engage in manual identification of (context) features involve a stage in which the researcher goes through a sample of occurrences of the target item and annotates them based on morphosyntactic features, semantic categories of co-occurring items, and so on. Statistical approaches delegate this identification to automatic systems, which, for instance, count the co-occurrence frequency of different lexemes and perform statistical tests to transform raw frequencies into association measures. One crucial difference lies in how the relevance of a feature is determined: by the linguistic competence and expertise of the lexicologist in the former group of approaches and by statistical methods in the latter.

Secondly, approaches that engage in manual detection of patterns take the output of the first stage to classify the results into meaningful, interpretable senses. Statistical approaches measure the correlation between features or compute distances between items based on their shared features.

Table 4.1: Cross-tabulation of manual and statistical approaches for two stages of corpus-based semantics: identifying features and detecting patterns.

		identifying features	
		manual	statistical
detecting patterns	manual	philology and lexicography	collocation analysis
	statistical	behavioral profile approach	vector space approach

As shown in Table 4.1 (adapted from Heylen et al. 2015: 154), the combination of the components yields four types of approaches.

The traditional philological and lexicographical work, preceding the availability of statistical methods, is characterized by the manual identification of contextual features and manual detection of patterns based on configuration of these features. This could have been the case with the annotators of *heffen* if they had had to induce the sense categories from their sample.

Collocation analyses leave the identification of features to automatic methods, which typically return ranks of collocates based on association strengths (Sinclair 1991: 170; Stubbs 1995: 23; McEnery, Xiao & Tono 2010; McEnery & Hardie 2012: 122:123). The researcher must then interpret those ranks and find meaningful relations between the items in those lists. In our corpus, the highest ranked collocates of *heffen* based on pointwise mutual information (PMI) include infrequent terms related to *belasting* 'taxes', which points towards the financial sense 'to levy', and more frequent ones such as *glas* 'glass', *hand* 'hand', *hoog* 'high' and *hemel* 'heaven', pointing towards the concrete 'to lift' sense. These results can offer a first sketch of the distributional profile of the lemma, but collapse the behaviour of its different senses into one list.

The complementary alternative to collocations is given by behavioral profiles or multifactorial feature analysis, where the researcher manually chooses and codes the features of interest, such as the kind of direct object or subject, or tense, mood and aspect of the target verb. These are typically schematic features that require an interpretation of observed linguistic forms by the researcher (e.g. *hand/arm* as BODY PART). By aggregating over multiple occurrences, the resulting feature configurations can be transformed into distances and fed into clustering methods or correspondence analysis for automatic pattern identification (Glynn 2014b, 2016; Gries 2006, 2012; Jansegers & Gries 2017, among others).

Finally, distributional[6] models, the main topic of this chapter, make use of automatic methods in both stages: the context features are identified and weighted automatically, and their values are taken as components of the profiles, which are called "vectors"[7] (See Lenci 2018 for a friendly introduction). Similarly to the behavioral profiles approach, we can calculate distances between the vectors and submit them to further statistical analysis to identify semantic patterns. In cognitive linguistics, they have been used in lexical semantics (Heylen, Speelman & Geeraerts 2012; Heylen et al. 2015), diachronic construction grammar (Hilpert & Correia Saavedra 2017; Hilpert & Flach 2020; Perek 2016, 2018), lectometry (Ruette, Ehret & Szmrecsanyi 2016; De Pascale 2019), and lexical typology (Koptjevskaja-Tamm & Sahlgren 2014). This approach will be explained in more detail in the next section.

2.2 Semantic vector space models

Semantic vector space models can be seen as a further development of collocational analysis, relying on the so-called Distributional Hypothesis (Harris 1954; Firth 1957), hence the alternative name *distributional semantic modelling*. As shown in Table 4.1, vector space models rely on statistical techniques both (1) for identifying relevant semantic features (like collocation analysis) and (2) for finding patterns in those features that correspond to (a network of) prototypically structured senses (like behavioral profile analysis). The choice of computational approach in both of these steps leads to different types of vector space models, which we will briefly introduce here: first we will describe the logic behind type-level vectors, i.e. aggregating over all instances of a lexeme, and then we will introduce token-level models.

---

[6] From a broad perspective, any approach basing meaning analysis on patterns of use can be considered a distributional approach to semantics, but a more narrow perspective focuses on distributional semantic models, such as vector space models.
[7] The entity described as "vector" or "profile" is a string of numbers: By naming it "profile", we focus on the fact that they constitute a description of the target item in terms of (meaningful) dimensions. By calling it "vector", we situate the item in the mathematical field, a one dimensional tensor, a column or row of a matrix, a string of coordinates in multiple dimensions that can be compared with another string of coordinates (i.e. vector) by various algebraic operations such as calculating the angle between them.
 Because the practical, mathematical properties are of more relevance in vector space models, we will call them "vectors", but they are still profiles, i.e. numeric representations and descriptions, of the items under investigation.

2.2.1 From word-feature co-occurrences to semantic vectors

In all approaches, semantic vector construction starts from frequency data about the co-occurrence of lexemes and context features and results in a continuous vector representation that models the semantics of a lexical item. However, different approaches exist to the two aspects of feature analysis we discussed above, viz (a) determining the relevance of features and (b) deriving latent, schematic features from observed lexical ones. In statistical modelling terms, (a) relates to selecting and weighting features in a vector and (b) to reducing the dimensionality of the vectors. The combination of these two modelling choices allows us to distinguish the two main approaches to word vector semantics: count-based models (aka distributional semantic models) and prediction-based models (aka word embeddings, see Baroni, Dinu & Kruszewski 2014 for a comparison).

Historically, count-based models were developed first, building further on the methodology of traditional collocation analysis (for an overview, including word-document and pair-pattern models, see Turney & Pantel 2010). The name derives from the fact that they extract co-occurrence counts from a corpus first, and only then proceed to feature weighting and, optionally, to dimensionality reduction. Just like in collocation analysis, context features – be they lexical collocates in a window or morpho-syntactic colligations – are weighted for relevance to the lexical item by transforming raw co-occurrence frequencies into association strengths using measures like t-score, positive pointwise mutual information, log-likelihood, etc. These association strengths are the values in a lexeme's vector and the vectors for all lexemes are combined in a matrix which has all context features as its dimensions. Given such a matrix, two lexemes are similar insofar they have similar association measures with the same context features: they are highly attracted to the same contexts.

From a corpus linguistic perspective, the matrix contains the collocational profiles for all lexical items. Because distributional models usually take into account many different context features (typically tens of thousands), these matrices are high-dimensional. In addition, since any given lexical item will only co-occur with a small subset of context features, depending on the frequency of the lexical item, they are also sparse. Sparse vectors may miss out on relevant generalizations over individual context features: even though *arms* and *hands* are semantically related, they are treated as different features. However, these relations between context features can be inferred from their tendency to be strongly associated with the same items. These patterns can be captured through dimensionality reduction techniques like Singular Value Decomposition, which turn the sparse word vectors into dense vectors with a reduced set of dimensions (a few hundred).

However, although these dimensions can be thought of as latent, schematic context features, their linguistic interpretability varies greatly with the specific method used.

Prediction-based models, on the other hand, proceed directly, and simultaneously, to the weighting and dimensionality reduction steps by training a neural network to predict either the target word based on one or more context words (continuous bag-of-words, CBOW), or some context words based on the target (Skip-Gram). The best known model, Word2Vec (Mikolov et al. 2013), has 1 hidden layer of a few hundred neurons whose weights are constantly updated as the neural network is trained on co-occurrence data from a corpus. Once the neural network is accurate enough, the weights in the hidden layer are used as the values of the word vector, "embedding" the word in a relatively low dimensional semantic space (hence the term *word embedding*). Although these dimensions themselves are linguistically completely uninterpretable, they allow vector comparisons between words that detect semantic similarity or analogy surprisingly well. Currently, word vector models based on neural networks are state-of-the-art for applied NLP tasks, such as automatic summarization or information retrieval. Yet, the relative un-interpretability of how these models capture meaning makes them less attractive for a linguistically focused semantic analysis.

2.2.2 From semantic vectors to word senses

The word vectors described above are type-level vectors: they aggregate over all occurrences of a word. Although they summarize the contextually defined (semantic) dimensions relevant to a word's meaning in a single vector, they do not model how individual occurrences of a word express a specific meaning or usage pattern. For what is known as Word Sense Induction in Computational Linguistics, but also for the kind of prototype-linguistic analysis of a word's semasiological structure that we pursue in this paper, we need a vector representation on the token-level, i.e. a vector that captures the semantics of each individual occurrence of a lexical item. Both count-based and prediction-based approaches to vector semantics compute token vectors (in the latter approach called "contextualized word embeddings") based on the type-vectors of the target lexeme and its co-occurring words in a specific usage event. They then combine these type vectors in specific ways to obtain a token vector representation. Count-based methods perform vector operations (addition, multiplication, etc.) on the type vectors to calculate a token vector: e.g. the vector of a token is a combination of the vectors of the words in its immediate context. In contrast, prediction-based models like BERT (Devlin et al. 2019) use the type vectors as input to train an additional neural network that predicts masked context words in individual sentences. The values of one of the hidden layers are then used as the token vector values. Some approaches will perform further computations (e.g. transformations or dimensionality reduction) or calculate derivations from these initial token vectors, e.g. "substitution" vectors in the current state-of-the-art approach by Amrami and Goldberg (2019).

Note that all approaches to token vector modelling have many different parameters that can be set in many different ways, leading to an exponentially increasing number of vector modelling possibilities for the same set of word tokens. However, in all approaches, the final vector modelling output is a matrix of token vectors for which pairwise similarities are calculated and stored in a token-by-token distance matrix. This matrix is then the input for the further identification of word senses, typically through some form of clustering analysis.

In fact, our visual analytics approach, presented below, takes advantage of the fact that all token-level models produce a token-by-token distance matrix and, in addition, it is specifically geared to comparing the output of many different token vector models on the same set of word occurrences. We argue that such a systematic comparison of different models is essential for the use of distribution modelling as a usage-based methodology in cognitive lexical semantics. Token vectors are able to encode semantic features of lexical usage events, and unlike the manually annotated usage features in behavioral profiles, they have the advantage of being derived completely bottom-up from statistical patterns in usage data. Yet, also unlike behavioral profile features, the semantic features that token vectors capture are not known *a priori*: They emerge through the modelling and they will differ from model to model, depending on the model's parameters. Moreover, the semantic features encoded in a token vector are usually not straightforwardly interpretable from the vector itself but need to be interpreted by linking back to the usage events (occurrences) they model.

2.3 204 models of Dutch *heffen*

For the case study of *heffen*, we have generated 204 different models of the same set of occurrences described above. We will introduce the parameter settings very briefly, but they won't be discussed in detail in the following section. A more thorough explanation can be found in the appendix.[8] For token-level

---

[8] The model-building workflow, up to the token-per-token distance matrices, was performed in Python 3 with the nephosem module developed within the research group (see https://qlvl.

count-based models, the parameter settings apply to two different levels: selection and weighting of first-order context words, and selection and weighting of second-order context words.

First-order parameters determine the immediate context selected to represent each occurrence. In our case, the first decision is between dependency-based models or bag-of-words models: the former selects context words based on their dependency relations to the target, while the latter ignores syntactic information. Instead, bag-of-words models differ in their window size (3, 5, or 10 tokens to either side of the target), in whether they apply part-of-speech filters (including only verbs, nouns, adjectives and adverbs or allowing most categories instead), and in whether they include context words outside the sentence of the target. There is also variation within the dependency-based models: "LEMMAREL" models only select context words that match a predefined set of dependency relations (e.g. direct object of the target verb), while "LEMMAPATH" models measure the length of the dependency path between the context words and the target and only select those under a certain threshold.

In addition to the bag-of-words- and dependency-specific first-order parameters, the "PPMI" parameter can take three values: "weight", "selection" and "no". In the first two cases, the PMI between each context word and *heffen* was calculated, and only those with a value larger than 0 were included; in the third case, no such filter was applied. The difference between the first two values relies on the relative importance of the context words. As we mentioned before, tokens are represented by averaging over the type-level vectors of its immediate context words. When the "PPMI" parameter takes the value "weight", this is a weighted average: the type-level vectors of context words with higher association strength with *heffen* will be more relevant than those with a lower association strength.

Second-order parameters, in contrast, define the type-level vectors of the first-order context words. Some important parameters are window size and weighting, i.e. the association measure that makes up the values in the vectors and the window size based on which it is calculated. In this case, these parameters are set constant to positive PMI (i.e. when PMI is negative it is set to 0) based on a window of 4 words to either side. The second-order parameters along which our models do vary are part-of-speech and vector length. The former is similar to the first-order part-of-speech parameter, but instead of applying the filter to the context words of the target, it applies it to the context words of the

---

github.io/nephosem for the code and documentation of nephosem and https://montesmariana.github.io/semasioFlow/tutorials/createClouds.html for a tutorial of the code used in this chapter).

type-level vectors. "Length", on the other hand, determines how many context words will be included, i.e. the length of the second-order vector and, in consequence, the dimensionality of the token-by-feature matrix. When it takes the value 5000, these are the 5000 most frequent lemmas in the corpus, after applying the part-of-speech filter. The alternative value is FOC, which means that the same list of first-order context is copied as second-order context features. This leads to a much lower dimensionality, in the range of the hundreds instead of thousands. More discussion on the differences between these values can be found in the appendix.

Each model is a configuration of parameter settings: for each combination of parameter values, we obtain a different model. This is reflected in the name of the model, e.g. "heffen.LEMMAPATHweight.PPMIselection.LENGTHFOC.SOCPOSall" represents a model of *heffen* that, for each instance, selected all the context words with a maximum dependency-path length of 3 and a minimum PMI with *heffen* of 0, weighted each context word by the length of the dependency path (direct dependency has maximum weight), and used all the selected first-order features as second-order features.

In the next section, we will discuss how a visual analytics approach can both support the comparison of different models and the interpretation of the lexical semantics captured by individual models. We will focus on count-based models because of their closer relationship to traditional collocation analysis and hence their easier linguistic interpretability, but, unless explicitly mentioned, the visual analytics approach is applicable to any type of token vector modelling.

3 Visualizing multidimensional data

The high level of automatization of vector space models makes it possible to analyze semantic patterns in huge amounts of corpus data. While this has the advantage of making semantic analyses more data-driven, this also implies a lower level of control for the linguist, who is confronted with advanced statistical output that is not straightforwardly interpretable in terms of the linguistic phenomena under investigation. In the case of vector space models, and especially an approach that combines multiple parameter settings to generate a multitude of models, the output is an array of distance matrices that "somehow" models different aspects of probabilistic semantic structure. To interpret and understand statistical modelling from a linguistic perspective, we turn to *visual analytics*.

Visual analytics aims to integrate statistical data analysis with techniques from information visualization so that human analysts can recognize, interpret and reason about the statistical patterns that the data analysis reveals (Card, Mackinlay & Shneiderman 1999). Importantly, a visual analytics approach offers a manipulable, interactive visualization that, unlike static diagrams, enables the exploration of a space of parameter values and modelling outputs.

Lexical semantic research with vector space models would benefit from a tool that aids i) the visualization of distance matrices based on high-dimensional data, ii) the comparison of multiple models and iii) more detailed examination of the input to these models. In the next three sections, we will describe a visual analytics tool that addresses all three issues. It was already introduced in Wielfaert et al. (2019), but has undergone some modifications since that description. While there are some differences in layout and available features, the foundational scope and main rationale are the same.[9]

First, regarding point i), for data as complex as the distance matrices returned by vector space models,[10] one way of visualizing it consists of reducing the hundreds of dimensions to only two, which can be mapped into a horizontal and a vertical axis in a scatterplot. Section 3.1 will present a few options for this step, that we run on R (R Core Team 2020). The input needed by the visualization includes the coordinates of each token for each model, as well as other variables of interest, such as the sense tags and even snippets of context corresponding to each occurrence.

Second, individual models can be compared visually, placing their 2D representations side by side, but we can also calculate and visualize the dissimilarities between them.[11] These dissimilarities, in the form of a distance matrix, may undergo the same kind of transformation of the first point to be visualized as a scatterplot. Section 3.2 presents the three main levels of the tool, designed to go from a birds-eye view over multiple models to the more detailed inspection of individual cases.

In relation to iii), Section 3.3 describes further interactive features that allow the user to access the input of each model for a more complete and interpretable comparison. In particular, we will show how we can link the scatterplots of the

---

[9] The tool was written in Javascript with help mostly from the D3 library (Bostock, Ogievetsky & Heer 2011) and can be accessed at https://qlvl.github.io/NephoVis/. The reader is encouraged to explore the various models offered in the site. For this case study we looked at plots found in https://qlvl.github.io/NephoVis/level1.html?type=heffen and subsequent levels.
[10] Behavioral profiles also work with distance matrices and typically visualize them via dendrograms or (multiple) correspondence analysis (Jansegers & Gries 2017; Glynn 2014b, 2016).
[11] We quantified the extent to which the semantic neighbourhood of tokens differs between models by computing the mean Euclidean distance between the double logged similarity ranks vector of tokens to each other across models.

models to the context words selected by each model for each token. This information must be computed elsewhere (in our case, as part of our model-building workflow, in the SemasioFlow Python 3 module) and incorporated to the model metadata as lists of context words per token per model. Further information on the context words, such as frequency and PMI with *heffen*, may be included as well.[12]

We will illustrate the tool with 204 models of *heffen*, as described above. While presenting the features themselves, we hope to demonstrate how they can aid semantic research in a Cognitive Linguistics framework; our findings will be summarized in Section 3.4.

3.1 Visualizing a distance matrix as a scatterplot

The first issue we mentioned is how to visualize distance matrices based on high-dimensional data. Vector space models represent linguistic items as strings of numbers, which are called dimensions. The numbers can be thought of as coordinates on these dimensions, so that the difference in the coordinates of two items is interpreted as the distance between these items along a given dimension.

Dimensionality reduction refers to algorithms that try to locate different items on a low-dimensional space (e.g. 2D) preserving their distances in the high-dimensional space (e.g. 5000D) as well as possible. The literature tends to go for either multidimensional scaling (MDS) or t-stochastic neighbor embeddings (t-SNE), which may be run on R with the function metaMDS() of the vegan package (Oksanen et al. 2019) and Rtsne() of the homonymous package (Krijthe 2015), respectively.

The former is an ordination technique, like principal components analysis (PCA). It tries out different low-dimensional configurations and tries to maximize the correlation between the pairwise distances in the high-dimensional space and those in the low-dimensional space: items that are close together in one space should stay close together in the other, and items that are far apart in one space should stay far apart in the other. It can be evaluated via the stress level, the complement of the correlation coefficient: if the correlation between the pairwise distances is 0.85, the stress level is 0.15. Unlike PCA, however, the dimensions are not meaningful per se; two different runs of MDS may result in plots that mirror each other while representing the same thing. In cognitive

---

[12] For more information on the kind of input required for the visualization, the reader is directed to the README file in the repository of the code (https://github.com/QLVL/NephoVis), which includes links to the Python and R packages used as well.

linguistics literature both metric (Hilpert & Correia Saavedra 2017; Hilpert & Flach 2020; Koptjevskaja-Tamm & Sahlgren 2014) and nonmetric MDS (Heylen et al. 2015; Perek 2016; Heylen, Speelman & Geeraerts 2012; De Pascale 2019) have been used.

The second technique, t-SNE (van der Maaten & Hinton 2008, 2012), has also been incorporated in cognitive distributional semantics (Perek 2018; De Pascale 2019). The algorithm is quite different from MDS, but for our purposes the crucial point is that it prioritizes preserving local similarity structure instead of the global structure: items that are close together in the high-dimensional space should stay close together in the low-dimensional space, but those that are far apart in the high-dimensional space may be even farther apart in low-dimensional space. This leads to nice, tight clusters but the distance between them is less interpretable than in an MDS plot. T-SNE is the state-of-the-art visualization technique for word vectors in computational linguistics (Smilkov et al. 2016).

In both cases we need to state the desired number of dimensions before running the algorithm –for visualization purposes, the most useful choice is 2. Three dimensions are difficult to interpret if projected on a 2D space, such as a screen (Wielfaert et al. 2019: 222; Card, Mackinlay & Shneiderman 1999: 18). In addition, t-SNE requires setting a parameter called *perplexity*, which basically sets how many neighbors the preserved local structure should cover. The figures in Sections 3.2 and 3.3 have all been created with t-SNE, setting the perplexity parameter to 30, but the result of other perplexity values and nonmetric MDS solutions are available in the online version by clicking on "Switch solution" on levels 2 and 3 (see below for instructions).

3.2 Interactive comparison of models

The second issue we presented is the comparison of multiple models of the same tokens. Computational linguists will evaluate the models by comparing them to a benchmark, such as manual sense annotation, and will choose the model that best agrees with it. However, this form of testing does not address in which way the different models have deviated from the benchmark. If we don't assume that there is one correct "solution" to the question of the semasiological structure of our lexeme, but instead wonder how different selections of contextual information can model different aspects of said structure, then a more qualitative comparison is in order.

With such an exploration in mind, and following Shneiderman's Visual Information Seeking Mantra: "Overview first, zoom and filter, then details-on-demand" (1996: 97), the tool organizes the full range of available information along three levels. The basic graphic representation is a scatterplot with coordinates stemming from a dimensionality reduction technique as described in Section 3.1. The three levels represent individual token-level models (Level 3), multiple token-level models next to each other (Level 2) and distances *between* token-level models (Level 1). While the tool itself takes us from the overview in Level 1 to the detailed examination in Level 3, for exposition purposes we will go in the opposite direction.

Level 3 of the visualization tool shows a zoomable scatterplot in which each glyph represents a token, i.e. an instance of the target lexical item. The name of the model, coding the parameter settings as described in Section 2.3 and the Appendix, is indicated on the top. It is possible to map colors and shapes to categorical variables (such as sense labels) and sizes to numerical variables (such as number of available context words[13]) and to select tokens with a given value by clicking on the corresponding legend key.

For example, in Figure 4.1 the *heffen* tokens are colored by the sense tags *heffen_1* ('to lift', in yellow) and *heffen_2* ('to levy', in blue). In this model, we can see that both senses are clearly separated, with only a few tokens mixed with others from a different sense. By hovering over them, we can read their context, such as in Figure 4.2, where the first-order context words selected by this model to represent this token are in highlighted boldface. This allows us to identify first-order context words that might be responsible for the position of a token. The occurrence shown in Figure 4.2 is reproduced in (3): the context words taken by the model, such as *als* 'if', *ze* 'she/they/them', and *dan* 'then', in boldface in the example, are not good cues for any of the senses, but *als* 'if' and *ze* 'she/they/them' tend to occur among the tokens in the tight group nearby. The key context word, *belasting* 'tax', occurs outside the sentence of the target, so that it is ignored by this model, which is based on dependency relations.

(3)   Ik ben tegen deze belasting. Maar **als** je **ze dan toch heft**, **dan** is de vooropgezette periode van vijf maanden niet logisch.
'I am against this tax, but **if** you **do levy it**, **then** the suggested period of five months is not logical.'

---

13 In these discussions we will refer to the contextual features selected by a given model as "context words", to avoid ambiguity with the features of the tool. However, it must be remembered that these need not be words. In addition, a further distinction must be made between words occurring in the context of the target and the subset actually selected for modelling. For the purpose of this tool, only those selected by the model under examination are relevant.

Moreover, the concrete sense 'to lift' is split in two tight groups, albeit close to each other, suggesting usage patterns that are as distinct from each other as the two senses we expected. We can select multiple tokens by clicking on them, by using a selection brush, by typing their unique identifier and by searching for specific context words. In addition, a box in the lower left corner shows the tokens included in other models but lost in the focused model because of lack of context words.

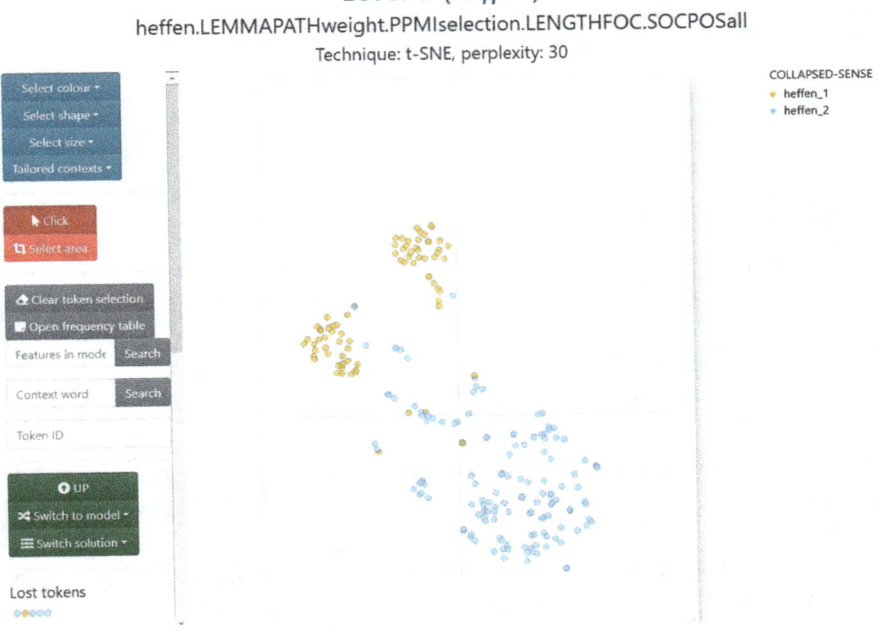

Figure 4.1: Scatterplot of tokens of *heffen*, Level 3 of the visualization tool.

Level 2 of the visualization shows an array of plots next to each other. Each of them represents a different model and the same basic features from Level 3 are available: color, shape and size coding, selection by clicking and brushing, and finding the context by hovering over the tokens. An example of 8 plots of *heffen* is shown in Figure 4.3; the third plot is the one shown in Figures 4.1 and 4.2. The tokens lost by each model are lined up in columns to the right of each plot. We can already see that most of the plots share the configuration found in Level 3, with a clear separation between the senses but also a stark split of 'to lift' in two groups. They do exhibit different levels of overlap: one of the 'to lift'

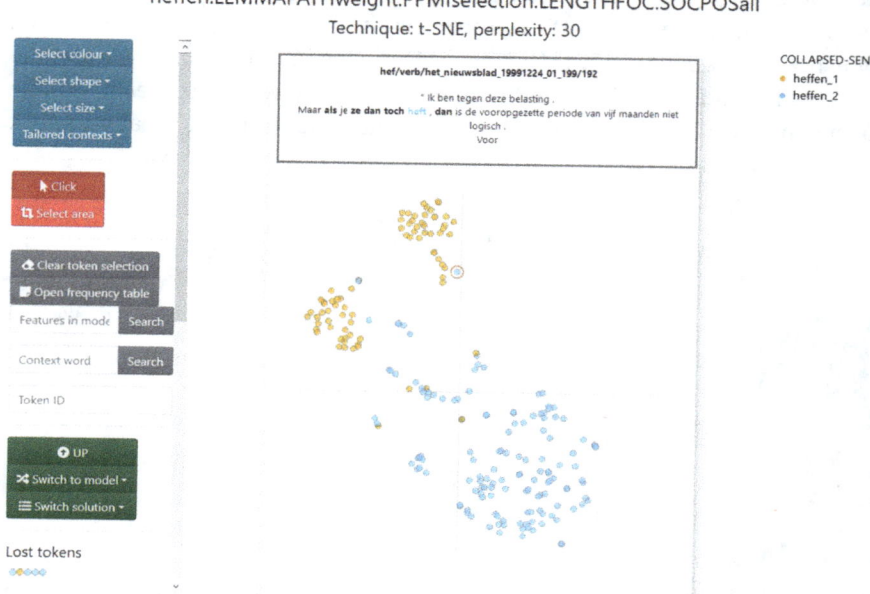

Figure 4.2: Hovering over a token in Level 3 shows its context.

groups is integrated with the 'to levy' tokens in model 8, the three-way split is less clear in model 4, and the three groups are aligned and close to each other in model 5.

Because they are model-dependent, highlighted context and searching tokens by context word are meaningless in this level, where multiple models are being shown simultaneously. The key contribution of this level, next to the superficial visual comparison of the shape of each plot, is the ability to select one or more tokens in a plot and highlighting them in the rest of the plots as well. Thanks to this functionality, the user can compare the relative position of a group of tokens in a model against that in a different model.

In Figure 4.4, for example, the rightmost 'to lift' group of model 3 is selected and its tokens are highlighted in all models. We can see that the same group sticks together, almost complete, in all models; it's the group on the edge of the alignment in model 5, and the group that merges with 'to levy' in model 8. This also means that the other group is always the same as well. In addition, we can see that one of the 'to lift' members of the selected group is

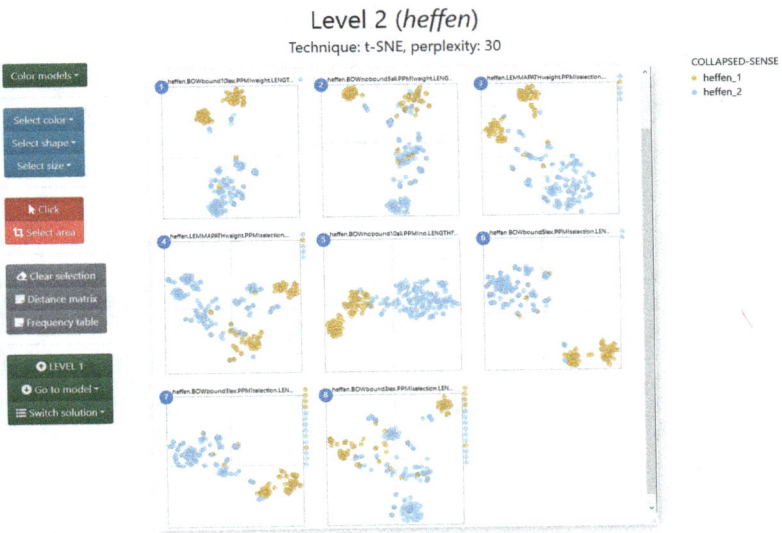

Figure 4.3: Eight scatterplots of tokens of *heffen*, Level 2 of the visualization tool.

lost by models 7 and 8, and that the 'to levy' token discussed above is classified better in models 1, 5, 6 and 7 (i.e. it is surrounded by other 'to levy' tokens).

Level 1 shows one zoomable scatterplot, similar to Level 3, but with each glyph representing one model, instead of one token. As a reminder of the difference, the default shape in Level 1 is a wye ("Y"), while that in the other levels is a circle. The data represented by this scatterplot is not the distance between tokens anymore, but that between models, as described at the beginning of Section 3. This scatterplot aims to represent the similarity between models and allows the user to select the models to inspect according to different criteria. Categorical variables (e.g. whether sentence boundaries are used) can be mapped to colors and shapes, as shown in Figure 4.5, and numerical variables (e.g. number of tokens in the model) can be mapped to size. A selection of buttons on the left panel, as well as the legends for color and shape, can be used to filter models with a certain parameter setting. Otherwise, models can be selected by clicking on the glyphs that represent them.

The increasing granularity from Level 1 to Level 3 and the manner of access to different functionalities respect the mantra "Overview first, zoom and filter, then details-on-demand" (Shneiderman 1996). The individual plots in Levels 1 and 3 are literally zoomable; and in all cases it is possible to select items (either models, in Level 1, or tokens, in the other two), i.e. to filter them, for more detailed inspection. Finally, a number of features show details on demand, such

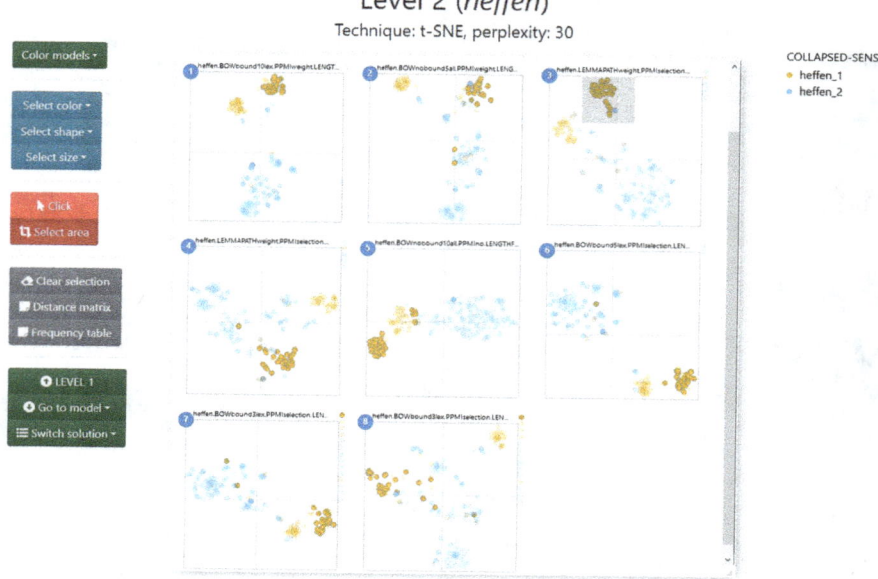

Figure 4.4: Eight scatterplots of tokens of *heffen*, Level 2 of the visualization tool. A group of 'to lift' tokens are selected in model 3 and highlighted in all of them.

as the names of the models in Level 1 and the context of the tokens in the other two levels.

In practice, the user will start with Level 1, the scatterplot of models, and can look for structure in the distribution of the parameters on the plot. For example, color coding may reveal that models with nouns, adjectives, verbs and adverbs as first-order context words are very different from those without strong filters for part-of-speech, while the use of sentence boundaries makes little difference. Depending on whether the user wants to compare models similar or different to each other, or which parameters they would like to keep fixed, they will use individual selection or the buttons to choose models for Level 2. In our case, we click on "Select medoids", which selects the 8 models returned by a partitioning algorithm,[14] which offers a wide range of variation in a manageable number of plots.

In Level 2 the user can already compare the shapes that the models take in their respective plots, the distribution of categories like sense labels, and the

---

[14] The list of medoids from the pam() function of the cluster R package (Maechler et al. 2019) based on the distances between models, with $k=8$.

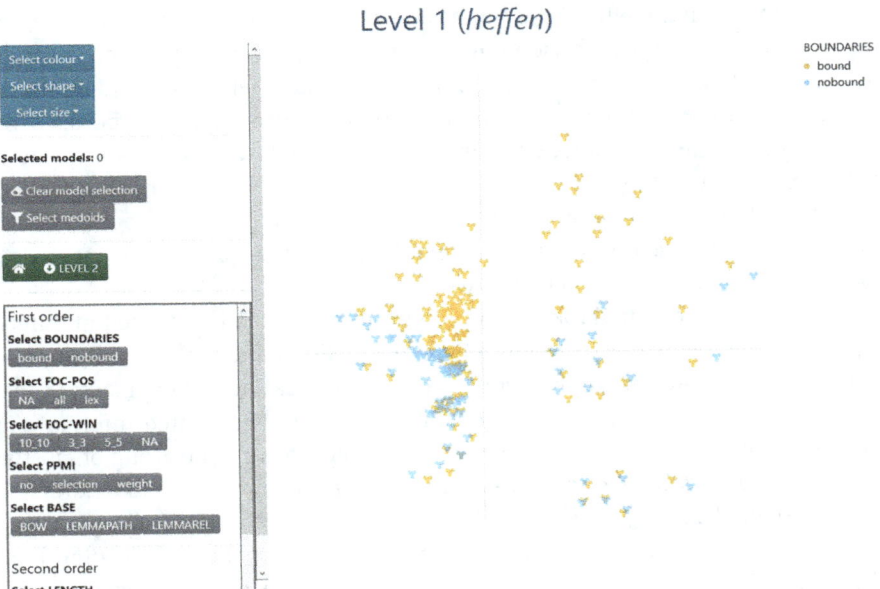

Figure 4.5: Level 1 scatterplot of *heffen* models, colored by whether sentence boundaries were applied.

number of lost tokens. In addition, the "distance matrix" button offers a heatmap of the pairwise distances between the selected models. In the case of *heffen*, the restrictive collocational patterns it presents lead to crisp clusters in the visualization and consistent organization across models. However, models with less clearly defined structure may prove harder to understand. In both cases, the brushing and linking functionality highlights whether tokens that are grouped in one model are also grouped in a different model. From here, the user might switch back and forth between Level 2 and Level 3 for a more detailed inspection of the models.

3.3 Examining context words

The third and final issue the visualization tool addresses is the detailed inspection of the input of the models in relation to the output. While it is possible to look at the individual context of each token by hovering over them, it loses track of the larger patterns we want to understand. That is the purpose of the frequency tables in levels 2 and 3.

In any given model, tokens might be close together because they share a context word, and/or because their context words are (based on the second-order modelling) similar to each other. First-order parameters are, by definition, directly responsible for the selection of context words that will be used to model each token. Therefore, when inspecting a model, we might want to know which context word(s) pull certain tokens together, or why tokens that we expect to be together are far apart instead. In other words, if each model offers a different perspective on the distributional behavior of a token, we want to understand what informs said perspective.

In Level 3, individual tokens and groups of them may be selected in different ways. Given such a selection, clicking on "Frequency table" will open a table with one row per context word, a column indicating in how many of the selected tokens it occurs, and more columns with pre-computed information (e.g. PMI values). Figure 4.6 shows the result after selecting the group of mostly 'to lift' tokens highlighted in Figure 4.4, in the same model shown in Figures 4.1 and 4.2 (model 3 in Figure 4.4).

The first two columns in the table are computed by the visualization tool itself, which recovers the context words listed for each of the selected tokens and counts with how many of these selected tokens they co-occur. The top three context words form a typical expression with the target, namely *De handen ten hemel heffen*, 'lift one's hands to the heavens', which describes a gesture of exasperation. The other most frequent ones are personal pronouns and determiners, later followed by *arm* 'arm', in a variant of the same expression.

The following five columns include pre-computed frequency information, such as the raw co-occurrence frequency and PMI value between the context word and the target based on windows of 10 and 4, and raw frequency in the corpus. If we rearrange the table ranking by the PMI value based on a window of 10, we can see *vinger* 'finger' and its diminutive, *arm* 'arm' and *handpalm* 'palm of the hand', as well as some emotions such as *hulpeloos* 'helpless' and *wanhoop* 'despair', which are much less frequent. These values can be interesting if we would like to strengthen or weaken filters for a smarter selection of context words. This particular model uses dependency-based information as well as a PMI threshold of 0 to select context words.

In Level 2, while comparing different models, the frequency table takes a different form. There is still one context word per row, but the number of tokens with which it co-occurs will depend on the model.

The columns in this table are all computed by the visualization based on the lists of context words per token per model. Next to the column with the name of the context word, the most basic table (Figure 4.7) shows one column called "total" and one per model, headed by the corresponding number. The

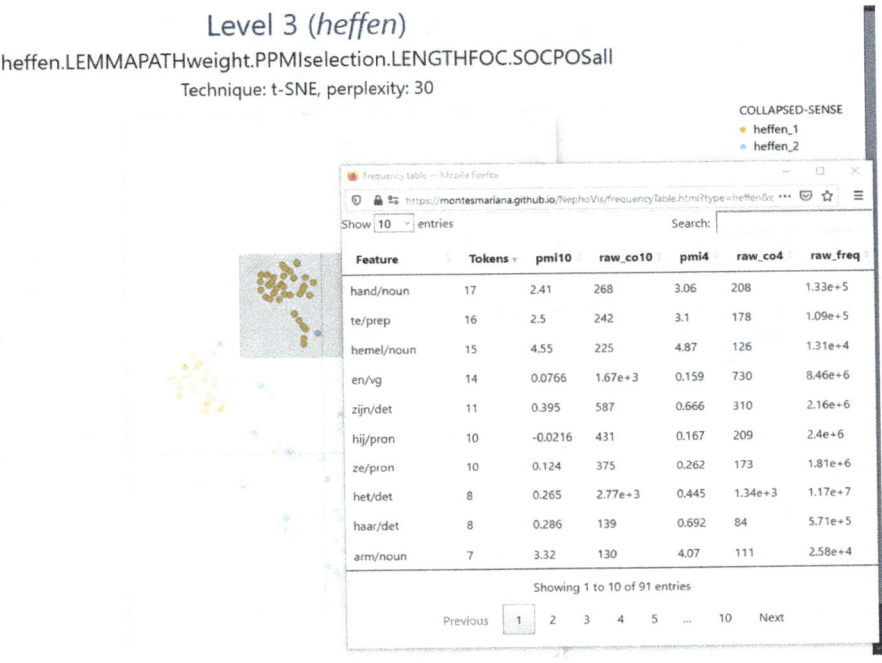

Figure 4.6: Frequency table in Level 3 of the visualization.

columns for each model match the second column in their Level 3 frequency table: they indicate with how many of the selected tokens the context word co-occurs. The "total" column, in contrast, reveals the union of this selection: with how many of the selected tokens the context word co-occurs in at least one model. For the selection in Figure 4.7, it shows that the context-word that co-occurs with most tokens is the determiner *de* 'the', but it is only taken by model 5. In all other cases, *hand* 'hand' and *hemel* 'hemel' stand out instead.

This table counts how many of the selected tokens co-occur with each of the context words and offers a dropdown button in the top left corner suggesting a small range of transformations, such as odds ratio, Fisher Exact, cue validity, etc. The default option shows the absolute frequencies within and outside the selection, as illustrated in Figure 4.8, where the green columns count the number of selected tokens that co-occur with each context word, and the white columns count the number of tokens outside of the selection co-occurring with those context words.

The new numbers relativize the information we saw in Figure 4.8. On the one hand, we can see that all the tokens with *hand* 'hand' as context word are

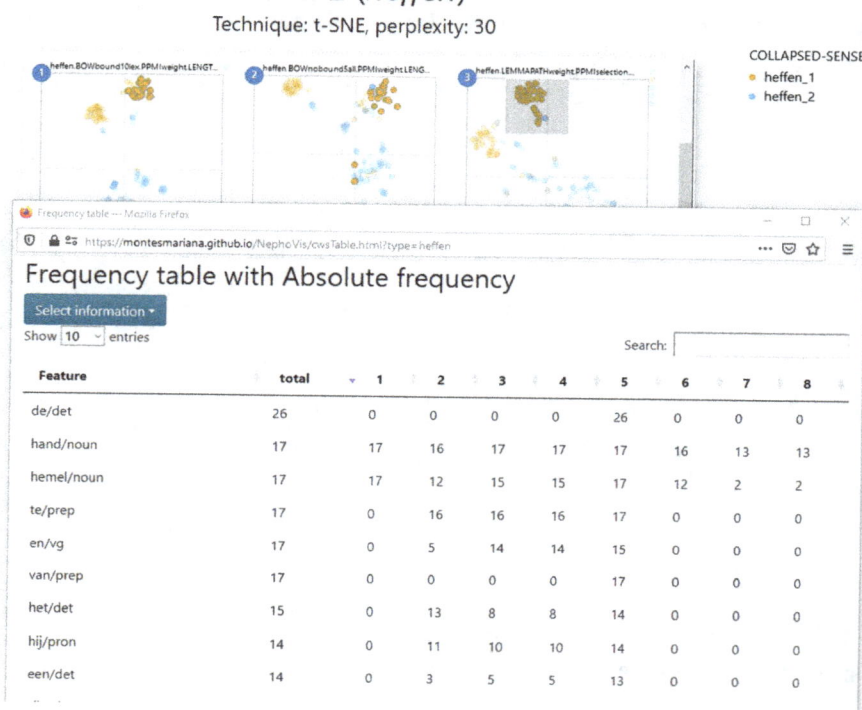

Figure 4.7: Basic Frequency table in Level 2 of the visualization.

included in the selected group. In contrast, some context words that occur with that much frequency in the group also co-occur with other tokens outside the selected cluster: from only one in the case of *hemel*, to dozens in the case of the function words *de* 'the', *te* 'to', *en* 'and' and *van* 'of/from'. On the other hand, function words are not taken at all by models 1, 6, 7 and 8.

Similar inspections could be performed on other sections of the plots. First, by highlighting the other group of 'to lift' tokens we could see that they all co-occur with *glas* 'glass', in expressions related to toasts: *het glas heffen op X* 'lift the glass for X'. Second, by highlighting that group and the 'to levy' tokens in model 5, we can see that they share passive auxiliaries that the other 'to lift' tokens don't co-occur with in our sample.

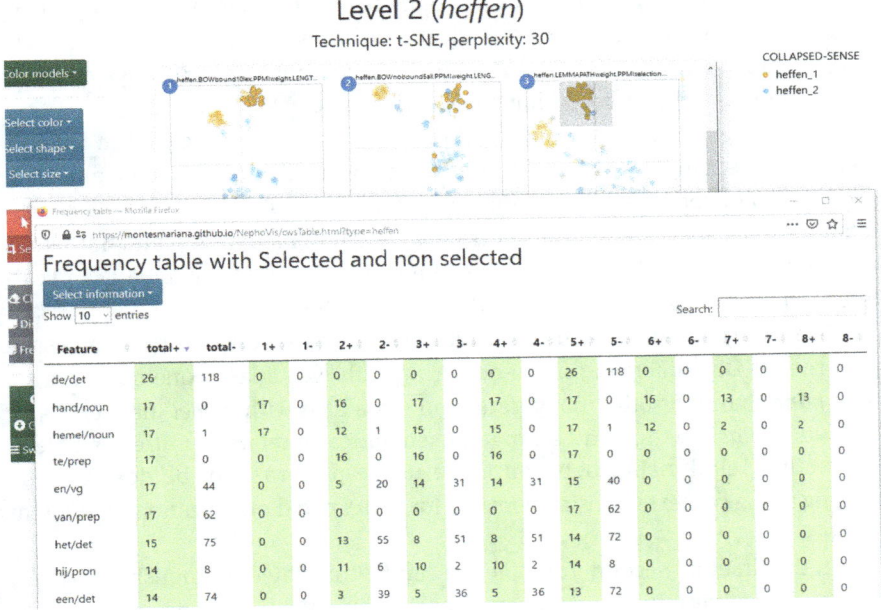

Figure 4.8: Default Frequency table in Level 2 of the visualization, showing frequency in selected and non-selected tokens.

3.4 Token model visualization and cognitive semantics

In Sections 3.2 and 3.3 we explored the features of the visualization tool and took a peek on what the models could tell us about the Dutch verb *heffen* based on a sample from a corpus of contemporary newspapers. In this section we will summarize the observations that can be made based on a more thorough usage of the features described above. It is not possible to describe the full exploration in these pages, but the reader is welcome to walk their own path in the online version. We won't go into the details of what Level 1 tells us or the relationship between parameter settings and the resulting models, either, because that would entail a longer discussion on the selection of parameter settings that goes beyond the scope of this paper.

As introduced before, we start out by annotating concordance lines of *heffen* based on two senses: a concrete one, translatable as 'to lift', and an abstract one, 'to levy'. We expected the vector space models to be able to recognize such a distinction, because their direct objects should have different distributional behaviors. We also know that most of the 'to lift' circumstances in Dutch are actually covered by the derived form *opheffen*, but an empirical comparison would entail a different, onomasiological case study. Nevertheless, this knowledge already suggests that our target word occurs in a limited range of situations, and might therefore exhibit some very crisp clusters.

Both expectations are borne out in most of the models we find in Level 2, when we select the medoids. Each plot shows three distinct clusters, and both senses tend to appear far away from each other. Regardless, there are some variations. Model 5 shows the three clusters aligned; in models 2, 4 and 8, there is a tight cluster of 'to levy' tokens and the rest is separated, maybe even scattered, and overlaps with some 'to lift' tokens in model 8.

The more constant tripartite structure suggests a network of three main usage patterns for Dutch *heffen*: one co-occurring with *glas* 'glass', one co-occurring with *hand* 'hand' or other body parts and often also with *hemel* 'heaven', and one with *belasting* 'tax' and a range of semantically related entities as object. The actual relationship between these usage patterns can be described by looking at the context words responsible for their spatial organization in different models.

In the first and second group *heffen* can be translated to English as 'to lift', but the former pertains to instances of toasts, while the latter represents various gestures, such as lifting hands, arms or the head in prayer or exasperation and lifting a finger to point something out. The third group can be translated to English as 'to levy' and has a couple of frequent, typical objects, such as *belasting* 'tax', *tol* 'toll' and *accijns* 'excise duty', as well as frequent subjects like *overheid* 'government' and *gemeente* 'commune'.

If we had had to manually annotate these features we would have had to devise an adequate classification with the right level of abstraction; as we can see in these scatterplots, this was taken care of by the models themselves in a bottom-up, automated way. The type-level vectors of *belasting* 'tax', *tol* 'toll' and *accijns* 'excise duty' were similar enough to bring together the tokens co-occurring with them, pulling them apart with those co-occurring with body parts.

In addition, model 5 suggests another criterion to group the usage patterns, namely the co-occurrence with the passive auxiliary *worden*. This feature seems to characterize both the 'to levy' sense and the *glass* 'glas' cluster, excluding the *hand* 'hand' cluster. Model 4, in contrast, splits the 'to levy' cluster in small groups based on combinations of absence and presence of *belasting* 'tax', *op* 'on', *te* 'to' and the passive auxiliary *worden*. In other words, different models may offer complementary information in relation to the usage patterns of a lemma.

Still, at the level of the senses, a model can suggest clusters, but not the relationship between them – it does not replace radial networks. However, at the level of the occurrences, we can see the prototypical structure in the variable density of the semantic space. For example, one 'to levy' subset that groups tightly in some models is defined by the co-occurrence of the most frequent object in this sense, namely *belasting* 'tax', but other possible objects are scattered around it, farther or closer from it depending on how similar their type-level vectors are to this prototypical object (in combination with other context words).

Another interesting finding is a small set of Netherlandic tokens co-occurring with *entrée*, which can mean 'appetizer' or 'entrance'. The relevant sense in this case is 'entrance/access fee'. However, in the former sense and for certain second-order parameter settings, it has a similar distributional behaviour with *glas* 'glass' and other terms in the frame of eating and drinking, so we might find these few tokens in the vicinity of the large *glas* 'glass' cluster. Meanwhile, because in the latter sense it is synonymous with *toegang* 'entrance' and *toegangsprijs* 'entrance fee', a couple of tokens with those context words are also pulled towards the *glas* 'glass' area.

4 Conclusion

In this chapter, we presented a data analytics approach to lexical semantics that combines distributional semantic modelling of word meaning in corpus data with an interactive visualization of the modelling output. More specifically, we introduced token-level semantic vectors as a statistical technique to model the semasiological structure of lexemes that emerges from contextual usage patterns, including phenomena like polysemy and prototypicality. We argued that token vector models are a logical extension of the Cognitive Linguistic toolkit for lexical semantics by comparing them to other usage-based approaches to polysemy. We gave a concise overview of the different approaches to token vector modelling and stressed (1) that there are many ways to model the same set of word tokens, and (2) that different models capture different semantic features that can only be understood by exploring the models' output post-hoc. With a case study of the Dutch polysemous verb *heffen*, we showed how a visual analytics approach can help to understand, interpret and compare the statistical usage patterns that different semantic vector space models capture. More specifically, we demonstrated how linked, interactive scatterplots can reveal to what extent the same senses and subsenses are identified by different token models as clusters of usage events. Finally, we discussed how the interactive token-level scatterplots in our visualization tool can be interpreted within a cognitive linguistic framework.

Appendix: Model parameters

In this appendix we include a more thorough description of the parameter settings used to create the 204 models of *heffen*. For each value, we include a description and how it is coded in the name of the models, which are made of four sections separated by periods. Note that these are not all the possible variations, but the ones used in this study.

The corpus is lemmatized and tagged for part-of-speech, and a context feature is a pair of lemma and part-of-speech. In principle, to be selected as first- or second-order feature they may have any part-of-speech except for punctuation and have a minimum frequency of 1 in 2 million (absolute frequency of 227) after discarding punctuation from the token count. There are 60533 such types in the corpus.

First-order parameters

Bag-of-words models

There are three first-order parameters that are specific to bag-of-words models. Their values are listed next to each other in the first section of the names of the models.

Parameter Name	Settings Value	Description	Model name example
Sentence boundaries (BOUND)	bound	Filters out context words outside the sentence of the target	**bound**10lex
	nobound	Includes context words inside and outside the sentence of the target	**nobound**10lex
Part-of-speech (FOC-POS)	lex	Selects nouns, verbs, adjectives and adverbs around the target token	bound10**lex**
	all	Only excludes punctuation and very infrequent parts-of-speech	bound10**all**

(continued)

Parameter	Settings		Model name example
Name	Value	Description	
Window size	3_3	Selects context words in up to three slots to either side of the target	bound3lex
	5_5	Selects context words in up to five slots to either side of the target	bound5lex
	10_10	Selects context words in up to ten slots to either side of the target	bound10lex

Dependency-based models

Dependency-based models select first-order context words based on their syntactic relationship to the target token. The specific kind of filter is coded in the first section of the model name.

LEMMAREL models select the context words that match specific dependency paths. LEMMARELgroup1 includes direct objects, active and passive subjects (with up to two modals in between for the active subject), reflexive complement and prepositions depending directly on the target. LEMMARELgroup2 expands group1 with conjuncts of the verb, complementizers, nouns depending through a preposition and verbal complements or elements of which the target is a verbal complement.

LEMMAPATH models don't filter out specific dependency relations but only look at the length of the path. For example, the subject of *heffen* is one step away from it; the determiner of the subject is two steps away from *heffen*, etc. LEMMAPATHselection2 only includes lemmas with a path of up to two steps from the target token, while LEMMAPATHselection3 and LEMMAPATHweight expand it to three-step paths. In addition, LEMMAPATHweight affects the contribution of each context word based on the length of the path.

Suppose we have a sequence like *het glas wordt geheven* 'the glass is raised': the target word is *geheven*; the passive auxiliary *wordt* is one step away; the subject *glas* 'glass' is two steps away, because it's coded as subject of the auxiliary, and its determiner *de* 'the' is three steps away. In a LEMMARELgroup1 selection, only *glas* 'glass' is included as context word, while group2 also includes the passive auxiliary. In the case of LEMMAPATH, selection2 excludes the determiner but selection3 includes it. LEMMAPATHweight, on the other hand, will multiply the vector of the passive auxiliary by 1, the one of *glas* 'glass' by $2/3$, and the one of the determiner by ⅓, based on the length of the dependency paths that connect them to the target.

PPMI

The PPMI parameter performs both selection and weighting of first-order context words, as shown in the table below. It is coded in the second part of the names of the models. For this parameter we have used PMI values between the context words and the target (i.e. *heffen*) based on a window size of 10, but it would be possible to use other association measures and/or other window sizes.

	weighting	no weighting
selection	PPMIweight	PPMIselection
no selection	–	PPMIno

Context word selection implies that the candidate context words are filtered by their PMI values –in our case, the threshold is 0, but it could be higher. Weighting implies that the contribution of a context word is given by its association strength with the target.

For instance, in a case like *het glas wordt geheven* 'the glass is raised', the PMI values (based on a symmetric window of 10 words to each side) between *heffen* and the context words *het* 'the', *glas* 'glass' and the passive auxiliary *worden* are 0.265, 4.87 and 0.876 respectively. This means that all three context words are included in any model, but that, while PPMIselection and PPMIno models will represent the token with the average between the three type-level vectors, PPMIweight will compute a weighted average, allowing the vector of *glas* 'glass' to have much more pull than the other vectors in determining the representation of the token.

Second-order parameters

Second-order parameters pertain to the type-level vectors that represent the context words selected by first-order parameters. In principle, they include settings that define the kind of association measure that makes up their values and how it is calculated, but for this case study we have settled with positive PMI based on a symmetric window of 4 words to each side. Instead, we vary along the part-of-speech and vector length.

The fourth slot in the names of the models codes the second-order part-of-speech filter. SOCPOSnav indicates that only lectally-neutral nouns, verbs and adjectives have been selected as second-order features –this is related to other studies comparing models based on Netherlandic and Belgian sources. SOCPO-Sall only excludes punctuation and infrequent parts-of-speech tags.

Vector length can take two values: 5000 and FOC, coded as LENGTH5000 and LENGTHFOC respectively in the third section of the names of the models. The former means that the second order features are the 5000 most frequent lemmas after the part-of-speech filter. There is not much difference between these models and others with the 10000 most frequent lemmas as second order features. The latter value, FOC, means that the same features selected by the first-order parameters are used as second-order features. On the one hand, they are not limited by frequency rank; on the other, they are tailored to the contexts in which our sample of tokens occur and the way the first-order parameters have filtered them. This makes the difference between the two values of LENGTH more complicated than just the number of dimensions, which, for LENGTHFOC models of *heffen*, ranges between 133 (for LEMMAREL models with PPMI selection) and 1325 (for bag-of-words models with no filters).

References

Amrami, Asaf & Yoav Goldberg. 2019. Towards better substitution-based word sense induction. *arXiv preprint arXiv:1905.12598*.

Arppe, Antti, Gaëtanelle Gilquin, Dylan Glynn, Martin Hilpert & Arne Zeschel. 2010. Cognitive Corpus Linguistics: Five points of debate on current theory and methodology. *Corpora*

Baroni, Marco, Georgiana Dinu & Germán Kruszewski. 2014. Don't count, predict! a systematic comparison of context-counting vs. context-predicting semantic vectors. In *Proceedings of the 52nd Annual Meeting of the Association for Computational Linguistics (Volume 1: Long Papers)*, 238–247.

Boon, C.A. den & Ruud Hendrickx. 2017. *Dikke Van Dale Online*.

Boon, Ton den & Dirk Geeraerts. 2007. *Van Dale klein woordenboek van de Nederlandse taal*. Utrecht: Van Dale.

Bostock, M., V. Ogievetsky & J. Heer. 2011. D^3 Data-Driven Documents. *IEEE Transactions on Visualization and Computer Graphics* 17(12). 2301–2309.

Card, Stuart K., Jock D. Mackinlay & Ben Shneiderman. 1999. *Readings in information visualization: Using vision to think (The Morgan Kaufmann Series in Interactive Technologies)*. San Francisco, Calif: Morgan Kaufmann Publishers.

De Pascale, S. 2019. *Token-based vector space models as semantic control in lexical lectometry*. PhD Dissertation.

Devlin, Jacob, Ming-Wei Chang, Kenton Lee & Kristina Toutanova. 2019. BERT: Pre-training of Deep Bidirectional Transformers for Language Understanding. In *Proceedings of the 2019*

Conference of the North American Chapter of the Association for Computational Linguistics: Human Language Technologies, Volume 1 (Long and Short Papers), 4171–4186. Minneapolis, Minnesota: Association for Computational Linguistics.

Firth, John R. 1957. A synopsis of linguistic theory, 1930-1955. *Studies in linguistic analysis*. Basil Blackwell.

Geeraerts, Dirk. 1993. Vagueness's puzzles, polysemy's vagaries. *Cognitive Linguistics* 4. 223–272.

Geeraerts, Dirk. 2000. Salience phenomena in the lexicon. A typology. In Liliana Albertazzi (ed.), *Meaning and Cognition*, 125–136. Amsterdam; Philadelphia: John Benjamins.

Geeraerts, Dirk. 2016. Entrenchment as onomasiological salience. In Hans-Jörg Schmid (ed.), *Entrenchment and the Psychology of Language Learning*, 153–174. Berlin: De Gruyter.

Glynn, Dylan. 2014a. Polysemy and synonymy: Cognitive theory and corpus method. In Dylan Glynn & Justyna A. Robinson (eds.), *Corpus methods for semantics: Quantitative studies in polysemy and synonymy*, 7–38. Amsterdam; Philadelphia: John Benjamins Publishing Company.

Glynn, Dylan. 2014b. The many uses of *run*: Corpus methods and Socio-Cognitive Semantics. In Dylan Glynn & Justyna A. Robinson (eds.), *Corpus methods for semantics: Quantitative studies in polysemy and synonymy*, 117–144. Amsterdam; Philadelphia: John Benjamins Publishing Company.

Glynn, Dylan. 2016. Quantifying polysemy: Corpus methodology for prototype theory. *Folia Linguistica*. De Gruyter Mouton 50 (2).413–447.

Gries, Stefan Th. 2006. Corpus-based methods and cognitive semantics: The many senses of "to run." In Stefan Thomas Gries & Anatol Stefanowitsch (eds.), *Corpora in cognitive linguistics: Corpus-based approaches to syntax and lexis*, 57–99. Berlin; New York: Mouton de Gruyter.

Gries, Stefan Th. 2012. Behavioral profiles. A fine-grained and quantitative approach in corpus-based lexical semantics. (Ed.) Gary Libben, Gonia Jarema & Chris Westbury. *Methodological and Analytic Frontiers in Lexical Research*.

Harris, Zellig S. 1954. Distributional structure. *Word*. Taylor & Francis 10 (2–3). 146–162.

Heylen, Kris, Dirk Speelman & Dirk Geeraerts. 2012. Looking at word meaning. An interactive visualization of Semantic Vector Spaces for Dutch synsets. In *Proceedings of the eacl 2012 Joint Workshop of LINGVIS & UNCLH*, 16–24. Avignon.

Heylen, Kris, Thomas Wielfaert, Dirk Speelman & Dirk Geeraerts. 2015. Monitoring polysemy: Word space models as a tool for large-scale lexical semantic analysis. *Lingua* 157. 153–172.

Hilpert, Martin & David Correia Saavedra. 2017. Using token-based semantic vector spaces for corpus-linguistic analyses: From practical applications to tests of theoretical claims. *Corpus Linguistics and Linguistic Theory* 0(0). https://doi.org/10.1515/cllt-2017-0009.

Hilpert, Martin & Susanne Flach. 2020. Disentangling modal meanings with distributional semantics. *Digital Scholarship in the Humanities* https://doi.org/10.1093/llc/fqaa014

Jansegers, Marlies & Stefan Th Gries. 2017. Towards a dynamic behavioral profile: A diachronic study of polysemous sentir in Spanish. *Corpus Linguistics and Linguistic Theory* 16(1). https://doi.org/10.1515/cllt-2016-0080.

Koptjevskaja-Tamm, Maria & Magnus Sahlgren. 2014. Temperature in the word space: Sense exploration of temperature expressions using word-space modelling. In Benedikt Szmrecsanyi & Bernhard Wälchli (eds.), *Aggregating Dialectology, Typology, and Register*

Analysis, 231–267. Berlin, Boston: DE GRUYTER. https://doi.org/10.1515/9783110317558.231.
Krijthe, Jesse H. 2015. *Rtsne: T-Distributed Stochastic Neighbor Embedding using Barnes-Hut Implementation*. https://github.com/jkrijthe/Rtsne.
Lenci, Alessandro. 2018. Distributional Models of Word Meaning. *Annual Review of Linguistics* 4(1).
Maechler, Martin, Peter Rousseeuw, Anja Struyf, Mia Hubert & Kurt Hornik. 2019. *cluster: Cluster Analysis Basics and Extensions*.
McEnery, Tony & Andrew Hardie. 2012. *Corpus linguistics: Method, theory and practice (Cambridge Textbooks in Linguistics)*. Cambridge; New York: Cambridge University Press.
McEnery, Tony, Richard Xiao & Yukio Tono. 2010. *Corpus-based language studies: An advanced resource book (Routledge Applied Linguistics)*. Reprinted. London: Routledge.
Mikolov, Tomas, Kai Chen, Greg Corrado & Jeffrey Dean. 2013. Efficient Estimation of Word Representations in Vector Space.
Montes, Mariana & Thomas Wielfaert. 2021. *QLVL/NephoVis: Altostratus*. Zenodo. https://doi.org/10.5281/ZENODO.5116843.
Oksanen, Jari, F. Guillaume Blanchet, Michael Friendly, Roeland Kindt, Pierre Legendre, Dan McGlinn, Peter R. Minchin, et al. 2019. *vegan: Community Ecology Package*. https://CRAN.R-project.org/package=vegan.
Perek, Florent. 2016. Using distributional semantics to study syntactic productivity in diachrony: A case study. *Linguistics* 54(1). 149–188.
Perek, Florent. 2018. Recent change in the productivity and schematicity of the way-construction: A distributional semantic analysis. *Corpus Linguistics and Linguistic Theory*. De Gruyter Mouton 14 (1).65–97.
R Core Team. 2020. *R: A Language and Environment for Statistical Computing*. Vienna, Austria: R Foundation for Statistical Computing. https://www.R-project.org/.
Ruette, Tom, Katharina Ehret & Benedikt Szmrecsanyi. 2016. A lectometric analysis of aggregated lexical variation in written Standard English with Semantic Vector Space models. *International Journal of Corpus Linguistics*. John Benjamins 21 (1).48–79.
Shneiderman, Ben. 1996. The Eyes Have It: A Task by Data Type Taxonomy for Information Visualizations. In *IEEE Visual Languages*, 96–13.
Sinclair, John. 1991. *Corpus, concordance, collocation (Describing English Language)*. 3. impr. Oxford: Oxford Univ. Press.
Smilkov, Daniel, Nikhil Thorat, Charles Nicholson, Emily Reif, Fernanda B. Viégas & Martin Wattenberg. 2016. Embedding Projector: Interactive Visualization and Interpretation of Embeddings. arXiv:1611.05469.
Stubbs, Michael. 1995. Collocations and semantic profiles: On the cause of the trouble with quantitative studies. *Functions of Language* 2(1). 23–55
Turney, Peter D & Patrick Pantel. 2010. From Frequency to Meaning: Vector Space Models of Semantics. *Journal of Artificial Intelligence Research* 37. 141–188.
van der Maaten, Laurens & Geoffrey Hinton. 2008. Visualizing Data using t-SNE. *Journal of Machine Learning Research* 9. 2579–2605.
van der Maaten, Laurens & Geoffrey Hinton. 2012. Visualizing non-metric similarities in multiple maps. *Machine Learning* 87(1). 33–55.

Van Sterkenburg, Piet, Peter Verhoeven & Jaap Parqui. 2006. *Van Dale groot woordenboek hedendaags Nederlands*. Derde druk in de nieuwe spelling ed. Utrecht: Van Dale lexicografie.

Wielfaert, Thomas, Kris Heylen, Dirk Speelman & Dirk Geeraerts. 2019. Visual Analytics for Parameter Tuning of Semantic Vector Space Models. In Miriam Butt, Annette Hautli-Janisz & Verena Lyding (eds.), *LingVis: Visual analytics for linguistics (CSLI Lecture Notes no. 220)*, 215–245. Stanford, California: CSLI Publications, Center for the Study of Language and Information.

Xiaoyu Tian, Weiwei Zhang, Dirk Speelman
Lectal variation in Chinese analytic causative constructions: What trees can and cannot tell us

1 Introduction

Years after its quantitative turn (cf. Janda 2013), Cognitive Linguistics experienced substantial methodological developments, which make it a suitable framework for exploratory studies that tap into large datasets and take into account multiple language-internal and language-external factors to model language variation (e.g. Colleman 2010; Zhang, Speelman, and Geeraerts 2011; Levshina, Geeraerts, and Speelman 2013a; Bernaisch, Gries, and Mukherjee 2014; Röthlisberger, Grafmiller, and Szmrecsanyi 2017). In addition to traditional hypothesis-testing regression modeling, more advanced statistical tools such as tree-based methods become more widely used to cope with the problems typically found in corpus data, such as data sparsity and collinearity (e.g. Tagliamonte and Baayen 2012; Bernaisch, Gries, and Mukherjee 2014; Szmrecsanyi et al. 2016). Recently, scholars have noticed the shortcomings of tree-based methods and proposed to combine them with regression models to yield more robust and interpretable results (cf. Strobl, Malley, and Tutz 2009; Gries 2019). In line with these methodological developments, this study explores the near-synonymous Chinese causative constructions from a cross-variety perspective using conditional random forests, conditional inference trees and multinomial logistic regression analysis.

Acknowledgement: The authors are grateful to the Linguistic Data Consortium for providing the corpus of *"Tagged Chinese Gigaword 2.0"*. This project was supported by a China Scholarship Council grant to the first author (grant No.202006900017) and a Marie Skłodowska-Curie grant to the second author (European Union's Horizon 2020 research and innovation programme, agreement No. 793920). The usual disclaimers apply.

Xiaoyu Tian, Department of Linguistics, University of Leuven & Institute of Linguistics, Shanghai International Studies University, e-mail: xiaoyu.tian@kuleuven.be
Weiwei Zhang, Department of Linguistics, University of Leuven & Institute of Linguistics, Shanghai International Studies University, e-mail: weiwei.zhang@kuleuven.be
Dirk Speelman, Department of Linguistics, University of Leuven, e-mail: dirk.speelman@kuleuven.be

ə Open Access. © 2022 Xiaoyu Tian et al., published by De Gruyter. This work is licensed under the Creative Commons Attribution-NonCommercial-NoDerivatives 4.0 International License.
https://doi.org/10.1515/9783110687279-006

According to Talmy (2000: Ch. 7), causation is a force-dynamic pattern that involves two main participants: the antagonist (labeled as the CAUSER in this study) and the agonist (labeled as the CAUSEE in this study). The causer instigates a causing event or state, which affects the causee, who brings about the caused event. Linguistic means to express causation are called causatives or causative constructions. Based on the formal differences between the expressions of the cause and the effect, Comrie (1981) made a three-way distinction of causative constructions: morphological causatives, lexical causatives and analytic causatives. In morphological causatives, "the causative is related to the non-causative predicate by [productive] morphological means" (Comrie 1981: 167). When the relation between the cause and the effect is "handled lexically, rather than by any productive process", lexical causatives are involved (Comrie 1981: 168). Analytic causatives refer to cases where "there are separate predicates expressing the notion of causation and the predicate of the effect" (Comrie 1981: 167). The current study focuses on the analytic causative constructions in Chinese.

Chinese analytic causative constructions involve several different markers, among which the most used ones in contemporary written Chinese are *shi*, *ling* and *rang* (Liu 2000; Niu 2007), as in example (1):

(1) 他　　使/令/让　　我　　想起　了　一　个　朋友。[1]
　　Ta　**shi/ling/rang**　*wo*　*xiangqi*　*le*　*yi*　*ge*　*pengyou.*
　　He　　make　　　me　　think of　PST　one　CLF　friend
　　'He makes me think of a friend.'
　　CAUS　CAUSATIVE　　　CAUSEE　EFFECTED
　　ER　　MARKER　　　　　　　　　PREDICATE

Although extensive research has been carried out on Chinese analytic causative constructions, only few studies have attempted to investigate the choice of causative markers and their lectal variation using corpus data and advanced statistical tools (cf. Liesenfeld, Liu, and Huang 2020; Tian and Zhang 2020). This paper aims to address this gap by answering the following two questions: (1) What are the syntactic and semantic factors that affect the alternation of analytic causative constructions with the markers of *shi*, *ling* and *rang*? (2) What is

---

[1] Example (1) is created by the first author through introspection. Other examples of this chapter are from the "Tagged Chinese Gigaword Version 2.0". Some of them are rephrased and unimportant details are omitted to save space.

the extent to which varieties of Chinese differ in the choice of *shi, ling* and *rang* as the causative marker?

The structure of the paper is outlined as follows: Section 2 reviews the previous studies on analytic causative constructions; Section 3 introduces the data and the methods; in Section 4, we present the statistical results, the implications of which are then discussed in Section 5; Section 6 provides some concluding remarks.

2 Previous studies on analytic causative constructions

2.1 Analytic causative constructions: A cross-linguistic review

Languages that have analytic causative constructions usually possess several different causative markers or auxiliaries, such as *make/have/cause* in English, *doen/laten* in Dutch, and *shi/ling/rang* in Chinese. In favor of the "Principle of No Synonymy" (Goldberg 1995: 67), cognitive linguists speculate that there should exist semantic or usage differences between different causative markers and investigate the alternation of analytic causative constructions. These studies mainly centered on English (e.g. Stefanowitsch 2001; Gilquin 2010) and Dutch (e.g. Verhagen and Kemmer 1997; Stukker 2005; Speelman and Geeraerts 2009; Levshina 2011). Some research then tackled the problem of lectal variation (e.g. Belgium Dutch vs. Netherlandic Dutch, cf. Speelman and Geeraerts 2009, Levshina 2011, Levshina, Geeraerts, and Speelman 2013a) or cross-linguistic variation (e.g. English vs. Dutch, cf. Levshina, Geeraerts, and Speelman 2013b) in analytic causative constructions.

To explain the difference between Dutch causative verbs *doen* ("do") and *laten* ("let"), Verhagen and Kemmer (1997) proposed the "(in)direct causation hypothesis", which was further developed by Stukker (2005). According to this hypothesis, if the causer produces the effected event directly without any inference "downstream", then direct causation is involved and speakers tend to choose *doen*; if besides the causer, the causee is the most immediate source of energy in the effected event and has some degree of "autonomy" in the causal process, then indirect causation is involved, and speakers tend to use *laten* (Stukker 2005: 50).

In light of the "(in)direct causation hypothesis", many scholars conducted quantitative research to investigate the alternation of analytic causative constructions. For instance, Speelman and Geeraerts (2009) employed logistic regression analysis to evaluate the effect of several linguistic internal and external predictors (e.g. the animacy of the causer, the coreferentiality between the causer and the causee, the transitivity of the effected predicate, the genre and variety, etc.) on the choice of *doen* and *laten*. The statistical results showed that the "(in)direct causation hypothesis" cannot fully explain the alternation between *doen* and *laten*. They also found significant lectal variation in the distribution of *doen* and *laten*, with *doen* appearing more frequently in Belgian Dutch than in Netherlandic Dutch.

Then, Levshina, Geeraerts, and Speelman (2013a) enhanced the multivariate approach by adding some new semantic variables to the model, including the semantic class of both the causer and the causee, the semantic class of the event expressed by the effected predicate (physical or mental), etc. The result supports the "(in)direct causation hypothesis" and lectal factors only display weak influences indirectly in this study.

The study of analytic causative construction alternation is not limited to Dutch. For instance, Levshina, Geeraerts, and Speelman (2013b) created a common conceptual space of analytic causatives in English and Dutch and found that different animacy configurations of the causer and the causee constitutes the most important two dimensions in the conceptual space. They also pointed out some commonalities in the semantics of causation between English and Dutch, although there are no strict cross-linguistic correspondences between the two languages.

2.2 Chinese analytic causative constructions with *shi*, *ling* and *rang*

Previous research on Chinese analytic causative constructions mainly focused on their differences from other syntactic means expressing causation (e.g. Fan 2000; Xiang 2002; Xiong 2004; Zhou 2004) or the grammaticalization of causative markers (e.g. Xu 2003; Zhang 2005; Niu 2007; Cao 2011). Only a few studies explored the onomasiological choice of causative markers (e.g. Yang 2016; Liesenfeld, Liu, and Huang 2020) and its lectal variation (Tian and Zhang 2020) based on corpus data.

Interesting results regarding the function and usage of *shi*, *ling* and *rang* have been found in previous research. First, *shi* and *ling* have lost the imperative meaning and most frequently serve as causative markers, whereas *rang* is still intensively used to denote a permissive meaning (Niu 2007). Second, *ling* tends to co-occur with the word *ren* (meaning "people" or "person") followed by a single verb and the construction [*ling ren* + result] exhibits a lexical fixation tendency, which is more likely to occur in a relative clause (Niu 2007; Zhang 2005). Third, *shi* tends to co-occur with verbs that indicate changes of results, while *rang* is more likely to be followed by verbs referring to activities and movements

(Yang 2016). In addition, scholars also found that the distributions of *shi*, *ling* and *rang* are sensitive to register differences: *Shi* and *ling* appear more often in written language, while *rang* tends to occur in spoken language (Wan 2004; Miyake 2005, Yang 2016).

Ni (2012) explained the alternation between *shi* and *rang* in Chinese analytic causative constructions with the "(in)direct causation hypothesis" proposed by Verhagen and Kemmer (1997). She suggests that *shi* is similar to *doen* in Dutch and involves direct causation, whereas *rang* is similar to *laten* and often expresses indirect causation. However, her study is based on 250 observations and she only explored four variables (i.e. the transitivity of the effected predicate, the animacy of the causer and the causee, modal verbs co-occurring with *shi* and *rang*, whether the causative construction is *wh*-cleft), therefore, her conclusions still need to be tested with more data and more robust statistical methods.

In general, Chinese analytic causative constructions are still understudied in terms of the following aspects. First of all, researchers have not systematically examined the influence of various syntactic and semantic features of construction components on the choice of markers. Secondly, previous studies barely considered that people from different varieties of Chinese might differ in their choices of causative markers, whereas the lectal variation has been attested in studies on Dutch causatives (Speelman and Geeraerts 2009; Levshina 2011; Levshina, Geeraerts, and Speelman 2013a). Thirdly, methodologically speaking, the traditional approaches in Chinese causative studies largely involve introspection or small-scale corpus-illustrated description, based on which it is difficult to make further theoretical interpretations.

Therefore, with regiolectally-balanced corpus data, this study adopts advanced statistical methods, viz. conditional random forests, conditional inference trees and multinomial logistic regression analysis, to disentangle the syntactic, semantic and lectal factors that influence the choice of Chinese causative markers *shi*, *ling* and *rang*.

3 Data and methods

3.1 Data resource and extraction

For this study, we tapped into the corpus of "Tagged Chinese Gigaword Version 2.0" (Huang 2009),[2] which contains more than 800 million words of

---

[2] The website of the corpus: https://catalog.ldc.upenn.edu/LDC2009T14.

newswire texts covering Mainland Chinese, Taiwan Chinese and Singapore Chinese (see Table 5.1).

Table 5.1: Information of the corpus of "Tagged Chinese Gigaword Version 2.0".

Source of data	Year	Number of characters
Central News Agency (Taiwan Chinese)	1991–2004	501,456,000
Xinhua News Agency (Mainland Chinese)	1991–2004	311,660,000
Lianhe Zaobao Newspaper (Singapore)	2000–2003	18,632,000
Total	/	831,748,000

For practical reasons, we restricted ourselves to a subset of the corpus by selecting around 2 million words from each variety.[3] In total, we retrieved 12,385 observations containing *shi*, *ling* and *rang* using Antconc (Anthony 2019) and then manually excluded spurious hits. The data cleaning criteria are as follows:
i) Delete repeated occurrences.
ii) Delete occurrences where *shi*, *ling* and *rang* are used as morphemes, e.g., *da-shi* 'ambassador', *ming-ling* 'order', *rang-zuo* 'offer seat to', etc.
iii) Delete occurrences where *shi*, *ling* and *rang* denote non-causative meanings. For instance, *ling* sometimes expresses 'order', and *rang* can be used to denote a permissive or passive meaning.

The third criterion involves some difficulties when it comes to distinguishing causative meanings from permissive meanings expressed by *rang*. For the difficulty cases, we rely on the Force Dynamic theory proposed by Talmy (2000): the causative category applies when the force of the Antagonist[4] overcomes that of the Agonist,[5] leading to a resultant state or activity of that "is the opposite of [the Agonist's] intrinsic actional tendency" (Talmy 2000: 418) in another situation, where the Antagonist that has been affecting the Agonist is removed and thus allows the Agonist to manifest its intrinsic tendency, the permissive category applies. We use (2) and (3) as examples for illustration:

---

[3] The corpus consists of news texts monthly from 1991 to 2004 for Mainland and Taiwan Chinese and from 2000 to 2003 for Singapore Chinese. We selected one file from each variety to make sure that they are comparable in both time and size. The texts of Mainland and Singapore Chinese are from September 2003 and that of Taiwan Chinese are from October 2003.
[4] The Antagonist in causative constructions is labeled as the CAUSER in this study.
[5] The Agonist in causative constructions is labeled as the CAUSEE in this study.

(2) 如果   让   菊花   按照   生产   规律
    Ruguo **rang** juhua   anzhao   shengchan   guilv
    If   let   chrysanthemum follow   growing   regularity
    开放, 市民   将   无法   十月
    kaifang, shimin jiang   wufa   shiyue
    blossom citizens will   not be able to   October
    初
    chu
    beginning
    zai shiyyuechu'
    in
    赏花。
    shanghua.
    admire flowers

'If we let the chrysanthemums blossom naturally, the citizens won't be able to admire them in early October.'

(3) 高科技   让   菊花   提前   盛开。
    Gaokeji   **rang**   juhua   tiqian   shengkai.
    The high technology make   chrysanthemum in advance   blossom

'The high technology makes the chrysanthemums blossom in advance.'

In (2), the chrysanthemums will manifest their intrinsic tendency and blossom naturally if there is no other force affecting this process, so the permissive category of Talmy (2000) applies and *rang* expresses a permissive meaning. In (3), however, the force of the high technology overcomes that of the chrysanthemums and causes them to blossom in advance against their intrinsic tendency, so in this context the causative category of Talmy (2000) applies and *rang* is used as a causative marker.

The cleaning procedures leave us with more than 10,000 observations, which still involves tremendous manual work for the variable coding. Therefore, we randomly selected 30% of the observations with *shi*, *ling* and *rang* respectively for the data annotation and analysis (see Table 5.2).

Table 5.2: Overview of the numbers of extracted and randomly selected occurrences.

	Mainland Chinese	Taiwan Chinese	Singapore Chinese	Total	Randomly Selected (30%)
shi	1425	659	1290	3374	1012
rang	669	1954	2598	5221	1566
ling	249	351	1022	1622	486
Total	2343	2964	4910	10217	3064

3.2 Variable annotation

The dependent variable of this study is a categorical one involving three different levels, i.e. *shi*, *ling* and *rang*. Based on the literature (e.g. Speelman and Geeraerts 2009; Levshina 2011; Niu 2014), the 3,064 observations were annotated with 27 independent variables (see Table 5.3 for an overview). All variables except for Variety were coded manually by the first author following the annotation scheme. To evaluate the reliability of the manual annotation, two coders independently annotated the 26 variables other than Variety for 100 randomly selected observations. We then calculated the kappa statistic (Carletta 1996) of the inter-rater agreement,[6] and the kappa *k* values range from 0.879 to 1, which indicates an excellent inter-rater reliability (Orwin 1994: 152).

Due to the lack of space, in the following text we only illustrate the seven variables that show significance in the random forest model (see Section 4.1). A complete annotation scheme with detailed explanations and examples is provided at https://osf.io/342re/.

- PredSynt: it refers to the syntactic form of the effected predicate and has five levels of *tr* (transitive verb, cf. (4a)), *intr* (intransitive verb, cf. (4b)), *copula* (cf. (4c)), *adj* (adjective, cf. (4d)),[7] and *idiom* (i.e. a fixed expression, cf. (4e)).

(4) a. 我 觉得 有必要 让 他 了解 真相。
 Wo juede youbiyao rang ta liaojie zhenxiang.
 I think necessary let him know truth
 'I think it is necessary to let him know the truth.'
 (PredSynt = *tr*)

 b. 新 技术 可 使 利润 提高。
 Xin jishu ke shi lirun tigao.
 New technology can make profit increase
 'The new technology can make the profit increase.'
 (PredSynt = *intr*)

---

6 This procedure is implemented using the {irr} package (Gamer et al. 2019) in R.
7 It is worth noting that Chinese analytic causative constructions allow the effected predicate to be a bare adjective. In other words, the three causative markers (i.e. *shi*, *ling* and *rang*) are interchangeable when a bare adjective serves as the effected predicate. It is different from English, where one can only use *make*, while other causative markers such as *let* or *have* do not work for a bare adjective effected predicate.

c. 她 使 中国队 成为 了 冠军。
      Ta shi zhongguodui chengwei le guanjun
      She make China Team become PST champion
      'She made the China Team become the champion.'
      (PredSynt = *copula*)
   d. 这 使 我 难过。
      Zhe shi wo nanguo.
      This make me sad
      'This makes me sad.'
      (PredSynt = *adj*)
   e. 这个 新闻 令 人 大跌眼镜。
      Zhege xinwen ling ren dadieyanjing
      This news make people drop glasses
      'This news is extremely surprising.'
      (PredSynt = *idiom*)

- Variety: it stands for language varieties. It was encoded automatically and has three possible values: *ml* (Mainland Chinese), *tw* (Taiwan Chinese), and *sg* (Singapore Chinese).
- CeSynt: it stands for the syntactic form of the causee. We assigned four possible values for this variable: *np* (noun phrase, cf. (5a)), *pron* (pronoun, cf. (5b)), *cl* (clause, cf. (5c)) and *ren* ("people/person" in Chinese, cf. (5d)). For practical reasons, *ren* is coded as a separate value since the previous studies (e.g. Wan 2004; Zhang 2005; Niu 2007) detected that *ling* is strongly collocated with *ren*. We expect that *ling* should be favored when the syntactic form of the causee is assigned the value of *ren*.

(5) a. 我 要 让 社区 更 美丽。
       Wo yao rang shequ geng meili.
       I want to make community more beautiful
       'I want to make the community more beautiful.'
       (CeSynt = *np*)
    b. 他 让 我 失望。
       Ta rang wo shiwang.
       He make me disappoint
       'He makes me disappointed.'
       (CeSynt = *pron*)

c. 大雨　　　　使　　按期　　完工　　　　　更　　困难。
　　Dayu　　　shi　　anqi　　wangong　　　geng　kunnan.
　　Intensive rainfall　make　on time　complete project　more　difficult
　　'The intensive rainfall makes it more difficult to complete the project on time'
　　(CeSynt = *cl*)

d. 她的　　邀请　　令　　人　　无法　　抗拒。
　　Tade　yaoqing　ling　ren　wufa　　kangju.
　　He　　invitation　make　people　no way to　resist
　　'Her invitation is irresistible.'
　　(CeSynt = *ren*)

- CsedProsody: this variable deals with the prosody of the caused event, i.e. the event expressed by the effected predicate. It has three possible values: *neg* (negative, cf. (5b)), *ntrl* (neutral, cf. (5d)) and *pstv* (positive, cf. (5a)).
- ClauseType: it refers to the clause type where the causative construction is found. We assigned five possible values to this variable: *avb* (adverbial clause, cf. (6a)), *cpl* (complemental clause, cf. (6b)), *cpd* (compound sentence, cf. (6c)), *main* (cf. (6d)), *rltv* (relative clause, cf. (6e)) and *smpl* (simple sentence, cf. (5d)). We expect that *ling* has a higher probability of occurring in relative clause as is observed in the literature (Niu 2007, Zhang 2005).

(6) a. 为　　使　　父母　　高兴，　他　努力　学习。
　　　Wei　shi　fumu　　gaoxing,　ta　nuli　xuexi.
　　　To　　make　parents　happy　　he　hard　study
　　　'In order to make his parents happy, he studies hard.'
　　　(ClauseType = *avb*)

b. 这个　广告　　　　宣称　　　可　使　　孩子　　长高。
　　Zhege　guanggao　　xuancheng　ke　shi　haizi　　zhanggao.
　　This　advertisement　claim　　　can　make　children　grow taller
　　'This advertisement claims that it can make children grow taller.'
　　(ClauseType = *cpl*)

c. 网络　　不仅　　使　　生活　　方便，　　也　　提供
　　Wangluo　bujin　　shi　shenghuo　fangbian,　ye　　tigong
　　Internet　not only　make　life　　convenient　also　provide
　　信息。
　　xinxi.
　　infomation

'The Internet not only makes life convenient, but also provides information.'
(ClauseType = *cpd*)

d. 由于   观众   很多,   使   场面   多次   失控。
   Youyu guanzhong henduo, shi   changmian duoci shikong
   Because audience a lot   make situation   many   out
                                                times of control

   'Because there is a big audience, it makes the situation out of control several times.'
   (ClauseType = *main*)

e. 昨天   真   是   令   人   难忘   的   一   天。
   Zuotian zhen shi ling   ren   nanwang   de   yi   tian.
   Yesterday truly is make   people hard to forget REL one day

   'Yesterday truly was a memorable day.'
   (ClauseType = *rltv*)

– PredSem: it stands for the semantic class of the effected predicate. There are three possible values for this variable: *atelic* (cf. (6b)), *telic* (cf. (7)), and *state* (cf. (6e)). The previous research shows that *ling* tends to co-occur with a stative predicate (Zhang 2005).

(7) 这   微笑   使   人   失去   了   判断力。
    Zhe weixiao shi   ren   shiqu   le   panduanli
    The smile   make people   lose   PST   judgement

    'The smile made people lose their judgement.'
    (PredSem = *telic*)

– CsedSemT: this variable refers to the semantic class of the target domain (i.e. the figurative meaning) of the caused event, as opposed to the source domain (i.e. the literal meaning) when metaphors are involved. It has three possible values: *ment* (mental caused event, cf. (6e)), *phy* (physical caused event, cf. (6b)) and *social* (social caused event, cf. (6d)).

Table 5.3: Independent variables.

Label	Predictor	Value
CrLocus	Locus of the causer	*adjacent, adjacent2, distant, implicit*
CrSynt	Syntactic form of the causer	*cl* (clause), *na, np* (noun phrase), *pron* (pronoun), *vp* (verbal phrase)
CrSem	Semantic class of the causer	*anim* (animate), *event, inanim* (inanimate), *na*
CrPers	Person of the causer	*1, 2, 3, na*
CrDef	Definiteness of the causer	*def* (definite), *indef* (indefinite), *na*
CrIntent	Intentionality of the causer	*intent* (intentional), *unintent* (unintentional)
CeSynt	Syntactic form of the causee	*cl, np, pron, ren* (meaning "people/person")
CeSem	Semantic class of the causee	*anim, event, inanim*
CePers	Person of the causee	*1, 2, 3, na*
CeDef	Definiteness of the causee	*def, indef*
CeControl	Whether the causee can control the caused event	*no, yes*
CeRole	Thematic role of the causee	*agent, befry* (beneficiary), *expcer* (experiencer), *patient, theme,*
CoRef	Coreference between the causer and the causee	*no, yes*
CseModality	Modal verb modifying the causative marker	*ability, incl* (inclination), *nece* (necessity), *none, poss* (possibility)
CseAdv	Adverb modifying the causative marker	*degree, none, oth* (other), *range, time*
CseNeg	Polarity of the causative marker	*no, yes*
PredSynt	Syntactic form of the effected predicate's	*adj* (adjective), *copula, idiom, intrans* (intransitive verb), *trans* (transitive verb)
PredSem	Semantic class of the effected predicate	*atelic, state, telic*
CsedProsody	Prosody of the caused event	*neg* (negative), *ntrl* (neutral), *pstv* (positive)
CsedModality	Modal verb modifying the effected predicate	*ability, incl* (inclination), *nece* (necessity), *none, poss* (possibility)

Table 5.3 (continued)

Label	Predictor	Value
CsedAdv	Adverb modifying the effected predicate	*degree, manner, none, range, time*
CsedNeg	Polarity of the effected predicate	*no, yes*
CsedSemS	Semantic class of caused event (source domain)	*ment* (mental), *phy* (physical), *social*
CsedSemT	Semantic class of caused event (target domain)	*ment* (mental), *phy* (physical), *social*
ClauseType	Clause type where the causative construction is found	*avb* (adverbial), *cpl* (complemental), *cpd* (compound), *main, rltv* (relative), *smpl* (simple)
Structure	Number of the effected predicate	*mul* (multiple), *sg* (single)
Variety	Language variety	*ml* (Mainland), *sg* (Singapore), *tw* (Taiwan)

3.3 Statistical analyses

The statistical analyses of this study are conducted in R software (R Core Team 2014) and the code can be found in the Appendix of this chapter. Given that our study looks into an extensive set of predictor variables, which moreover may interact in potentially ways, we opted not to directly feed all predictor variables into a massive logistic regression model. Instead, we chose to first try and identify which are the most important predictors by means of a conditional random forest analysis, an approach which has gained popularity in recent multifactorial studies (e.g. Tagliamonte and Baayen 2012; Bernaisch, Gries, and Mukherjee 2014; Szmrecsanyi et al. 2016; Deshors and Gries 2016). Compared to logistic regression models, tree-based methods such as conditional inference trees and conditional random forests are less affected by predictor collinearity and data sparsity, which is typically exhibited in corpus data (cf. Gries 2019). Moreover, tree-based methods can process a large number of variables simultaneously and can handle high-order interactions well (Strobl, Malley, and Tutz 2009), which suits the characteristics of our data.

We first built a conditional random forest model with all the 27 independent variables using the {party} package in R (Hothorn, Hornik and Zeileis 2006). A conditional random forest is an ensemble of multiple conditional inference trees.

A conditional inference tree partitions the data into two subsets based on whichever predictors that co-vary most strongly with the responses and recursively repeats this process, each time picking the predictor that works best at that point in the tree, until no further split can be made to significantly improve the classification accuracy. Random forest models add two layers of randomness in this procedure to reduce the variability of prediction: first, each tree in the forest is grown based on randomly bootstrapped data; second, each split of each tree is decided based on a randomly selected subset of the predictors (cf. Gries 2019). The researcher needs to specify two parameters when creating a random forest model: the number of trees that the forest grows (*ntree*) and the number of variables considered when making each split of each tree (*mtry*). By aggregating predictions of all the conditional inference trees, a random forest model assigns a variable importance score to each predictor[8](as in Figure 5.1).

After having the variable importance of each predictor, our next step was to build a single conditional inference tree, again using the {party} package, this time only using the variables that showed significant effects in the random forest. Previous studies using tree-based methods (e.g. Bernaisch, Gries, and Mukherjee 2014; Szmrecsanyi et al. 2016) usually start by building a conditional inference tree with all the variables in the first step and then create a random forest, using the conditional inference tree as a first tentative, but possibly fragile model, and using the forest for a more robust assessment of the variable importance of the predictors. Indeed, individual conditional inference trees are known to be easily affected by the problem of instability because each split of the tree is made based on the previous splits and a small change in the data may alter the whole structure (Strobl Malley, and Tutz 2009; Kuhn and Johnson 2016: 174; Levshina, in press). We acknowledge this vulnerability, and by no means consider the conditional inference tree we build in the second step to be superior to the random forest we build in the first step. It merely helps interpret the random forest, because it visualizes how exactly the important predictors affect the alternation and how they interact, which is information that is hidden in the forest analysis. We accept, however, that the conditional inference tree analysis remains potentially less robust than the random forest analysis. We do believe, though, that building the tree with just the predictors deemed important by the forest can somewhat reduce undesired variability of the results of the tree analysis.

Both tree-based methods described above are powerful tools. Unfortunately, however, both have their limitations. On the one hand, conditional random

---

8 There are different kinds of variable importance measures, e.g. "Gini importance" and "permutation accuracy importance". For more details, see Strobl, Malley, and Tutz (2009).

forest analysis is a "black-box" method whose result is hard to interpret (Strobl, Malley, and Tutz 2009). It shows us which variables are important, but not how exactly they are important. On the other hand, an individual conditional inference tree might yield less robust results and, moreover, also may keep some of the global patterns in the data hidden, because of the way each node in the tree is the result of a 'winner takes it all' kind of procedure. More specifically, at each point in the tree, only the single most important pattern in that part of the tree is highlighted, potentially hiding other important patterns.

Therefore, our third and final step is to complement the tree-based methods with logistic regression modelling, as is suggested and implemented in several studies (e.g. Strobl, Malley, and Tutz 2009; Gries 2019; Deshors and Gries 2020). This procedure serves two purposes: the first one is to verify whether the results of tree-based methods and of logistic regression modelling are consistent; the second one is to further investigate the interactions between Variety and other variables. The latter goal is driven by our research interest, which lies in the lectal variation. Given that the dependent variable of our study is a categorical one that includes three values, i.e., *shi*, *ling* and *rang*, we built a multinomial logistic regression model.

Multinomial logistic regression models can be built in R software using any of the packages {mlogit} (McFadden 1973, 1974; Train 2009), {polytomous} (Arppe 2008, 2009) or {nnet} (Ripley 1996; Venables and Ripley 2002) (cf. Levshina 2015: Section 13 for the differences between these packages). We opted for the {nnet} package in this study. We started out with a model with the seven significant variables that are significant in the random forest model as well as the two-way interactions between Variety and the other six variables and used a backward model selection procedure to obtain a final model, which is presented in Section 4.3.

The annotated 3064 observations were randomly divided into a training dataset (70%) and a test dataset (30%). All the three models were created based on the training dataset and then were used to predict the responses in the 30% test dataset to evaluate their performance.

4 Results

4.1 Conditional random forests

We created a random forest model with 1000 inference trees (ntree =1000) and each split of each tree is made based on five randomly selected variables (mtry = 5). The model yields importance scores for all the variables, as is shown in Figure 5.1.[9]

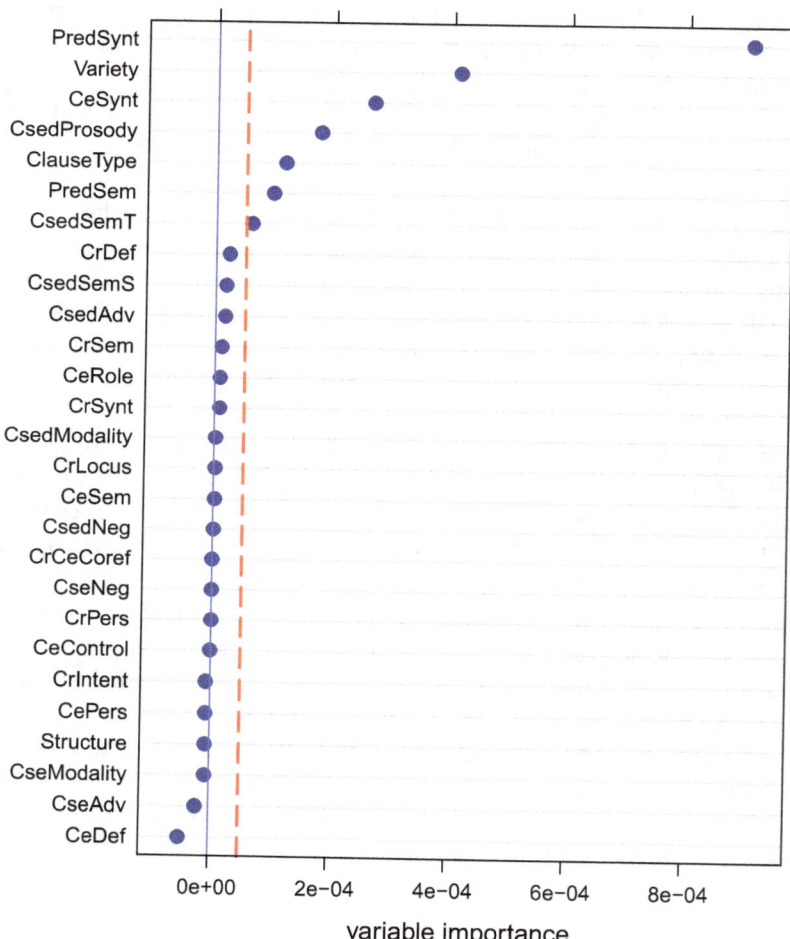

Figure 5.1: Importance measure of all variables.

---

[9] We built five random forest models by using different seeds when splitting the data into the training dataset and the test dataset. In all these five models, PredSynt, Variety, CeSynt, Csed-Prosody and ClauseType are always significant, which means that the results of the random forest models are highly stable and reliable.

According to the random forest model, the syntactic form of the effected predicate (PredSynt) is the most important variable, followed by Variety, the syntactic form of the causee (CeSynt), the prosody of the caused event (CsedProsody), the type of the clause in which the causative construction is found (ClauseType), the semantic class of the effected predicate (PredSem) and the semantic class of the caused event (target domain) (CsedSemT). The other variables do not have a significant effect on the choice of *shi*, *ling* and *rang*.

The prediction accuracy of the random forest on the 30% test dataset is 71.43% (Table 5.4), which is better than the accuracy rate of always choosing the most frequent marker (i.e. *rang*) (51.15%) and much better compared to 33.33%, the correct chance if the responses are chosen randomly.

Table 5.4: Confusion matrix of the conditional random forest model on 30% test dataset.

Predicted		Observed		
		ling	rang	shi
	ling	82	47	16
	rang	17	381	71
	shi	1	110	192

The importance scores assigned to the variables by the random forest model are hard to interpret. For instance, we know from Figure 5.1 that PredSynt is the most important variable, but the model does not show how different values of this variable affect the probability of choosing *shi*, *rang* or *ling*. Therefore, we complement this method with a conditional inference tree (Section 4.2) and a multinomial logistic regression model (Section 4.3).

4.2 Conditional inference trees

We built a conditional inference tree with the seven variables that turned out to be significant in the random forest model. The result is shown in Figure 5.2.

We can see from the model that the alternation of *shi*, *ling* and *rang* involves a complex interplay of different variables. The first split is made based on the syntactic form of the causee (CeSynt), where the most important reason of that split seems to be that *shi* is hardly ever used when the causee is expressed by the word *ren* (CeSynt = ren). Whether in the latter situation the chosen causative is *rang* or

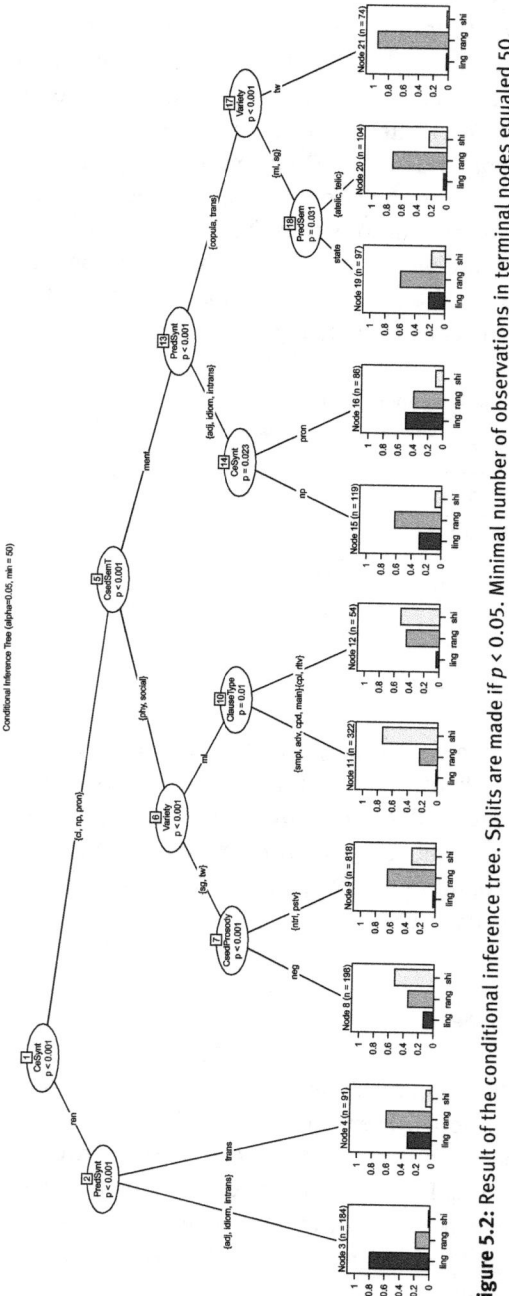

Figure 5.2: Result of the conditional inference tree. Splits are made if $p < 0.05$. Minimal number of observations in terminal nodes equaled 50.

ling, turns out, according to the model, to correlate strongly with the syntactic form of the effected predicate (PredSynt, cf. Node 2). More specifically, if the effected predicate is an idiom, an adjective or an intransitive verb, *ling* is strongly favored (Node 3), as in (8). If it is a transitive verb, the proportion of *rang* exceeds that of *ling* (Node 4).

(8) 这个   奇迹   令   人   叹为观止。
    Zhege qiji   ling   ren   tanweiguanzhi.
    This   miracle make   people   knock one's socks off
    'This miracle knocked people's socks off.'
    (CeSynt = *ren*; PredSynt = *idiom*)

When the causee is expressed by other forms than *ren*, the interactions of variables are much more complex, as is shown in the right side of the first split. The first variable coming into play in that part of the tree is the semantic class of the caused event (target domain) (CsedSemT, Node 5), which divides the local subset of the data into a subset to the left (CsedSemT = *physical* or social) with relatively more *shi* and less *ling*, compared to the second branch, and a subset to the right (CsedSemT = *mental*), with relatively more *ling* and less *shi*, compared to the first branch.

If a physical or social event is expressed by the effected predicate, Variety comes into play, where Mainland Chinese (the second branch of Node 6) shows a stronger preference for *shi* than Singapore and Taiwan Chinese (the first branch of Node 6). In the latter two varieties, the proportion of *shi* only slightly exceeds that of *rang* when the event is negative (Node 8) while *rang* is predominant if the event is positive or neutral (Node 9). In Mainland Chinese, on the other hand, *shi* always takes up the highest proportion, although its advantage over *rang* lessens when the causative construction is in a complemental or a relative clause (Node 12).

The picture is more complex when the effected predicate expresses a mental event, where the syntactic form of the effected predicate (PredSynt) shows an effect again (Node 13). In the first branch of Node 13, *ling* shows again its preference for an effected predicate expressed by an idiom, an adjective or an intransitive verb, and it becomes the most favored marker if the causee is a pronoun (Node 16).

In the second branch of Node 13, i.e., when the syntactic form of the effected predicate is a copula or a transitive verb, *rang* is always the most favored marker, although the preferences of the three varieties differ again. In Taiwan Chinese, *rang* is predominant and the other two markers are barely used (Node 21), whereas in Mainland and Singapore Chinese, the proportion of *ling* notably increases when the semantic class of the effected predicate is stative (Node 19).

The prediction accuracy of the conditional inference tree on the test dataset is 65.21% (Table 5.5), which is better than the accuracy rate of always choosing *rang* (51.15%), the most frequent marker and much better compared to 33.33%, the correct chance if the responses are chosen randomly.

Table 5.5: Confusion matrix of the condition inference tree model on 30% test data.

Predicted	Observed		
	ling	*rang*	*shi*
ling	77	48	20
rang	36	361	72
shi	3	140	160

4.3 Multinomial logistic regression

Then we fitted a multinomial logistic regression model with the seven variables that are significant in the random forest model as well as the two-way interactions between Variety and the other six variables. We started out with a model with all these predictions and interactions and continued by removing non-significant terms, each time removing the term with the highest *p*-value, until all remaining terms were significant at an alpha-level of 0.01.[10] The final model is:

> Item ~ PredSynt + Variety + CeSynt + CsedProsody + ClauseType + CsedSemT + Variety: CsedSemT[11]

The reference value of the dependent variable is *ling*. An odds ratio greater than 1 indicates that the probability of *rang* or *shi* increases compared with *ling*. An odds ratio smaller than 1 indicates the opposite, viz. a decrease of the probability of *rang* or *shi*, compared to *ling*.

---

[10] This procedure is implemented with the function Anova() in the R package {car}. The output of the model is created using the function tab_model() in the R package {sjPlot}.
[11] We noticed that there are only seven observations with the value CeSynt = *cl*. In order to avoid the effect of data sparsity, we removed the seven observations from the data and built the multinomial logistic regression model.

Table 5.6: Summary of the multinomial logistic regression model.

Predictors	Odds Ratios	CI	p	Response
(Intercept)	1.43	0.50 – 4.08	0.504	*rang*
PredSynt [copula]	2.87	0.63 – 13.01	0.172	*rang*
PredSynt [idiom]	0.87	0.49 – 1.54	0.634	*rang*
PredSynt [intrans]	0.94	0.57 – 1.55	0.818	*rang*
PredSynt [trans]	3.69	2.27 – 6.00	**<0.001**	*rang*
Variety [sg]	0.74	0.41 – 1.36	0.335	*rang*
Variety [tw]	0.97	0.49 – 1.93	0.925	*rang*
CeSynt [pron]	1.04	0.68 – 1.61	0.853	*rang*
CeSynt [ren]	0.16	0.10 – 0.24	**<0.001**	*rang*
CsedProsody [ntrl]	3.43	2.31 – 5.09	**<0.001**	*rang*
CsedProsody [pstv]	3.00	2.06 – 4.38	**<0.001**	*rang*
ClauseType [compl]	4.98	1.07 – 23.15	0.041	*rang*
ClauseType [cpd]	1.53	0.44 – 5.30	0.503	*rang*
ClauseType [main]	1.46	0.42 – 5.10	0.551	*rang*
ClauseType [rltv]	0.19	0.07 – 0.49	**0.001**	*rang*
ClauseType [simple]	0.69	0.29 – 1.62	0.396	*rang*
CsedSemT [phy]	2.93	0.60 – 14.17	0.182	*rang*
CsedSemT [social]	1.19	0.49 – 2.87	0.703	*rang*
Variety [sg] * CsedSemT[phy]	0.81	0.15 – 4.39	0.805	*rang*
Variety [tw] * CsedSemT[phy]	2.55	0.36 – 18.02	0.349	*rang*
Variety [sg] * CsedSemT[social]	2.16	0.81 – 5.77	0.126	*rang*
Variety [tw] * CsedSemT[social]	4.15	1.34 – 12.87	0.014	*rang*
(Intercept)	1.96	0.63 – 6.04	0.244	*shi*
PredSynt [copula]	5.96	1.31 – 27.15	0.021	*shi*
PredSynt [idiom]	0.58	0.30 – 1.15	0.120	*shi*
PredSynt [intrans]	0.75	0.42 – 1.34	0.334	*shi*
PredSynt [trans]	2.27	1.29 – 3.99	**0.004**	*shi*
Variety [sg]	0.42	0.20 – 0.87	0.020	*shi*

Table 5.6 (continued)

Predictors	Odds Ratios	CI	p	Response
Variety [tw]	0.09	0.02 – 0.29	**<0.001**	shi
CeSynt [pron]	0.95	0.59 – 1.53	0.833	shi
CeSynt [ren]	0.08	0.04 – 0.15	**<0.001**	shi
CsedProsody [ntrl]	1.36	0.88 – 2.12	0.167	shi
CsedProsody [pstv]	1.60	1.06 – 2.41	0.026	shi
ClauseType [compl]	2.93	0.61 – 14.10	0.179	shi
ClauseType [cpd]	1.29	0.36 – 4.72	0.695	shi
ClauseType [main]	1.65	0.46 – 5.96	0.441	shi
ClauseType [rltv]	0.18	0.06 – 0.53	**0.002**	shi
ClauseType [simple]	0.58	0.24 – 1.40	0.225	shi
CsedSemT [phy]	12.92	2.65 – 63.13	**0.002**	shi
CsedSemT [social]	8.66	3.45 – 21.74	**<0.001**	shi
Variety [sg] * CsedSemT[phy]	0.47	0.08 – 2.65	0.394	shi
Variety [tw] * CsedSemT[phy]	5.80	0.64 – 52.59	0.118	shi
Variety [sg] * CsedSemT[social]	0.73	0.25 – 2.08	0.554	shi
Variety [tw] * CsedSemT[social]	7.40	1.63 – 33.58	**0.009**	shi
Observations	2141			
R^2 Nagelkerke	0.476			

According to the model, when the syntactic form of the effected predicate is a transitive verb (PredSynt = *trans*), the probabilities of both *rang* and *shi* significantly increase ($p < 0.01$). When the causee is expressed by the word *ren* (CeSynt = *ren*), the probabilities of both *rang* and *shi* significantly decrease ($p < 0.001$). Another variable configuration that disfavors *rang* ($p = 0.001$) and *shi* ($p = 0.002$) is when ClauseType = *rltv* (relative), i.e., when the causative construction occurs in a relative clause. When the effected predicate expresses neutral or positive events, the probability of *rang* will significantly increase ($p < 0.001$). The probability of using *shi* significantly increase when the effected predicate expresses physical ($p = 0.002$) or social events ($p < 0.001$). These main effects in the multinomial logistic regression model corroborate the result of the conditional inference tree.

The interaction between Variety and CsedSemT is illustrated in Figure 5.3.[12]

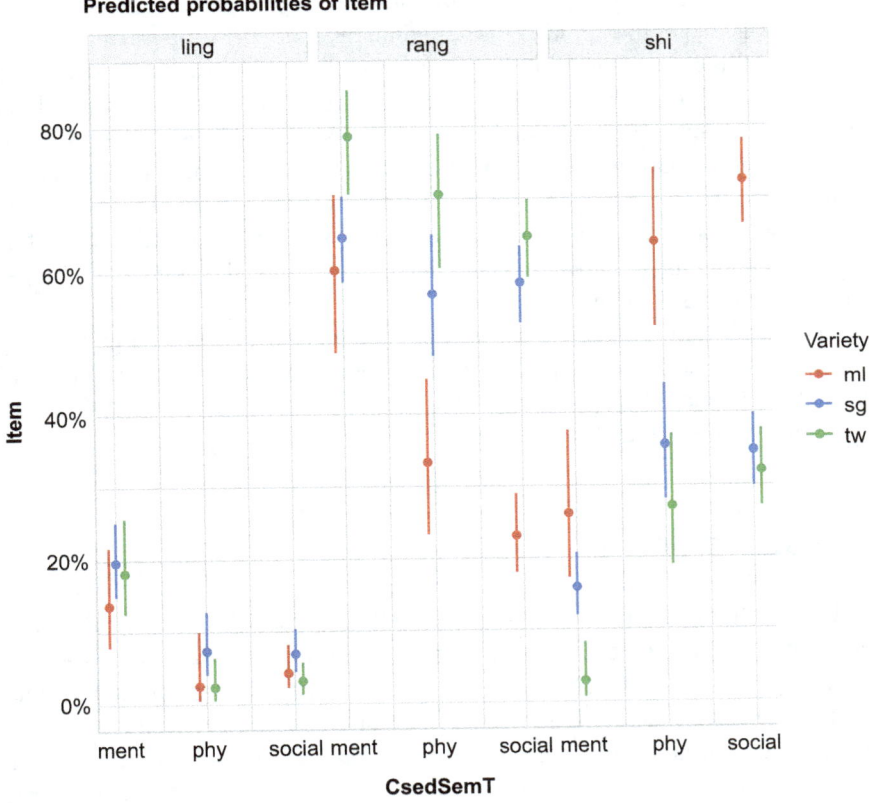

Figure 5.3: The interaction plot between Variety and CsedSemT.

Figure 5.3 presents the probabilities of *ling* (left side), *rang* (middle) and *shi* (right side) in Mainland Chinese (red), Singapore Chinese (blue) and Taiwan Chinese (green) with different values of CsedSemT, i.e. the semantic class of the caused event (target domain).

We can see from the plot that the probability of *shi* is always higher in Mainland Chinese than in the other two varieties, whereas Singapore Chinese and especially Taiwan Chinese prefer to choose *rang*, irrespective of the values of CsedSemT. The probability of *ling* remains low in all three varieties, with a

---

[12] The plot is generated with the functions ggeffect() in the R package {ggeffects}and plot().

notable increase when the semantic class of the caused event (target domain) is a mental activity.

The variability of the probability of *shi* and *rang* with different values of CsedSemT is bigger in Mainland Chinese than in Singapore Chinese and Taiwan Chinese. Although the probabilities differ, the effect of CsedSemT is similar in Mainland Chinese and Taiwan Chinese. More specifically speaking, in Mainland Chinese and Taiwan Chinese, the probability of *shi* is the lowest when it is followed by mental caused event (target domain) and the highest when it is followed by social caused event (target domain), and the probability of *rang* is exactly the opposite. In Singapore Chinese, on the other hand, the probabilities of *shi* are nearly the same when it is with social or physical caused event (target domain), and this finding also holds for *rang*.

The prediction accuracy of the multinomial logistic regression in 30% test dataset is 67.14%. The C values of the model when predicting *ling*, *rang* and *shi* are 0.92, 0.75 and 0.81 respectively, indicating a good predictive power (Hosmer and Lemeshow 2000: 162).

5 Discussion

With the help of the advanced statistical methods, viz. conditional random forests, conditional inference trees and multinomial logistic regression analysis, this study manages to simultaneously investigate multiple language-internal and language-external factors based on corpus data and achieve a more realistic model of the variation in Chinese analytic causative construction alternation. The model results unveil the complex interplay between the syntactic, semantic and lectal factors that affect the choice of Chinese causative markers *shi*, *ling* and *rang*, yielding some important findings that speak to the research questions laid out in Section 1.

(1). What are the syntactic and semantic factors that affect the choice of *shi*, *ling* and *rang*?

Based on bottom-up data analytics, this study provides objective and verifiable evidence which confirms some previous findings regarding the use of *shi*, *ling* and *rang* while providing some new insights.

Both conditional inference tree and multinomial logistic regression analyses confirm that the [*ling ren* + result] construction, where *ling* and *ren* form a fixed expression while the result is expressed by an effected predicate in form of an adjective or an intransitive verb, has become the most prevalent usage for *ling* (Figure 5.2, Node 3). Given the low frequency of *ling* occurring in other contexts (the terminal nodes other than Node 3 in Figure 5.2) and the low probability of using *ling* in general (Figure 5.3), we concur with Niu (2007) in that *ling* is losing its status of functioning as a causative marker and is on the process of becoming a morpheme in the fixed expressions of [*ling ren* + adj./intransitive verb]. This tendency of *ling* also explains why it is significantly more likely to occur in a relative clause (see Table 5.6), which is normally shorter than other clause types in Chinese and has a similar function with adjectives in terms of modifying a noun. Therefore, the fixed expressions of [*ling ren* + adj./intransitive verb] are more ideal choices than other longer and more complicated causative constructions. In addition, the *ling*-construction tends to express a mental event instead of a physical or social event (see Figure 5.3), which supports the findings on the usage of *ling* in Zhang (2005).

While studies on Chinese analytic causative constructions usually compare *shi* with *rang* (e.g. Hu 2002; Chen 2005; Ni 2012; Yang 2016), our models show that *shi* tends to occur in a different context with *ling* rather than *rang*. For instance, the frequency of *shi* is extremely low when *ling* is the most favored marker (Node 3 in Figure 5.2) and vice versa (Node 11 in Figure 5.2). As *shi* and *ling* grammaticalized into causative markers in similar historical periods and their grammaticalization occurred much earlier than *rang* (cf. Xu 2003; Cao 2011), we speculate that there may exist a competitive relationship between *shi* and *ling* during their grammaticalization processes, which caused the division of labor between these two markers. Of course, more diachronic research is required to verify this speculation.

Rang, on the other hand, as a much younger and more versatile marker, covers more usage contexts, as is shown by the relatively high proportions of *rang* in many terminal nodes of the conditional inference tree (see Figure 5.2). However, this does not mean that *rang* is equally distributed in all the contexts. For instance, *rang* shows a strong preference for effected predicates that are transitive verbs (see Figure 5.2 Node 4, 19–21 & Table 5.6). This finding confirms Ni (2012)'s assessment that *rang* has some similarity with the Dutch causative marker of *laten* (Speelman & Geeraerts 2009; Levshina, Geeraerts, and Speelman 2013a), which also favors transitive effected predicates.

As for Ni (2012)'s proposition of accounting for the distribution of *shi* and *rang* with the "(in)direct causation hypothesis" (Verhagen and Kemmer 1997), our study, by investigating more variables, calls for caution to reach such a conclusion. Firstly, the "(in)direct causation hypothesis" distinguishes direct and indirect causation by identifying whether the causer or the causee constitutes the source of energy over the whole causation process (cf. Verhagen and Kemmer 1997 and Section 2.1 of this paper), which assumes that different syntactic and semantic configurations of the causer and the causee should be the most important factors. However, our models suggest that when taking multiple variables into account, the features of the causer and the semantic features of the causee do not stand out as the most influential ones affecting the choice of *shi* and *rang*, which means the "(in)direct causation hypothesis" may not be a suitable theory to explain the distribution of these two markers. Secondly, as is discussed above, the competition between *shi* and *ling* in different contexts is more intense than that between *shi* and *rang*, and the difference between *shi* and *rang* can be attributed to language external factors, such as register (cf. Wan 2004; Miyake 2005, Yang 2016) and language variety (see below for a detailed discussion).

(2). What is the extent to which varieties of Chinese differ in the choice of analytic causative constructions?

We explored the regional variation of Chinese analytic causative constructions by incorporating the variable of Variety into our models. The random forest model determines whether Variety stands out in the competition of all factors affecting the choice of *shi*, *ling* and *rang*, while the conditional inference tree and the multinomial logistic regression model can provide more information by showing the interactions between Variety and the language-internal factors.

All three models presented in Section 4 point to significant lectal differences in Chinese analytic causative construction alternation. More specifically, Variety ranks the second most important variable in the random forest model; in the conditional inference tree analysis, Variety manifests complex interactions with other variables by showing up twice in the splits; the multinomial logistic regression model also reveals a significant interaction between language varieties and the semantic class of the caused event.

A closer look at the results shows that the lectal variation mainly lies in the choices of *shi* and *rang*, whereas the frequency of *ling* remains rather low in all the three varieties and is mainly affected by the language-internal factors. According to the conditional inference tree and the multinomial logistic regression analysis, Mainland Chinese favors *shi* while Singapore and especially Taiwan Chinese favor *rang* (see Figure 5.2 & 5.3).

There are two possible explanations for this lectal variation. First, previous studies have reported that register plays an important role in the distributions of *shi* and *rang*. More specifically, *shi* is frequently used in written Chinese, while in spoken Chinese people prefer to choose *rang* (Wan 2004; Miyake 2005, Yang 2016). Although we controlled the register in the current study by only looking at newswire data for all the three varieties, the news articles from the different varieties may display stylistic variation. For instance, the news articles in Taiwan and Singapore Chinese may be more informal than in Mainland Chinese, leading to a lectal difference in the distributions of *shi* and *rang*. A second explanation is that like the usage of *doen* and *laten* in Netherlandic Dutch and Belgian Dutch (Speelman and Geeraerts 2009; Levshina, Geeraerts, and Speelman 2013a), the division of labor between *shi* and *rang* differs across the three varieties. In Mainland Chinese, *shi* and *rang* are both frequently used and show different preferences for the semantic class of the caused events, whereas in Taiwan and Singapore Chinese, *shi* becomes an obsolescent marker that has been gradually replaced by *rang*. However, more cross-variety and cross-register investigations are needed to verify which explanation reflects the real picture of language use.

6 Concluding remarks

To conclude, this study contributes to the discussion on Chinese analytic causatives by exploring syntactic and semantic factors that constrain the choice of *shi*, *ling* and *rang*, which are the three most frequently used causative markers in contemporary written Chinese. By incorporating a cross-variety perspective, we also found significant lectal variation in the alternation of Chinese analytic causative constructions. As a case study that explores multiple factors based on a large dataset, this study provides a showcase of how bottom-up data analytics in the framework of Cognitive Linguistics can help to draw new insights on construction alternation studies. More specifically, it provides empirical evidence pertaining to Chinese analytic causative constructions on the benefits of combining tree-based methods and logistic regression modelling.

However, the results reported here should be considered in the light of some potential limitations. The first limitation concerns the design of variables. In this case study, we only included one language external factor, i.e., Variety, in our models. Other variables which have been discussed in the literature of Chinese analytic causatives (e.g, the register of the texts) should also be explored in future studies to achieve a more adequate account. Second, we point out that the competition between *shi* and *ling* may be attributable to their grammaticalization processes, however, without an empirical study based on diachronic data, this conclusion should be taken with caution.

Appendix: R codes of the study

```
# Activating necessary packages:
> library(readr); library(party); library(caret); library(dplyr);
library(lattice); library(pdp); library(nnet); library(car); library
(ggeffects); library(sjmisc)

# Preparing the data:
> data <- read_csv("dataname.csv")
> slr <- data %>%
Select (Item, CrLocus, CrSynt, CrSem, CrPers, CrDef, CrIntent,
CseModality, CseAdv, CseNeg, CeSynt, CeSem, CePers, CeDef, CeControl,
CeRole, CsedModality, CsedAdv, CsedNeg, Coref, PredSynt, PredSem,
CsedProsody, CsedSemS, CsedSemT, Structure, ClauseType, Variety)
> slr[] <- lapply(slr, factor)

# Data splitting (70% training set, 30% test set):
> set.seed(18)
> trainsamples <- createDataPartition(slr$Item, times = 1, p = 0.70)
> trainsamples <- unlist(trainsamples)
> data_train <- slr[trainsamples, ]
> data_test <- slr[-trainsamples, ]

# Creating a random forest using {party} package:
> m_cf <- cforest(Item ~ ., data=data_train, control = cforest_unbiased
(ntree= 1000, mtry = 5))
> m_cf.varimp <- varimp(m_cf, conditional=TRUE)
> dotplot(sort(m_cf.varimp), main="Random forest (ntree=1000)",
xlab="variable importance", panel=function(x,y){
    panel.dotplot(x,y,col="darkblue", pch=16, cex=1.2)
    panel.abline(v=abs(min(m_cf.varimp)), col="red", lty="longdash",
    lwd=2)
    panel.abline(v=0, col="blue")})

# Prediction of random forest on the 30% test data:
> pred <- predict (m_cf, newdata = data_test, OOB = TRUE, type = "response")
> table(observed=slr$Item[-trainsamples], predicted=pred)
```

```
# Building a conditional inference tree with the variables evaluated to be
significant by the random forest using {party} package:
> ctree_model <- ctree(Item~Variety + CsedSemT + CeSynt + CsedProsody +
ClauseType + PredSynt + PredSem, data=data_train, controls =
ctree_control(testtype = "MonteCarlo", mincriterion = 0.95, minbucket = 50))
> ctree_model
> plot(ctree_model, main="Conditional Inference Tree (alpha=0.05, min = 50)")

# Prediction and model evaluation on testing dataset (30%):
> data_test$pred <- predict(ctree_model, data_test[,-1])
> confusionMatrix(data_test$Item, factor(data_test$pred))

# Building a multinomial logistic regression model with the seven variables
proved to be significant in the random forest model as well as their
interactions with the variable Variety:
> fit0 <- multinom(Item ~ PredSynt + Variety + CeSynt + CsedProsody +
ClauseType + PredSem + CsedSemT + Variety:PredSynt + Variety:CeSynt + Variety:
CsedProsody + Variety:ClauseType + Variety:PredSem + CsedSemT:Variety,
data=data_train)
> Anova(fit0)

# Removing the insignificant variables and fitting the final model:
> fit <- multinom(Item ~ PredSynt + Variety + CeSynt + CsedProsody + ClauseType
+ CsedSemT + Variety:CsedSemT, data=data_train)
> Anova(fit)
> summary(fit)
> tab_model(fit)

> data_test$pred <- predict(fit, data_test[,-1])
> confusionMatrix(data_test$Item,factor(data_test$pred))

# Drawing the interaction plot:
> Var_CsedSemT<-ggeffect(fit, type = "pred", terms = c("CsedSemT",
"Variety"), ci.lvl = 0.95)
> plot(Var_CsedSemT)
```

References

Anthony, Laurence. 2019. *AntConc* (Version 3.5.8) [Computer Software]. Tokyo, Japan: Waseda University. Available from https://www.laurenceanthony.net/software.

Arppe, Antti. 2008. *Univariate, bivariate and multivariate methods in corpus-based lexicography – a study of synonymy*. Publications of the Department of General Linguistics, University of Helsinki, No. 44. URN: http://urn.fi/URN:ISBN:978-952-10-5175-3.

Arppe, Antti. 2009. Linguistic choices vs. probabilities – How much and what can linguistic theory explain? In Featherston, S. & S. Winkler (eds.) *The Fruits of Empirical Linguistics. Volume 1: Process*. Berlin: de Gruyter. 1–24.

Bernaisch, Tobias, Gries, Stefan Th. & Joybrato Mukherjee. 2014. The dative alternation in South Asian English(es): Modelling predictors and predicting prototypes. *English World-Wide*, 35 (1): 7–31.

Carletta Jean. 1996. Assessing agreement on classification tasks: The kappa statistic. *Computational Linguistics*, 22 (2): 249–254.

Cao, Jin. 2011. Shilingju cong shanggu hanyu dao zhonggu hanyu de bianhua [The change of *shi/ling* causative construction from Old Chinese to Middle Chinese]. *Yuyan Kexue* (6): 602–617.

Chen, Xiaoying. 2005. Dai jianyu de *shi* yu *rang* zhi bijiao. [The comparison of *shi* and *rang* with pivotal constructions]. *Guangxi Social Sciences* (2): 156–158.

Colleman, Timothy. 2010. Beyond the dative alternation: The semantics of the Dutch aan-Dative. In Dylan Glynn & Kerstin Fischer (eds.), *Quantitative methods in Cognitive Semantics: Corpus-driven approaches*, 271–303. Berlin/New York: De Gruyter Mouton.

Comrie, Bernard. 1981. *Language universals and linguistic typology: Syntax and morphology*. Chicago: The University of Chicago Press.

Deshors, Sandra C. & Stefan Th. Gries. 2016. Profiling verb complementation constructions across New Englishes: A two-step random forests analysis of -ing vs. to- complements. *International Journal of Corpus Linguistics* 21(2). 192–218.

Deshors, Sandra C. & Stefan Th. Gries. 2020. Mandative subjunctive vs. *should* in world Englishes: A new take on an old alternation. *Corpora* 15 (2). 213–241.

Fan, Xiao. 2000. Lun zhishi jiegou [About causative constructions]. In Chinese Language Magazine (ed.). *Yufa Yanjiu he Tansuo*. Beijing: The Commercial Press. 135–151.

Gamer, Matthias, Jim Lemon, Ian Fellows & Puspendra Singh. 2019. IRR: Various coefficients of interrater reliability and agreement. *R package version, 0.84.1.* https://CRAN.R-project.org/package=irr.

Gilquin, Gaëtanelle. 2010. *Corpus, cognition and causative constructions*. Amsterdam / Philadelphia: John Benjamins.

Goldberg, Adele E. 1995. *Constructions: A Construction Grammar Approach to Argument Structure*. Chicago: University of Chicago Press.

Gries, Stefan Th. 2019. On classification trees and random forests in corpus linguistics: Some words of caution and suggestions for improvement. *Corpus Linguistics and Linguistic Theory*.

Hosmer, David W. & Stanley Lemeshow. 2000. *Applied Logistic Regression*. New York: Wiley.

Hu, Yunwan. 2002. Dai jianyu de *shi* he *rang* zhi bijiao yanjiu. [The comparison research of *shi* and *rang* with pivotal constructions]. *Songliao Journal* (1): 86–86, 93.

Huang, Chu-Ren. 2009. *Tagged Chinese Gigaword Version 2.0 LDC2009T14*. Web Download. Philadelphia: Linguistic Data Consortium.

Hothorn, Torsten, Kurt Hornik & Achim Zeileis. 2006. Unbiased Recursive Partitioning: A Conditional Inference Framework. *Journal of Computational and Graphical Statistics*, 15 (3): 651–674.

Janda, Laura A. 2013. *Cognitive Linguistics-The Quantitative Turn: The Essential Reader*. Berlin/New York: Walter de Gruyter.

Kuhn, Max & Kjell Johnson. 2016. *Applied Predictive Modeling*. New York: Springer.

Liesenfeld Andreas, Meichun Liu & Chu-Ren Huang. 2020. Profiling the Chinese causative construction with rang (讓), shi (使) and ling (令) using frame semantic features. *Corpus Linguistics and Lingustic Theory*. Aop.

Levshina, Natalia. 2011. *Doe Wat Je Niet Laten Kan: A Usage-based Analysis of Dutch Causative Constructions*. Leuven: Catholic University of Leuven dissertation.

Levshina, Natalia. 2015. *How to Do Linguistics with R: Data exploration and statistical analysis*. Amsterdam: John Benjamins.

Levshina, Natalia. In press. Conditional inference trees and random forests. In: Magali Paquot & Stefan Th. Gries (eds.), *Practical Handbook of Corpus Linguistics*. New York: Springer.

Levshina, Natalia, Dirk Geeraerts & Dirk Speelman. 2013a. Towards a 3D-grammar: Interaction of linguistic and extralinguistic factors in the use of Dutch causative constructions. *Journal of Pragmatics*, (52): 34–48.

Levshina, Natalia, Dirk Geeraerts & Dirk Speelman. 2013b. Mapping constructional spaces: A contrastive analysis of English and Dutch analytic causatives. *Linguistics* 51(4): 825–854.

Liu, Yonggeng. 2000. Shilinglei dongci he zhishici [Imperatives and causatives]. *Journal of Xinjiang University (Social Science)* (1): 93–96.

McFadden, Daniel. 1973. Conditional Logit Analysis of Qualitative Choice Behaviour. In Paul Zarembka (ed.). *Frontiers in Econometrics*. New York: Academic Press.

McFadden, Daniel. 1974. The measurement of urban travel demand. *Journal of Public Economics*, 3(4): 303–328.

Miyake, Takayuki. 2005. A usage-based analysis of the causative verb shi in Mandarin Chinese. In Takagaki, T., Zaiman S., Tsuruga, Y., Moreno-Fernandez, F. & Kawaguchi, Y. (eds.). *Corpus-based Approaches to Sentence Structures*. Amsterdam/Philadelphia: John Benjamins Publishing Company. 77–94.

Ni, Yueru. 2012. *Categories of Causative Verbs: A Corpus Study of Mandarin Chinese*. Utrecht: Utrecht University MA thesis.

Niu, Shunxin. 2007. Putonghua zhishici de sange yufahua jieduan [Three grammaticalization phrases of mandarin causative verbs]. *Shehui Kexuejia* (3): 206–209.

Niu, Shunxin. 2014. *Hanyuzhong Zhishi Fanchou de Jiegou Leixing Yanjiu [A Typological Study of Causatives in Chinese]*. Tianjin: Nankai University Publishing.

Orwin, Robert G. 1994. Evaluating coding decisions. In Harris Cooper & Larry V. Hedges (Eds.), *The handbook of research synthesis*. Russell Sage Foundation. 139–162.

R Core Team. 2014. R: A language and environment for statistical computing. R Foundation for Statistical Computing. Vienna. URL http://www.R-project.org/.

Ripley, Brian D. 1996. *Pattern Recognition and Neural Networks*. Cambridge: Cambridge University Press.

Röthlisberger, Melanie, Jason Grafmiller & Benedikt Szmrecsanyi. 2017. Cognitive indigenization effects in the English dative alternation. *Cognitive Linguistics*, 28(4): 673–710.

Speelman, Dirk & Dirk Geeraerts. 2009. Causes for causatives: The case of Dutch doen and laten. In T. Sanders & E. Sweetser (eds.). *Linguistics of Causality*, 173–204. Berlin: Mouton de Gruyter.

Stefanowitsch, Anatol. 2001. Constructing causation: A Construction Grammar approach to analytic causatives. Houston, TX: Rice University dissertation.

Strobl, Carolin, James Malley & Gerhard Tutz. 2009. An introduction to recursive partitioning: Rationale, application, and characteristics of classification and regression trees, bagging, and random forests. *Psychological Methods* 14 (4): 323–348.

Stukker, Ninke. 2005. *Causality marking across levels of language structure*. University of Utrecht dissertation.

Szmrecsanyi, Benedikt, Jason Grafmiller, Benedikt Heller & Röthlisberger Melanie. 2016. Around the world in three alternations: Modeling syntactic variation in varieties of English. *English World-Wide 37*(2). 109–137.

Tagliamonte, Sali A. & Harald R. Baayen. 2012. Models, forests, and trees of York English: Was/ were variation as a case study for statistical practice. *Language Variation and Change* 24(2). 135–178.

Talmy, Leonard. 2000. *Toward a Cognitive Semantics Vol.I Concept Structuring Systems*. Cambridge, MA.: The MIT Press.

Tian, Xiaoyu & Weiwei Zhang. 2020. Hanyu biantizhong fenxixing zhishi goushi bianyi yanjiu: Duofenlei luojisidi huigui jianmo [Chinese analytic causative constructions and their lectal variation: A multinomial logistic regression]. *Foreign Languages and Their Teaching* (3). 22–33.

Train, Kenneth E. 2009. *Discrete Choice Methods with Simulation*. Cambridge: Cambridge University Press.

Venables, W. N. & Brian D. Ripley. 2002. *Modern Applied Statistics with S (fourth edition)*. Berlin: Springer.

Verhagen, Arie & Suzanne Kemmer. 1997. Interaction and causation: Causative constructions in modern standard Dutch. *Journal of Pragmatics*, (27): 61–82.

Wan, Xinzheng. 2004. *Xiandai Hanyu Zhishi Goushi Yanjiu* [Research of Causative Constructions in Modern Chinese]. Shanghai: Fudan University PhD dissertation.

Xiang, Kaixi. 2002. Hanyu de shuangshili goushi [Double-force constructions in Chinese]. *Yuyan Yanjiu* (2): 70–77.

Xiong, Zhongru. 2004. *Xiandaihanyuzhongde zhishi jushi [Causative constructions in Modern Chinese]*. Hefei: Anhui University Press.

Xu, Dan. 2003. *Shi* ziju de yanbian, jiantan *shi* de yufahua [The grammaticalization of *shi*-construction and the evolution of *shi*]. In Wu (ed.). *Yufahua yu Yufa Tansuo*. Beijing: The Commercial Press.

Yang, Jiangfeng. 2016. *Hanyu Yuhui Zhishi Jiegou de Duoweidu Yanjiu* [A Multi-Dimensional Study of Periphrastic Causative Construction in Mandarin Chinese]. Doctoral dissertation, Zhejiang University.

Zhang, Lili. 2005. Cong shiyi dao zhishi [From order to causation]. *Taida Wenshi Zhexue Bao*: 119–152.

Zhang, Weiwei, Dirk Speelman & Dirk Geeraerts. 2011. Variation in the (non) metonymic capital names in Mainland Chinese and Taiwan Chinese. *Metaphor and the Social World* 1(1). 90–112.

Zhou, Hong. 2004. *Xiandaihanyu Zhishi Fanchou Yanjiu* [Research of Causative Category in Modern Chinese]. Shanghai: East China Normal University PhD dissertation.

Molly Xie Pan
Personification metaphors in Chinese video ads: Insights from data analytics

1 Introduction

Advertising is crucial to successful brand communication that is associated with positive brand equity, i.e. the high economic value (Aaker and Biel 2013). Expanding brand equity requires building positive brand images and vivid brand personalities to shape a brand (Aaker 1997; Roy et al. 2016; Singh 2013; Sung and Kim 2010). Brand personality refers to "the set of human characteristics associated with a brand"(Aaker 1997: 347) and contributes to establishing the uniqueness of a brand. Research on consumer behaviour showed that not all human personality traits are appropriate to be attributed to brands (Aaker 1997; Caprara et al. 2001). The framework of brand personality proposed by Aaker (1997) had five dimensions, i.e. sincerity, excitement, competence, sophistication, and ruggedness. The practical issue for marketers then turned out to be how to use words and images to effectively deliver and reinforce the most distinct and competitive traits of a brand (Caprara et al. 2001). Several studies have demonstrated that metaphor in texts and images contributed to communicating the intangible brand personality and exerted a positive influence on brand perceptions (Ang and Lim 2006; Delbaere et al. 2011; Koller 2009).

Metaphor in advertising is ubiquitous, stimulating, and encouraging (Jeong 2008; Kim et al. 2012; McQuarrie and Mick 1996, 2003; Mulken et al. 2010; Pérez-Sobrino et al. 2019). It refers to comparisons between two different objects, providing a better picture of one by depicting deviation from expectations, according to the literature in marketing research (Jeong 2008; Kim et al. 2012; McQuarrie and Mick 1996, 1999). Inspirations from Cognitive Linguistics refined the definition of metaphor as a conceptual mechanism that allows the audience to "understand and experience one thing in terms of another" (Lakoff and Johnson 1980: 5). When communicating the intangible human characteristics by inviting viewers to understand and experience the product/brand in terms of a human-related concept, a personification metaphor is created (Delbaere et al. 2011).

Molly Xie Pan, College of Foreign Languages and Literature, Fudan University, e-mail: mollyxiaoxie@foxmail.com

https://doi.org/10.1515/9783110687279-007

An example can be found in Figure 6.1, which is an ad for the brand Hortfruti in Brazil. The metaphor CLEMENTINE IS AN ORGAN DONOR can be derived from the interaction between visuals and verbal language. The signpost shows that the personified clementine is walking to organ donation. The text at the right corner shows that "only the good one gets in". The product, as shown in this ad, engaged in the human behaviour of donation. This metaphor may transfer some positive human characteristics such as kindness and selflessness to the product, i.e. clementine. Since this metaphor could be a multimodal manifestation of the Conceptual Metaphor FOOD ARE PEOPLE, viewers might be willing to be a kind and selfless person as the personified clementine. However, the mapping from the organ donor cannot be fully inferred without considering the background of this brand, which is Brazil's number one premium retailer of healthy foods. This ad appears to impart the message that the selection of fruits is as strict as that in organ donation, implying that the company values healthy fruits.

Figure 6.1: The Ad for Hortfruti, Text: Only the good one gets in, Retrieved from http://www.vismet.org/VisMet/display.php.

According to Delbaere et al. (2011), using the personification metaphor could be a tacit way of triggering anthropomorphism, which contributes to creating a brand/product liking. Anthropomorphism is the tendency "to imbue the real or imagined behaviour of nonhuman agents with humanlike characteristics, motivations, intentions, or emotions" (Epley et al. 2008: 864). It is common for people to anthropomorphise objects (Delbaere et al. 2011; Epley et al. 2008; Laksmidewi et al. 2017), such as personifying pets or seeing faces in the clouds. Empirical evidence (Laksmidewi et al. 2017) has demonstrated that ads with personification metaphors where the product engaged in human behaviour appeared to elicit more positive emotions and contribute to shaping positive brand personality and yield greater brand liking. Research from a cognitive linguistic perspective also demonstrated how the metaphor BRANDS ARE PEOPLE structured corporate brands by investigating corporate corpus, including illustrations, logos, and layout. However, the manifestations and characteristics of personification metaphors in video ads are underexplored to date.

Video ads enhance customers' experience through multi-sensory interaction of sight, sound, and motion, compared with print ads that are text-only or text-picture appeals (Appiah 2006). Information presented in multi-modal formats enables customers to perceive corporate brands in a more vivid communication mode. Since globalization increases audience worldwide, video ads have been ubiquitous and attracted increasing investments from marketers. For instance, according to a survey report from eMarketer (an organization providing information on the business for research), the investment on video ads has been embracing a compound annual growth rate of 12.8% from 2019 to 2023.[1] The expenditure on programmatic digital video ads in China is about RMB 41.95 billion ($6.34 billion) in 2019, accounting for 20.2% of programmatic display ad spend, which will be expected to rise to 56.5% by 2021.[2] Therefore, researching how personification metaphors are exploited in video ads bears important implications for effective brand communication in the current digital age.

Video ads provide metaphors with more chances to manifest themselves in any mode of communication, which allows personification metaphors to be exploited flexibly. For instance, in the ad for Express Mail Service by China Post, the packages are on seats of an aero plane and air hostesses are serving these packages as they are passengers. Specifically, a scene shows that the stewardess helps a package to fasten the seatbelt, as shown in Figure 6.2. The personification metaphor EMS PACKAGES ARE PASSENGERS is visually constructed by replacing real passengers as EMS packages. The EMS staff who are responsible for these packages are metaphorized as air hostesses who serve passengers. The metaphor EMS STAFF ARE AIR HOSTESSES can be derived from this scenario by considering the contextual information. The central claim of this ad is 全心,全速, 全球 [Translation: 'With heart and soul, a full-speed, and global service'].

In the ad for Hortfruiti, the target of the personification metaphor, clementine, belongs to the advertised product. This personification metaphor directly advertises the features of the product, which is good and healthy. However, EMS packages, the target of personification metaphor in this ad, are more likely to receive the service of the product, rather than being a part of the service.

---

[1] https://www.emarketer.com/content/digital-video-2019 .
[2] https://www.emarketer.com/content/china-programmatic-digital-display-ad-spending .

Figure 6.2: Screenshots from the Ad for EMS.[3]

This personification metaphor appears to work with the other non-personification metaphor to create a metaphorical scenario to engage viewers in imagining EMS service as the flight service, supporting the ad's central claim that the service of EMS is considerate, professional, and international.

This use of metaphors in video ads is labelled as *supporting metaphors*, according to Pan (2020), where the metaphor shows messages that are in alignment with the central claim of the ad to play a supporting role in directly advertising the product. The use of directly involving the product as its target and advertising its features in video ads is labelled as *features-highlighting metaphors*. This is similar to how the personification metaphor is used for advertising fruits of Hortfruiti. Another use of metaphor in video ads is to highlight the needs of the envisaged audience by creating a problematic or desirable metaphorical scenario where the product is introduced as the solution to a problem or the platform to achieve the desirable outcome (Pan 2020). *Needs-highlighting metaphors* normally do not involve the product as its target or source.

Since the systematic investigation on how personification metaphors are used in video ads is limited in the extant literature, it is unknown whether the types of products influence the uses of personification metaphors. Postulations have been made that metaphors might behave differently (Forceville 2008) and exert different effects when advertising different types of products (Ang and Lim 2006; Chang and Yen 2013). Research has found that for products with tangible attributes like toothpaste, metaphor enhanced perceptions of the dimensions of sophistication and excitement in brand personality perception, whereas metaphors weakened the perceptions of sincerity and competency perception for products with symbolic attributes like perfume (Ang and Lim 2006). It seemed that when the products are

---

3 https://v.youku.com/v_show/id_XNzc0NzgwNDky.html?spm=a2h0k.8191407.0.0&from=s1.8-1-1.2.

tangible and concrete, personification metaphors are more likely to be created by altering the visuals of the product. Nevertheless, it is an empirical question that how personification metaphors are exploited and worked in video ads when advertising different types of products. We may assume that personification metaphors are equally important for different types of products as the brand itself bears an intrinsically intangible nature, which requires personification metaphors to communicate brand personality as a crucial component in shaping a brand.

This chapter will report a corpus-driven study on the uses of personification metaphors in video ads for advertising different types of products. It aims at systematically exploring the characteristics of personification metaphors, including how personification metaphors are manifested within the dynamic multimodal discourse and how personification metaphors interact with other metaphors. Given the unstructured and underexplored nature of the metaphorical phenomena in the real-world video ads, this study adopts a data analytics approach first to gauge the overall picture of the associations between personification attributes (i.e. being personification or not), metaphor's uses, and product types. Then, it demonstrates how findings from data analytics guide further discourse analysis. I will introduce the method including corpus and coding schemes of metaphors, uses, and personification attributes in the next section, followed by findings and discussions. Research questions to be addressed are:
(1) Is there a statistically significant association among personification attributes, product types, and metaphor's uses?
(2) How do personification metaphors manifest and be exploited in Chinese video ads?

2 Methods

This study worked on a corpus of metaphorical Chinese video ads ($N = 66$), which was built as a part of a larger study where the original corpus was built by stratified random sampling. Here, I introduce how the original corpus was built, followed by coding schemes of metaphors, personification metaphors, metaphor's uses, and details of the analysis.

2.1 Corpus building

The original corpus consisted of 100 Chinese video ads collected by stratified random sampling. Ten strata were built considering product types and online platforms retrieving these ads. Product types included search products and experience products, which were distinguished by the tangibility of the major attributes of products under the realm of the Economics of Information (EOI) (Bloom 1989; Ford et al. 1990). Search products possess prominent attributes that are tangible and concrete, which can be manufactured with a given standard and be evaluated effectively prior to the act of purchasing (Bloom and Reve 1990; Jiménez and Mendoza 2013). Prototypical examples are pens, cups, and lamps. Attributes of experience products are predominantly intangible and abstract, which are difficult to be evaluated effectively before purchasing (Bloom and Reve 1990; Jiménez and Mendoza 2013), such as insurance services, haircuts, and travel services. Online platforms to retrieve video ads included five platforms supported by the BAT companies, i.e. Baidu, Alibaba, and Tencent, which have been expected to dominate the Chinese digital market from 2016 to 2021, according to the report from emarketer.[4] When collecting video ads, the keyword 广告 [Advertisements] was typed in the platforms and ads with the numbers generated by research randomizer[5] were selected. Repeated ads were excluded during the process. Table 6.1 displays an overview of the corpus.

Table 6.1: An overview of the original corpus.

Online Websites	Search Products	Experience Products	Total
Iqiyi	10	10	20
Tencent	10	10	20
Youku	10	10	20
Shuying	10	10	20
TVC	10	10	20
Total	50	50	100

---

[4] https://www.emarketer.com/Article/Chinarsquos-Digital-Video-Ad-Spending-Overtake-TV-by-2021/1016452.
[5] https://www.randomizer.org/.

2.2 Coding schemes

The identification of metaphors and their uses adopted a bottom-up approach which maximizes the diversity and accuracy of coding (Cameron and Maslen 2010; Deignan 2005), especially when it comes to a multimodal discourse where the meaning-making is dynamic and diverse. Inter-rater reliability examinations were carried out on identifying both metaphors and uses.

2.2.1 Identifying metaphors and personification metaphors

Metaphor identification in this study followed the six-step procedure of Creative Metaphor Identification Procedure (C-MIPVA) by Pan and Tay (2021). According to C-MIPVA, creative metaphors in video ads have dual traits. On the one hand, they could be multimodal manifestations of novel uses of conceptual resources within the dynamic processes where interactions of different modes make the metaphorical meanings; on the other hand, they are created to fulfil the ultimate goal of an ad which drives the design of metaphors. As products of goal-oriented design in mass communication, the assumption of relevance in Relevance Theory (Forceville 2014; Wilson and Sperber 2002) suggested that designers have made the most creative and relevant videos to their best knowledge. This procedure, therefore, focuses on metaphors at the discourse level and emphasizes the importance of native speakers' intuition when identifying the noticeable metaphorical phenomena.

Figure 6.3 shows the six-step procedure of C-MIPVA. The essence of the procedure is to identify pairs of concepts connected by five concrete filmic techniques and to further determine whether the connection of paired concepts creates metaphorical meanings within the context based on native speakers' intuition. The identification of concepts resorts to explicit cues in the video, which could be in any mode of communication. C-MIPVA followed Forceville (2008) which proposed a working category of modes for video ads, including visuals, written language, spoken language, non-verbal sound, and music. Following C-MIPVA, creative metaphors at the discourse level in video ads were presented in italic small capitals (Pan and Tay 2021).

As reported in Pan and Tay (2021), inter-rater reliability examinations were carried out on 20 video ads that were randomly selected from the corpus. Annotators were three metaphor analysts who were native speakers of Chinese and had researched metaphors for more than two years. The identification of metaphor went through a process of calibrating understanding of the coding scheme, independent coding of the 20 video ads, quantifying the degree of agreement,

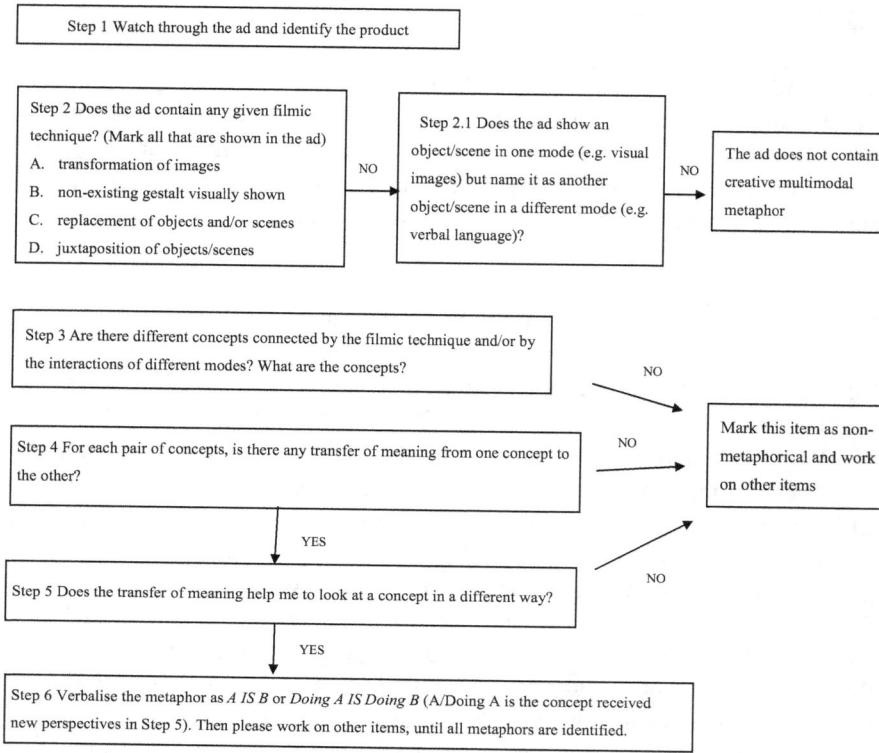

Figure 6.3: An overview of the six-step procedure in C-MIPVA (Pan and Tay 2021: 222).

and discussions to resolve the disagreement (Cameron and Maslen 2010; Pragglejaz Group 2007). The author then used the agreed criteria to code metaphors in the rest of the corpus. Results from Fleiss' Kappa provided statistical evidence for the reliable identification of metaphorical unit ($k = .78$) and results from percentage agreement showed strong support for the agreement on what the metaphor is (Percentage agreement = 80%).

This study proceeded further to identify personification metaphors from the metaphorical Chinese video ads corpus ($N = 66$). The author manually worked on the identification of personification metaphors by considering its definition that human-related attributes were transferred from the source to the non-human target. When coding a personification metaphor, the first step was to judge whether the source domain was human or metonymically linked to human. For instance, although the sources PATIENT, PARTNER, and MR.DI referred to specific identities, they all belong to the source domain of HUMAN and attributes of human were selectively transferred to the target. Apart from sources that specified the identities, concepts metonymically linked to humans were also considered. For instance, the source of HAND was also included as hand is a part of the human's body.

The second step is to judge whether the target was human or not. When the target was not human (e.g. WINTER), the metaphor was labelled as personification metaphor. For instance, the metaphor WINTER IS AN ENEMY attached the concept of *winter* with characteristics of an enemy, such as attacking our bodies. Viewers could derive human-related attributes from the non-human concept from this metaphor. This metaphor was, therefore, labelled as a personification metaphor. However, the metaphor EMS STAFF ARE AIR HOSTESSES was labelled as a non-personification metaphor because the target itself pointed to human. Metaphors with non-human sources were labelled as non-personification metaphors.

2.2.2 The coding scheme of metaphor's uses

All metaphors identified from the corpus (N = 197) were coded regarding the three uses (Pan 2020) derived from qualitative analyses of metaphorical ads in the corpus based on Relevance Theory (RT) (Forceville 2014; Wilson and Sperber 2002). The author worked with a doctoral student (a native speaker of Chinese) on 14 video ads, a random-selected sub-corpus of the metaphorical ads, including 65 creative metaphors which accounted for 36% proportion of the total metaphors. To maximize the inter-rater reliability, they went through a process of calibrating understanding of a coding scheme with examples, independent annotations, examining the degree of agreement, and discussing disagreed cases. Then the author used the agreed criteria to code the rest of the metaphors. Results from Cohen's Kappa provided statistical evidence for reliable coding (k = .74) (Cohen 1968). Table 6.2 shows the coding scheme for metaphor's uses.

Table 6.2: A coding scheme for metaphors' uses.

Steps	Descriptions
Step1	Watch the whole ad and get to know the context of each metaphor. For each metaphor,
Step 2	Judge whether the metaphor's target or source is the product. If yes, mark it as Features-Highlighting Metaphor. If no, go to step 3.

Table 6.2 (continued)

Steps	Descriptions
Step 3	Judge the relationship between the claim of this metaphor (conveyed by two terms and mapping) and the claim of the product. A. If the ad contains a central metaphor, consider whether this metaphor provides sub-mappings to support the metaphorical scenario lead by the Features-Highlighting Metaphor. B. If yes, mark it as Supporting Metaphor. If no, consider the following possibilities. C. The metaphor's claim is in alignment with the claim of the product. It provides more details of the product's traits. Mark it as Supporting Metaphor. D. The metaphor contributes to a problematic scenario, which needs a solution. The product can be a solution to the problem. Mark it as Needs-Highlighting Metaphor (D). E. The metaphor contributes to a beneficial scenario where the product can be a platform/motive to achieve the benefits. Mark it as Needs-Highlighting Metaphor (E). F. There is no clear relationship between the metaphor and the product. But the metaphor is eye-catching/entertaining/fancy. Mark it as Needs-Highlighting Metaphor (F).

2.3 Analysis

This study adopted a mixed-method approach where a set of data analytics was performed first to detect patterns of metaphors in the real-world corpus of ads and qualitative discourse analyses were followed up to zoom into specific cases informed by data analytics.

2.3.1 Data analytics

Unlike traditional statistical analysis which mainly tests hypotheses formed for controlled data, data analytics helps explore naturally occurred unstructured data and requires domain-specific knowledge to inform further actions. Since video advertising is an important marketing medium, analyzing metaphors in such a context requires knowledge about principles of mass communication, which underpins the design of metaphors and their characteristics. Considering the unstructured traits of metaphors in the naturally occurred multimodal discourse, data analytics serves an important role in exploring the large-scale corpus and deriving general patterns.

This study performed a set of data analytics, including Log-Linear Analysis, Multiple Correspondence Analysis (MCA), and Chi-Square Tests of Independence. Log-Linear Analysis examines to what extent the association between more than two categorical variables can be placed in a linear model (Christensen 1990; Tay 2018). It provides statistical evidence for how to fit a linear model can be when a set of categorical variables are included. In this study, Log-linear Analysis examined the overall associations between variables of personification, product types, and metaphor's uses with statistical results. MCA is helpful to visualize the associations between more than two categorical variables as geometrical distance and visualize the clusters formed by the individual case with an overview of how the individual case contributes to explaining the overall variance (Le Roux and Rouanet 2010; Tay 2020). The clusters generated by MCA in this study played an important role in guiding further discourse analyses of the characteristics of metaphors within the context. Chi-square Test of Independence generates statistical details of associations between two categorical variables. In this study, it provides statistical evidence for verifying postulations from discourse analyses and demonstrates the complementary strength provided by data analytics. These statistical tests were run by R,[6] free software for statistical computing. Codes were presented in the appendix.

2.3.2 Analytical framework

Qualitative analyses of this study were based on insights from research on multimodal metaphors (Forceville 2007, 2016; Forceville and Urios-Aparisi 2009) and Relevance Theory (Forceville 2014, 2020; Wilson and Sperber 2002). RT regards communication as a cognitive process that is grounded in a universal cognitive principle as human nature stemming from cognitive mechanisms (Wilson and Sperber 2002). It is, therefore, reasonable to apply RT into multimodal discourse (Abdel-Raheem 2017; Forceville 2014), although the majority of this framework has been developed from verbal language in face to face communication. Following the Cognitive Principle of Relevance (CPR), the interlocutors can automatically judge the degree of relevance of input by balancing the cognitive effect and processing effort. The information could be relevant to a person by "answering a question he had in mind, improving his knowledge on a certain topic, setting a doubt, confirming a suspicion, or correcting a mistaken impression" (Wilson and Sperber 2002: 3).

---

6 https://www.r-project.org/ .

When processing the information, the receivers tend to be attracted by more relevant information than other available information.

Several studies have demonstrated how RT can be applied as a systematic framework for analyzing multimodal discourse (Abdel-Raheem 2017, 2018; Braun 2016; Forceville 2014, 2020). While most of these studies analyzed static images, such as print ads, comics, and traffic signs, video advertising as a type of mass communication shares the common ground as other multimodal discourse in mass communication.

In the first place, video ads belong to the ostensive-inferential communication (Wilson 2003; Wilson and Sperber 2002), where both communicators and the audience are aware that the communicator has a purpose to be recognised when delivering a message. The audience derives the relevance by comprehending and inferring the message. When the information delivered by the message is recognized, the informative intention from the communicator is fulfiled. When the purpose of delivering such a message is recognized, the communicative intention from the communicator is fulfiled. In order to achieve these purposes, the communicators normally create the stimuli with optimal relevance. For instance, to achieve the best potential of advertising effect, designers will create a video ad with his/her best effort.

Secondly, the notions of *explicatures* and *implicatures* are appliable to video ads since the meaning delivered by the video itself meets the definition of 'explicatures' which can be unambiguously delivered through interactions of different modes, whereas the implicatures embrace diverse interpretations from the audience. Forceville (2014) emphasized that relevant input is always relevant to individuals in mass communication, i.e. individual difference plays an important role in deriving the explicatures and implicatures. Therefore, when viewing a video ad, viewers can regard the content of the ad as explicatures but the associated meanings derived from the video belong to implicatures. While individual differences might influence the focuses on certain explicatures, the assumption of optimal relevance generally ensures the salience of certain information that the designers intend to emphasize. In mass communication, the communicative intention is easy to fulfil (e.g. the viewer recognizes the video is an ad), whereas the informative intention might need the effort to be fully fulfiled (e.g. the viewer derives every detail in a video).

Case studies in this chapter adopted the analytical lens of RT to analyze metaphors in video ads based on the research of multimodal metaphors (Forceville 2014), where metaphors as a conceptual mechanism can manifest itself in any mode of communication, not just verbal language. The analytical lens of RT can be summarized as depicting explicatures, inferring implicatures by considering the relevance to an individual among the envisaged audience, the communicative and informative intention, and cognitive effect and processing effort.

3 Results and findings

This section reports statistical results and carried out case studies guided by findings from statistical results. It starts with the overall associations between PERSONIFICATION ATTRIBUTES, USES, and PRODUCT TYPES, followed by binary associations with ad examples.

3.1 An overview of associations

The associations between PERSONIFICATION ATTRIBUTES (PA), USES(U), and PRODUCT TYPES (PT) were first explored by Log-linear Analysis. Results showed a non-significant three-way interaction (p = .32), suggesting that a model with no three-factor interactions fits well. The likelihood ratio indicated a good fit of this model, X^2 (2) = 2.27, p = .32. The non-significant three-way interaction also suggested that if there are significant binary associations between any two variables, the associations do not change along the third variable (Tay 2018). Within the context, a lack of three-way interaction and two-way interaction between P and PT indicated that whether a metaphor is designed as a personification may not necessarily associate with how the metaphor is used for a specific type of product. In other words, there could be more general patterns of designing the dimension of personification for a certain use that are applicable to both types of products.

Although there is a non-significant three-way interaction, exploring the underlying structure of these three variables is important for having a general picture of the interplay among variables of multiple levels. MCA plots visualize the associations among variables as geometrical distance, describing the patterns through positioning each unit of analysis as a point in a low-dimensional space (Le Roux and Rouanet 2010). Cases with similar patterns in terms of the associations among variables normally cluster together.

Figure 6.4 illustrates the distribution of variables at the level of categories. In MCA, each dimension shows a linear combination of variables, and normally the first two dimensions represent the two dimensions that best capture the variance of the data (Caprara et al. 2001; Tay 2020). Figure 6.4 showed that the first dimension accounted for 32.6% of the variance and the second accounted for 27.1% of the variance, yielding a total variance of 59.7%. The angles from the origin and the closeness of variables in the same quadrant represent the geographic relations between these variables (Nenadic and Greenacre 2007). A far distance from the origin suggests a large deviation from the expected proportions. From Figure 6.4, we can observe that features-highlighting metaphors tend to occur in ads for search products; non-personification metaphors tend to be used for highlighting needs.

This map visualizes the degree of contribution through colours. The more contribution the variable makes, the warmer the colour is. The red colour indicates a large contribution to the variance. Here, the variable of personification metaphors contributes to most of the variance, implying that personification metaphors embrace more diversity in terms of associations with other variables. The map also showed that product types and some uses of metaphors were discriminating from other variables and made moderate contributions to explaining the variances. However, the supporting uses of metaphors made little contributions to the significant associations.

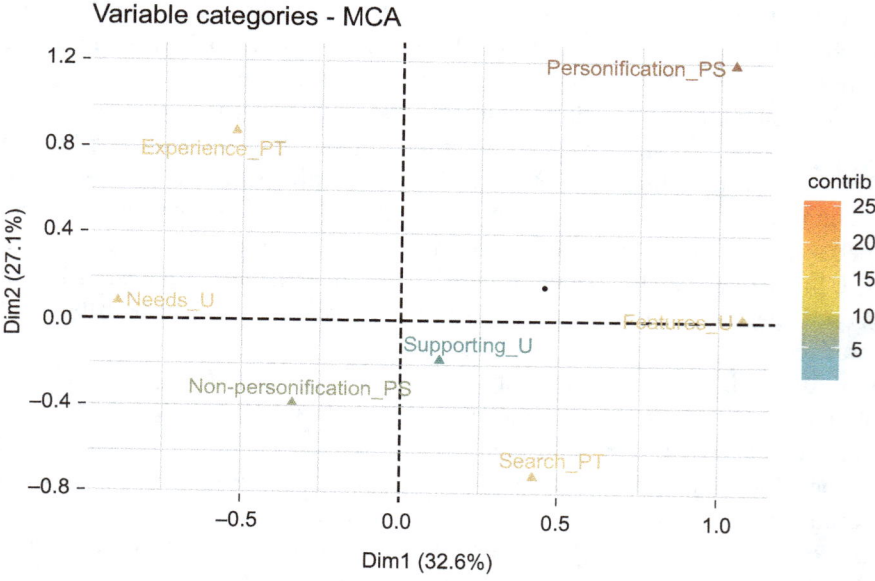

Figure 6.4: The MCA plot of associations between variable categories.

Plots from MCA can not only visualize the associations at the categorical level but also visualize how individual cases cluster as clouds and contribute to explaining the overall variances. Figure 6.5 presents how each analytical unit is grouped with units of similar patterns in terms of the underlying associations. This map is useful in guiding qualitative analyses within the context by makes tracking individual cases in the general picture feasible. However, to fully exploit the strengths of data analytics in the research trajectory, clusters shown in

Figure 6.5 can be interpreted together with the results of binary associations. I will present relevant ad examples after synergizing the statistical findings from Chi-square Tests of Independence and clusters shown in Figure 6.5.

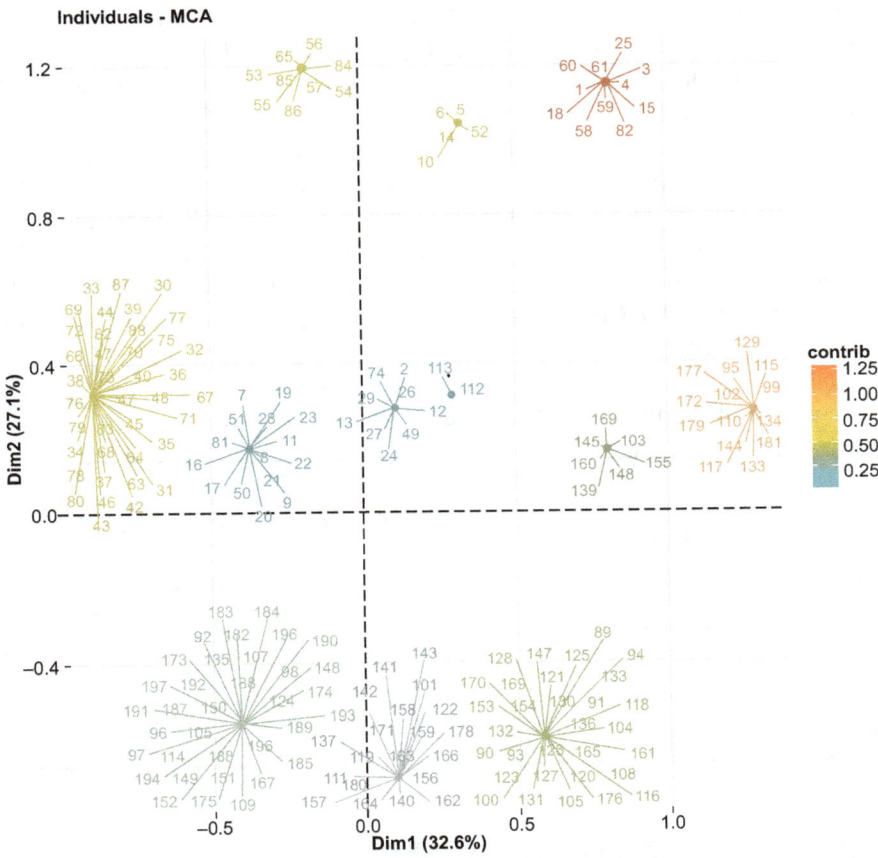

Figure 6.5: The MCA plot of associations among individuals.

3.2 The relationship between PRODUCT TYPE and PERSONIFICATION ATTRIBUTES

A Chi-Square Test of Independence was performed to compare the frequencies of personification metaphors and non-personification metaphors that occurred in ads for experience products and search products. Results showed a non-significant difference between PRODUCT TYPE and PERSONIFICATION, $X^2 = (1, N = 197) = 1.04$, $p = 0.31$, Cramer's $V = 0.07$. The effect size was very small (Cohen 1988). Table 6.3 shows that the adjusted residual did not reach a significant level (±1.9) (Tay 2018). The non-significant difference suggested that product types do not have a significant influence on using personification metaphors or not.

This adds to the interpretation of Figure 6.5 that although orange to red clusters on the top displayed that all personification metaphors were designed for experience products and only a few cases of personification metaphors (no. 103, 139, 145, and 146) in the brown cluster on the in the right quadrant were designed for search products, the difference for the preference of personification metaphors was not statistically significant. This is in line with the theoretical argument about the importance of using personification metaphors for brand building (Aaker 1997; Ang and Lim 2006), where either search products or experience products can benefit from exploiting personification metaphors to construct their brand personalities.

Table 6.3: PRODUCT TYPE and PERSONIFICATION ATTRIBUTES crosstabulation.

			PA		
			Personification	Non-personification	Total
PT	Experience	Count	25	63	88
		Adjusted Residual	1.19	−1.19	
	Search	Count	23	86	109
		Adjusted Residual	−1.19	1.19	
Total		Count	48	149	197

3.3 The relationship between USES and PERSONIFICATION ATTRIBUTES

A Chi-Square Test of Independence was carried out to examine the relationship between USES and PERSONIFICATION. Results revealed a significant association between the two variables, $X^2 = (1, N = 197) = 13.06$, $p = 0.001$, Cramer's $V = 0.26$. The effect size was a small to medium one (Cohen 1988), indicating that the personification attributes of a metaphor have a small to medium correlation with its use.

Table 6.4 showed the specific information about the distribution of frequencies. Darker cells indicated an over-expected occurrence of frequencies, whereas lighter cells showed that the frequencies were significantly less than expected. From Table 6.4, we can observe that personification metaphors had a tendency to be associated with features-highlighting metaphors, whereas non-personification metaphors tended to be associated with needs-highlighting metaphors. Supporting metaphors did not show a preference for the attributes of personification. These trends are consistent with findings from MCA, as displayed in Figure 6.5 that the variable of the supporting use was around the origin, whereas the uses of features-highlighting and needs-highlighting were discriminated from the centre.

Table 6.4: USES and PERSONIFICATION ATTRIBUTES crosstabulation.

			PA		Total
			Personification	Non-personification	
U	Features-H	Count	25	40	65
		Adjusted Residual	3.2	−3.2	
	Supporting	Count	12	35	47
		Adjusted Residual	.2	−.2	
	Needs-H	Count	11	74	85
		Adjusted Residual	−3.3	−3.3	
Total		Count	49	148	197

The significant pairs generated by the Chi-Square test are helpful in guiding us to locate relevant cases when investigating clusters in Figure 6.5. For instance, the red cluster on the top showed several cases with personification metaphors. By referring to the corpus, we found that three cases (no. 59, 60, 61) were features-highlighting metaphors from the ad *DiDiChuXing*. The brown cluster on the left of the map showed many cases of non-personification metaphors highlighting the needs of consumers. Then, we can zoom in to a specific ad and analyze these metaphors within the original context.

In the ad for the APP *DiDiChuXing (DiDi)*, a leading mobile transportation platform in China, the product is metaphorized as a young handsome gentleman called Mr.*Di*. The verbal language in spoken and written forms introduces Mr. *Di* as a good friend of the female narrator. The use of pronoun the *you* also directs viewers' attention to a person. The visuals shows a gentleman along with the story. The general audience could capture these explicatures regardless of having knowledge of the platform or not. In the second part of the ad, several juxtapositions of scenes with Mr. Di and the real scenes of using *DiDi* construct metaphors DIDICHUXING IS MR. DI (no. 59, 60, and 61), as shown in Figure 6.6. The compliments of Mr. Di with accompanying visuals illustrate the comprehensive and helpful functions of the product *DiDiChuXing*. The construction of *DiDiChuXing* as a professional gentleman who used to help the female narrator also imparts the implicatures that the service is of high safety for the female. Viewers who have the same needs during travelling, such as picking up service, transportation by the taxi, and recommendations of hotels and restaurants, especially female travellers might find this ad relevant to them.

Figure 6.6: Screenshots from *DiDiChuXing*.[7]

While several ads are involved in the brown cluster on the left of the map, here I show one example of how non-personification metaphors can be used for highlighting the needs of consumers. Four cases (no. 76–79) are from the ad for *MiGuShanPao*, a fitness app in China. This ad shows several scenarios of running and fitness training, where metaphors are constructed through interactions of spoken and written language with visuals. There is no visual incongruity created in this ad. The scenario of exercising creates a metaphor that EXERCISING IS BURNING where the concept of EXERCISING is cued by visuals and the concept of BURNING is communicated through spoken and written language. The scenario of an exercising person is commented as a growing seed, as shown in Figure 6.7, creating a metaphor of A PERSON IS A SEED. Similarly, legs are verbally commented

---

7 https://www.digitaling.com/projects/18842.html.

as motors and the punchline encourages the audience to be a fighter by showing visuals of a runner, constructing metaphors of LEGS ARE MOTORS and A RUNNER IS A FIGHTER.

Figure 6.7: Screenshots from the Ad for *MiGuShanPao*,[8]
Text: 一粒破土的种子 [Translation: 'A growing seed'].

The construction of these metaphors are explicatures that can be recognized with concrete cues. The first three metaphors have non-human related concepts as source domains. Although the source domain of the last metaphor is FIGHTER, the source is also a person-related concept. Therefore, all of these metaphors are non-personification metaphors. The target audience of this app could be young people, as implied by models appeared in the ad. All of these metaphors seem to impart the implicatures that the goals of exercising, such as burning calories and growing strongly, can be achieved with the accompany of this APP. The scenarios of exercising are invited to be imagined as other scenarios, such as burning, growing, moving, and fighting, which might be more dynamic and exciting than the actual processes. The delineated dynamic and exciting processes might be desirable for the target audience who need the motivation to keep doing exercise which could be tiring and demanding. By engaging viewers in the desirable scenarios, these metaphors highlight consumers' needs.

---

8 https://www.digitaling.com/projects/23692.html .

3.4 The relationship between PRODUCT TYPE and USES

A Chi-Square Test of Independence found a statistically significant association between PRODUCT TYPE and USES, $X^2 = (2, N = 197) = 9.96$, $p = 0.006$, Cramer's $V = 0.22$. The effect size was medium (Cohen 1988), suggesting that the uses of metaphors changed along the types of products. Table 6.5 illustrated the frequencies of variables, showing that needs-highlighting metaphors tended to be associated with experience products, whereas features-highlighting metaphors tended to be associated with search products. There was no strong tendency for supporting metaphors.

Table 6.5: PRODUCT TYPE and USES crosstabulation.

			U			
			Features-H	Supporting	Needs-H	Total
PT	Experience	Count	20	20	48	88
		Adjusted Residual	−2.8	−.3	2.9	
	Search	Count	45	27	37	109
		Adjusted Residual	2.8	.3	−2.9	
Total		Count	65	47	85	197

In Figure 6.5, on the left of dimension one, the orange cluster on the top and the brown cluster above dimension two showed groups of needs-highlighting metaphors designed for experience products. A close investigation of them within the original context revealed that the orange cluster showed cases of personification metaphors, whereas the brown cluster showed cases of non-personification metaphors. Since we have discussed an example of how non-personification metaphors highlight the needs of consumers in ad for the experience product *MiGuShanPao* (see section 3.5), here I show an example of how personification metaphors for experience products can highlight the needs of consumers.

Metaphors (no. 54 to 57) in the orange cluster are from the ad for *TMALL*, a leading online shopping platform in China. These metaphors are personification metaphors, metaphorizing products as partners. The major claim of this ad is 大胆爱新欢[Translation: 'Be brave to new love']. This ad shows breakup moments of five stories where metaphors are created by replacing the assumed scenes of human partners with scenes of used products, including a phone, cosmetics, pyjamas, baby clothes, and a pair of high heels. The interaction of spoken language and visuals create metaphors of A PHONE IS A PARTNER, A COLLECTION OF COSMETICS IS A PARTNER, PYJAMAS IS A PARTNER, BABY CLOTHES IS THE GIRLFRIEND OF ONE'S SON, and A PAIR OF HIGH HEELS IS A PARTNER. All of these metaphors are warranted with concrete and explicit cues in the ad and could be perceived without ambiguity by the general audience.

Figure 6.8 shows the example of A COLLECTION OF COSMETICS IS A PARTNER. The mappings from the sources to the target overall highlight the intimate relationship between products and consumers. Every story first shows breakup moments, engaging the audience in a gloomy mood. Then, the replacement of anticipated human partners might bring in surprise and the vibrant background music might add a sense of humour to the overall effect, making these metaphors impressive and thought-provoking. These personification metaphors seem to motivate consumers to look for new products by emphasizing the rationale of leaving a broken relationship. The envisaged audience might be motivated to browse the shopping platform if they find relevance in this ad.

Figure 6.8: Screenshots from TMALL,⁹ Spoken language:我早就不喜欢你了 [Translation: 'I dislike you for a long time'].

The two brown clusters on the right of dimension one showed many cases of features-highlighting metaphors designed for search products. Here, I show an example of how personification metaphors and non-personification metaphors worked together to highlight different aspects of a search product. In the big brown cluster below dimension two, several metaphors (no. 126, 127, 128, 130, 131,132, and 133) were from the ad Tommee Tippee's Feeding Bottle and were

---

9 https://www.tvcbook.com/showVideo.html?vid=939242&code=55f4TGaIdjzLa9TPSRS4bjL4o hi3uIA93I3BKpgqakDk9Ydv0hQR .

used for highlighting features of the product. This ad exploits the spoken language with the tone of the first person to construct the product (shown in visuals) as a person. For example, 我就是来自英国的 *Tommee Tippee* [Translation: 'I'm Tommee Tippee from the UK'], as shown in Figure 6.9. Then the ad introduces the multiple functions of the product by metaphorizing it as Big Ben, bridge piers, a sceptre, the underground, a guard, bus, Ferris wheel, rock music and a building. The filmic technique of juxtaposition is exploited to visually combine the product with these concepts and the written and spoken language point out mappings from the source to the target. For example, in the metaphor THE FEEDING BOTTLE IS A BUS, the spoken language explains that the product has the timing function when making milk formula, which is as punctual as the scheduled buses. These metaphors are created by interactions of visuals and verbal language, which can be perceived by general viewers. The personification metaphor which metaphorizes the product as a person seems to play the role of directing viewers' attention to the brand, which is exotic and reputable. Other metaphors overall highlight different aspects of the product, especially its functions.

Figure 6.9: Screenshots from Tommee Tippee,[10]
Text: 我就是来自英国的 *Tommee Tippee* [Translation: 'I'm Tommee Tippee from the UK'].

---

[10] http://www.tvcbook.com/showVideo.html?vid=70386&code=3af5MKotjdgM4uoyPB4z_qESdgZGArMK4axYhYkgjeqhoA .

4 Conclusion

Investigating the manifestation and characteristics of personification metaphors in ads contributes to successful brand communication as it is a metaphor that enables marketers to deliver the brand personality to the envisaged audience (Aaker 1997; Ang and Lim 2006; Koller 2009). This chapter has demonstrated how to synergize data analytics with discourse analysis through exploring personification metaphors in a corpus of Chinese video ads. A data analytics approach was adopted first to systematically exploring the unstructured and underexplored metaphorical phenomena in video ads. Insights from a set of data analytics benefit the discourse analysis of metaphors within the original context of video ads by generating significant associations and pointing out intriguing cases to follow up.

To summarize, we found a non-significant association between personification attributes and product types, suggesting that personification metaphors are exploited with an equal chance for different types of products. This finding highlighted the necessity of personification metaphor in advertising, as brand personality communication could be important regardless of product types. A statistically significant association was found between uses of metaphors and personification attributes, where the personification metaphors were more likely to be associated with the use of highlighting features of products but non-personification metaphors tended to be associated with the use of highlighting needs of consumers. This finding implied the important role of personification metaphors in advertising the attributes of products that human-related concepts might be exploited more frequently when marketers tried to directly advertise the features of their products. The association between product types and uses of metaphors was also statistically significant. Specifically, features-highlighting metaphors tended to occur in ads for search products, whereas needs-highlighting metaphors tended to occur in ads for experience products. This finding showed that the uses of metaphors varied across product types.

Discourse analysis on cases suggested by statistical results revealed that personification metaphors in video ads exploited multi-sensory modes to deliver meaning and to interact with non-personification metaphors, convergently advertising the product and the brand. The communication of brand personality, therefore, might be unlikely restricted with personification metaphors. Given the abundant opportunities to create metaphors with multiple source domains, non-personification metaphors with high frequency in the corpus may also be able to successfully communicate brand personality to the target audience. While personification metaphors are important and necessary to brand personality communication, video ads have fertile resources for marketers to exploit and create diverse metaphorical phenomena to enhance brand communication.

This chapter bears both theoretical and methodological contributions to cognitive linguistics. On the one hand, the underexplored issues of personification metaphor in video ads have been investigated systematically within the realm of Cognitive Linguistics; on the other hand, the synergy of a data analytics approach and discourse analysis has been demonstrated with substantial examples. Limitations of this corpus-driven study included a limited classification of product types and limited diversity of the corpus. Future studies can expand the list of product types and include non-Chinese video ads as culture differences might play a role in influencing the manifestation and uses of metaphors in advertising.

Appendix: Programming codes in R

```
library(readxl)
#Bring in data
p <- read_excel("p.xlsx")
View(p)

#Codes for Log-Linear Analysis
#Make a contingency table
pa = table (p$`Product Types`, p$Personification,p$Uses)
#Model of three variables
ln <-loglin(pa, list(c(1,2),c(1,3),c(2,3)))
ln
#Significance of three-way interaction
1-pchisq(ln$lrt,ln$df)

#Codes for Chi-Square Test of Independence
install.packages("lsr")
library(gmodels)
library(lsr)
#Make a contingency table of two variables
pb = table (p$Personification, p$Uses)
#chi-square test of independence
chisq.test(pb)
#effect size
cramersV(pb)
#View the adjusted residuals
CrossTable(p$Personification,p$Uses, asresid = TRUE, format = "SPSS")
```

```
#Codes for MCA
install.packages(c("FactoMineR", "factoextra"))
library("FactoMineR")
library("factoextra")
res.mca <- MCA(p, graph = FALSE)
print(res.mca)
get_eigenvalue(res.mca)
fviz_mca_var(res.mca, col.var = "contrib",
             gradient.cols = c("#00AFBB", "#E7B800", "#FC4E07"),
             repel = TRUE, # avoid text overlapping (slow)
             ggtheme = theme_minimal())
fviz_mca_ind(res.mca, col.ind = "contrib",
             gradient.cols = c("#00AFBB", "#E7B800", "#FC4E07"),
             repel = TRUE, # Avoid text overlapping (slow if many points)
             ggtheme = theme_minimal())
```

References

Aaker, A. David & Alexander L. Biel. 2013. *Brand equity & advertising: Advertising's role in building strong brands*. Psychology Press.

Aaker, Jennifer L. 1997. Dimensions of brand personality. *Journal of Marketing Research* 34(3). 347–356.

Abdel-Raheem, Ahmed. 2017. Decoding images: Toward a theory of pictorial framing. *Discourse & Society* 28(4). 327–352.

Abdel-Raheem, Ahmed. 2018. Multimodal humour: Integrating blending model, relevance theory, and incongruity theory. *Multimodal Communication* 7(1). 1–19.

Ang, Swee Hoon & Elison Ai Ching Lim. 2006. The influence of metaphors and product type on brand personality perceptions and attitudes. *Journal of Advertising* 35(2). 39–53.

Appiah, Osei. 2006. Rich Media, poor Media: The Impact of audio/video vs. text/picture testimonial ads on browsers' evaluations of commercial web sites and online products. *Journal of Current Issues & Research in Advertising* 28(1). 73–86.

Bloom, Paul N. 1989. A decision model for prioritizing and addressing consumer information problems. *Journal of Public Policy & Marketing* 8(1). 161–180.

Bloom, Paul N & Torger Reve. 1990. Transmitting signals to consumers for competitive advantage. *Business Horizons* 33(4). 58–66.

Braun, Sabine. 2016. The importance of being relevant?: A cognitive-pragmatic framework for conceptualising audiovisual translation. *Target. International Journal of Translation Studies* 28(2). 302–313.

Cameron, Lynne & Robert Maslen. 2010. Identifying metaphors in discourse data. In Lynne Cameron & Robert Maslen (eds.), *Metaphor analysis: Research practice in applied linguistics, social sciences and the humanities*, 97–115. London: Equinox.

Caprara, Gian Vittorio, Claudio Barbaranelli & Gianluigi Guido. 2001. Brand personality: How to make the metaphor fit? *Journal of Economic Psychology* 22(3). 377–395.

Chang, Chun-Tuan & Ching-Ting Yen. 2013. Missing ingredients in metaphor advertising: The right formula of metaphor type, product type, and need for cognition. *Journal of Advertising* 42(1). 80–94.

Christensen, Ronald. 1990. *Log-linear Models.* New York: Springer.

Cohen, Jacob. 1968. Weighted kappa: Nominal scale agreement provision for scaled disagreement or partial credit. *Psychological Bulletin* 70(4). 213.

Cohen, Jacob. 1988. *Statistical power analysis for the behavioural sciences* 2nd edn. Hillsdale, NJ: Erlbaum.

Deignan, Alice. 2005. *Metaphor and corpus linguistics.* Amsterdam and Philadelphia: John Benjamins Publishing.

Delbaere, Marjorie, Edward F McQuarrie & Barbara J Phillips. 2011. Personification in advertising. *Journal of Advertising* 40(1). 121–130.

Epley, Nicholas, Adam Waytz, Scott Akalis & John T Cacioppo. 2008. When we need a human: Motivational determinants of anthropomorphism. *Social Cognition* 26(2). 143–155.

Forceville, Charles. 2007. Multimodal metaphor in ten Dutch TV commercials. *Public Journal of Semiotics* 1(1). 15–34.

Forceville, Charles. 2008. Pictorial and multimodal metaphor in commercials. In Edward F. McQuarrie & Barbara J. Phillips (eds.), *Go figure! New directions in advertising rhetoric*, 178–204. New York/London: ME Sharpe.

Forceville, Charles. 2014. Relevance Theory as model for analysing visual and multimodal communication. *Visual Communication* 4. 51.

Forceville, Charles. 2016. Pictorial and Multimodal Metaphor. In M Klug & H Stöckl (eds.), *Handbuch Sprache im multimodalen Kontext [The Language in Multimodal Contexts Handbook].* 241–261. Berlin: Mouton de Gruyter.

Forceville, Charles. 2020. *Visual and multimodal communication: Applying the relevance principle* New York: Oxford University Press.

Forceville, Charles & Eduardo Urios-Aparisi (eds.). 2009. *Multimodal Metaphor.* Berlin and New York: Walter de Gruyter.

Ford, Gary T, Darlene B Smith & John L Swasy. 1990. Consumer skepticism of advertising claims: Testing hypotheses from economics of information. *Journal of Consumer Research* 16(4). 433–441.

Jeong, Se-Hoon. 2008. Visual metaphor in advertising: Is the persuasive effect attributable to visual argumentation or metaphorical rhetoric? *Journal of Marketing Communications* 14(1). 59–73.

Jiménez, Fernando R & Norma A Mendoza. 2013. Too popular to ignore: The influence of online reviews on purchase intentions of search and experience products. *Journal of Interactive Marketing* 27(3). 226–235.

Kim, Jooyoung, Youngshim Baek & Yang Ho Choi. 2012. The structural effects of metaphor-elicited cognitive and affective elaboration levels on attitude toward the ad. *Journal of Advertising* 41(2). 77–96.

Koller, Veronika. 2009. Brand images: Multimodal metaphor in corporate branding messages. *Multimodal Metaphor* 11. 45–72.

Lakoff, George & Mark Johnson. 1980. *Metaphors we live by.* Chicago: Chicago University Press.

Laksmidewi, Dwinita, Harry Susianto & Adi Zakaria Afiff. 2017. Anthropomorphism in advertising: The effect of anthropomorphic product demonstration on consumer purchase intention. *Asian Academy of Management Journal 22*(1). 1.

Le Roux, Brigitte & Henry Rouanet. 2010. *Multiple correspondence analysis*. Thousand Oaks: Sage.

McQuarrie, Edward F & David Glen Mick. 1996. Figures of rhetoric in advertising language. *Journal of Consumer Research 22*(4). 424–438.

McQuarrie, Edward F & David Glen Mick. 1999. Visual rhetoric in advertising: Text-interpretive, experimental, and reader-response analyses. *Journal of Consumer Research 26*(1). 37–54.

McQuarrie, Edward F & David Glen Mick. 2003. The contribution of semiotic and rhetorical perspectives to the explanation of visual persuasion in advertising. In Linda M. Scott & Rajeev Batra (eds.), *Persuasive imagery: A consumer response perspective*, 191–221. Mahwah, NJ: Lawrence Erlbaum Associates.

Mulken, Van Margot, Le Rob Pair & Charles Forceville. 2010. The impact of perceived complexity, deviation and comprehension on the appreciation of visual metaphor in advertising across three European countries. *Journal of Pragmatics 42*(12). 3418–3430.

Nenadic, Oleg & Michael Greenacre. 2007. Correspondence analysis in R, with two- and three-dimensional graphics: The capackage. *Journal of Statistical Software* (20). 1–13.

Pan, Xie. 2020. *Exploring creative metaphors in video ads: Manifestation, uses, and effectiveness*. Hong Kong SAR: The Hong Kong Polytechnic University PhD thesis.

Pan, Xie & Dennis Tay. 2021. Identifying creative metaphors in video ads In Ling. Lin, Isaac.N. Mwinlaaru & Dennis Tay (eds.), *Approaches to specialized genres: In memory of Stephen Evans* 216–240. Routledge.

Pérez-Sobrino, Paula, Jeannette Littlemore & David Houghton. 2019. The role of figurative complexity in the comprehension and appreciation of advertisements. *Applied Linguistics 40*(6). 957–991.

Pragglejaz Group. 2007. MIP: A method for identifying metaphorically-used words in discourse. *Metaphor and Symbol 22*(1). 1–40.

Roy, Pinaki, Kapil Khandeparkar & Manoj Motiani. 2016. A lovable personality: The effect of brand personality on brand love. *Journal of Brand Management 23*(5). 97–113.

Singh, Dipinder. 2013. The brand personality component of brand goodwill: Some antecedents and consequences. *Brand Equity & Advertising: Advertising's Role in Building Strong Brands* 83.

Sung, Yongjun & Jooyoung Kim. 2010. Effects of brand personality on brand trust and brand affect. *Psychology & Marketing 27*(7). 639–661.

Tay, Dennis. 2018. Metaphors of movement in psychotherapy talk. *Journal of Pragmatics 125*. 1–12.

Tay, Dennis. 2020. Co-constructing crisis with metaphor: A quantitative approach to metaphor use in psychotherapy talk. In Mimi Huang & Lise-lotte Holmgreen (eds.), *The language of Crisis: Metaphors, frames, and discourse* 231–255. Amsterdam: John Benjamins.

Wilson, Deirdre. 2003. Relevance and lexical pragmatics. *Italian Journal of Linguistics 15*. 273–292.

Wilson, Deirdre & Dan Sperber. 2002. Relevance theory. In Gregory. Ward & Laurence. Hon (eds.), *Handbook of Pragmatics*, 607–632. Oxford: Blackwell.

Han Qiu, Dennis Tay
The interaction between metaphor use and psychological states: A mix-method analysis of trauma talk in the Chinese context

1 Introduction

Psychological trauma is the experience of overwhelming negative emotional feelings as a result of an extremely distressing event, for example, car accidents, sexual harassment, and natural disasters. Typical post-traumatic feelings include anxiety, depression, anger, confusion, and so on. Trauma-related mental disorders, such as Acute Stress Disorder (ASD) and Post-traumatic Stress Disorder (PTSD), could cause clinical symptoms such as disturbing thoughts, feelings, dreams, mental and physical distress, and induce alterations in how a person thinks and feels (American Psychiatric Association 2013). The symptoms could last from 2 days to 4 weeks in the case of ASD and even longer for PTSD (American Psychiatric Association 2013).

Although issues related to psychological trauma are most often discussed in the context of psychology, trauma victims' language use, as an important source of information for clinical diagnosis and treatment, also attracted the attention of linguistic researchers. A particularly interesting aspect of trauma language is the use of metaphors, a linguistic act of talking and potentially thinking about something in terms of something else (Semino 2008). Metaphors are widely noticed in the description of complex emotional feelings and thought processes (Lakoff and Johnson 1980, 1999; Cameron 2007; Cameron and Maslen 2010; Kövecses 2010). According to Failsilber and Ortony (1987), metaphors occur at a higher rate in the expression of emotions than they do in the description of behaviors; as the intensity of emotion grows, the frequency of feeling metaphors increases

---

Acknowledgment: We are grateful to all our participants, who made this study possible despite their struggles. We would also like to thank Mr. Yulin Wang for his help in the interrater reliability tests, and the reviewer for the valuable comments.

Han Qiu, Department of English and Communication, The Hong Kong Polytechnic University, e-mail: amy-han.qiu@connect.polyu.hk
Dennis Tay, Department of English and Communication, The Hong Kong Polytechnic University, e-mail: dennis.tay@polyu.edu.hk

https://doi.org/10.1515/9783110687279-008

correspondingly. Experimental evidence has further shown that metaphors could be more affectively engaging than their literal counterparts (Citron and Goldberg 2014; Citron et al. 2019; Tay 2020). Since traumatic events are often beyond ordinary experience and sometimes ineffable, it is natural for trauma victims to use metaphors for more effective communication. For example, people who had experienced a fatal accident sometimes describe themselves as being "paralyzed" with fear and "forever sealed up" in the container of traumatic memories. Such expressions translate elusive and inexpressible emotions into tangible entities and experiences and reduce the difficulty for the hearer to access the speaker's experiential world. The way they are worded is intimately connected with the speaker's physical experiences, cognitive inclinations, and the surrounding socio-cultural context. Therefore, by examining systematic patterns of metaphors at the discourse level, researchers could also catch a glimpse of how people feel, think, and reason about the world (Cameron 2010).

The study of trauma metaphors carries both theoretical and practical implications. Firstly, studying metaphors in the context of trauma could shed new theoretical light on the contextualized nature of metaphor use. Previous research suggests that the experience of trauma encompasses several dimensions of individual life, for example, the nature of the traumatic event, emotions and evaluative judgments, socio-cultural knowledge, and personal experience (Ehlers and Clark 2000). This provides a valuable opportunity to investigate the dynamic interaction between metaphor use and relevant contextual factors. Secondly, we could use metaphor analysis as a reliable research tool to explore how people experience and make meaning of their traumatic experiences. The findings could serve as a ready handle for the clinical treatment of trauma (Witztum, van der Hart, and Friedman 1988; Wilson and Lindy 2013) and the application of metaphor-based therapeutic protocols (e.g., Kopp and Craw 1998; Sims 2003; Blenkiron 2005; Friedberg and Wilt 2010; Stott et al. 2010).

Previous research on trauma metaphors mostly followed the qualitative approach. Focusing on metaphor use by different trauma populations, such as victims of sexual abuse, veterans, and survivors of earthquakes, the studies provided valuable insights into the qualitative interactions between vehicle terms and topics of metaphors, and the interplay between trauma metaphors and contextual factors such as bodily experience, stages of recovery, and socio-cultural background (e.g., Tay 2014; Tay and Jordan 2015; Costa and Steen 2014; Foley 2015; Meili 2018; Rechsteiner et al. 2020; Littlemore and Turner 2020). Their findings revealed many nuanced characteristics of trauma metaphors, which not only inspired the theoretical investigation of contextualized metaphors but also foregrounded various contextual factors that are often neglected in psychological research. However, the study of qualitative characteristics may not always fulfill our need to detect general patterns of metaphor use. Acknowledging the strengths of qualitative analysis, another strand of research on contextualized metaphors pointed toward the complementary value of mixed-method analysis in exploring more schematic patterns of metaphors. For example, Moser (2007) combined configuration frequency analysis and content analysis to explore the distribution of self-related metaphors among six theoretical aspects of self-concepts. While the use of quantitative methods allows us to capture overall tendencies of metaphor use, qualitative analysis of single cases enables a more precise understanding of the patterns' situational, biographical, and social properties (Moser 2000). Combining log-linear analysis and discourse analysis, Tay (2017) examined how metaphors in psychotherapy interact with contextual factors such as therapeutic roles, topics, and time. The study illustrated how a discourse analytic perspective on quantitative metaphor usage patterns could generate theoretical and clinical insights that are invisible to purely qualitative analysis. As existing research on trauma metaphors mainly focused on the qualitative dimension, it would be interesting to explore how the application of statistical methods could bring a deeper understanding of trauma metaphors and open up prospects for future diagnostic and clinical research.

Another avenue of research lies in the interaction between metaphor use and the speaker's mental condition. Given that metaphors bear special relevance to emotion expression and the therapeutic process, a number of studies have investigated the metaphorization of trauma-related emotions such as anxiety and confusion and therapeutic themes like recovery and post-traumatic growth (e.g., Foley 2015; Costa and Steen 2014; Meili 2018; Littlemore and Turner 2020). However, the analyses were mainly based on people's introspective reports rather than objective measures of traumatization. Although introspections could provide convenient access to psychological phenomena that cannot be directly observed, the observations are not necessarily reliable; they could be even less accurate when the person is in an unstable state of mind, of which trauma is an exemplar. Moreover, introspection-based studies are limited in making cross-subject comparisons and determining correlational relationships. To identify patterns that are generalizable to a larger population, more valid and reliable measures of trauma are needed.

A feasible solution is to use psychometric tests, for example, the Posttraumatic Diagnostic Scale (PDS) (Foa 1995) and the Stanford Acute Stress Reaction Questionnaire (SASRQ) (Cardeña et al. 2000). In fact, psychometric data has been commonly used in psychological and therapeutic research on trauma narratives (see O'Kearney and Perrott 2006 for a review). Numerous linguistic constructs were found to be related to traumatization, such as emotional valence, sensory and perceptual information, thinking and understanding, and motion words. However, psychological and therapeutic research is more concerned with the substantive content of meanings than the linguistic forms of meaning-making; therefore, the studies took both literal and metaphorical expressions into account without making any distinctions. While metaphors are widely found to be more active and productive in articulating emotions than literal language, the patterns discovered for general trauma language do not necessarily apply to metaphorical expressions. To better understand the relationship between metaphors and trauma and facilitate the development of metaphor-based trauma treatment, we need to compare trauma victims' metaphor use against their psychometric scores of trauma to make more exact observations.

The present study investigates the interaction between metaphorical language and traumatization by incorporating psychometric data into statistical analyses of metaphors. A mixed-method analysis was conducted on metaphorical language and psychometric test scores collected from 46 trauma victims of the 2019 social unrest in Hong Kong (see Section 2 for more details). The participants' metaphors were examined for several variables that are related to trauma or emotion expression, and their quantitative patterns were analyzed at two different levels. The metaphor-level analysis took specific metaphorical expressions as the unit of analysis and combined categorical data analysis and discourse analysis to investigate the interrelationships among different metaphor variables. As some variables have multiple subcategories, we chose appropriate visualization tools to help identify patterns of analytic interest. The subject-level analysis, by contrast, focused on metaphor use by each subject and probed into the correlational relationship between metaphor use and the speaker's overall degrees of trauma. To better capture the dynamicity of the metaphor-trauma interaction, two statistical methods with complementary theoretical underpinnings (i.e., multiple regression and correlation analysis) were used to address the same research objectives. The patterns were further interpreted using linguistic examples from a discourse analytic perspective. More details about the variables and research methods will be given in Section 3.

It is important to note that this study does not intend to pinpoint the particularities of trauma metaphors; neither the sampling method nor the selection of variables allows us to draw such conclusions (see Section 5 for limitations of this study). It instead aims to open a new methodological perspective on exploring potentially trauma-related variables in metaphorical language and set the stage for future research. More specifically, this study aims to demonstrate the value of quantitative methods in complementing qualitative metaphor analyses, and highlight how the juxtaposition of linguistic data and psychometric data could lead to further psychological and clinical insights. The subject-level analysis also makes a special point on how the study of real-world metaphors could benefit from the idea of methodological pluralism.

In the following sections, we will first provide some background information on the research context, including the traumatic event, the participants, the interviews, and the psychometric data. We will then explain the procedure of metaphor identification, introduce the variables under examination, and present the results of interrater reliability tests. After introducing the research methods, we will present the statistical results and illustrate the patterns from a discourse analytic perspective. Implications, limitations, and future directions will also be discussed.

2 Data and metaphor identification

2.1 The traumatic event

Political tensions in Hong Kong arguably date back to its handover from the UK to China in 1997. Since mid-2019, however, they have escalated over a proposed extradition bill to transfer fugitives to jurisdictions including the Chinese Mainland. Pro-democracy factions accused the HKSAR government of undermining Hong Kong's autonomy under the "one country, two systems" constitutional principle, raising five key demands, including the full withdrawal of the extradition bill, universal suffrage, inquiry into police brutality, amnesty for arrested protestors, and retraction of their classification as rioters. Protests grew increasingly intense towards the end of 2019, turning into months of violence and property destruction. Some escalated into violent protesters-police conflicts, causing injuries to local citizens, police, and protesters and even deaths in some cases. The social unrest also resulted in substantial economic loss and led to a sharp decline in public confidence in the Hong Kong government. The overgeneralization of political divergences to everyday life added to the polarization of society and the disintegration of family and friends. Violence and physical assault also brought about a widespread sense of fear, frustration, and lack of certainty, leaving a significant psychological impact on residents' psychological wellbeing (Ni et al. 2020).

2.2 Participants

This study is part of a larger project on the use of trauma metaphors, and the data was collected from mid to late December 2019. Since the social unrest was still ongoing at the time of the research, this study focused on participants' acute stress reactions that last between two days to four weeks since the traumatic event, rather than PTSD, the diagnosis of which requires the symptoms to persist for more than a month (American Psychological Association, 2013). Forty-six participants (thirty-three female and thirteen male) were recruited using convenience sampling. All had witnessed or experienced highly distressing events such as violence and physical assault within the past four weeks. All participants were mainland Chinese who were working or studying in Hong Kong. All had received undergraduate education, and the mean age was 26.61 (SD=4.52). The participants were first invited to a semi-structured interview and then finished a psychometric test on acute stress reactions (see Section 2.3 and 2.4 for more details).

2.3 The interview data

The aim of semi-structured interviews was to probe into the interviewees' thoughts, feelings, and understanding of the traumatic event. Example questions include "What were the moments that impressed you the most?", "How has your life changed since the traumatic event?", and "Could you elaborate on your emotional experiences during that time?". Metaphorical language was carefully avoided in the interviewer's wording of prepared questions and follow-up clarifying questions (cf. Moser 2007). The interviewees were encouraged to describe their subjective experiences in as much detail as possible. Since the interview was designed to elicit trauma victims' natural use of metaphors rather than extract a metaphorical model of trauma, the interviewees were not explicitly instructed to use metaphors or talk about any specific aspects of the traumatic experience. All interviews were recorded with informed consent and transcribed for further analysis. The dataset consists of 178,747 Chinese characters (Mean=3869.15, SD=1750.77), totaling 16.67 hours of talk. The procedures of metaphor identification and relevant variables will be introduced in Section 3.

2.4 The psychometric data

Given the focus on acute stress reactions, the Chinese version of SASRQ (Cardeña et al. 2000, translated by Hou 2009) was chosen. It is a 30-item self-report on the subjects' experience of post-traumatic symptoms (e.g., dissociation, re-experiencing, and anxiety) from two days to four weeks since the traumatic event. The subject's degree of traumatization is measured on a 6-point Likert scale (0=not experienced, 5=very often experienced). Both the original questionnaire and the translated version were proved to have good reliability and validity (Cardeña et al. 2000). The internal consistency for scorings in this study is excellent (Cronbach's α=0.95), and the mean score is 39.09 (SD=23.75).

3 Methodology

3.1 Metaphor identification

Since metaphor production in the mental health context does not occur exclusively at the level of lexical unit (Fainsilber and Ortony 1987; Tay 2017), the discourse dynamics approach proposed by Cameron and Maslen (2010) was chosen for metaphor identification. Instead of extracting metaphors at the word level, this approach identifies metaphors at the level of word, phrase, and even larger chunks of language. Metaphoricity is determined based on contrast and transfer between basic and contextual meanings; stretches of metaphorical language are called "metaphor vehicle terms", and what is described by the vehicle is labelled as its "topic" (Cameron and Maslen 2010). To assist the identification of basic meanings, *the Contemporary Chinese Dictionary* (the 7th edition) was used. The process of metaphor identification is illustrated using the following examples:

(1) 以前觉得还可以,就是我们不谈,我们不说,我们置身事外,但是现在就发现不行,就是政治已经糊在你脸上了,就是你跑都跑不掉了。

'I thought it was ok: we could stay out of it as long as we don't talk about it. But now it doesn't work anymore. Politics has been **pasted to your face** now; you **can't run away from it** anyway.'

In example (1), both 糊在你脸上 ("have something slimy pasted to your face") and 跑都跑不掉了 ("cannot run away") show contrast and transfer between the basic meaning of the word and a more abstract contextual meaning: the experience of being involuntarily involved in the social unrest is interpreted as having something slimy pasted to the speaker's face, and the inability to avoid the situation is described as herself being unable to run away from it. The two expressions were thus identified as metaphor vehicle terms. Following this approach, 1,634 metaphor vehicle terms were identified, and the average is 35.52 per interview (SD=25.62).

3.2 Metaphor variables

Participants' metaphor use was further examined in terms of several variables that are relevant to trauma or emotion expression, including conventionality, target categories, perspectives, emotional valence, several key vehicle groupings and discourse topics, and metaphor density.

3.2.1 Conventionality

Conventionality of metaphors refers to how deeply entrenched an expression is in everyday use (Kövecses 2010). Conventional metaphors are socially established expressions that people use to talk about a relatively abstract concept, whereas novel metaphors are less well-established and involve the speaker's idiosyncratic understanding and creative thinking. The two types of metaphors have been found with differentiated emotional and therapeutic relevance, but the conclusions were inconsistent. Some researchers hold that novel metaphors are more affectively engaging and cognitively demanding than conventional metaphors (e.g., Bowdle and Gentner 2005; Semino 2011; Gelo and Mergenthaler 2012), whereas some believe that conventional metaphors, as reflections of internalized or subconscious actions (Moser 2000), bear no less therapeutic potential than novel metaphors do (e.g., McMullen 1989; Moser 2007).

In the present study, whether a metaphor vehicle term is conventional or novel could be determined using a dictionary (Steen et al. 2010: 34); if its contextual meaning is included as one of the standard senses of the word, then it is identified as a conventional metaphor, if not, then it is to be labeled as a novel metaphor. Using *The Chinese Contemporary Dictionary*, 716 novel metaphors and 918 conventional metaphors were identified in the dataset.

3.2.2 Target categories and perspectives

Target categories proposed by Kopp and Eckstein (2004) are the most fundamental topics of metaphors in psychotherapy. The original taxonomy includes the description of the self, others, situations, and how the speaker interprets these topics in relation to themselves. The categories aim to capture the metaphorical structure of the speaker's subjective reality (Kopp, 1995) and generate therapeutic insights about his/her cognitive and emotional statuses. Although the original taxonomy is largely compatible with the present interview data, the very nature of the traumatic event (i.e., people's personal life being disrupted by the social unrest) raises the need for a finer distinction between "social situation" and "personal situation". In this study, the original "situation" category was divided into "personal situation" and "social situation", and "self and situation" was split into "self and personal situation" and "self and social situation" accordingly.

Because Kopp and Eckstein (2004) did not provide explicit criteria for the identification of SELF and SELF AND SELF, we incorporated Lakoff's (1992) framework of "multiple selves" to make clearer distinctions. According to Lakoff (1992: 9), people's cognitive activities are often metaphorically conceptualized in terms of the interaction between two different facets of the person, i.e., the center of consciousness, will, and judgment (i.e., the "subject"), and the rest of the person (i.e., the "self"). The self could be perceived as consistent with, separated from, or even incompatible with the subject in terms of physical conditions, emotions, and thoughts. For the present study, metaphor vehicle terms in which the subject is conscious, compatible with the self, or has normal control over the self were labeled as SELF, and those in which the two are incompatible, or either is unconscious or uncontrollable, were labeled as SELF AND SELF. Those depicting the self's interaction with others, personal life, and social situation were labeled accordingly.

We can find that Kopp and Eckstein's (2004) target categories are described either with or without reference to the self. The dichotomous division is reminiscent of the notion of perspective proposed by Nigro and Neisser (1983), which is the point of view from which the speaker describes or evaluates a particular event or experience. The choice of perspective is closely associated with the speaker's experience of traumatic feelings (Berntsen, Willert, and Rubin 2003; McIssac and Eich 2004). In the field perspective, the memory is retrieved in a self-immersed way, with the subject being the actor or experiencer of the scene. In contrast, in the observer perspective, the experience is recollected from an external standpoint, with the subject observing him/herself and the surroundings "from the outside" with less emotional involvement. While previous research mainly examined perspective choices in general trauma language, the present study explores the relationship between metaphor perspectives and traumatic experience. The identification of perspectives is based on the division of target categories: those experienced with speakers "inside" themselves (i.e., SELF, OTHERS, PERSONAL SITUATION, and SOCIAL SITUATION) were categorized as the field perspective, and the rest, in which the self was both the subject and the object of the observation, were labeled as the observer perspective.

The original and the adapted version of target categories, together with the perspectives they belong to, are presented in Figure 7.1. The frequencies of metaphors in each target category and perspective are summarized in Table 7.1.

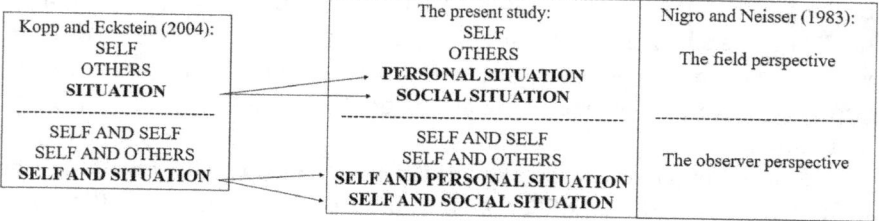

Figure 7.1: The original and the adapted taxonomy of target categories and the corresponding perspectives.

Table 7.1: Frequencies of metaphors in each target category and perspective.

Perspective	Target Category	Frequency
The field perspective	Self	341
	Others	255
	Personal situation	181
	Social situation	210
The observer perspective	Self and self	175
	Self and others	90
	Self and personal situation	104
	Self and social situation	278

3.2.3 Emotional valence

The use of emotional language, especially the heightened use of negative emotion words (Cohn, Mehl, and Pennebaker 2004; O'Kearney and Perrott 2006), has also been a central issue in the study of trauma narratives. To investigate the relationship between metaphor use and the expression of emotions, we coded all metaphor vehicle terms in terms of their emotional valences. Expressions that indicate a pessimistic, passive, or disapproving attitude are labeled as "negative", those expressing an optimistic, active, or approving attitude are identified as "positive", and those without an apparent emotional orientation are rated as "neutral". The frequencies of negative, neutral, and positive expressions were 826, 711, and 97.

Table 7.2: Crosstabulation for CONVENTIONALITY, TARGET CATEGORY, PERSPECTIVE, and EMOTIONAL VALENCE.

Perspective	conventionality	Target category	Valence		
			negative	neutral	positive
field	conventional	self	143	75	23
		others	71	56	7
		Personal situation	64	45	4
		Social situation	62	66	5
	novel	self	61	31	8
		others	62	52	7
		personal situation	43	22	3
		Social situation	38	34	5
observer	conventional	Self and self	26	60	7
		Self and others	15	25	2
		Self and personal situation	19	32	7
		Self and social situation	47	55	2
	novel	Self and self	35	43	4
		Self and others	27	15	6
		Self and personal situation	14	25	7
		Self and social situation	99	75	0

3.2.4 Trauma-related vehicle groupings and discourse topics

Drawing from previous research on general trauma language and trauma metaphors, we also examined all the metaphor vehicles for their relevance to several trauma- or emotion-related themes (see Table 7.3). Those describing concrete experiences and tangible objects, i.e., sensory information, war and threat, space and spatial relations, and physical activity, were identified based on the groupings of vehicles. Those that contained more abstract information, i.e., emotional feelings and processes, self-reference, and thinking and understanding, were extracted based on the discourse topics of metaphors.

Table 7.3: Frequencies of trauma-related vehicle groupings and discourse topics.

	Category	Frequency
Vehicle groupings	Sensory information	331
	War and threat	112
	Space and spatial relations	140
	Physical activity	353
Discourse topics	Emotional feelings	517
	Self-references	81
	Thinking and understanding	215

3.2.5 Metaphor density

According to Fainsilber and Ortony (1987), the experience of intense emotions might pose a more pressing need for the use of metaphors. To see if this argument applies in the context of trauma, we calculated "metaphor density" for each participant (Cameron 2003), i.e., the occurrence rates of metaphor vehicle terms per thousand words of transcription. Statistics of the present dataset ranged from 3.39 to 19.51 per thousand Chinese characters, and the average is 8.92 (SD=3.59).

3.3 Inter-rater reliability

Because metaphor identification using the discourse dynamics approach needs to make qualitative decisions on the boundaries and contextual meanings of metaphor vehicle terms, quantitative reliability measures are hardly applicable for the identification process. Instead, consistency of coding was achieved through the discussion between the researchers (Cameron and Maslen 2010).

Because the judgment of target categories, emotional valences, vehicle groupings, and discourse topics involves making categorical decisions, the reliability of coding needs to be checked. According to Bolognesi, Pilgram, and van den Heerik (2017), a coding scheme could only be considered reliably replicable if the coding provided by trained raters is comparable to that accomplished by novice raters who have different academic backgrounds and no prior coding experience. Therefore, a novice rater of non-linguistic background was invited and trained for reliability checks. The two raters worked independently on 15% of the data, which was randomly selected from the whole dataset. Krippendorff's alphas for the coding of EMOTIONAL VALENCE, TARGET CATEGORY, vehicle groupings, and discourse topics are 0.741, 0.865, 0.697, and 0.721, respectively. All values are greater than 0.667, suggesting acceptable reliability (Krippendorff 2004). As the determination of conventionality relied on dictionary meanings and perspectives were coded based on the conflation of target categories, no extra checks were needed.

3.4 Research methods

As indicated earlier, the metaphor-level analysis took each metaphor vehicle term as the unit of analysis. Categorical data analysis was used to probe into the interrelationships among TARGET CATEGORY, CONVENTIONALITY, and EMOTIONAL VALENCE. Since PERSPECTIVE is the combination of different TARGET CATEGORIES, it was not entered into the statistical analysis but only taken as a referential point for later discussion. Linguistic examples were then used to illustrate the patterns from a discourse analytic perspective and assist the discussion of potential implications.

The subject-level analysis focused on the correlations between metaphor use and overall degrees of traumatization. The participants' SASRQ scores were taken as the dependent variable in correlation and regression analysis. All abovementioned metaphor variables were entered as independent variables, including metaphor density, conventionality, valenced metaphors, target categories, perspectives, trauma-related vehicle groupings, and relevant discourse topics. Considering that the variables might be linked either independently or jointly to the speaker's degree of traumatization, two statistical methods with different theoretical underpinnings were performed: Pearson's correlations were computed to examine the strengths of relationships between the metaphor variables and the speaker's overall degree of trauma, and multiple regression was run to see which aspects of metaphors could be used to predict trauma. In the former, each metaphor variable was evaluated in terms of its correlation with SASRQ scores without considering the impact of a third variable. In contrast, in the latter, all predictor variables were entered into the analysis as a whole chunk, which means the interrelationships among variables were also taken into consideration. Linguistic examples were likewise used to interpret the statistical patterns and support further discussion.

4 Results and discussion

4.1 Metaphor-level analysis

For the categorical data analysis at the metaphor level, a log-linear analysis was firstly run, but the final model failed to retain the highest three-way interaction. Following Tay (2017), follow-up chi-square tests were then conducted to look for potential bivariate associations. The requirement for minimal sample size in chi-square tests was met, with all cells having an expected frequency larger than one and more than 80% having a value larger than five. Significant associations were found between TARGET CATEGORY and CONVENTIONALITY, $\chi^2(7)=81.46$, $p<.001$, Cramer's V=.223, and between VALENCE and TARGET CATEGORY, $\chi^2(14)= 84.79$, $p<.001$, Cramer's V=.161, indicating distinct metaphor usage profiles for different target categories. The CONVENTIONALITY*VALENCE association was not statistically significant, $\chi^2(2)=2.903$, $p=.234$, Cramer' s V=.042, which means the distribution of valence in conventional and novel metaphors had no fundamental difference.

To better visualize the relationships between different variable categories, a factor plot was generated using Multiple Correspondence Analysis (MCA) (see Figure 7.2). The analysis reduced the variance of the data to two dimensions, which captured a substantial proportion of variance: dimension one explained 41.68% of the total variance, and dimension two an additional 39.21%, making a total of 80.89%.

In MCA plots, the nature of associations could be interpreted based on the location of one category in relation to another; positively correlated categories are clustered at the same side of the origin, and negatively correlated ones are distributed on opposite sides. The strengths of associations are reflected by the distance of the category from the origin, with stronger ones denoted by further distance and vice versa. From Figure 7.2 we can see (1) all eight target categories were distributed in distinct quadrants and on different sides of the origin, revealing remarkable differences in their metaphor usage patterns. SELF and SELF AND SOCIAL SITUATION were the furthest away along dimension 1. SELF AND SELF, PERSONAL SITUATION, and SELF AND PERSONAL SITUATION were the furthest along dimension 2, which means these categories showed particularly salient features. (2) Novel and conventional metaphors were approximately equidistant on different sides of the origin on dimension 1, reflecting discriminating metaphor usage patterns. (3) All three valences were distributed in different quadrants, with negative and positive metaphors being further from the origin, thus showing bigger contrasts. (4) Target categories from different perspectives were clustered at different sides of the origin; those from the observer perspectives were distributed on the left side, positively associated with novel metaphors and the neutral valence, and those from the field perspective were on the right, positively associated with

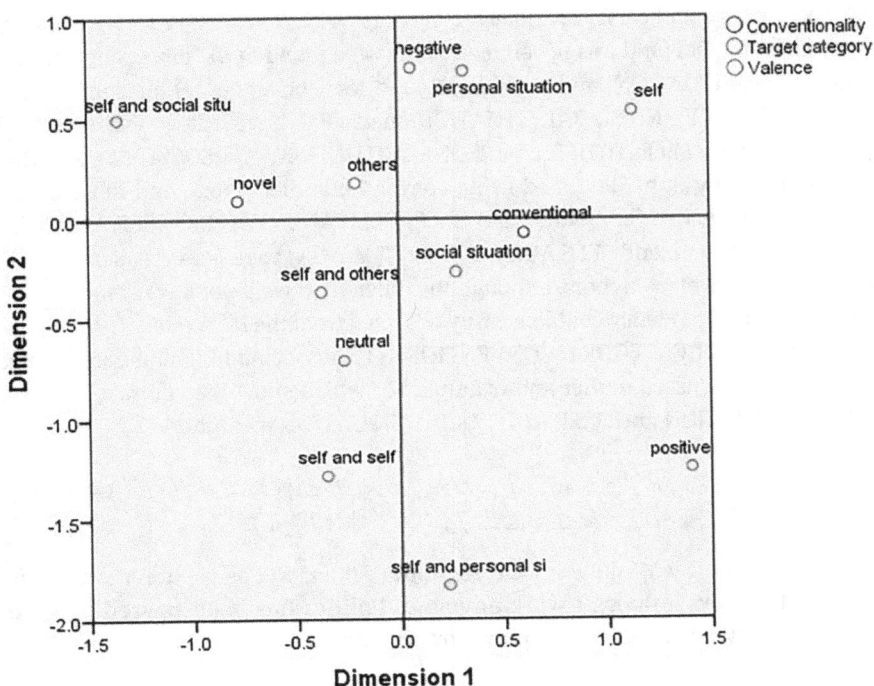

Figure 7.2: A factor plot of relevant variable categories.

conventional metaphors and the other two valences. In what follows, we will illustrate the two significant associations using genuine linguistic examples and discuss their theoretical and practical implications.

4.1.1 The TARGET CATEGORY*CONVENTIONALITY association

Target categories of trauma metaphors differed significantly in their preferences of conventional and novel metaphors. While some categories were more often described using established metaphors shared by the whole community, some were more likely to elicit speakers' creative and idiosyncratic understandings and trigger the use of novel metaphors.

Crosstabulation for the TARGET CATEGORY*CONVENTIONALITY association is shown in Table 7.4. The deviation of the observed frequency from expectation was examined using the adjusted residual. An adjusted residual above +2 (colored in light gray) means the category occurs significantly more often than expected alone ($p<.05$), and a value below –2 (colored in dark gray) suggests that the category is significantly less likely to occur (*p*<.05). We can see that significantly more conventional (and less novel) metaphors were found in the discussion of SELF and SOCIAL SITUATION, and more novel (and less conventional) metaphors were observed for SELF AND SOCIAL SITUATION. In general, target categories in the field perspective (i.e., SELF, OTHERS, PERSONAL SITUATION, and SOCIAL SITUATION) were more likely to be described using conventional metaphors, and those in the observer perspective (i.e., SELF AND SELF, SELF AND OTHERS, SELF AND PERSONAL SITUATION, and SELF AND SOCIAL SITUATION) were more frequently interpreted using novel metaphors, although the differences were not always statistically significant. This tendency could be easily observed from the MCA plot.

The TARGET CATEGORY*CONVENTIONALITY association is illustrated using example (1) discussed earlier and example (2), which show the contrast between SOCIAL SITUATION and SELF AND SOCIAL SITUATION metaphors:

(1) 以前觉得还可以，就是我们不谈，我们不说，我们置身事外，但是现在就发现不行，就是政治已经**糊在你脸上了**，就是你**跑都跑不掉了**。

'I thought it was ok: we could stay out of it as long as we don't talk about it. But now it doesn't work anymore. Politics has been **pasted to your face** now; you **can't run away from it** anyway.'

(2) 这个事情，我感觉啊，就是个小小**插曲**。

'This event, I feel, is just like **a small episode**.'

Example (1) is a novel metaphor about the speaker's idiosyncratic understanding of SELF AND SOCIAL SITUATION. Expressions about sensory information (i.e., having something "pasted" to her face) and physical movement (i.e., "run away from it") were creatively adapted to interpret how the speaker was connected to and affected by the social unrest. In example (2), an unexpected protest is conceptualized as "a small episode", which is a conventional metaphor widely used in Mandarin Chinese.

The difference in metaphor choices at the target category level might be explained by the salience of the topics in everyday communication. As personal life, interpersonal situations, and social events are essential elements of daily life and common topics in everyday communication, it would not be difficult for speakers to borrow pre-established expressions to express their feelings and opinions. By contrast, issues such as cognitive changes, perceived changes in life, and evaluations of the broader social context are only loosely connected to concrete and shared experiences but are more related to the speaker's idiosyncratic way of thinking and evaluating. The preference for idiosyncratic expressions from the

Table 7.4: Crosstabulation for TARGET CATEGORY and CONVENTIONALITY.

			conventionality		total
			conventional	novel	
Target category	self	count	241	100	341
		Expected Count	191.6	149.4	341.0
		Adjusted Residual	6.1	-6.1	
	others	count	134	121	255
		Expected Count	143.3	111.7	255.0
		Adjusted Residual	-1.3	1.3	
	Personal situation	count	113	68	181
		Expected Count	101.7	79.3	181.0
		Adjusted Residual	1.8	-1.8	
	Social situation	count	133	77	210
		Expected Count	118.0	92.0	210.0
		Adjusted Residual	2.2	-2.2	
	Self and self	count	93	82	175
		Expected Count	98.3	76.7	175.0
		Adjusted Residual	-.9	.9	
	Self and others	count	42	48	90
		Expected Count	50.6	39.4	90.0
		Adjusted Residual	-1.9	1.9	
	Self and personal situation	count	58	46	104
		Expected Count	58.4	45.6	104.0
		Adjusted Residual	-.1	.1	
	Self and social situation	count	104	174	278
		Expected Count	156.2	121.8	278.0
		Adjusted Residual	-6.9	6.9	
Total		count	918	716	1634
		Expected Count	918.0	716.0	1634.0

observer perspective might also reflect increased psychological distance from the self, which is a typical post-traumatic reaction that allows speakers to process their traumatic experience without being overwhelmed by negative emotions (Kross, Ayduk, and Mischel 2005).

Although the use of novel metaphors in psychotherapy is often related to the expression and regulation of non-adaptive emotions (Borbely 1998; Gelo and Mergenthaler 2012) and prioritized over that of conventional metaphors, findings of this study suggest that trauma victims' choices over conventional and novel metaphors are more topic-driven than emotion-oriented. The flexibility of choices observed at the target category level supports the argument that therapists should refrain from making prior assumptions about the therapeutic value of specific types of metaphor (McMullen 1985, 1989; Rasmussen and Angus 1996) and focus more on the contextual significance of the expression.

The examples also reveal the contrast between metaphors generated from the field and the observer perspective, although the differences were not statistically significant for all target category pairs (e.g., SELF and SELF AND SELF). The findings bear practical implications for the study of trauma narratives and the development and application of metaphor-based therapeutic protocols (e.g., Kopp and Craw 1998), which strive to provoke therapeutic insights through stimulating and exploiting client-generated metaphors. Given that target category pairs from different perspectives are very often instantiated using different types of metaphors, therapists might consider using instructed perspective shift (Wallace-Hadrill and Kamboj 2016) as a therapeutic tool to facilitate the exploitation of implicit metaphorical elements, the introduction of contrasting expressions, or the production of adaptive metaphors.

4.1.2 The TARGET CATEGORY*EMOTIONAL VALENCE association

Although traumatic experience is most often associated with a mixture of overwhelmingly negative emotions (Badour, Resnick, and Kilpatrick 2017), the target categories were not indiscriminately metaphorized using the negative valence. Quite the contrary, the significant association between TARGET CATEGORY and EMOTIONAL VALENCE suggests that trauma victims tended to metaphorize different topics using contrasting emotional tones. Crosstabulation for this association is shown in Table 7.5.

We can see the eight target categories differed significantly in their emotional inclinations. Positive expressions were more likely to occur than by chance alone when describing SELF and SELF AND PERSONAL SITUATION. But they were used at a significantly lower rate when discussing SELF AND SOCIAL

Table 7.5: Crosstabulation for TARGET CATEGORY and EMOTIONAL VALENCE.

			valence			total
			negative	neutral	possitive	
Target category	self	count	204	106	31	341
		Expected Count	172.4	148.4	20.2	341.0
		Adjusted Residual	3.9	-5.2	2.8	
	others	count	133	108	14	255
		Expected Count	128.9	111.0	15.1	255.0
		Adjusted Residual	.6	-.4	-.3	
	Personalsituation	count	107	67	7	181
		Expected Count	91.5	78.8	10.7	181.0
		Adjusted Residual	2.4	-1.9	-1.2	
	Socialsituation	count	100	100	10	210
		Expected Count	106.2	91.4	12.5	210.0
		Adjusted Residual	-.9	1.3	-.8	
	Self and self	count	61	103	11	175
		Expected Count	88.5	76.1	10.4	175.0
		Adjusted Residual	-4.4	4.3	.2	
	Self and others	count	42	40	8	90
		Expected Count	45.5	39.2	5.3	90.0
		Adjusted Residual	-.8	.2	1.2	
	Self and personal situation	count	33	57	14	104
		Expected Count	52.6	45.3	6.2	104.0
		Adjusted Residual	-4.0	2.4	3.4	
	Self and social situation	count	146	130	2	278
		Expected Count	140.5	121.0	16.5	278.0
		Adjusted Residual	.7	1.2	-4.0	
Total		count	826	711	97	1634
		Expected Count	826.0	711.0	97.0	1634.0

SITUATION. The negative valence occurred at a significantly higher rate in metaphors about SELF and PERSONAL SITUATION. However, when the two target categories were accessed from an observer perspective, significantly more neutral metaphors and fewer negative metaphors were produced. As we can see from the MCA plot (refer to Figure 7.2), target categories from the field perspective were generally closer to and on the same side with the negative and the positive valence. In contrast, their counterparts from the observer perspective were clustered on the other side around the neutral valence. The TARGET CATEGORY*VALENCE association is illustrated using the following examples:

(3) 就是我觉得可能就是一种比较无奈或者说**无力**的感觉。

'What I felt is probably helplessness, or say, **lack of strength**.'

(4) 通过那段经历来学会一些辩证思考,然后重新去反省自己过往的那些认知,然后把自己从当时的环境脱离开来, 作为**一个旁观者**去分析。

'Through my experience of the event, I learned to think in a dialectical way. I learned to reflect upon my cognition in the past, get myself detached from the environment, and analyze all these thoughts in the role of **an onlooker**.'

Example (3) is a SELF metaphor generated from the field perspective. In this expression, helplessness during the peak of the traumatic event is interpreted as the lack of strength in the physical sense and is experienced directly from her own viewpoint. As a SELF AND SELF metaphor and an observer metaphor, example (4) describes the speaker's reflection on her cognitive states using a neutral tone. The ability to engage in dialectical thinking is interpreted as the speaker becoming an onlooker who is detached from the traumatized self and observing the social environment in a rational way.

The contrast of emotional inclinations at the perspective level is generally consistent with previous studies on autobiographical memories (e.g., Robinson and Swanson 1993; McIssac and Eich 2004; Kross, Ayduk, and Mischel 2005; Mooren et al. 2019). This finding reveals the concordance between metaphorical thinking about abstract concepts and the recollection of concrete details. Target categories in the field perspective tended to be portrayed in a negative light, which is probably due to the speakers' immersion in negative emotions (Wallace-Hadrill and Kamboj 2016). By contrast, the observer perspective allows trauma victims to focus on the event in a self-distanced or ego-decentered way (Kross, Ayduk, and Mischel 2005) and is thus more likely to be associated with lower levels of emotionality (Wallance-Hadrill and Kamboj 2016). Self-regulatory metaphors like example (4) also corroborate the claim that the observer perspective could be adopted as an adaptive strategy to distance oneself from overwhelming emotions (Metcalfe and Mischel 1999; Kenny and Bryant 2007; Williams and Moulds 2007).

We can also observe a diverse set of emotional inclinations at the target category level. Some target categories carried more negative emotions than others, and some were more likely to be described in a neutral or positive tone for self-regulatory or self-persuasive purposes. It is also possible that some target categories are interpreted using mixed and even conflicting emotions; for example, SELF is significantly and positively associated with both negative and positive emotions. More interestingly, target categories directly relevant to the traumatic experience were found with rather conservative emotional inclinations. For example, SELF AND SOCIAL SITUATION, as a central theme of the traumatic event, was not so sensitive to the negative valence as expected, but the emotional focus was encoded implicitly in the proportional lack of positive metaphors. SOCIAL SITUATION, i.e., the counterpart of SELF AND SOCIAL SITUATION in the field perspective, was not explicitly marked by any specific valence but had a relatively balanced blend of all three valences. Although there has been extensive research on the relationship between emotion expression and psychological well-being (e.g., Batten et al. 2002; Cohn, Mehl, and Pennebaker 2004; Jaeger et al. 2014), whether a specific valence is related to better or worse psychological states remains unclear. According to Wardecker et al. (2017), a possible reason for such inconsistency is that the linguistic constructs might differ in the types of expression they contain. The findings of this study provide supporting evidence for this hypothesis. Although the study is insufficient to draw conclusions regarding the psychological basis of the divergences, the findings still highlight target categories as an important factor interacting with emotional expression, which underlines the need for future research to focus on more nuanced classifications of topics. In sum, this section demonstrates how the application of categorical data analysis and the use of visualization tools could open up a new perspective on the interaction among metaphor variables. The study also generates fresh insights into the contextualized nature of metaphors and the application of metaphor-based trauma treatment.

4.2 Subject-level analysis

In the subject-level analysis, correlation analysis and multiple regression were chosen to account for different forms of trauma-metaphor interaction, i.e., the association between trauma and a specific variable, and how trauma interacts with the joint effect of multiple variables.

Significant results of the correlation analysis are shown in Table 7.6. Speakers' overall degrees of trauma were positively and significantly correlated with negative metaphors (*r*=.318, *p*=.031), the observer perspective (*r*=.334, *p*=.023), SELF AND SELF (*r*=.339, *p*=.021), and self-reference (*r*=.311, *p*=.036). In other words, people of higher degrees of trauma tended to use more negative metaphors than the less traumatized. They were also more likely to adopt an external viewpoint and talk about self-related issues.

Table 7.6: Significant results of the correlation analysis.

		SELF AND SELF	Self-reference	The observer perspective	Negative metaphors
SASRQ scores	Correlation coefficient	.339*	.311*	.334*	.318*
	Sig. (2-tailed)	.021	.036	.023	.031

Due to the exploratory nature of this study, the stepwise method was chosen for the regression analysis. To avoid suppressor effects (Horst 1941), which occur when a variable has a significant effect only when another is held constant, backward elimination was adopted. The parameters for the final regression model and coefficients for significant predictors are presented in Table 7.7 and 7.8.

Table 7.7: Parameters of the final regression model.

Model		ANOVA				
		Sum of Squares	df	Mean Square	F	Sig.
the final modal	Regression	7182.745	3	2394.248	5.527	0.003
	Residual	18194.907	42	433.212		
	Total	25377.652	45			

The final model for multiple regression included three predictors, i.e., negative metaphors (β=.449, *p*=.002), OTHERS (β=−.375, *p*=.008), and PERSONAL SITUATION (β=−.267, *p*=.054). While the coefficient of negative metaphors had a positive value, those of OTHERS and PERSONAL SITUATION were negative. This means people of higher degrees of trauma were more likely to use more metaphors in the negative valence but were less inclined to talk about OTHERS and PERSONAL SITUATION. Conversely, those traumatized to a lesser extent

Table 7.8: Coefficients for predictors in the final regression model.

		Unstandardized Coefficients		Standardized coefficients	t	Sig.
		B	Std. Error	Beta		
the final model	(constant)	28.379	7.936		3.576	.001
	negative metaphors	5.404	1.648	.449	3.279	.002
	OTHERS	−5.427	1.938	−.375	−2.800	.008
	PERSONAL SITUATION	−6.215	3.135	−.267	−1.982	.054

tended to use fewer negative metaphors and talk more about OTHERS and PERSONAL SITUATION. The absolute value of the standardized beta value indicates the importance of the predictor in the model. Negative metaphors had the highest standardized beta value and thus the greatest importance in the model. By comparison, the values for OTHERS and PERSONAL SITUATION were smaller, which means their strengths were relatively less strong. The value of adjusted R^2 is .232, which means the three predictors together accounted for 23.2% of the total variance, $F(3,42)=5.527$, $p=.003$.

We can see the results of correlation analysis and multiple regression are generally consistent with and complementary to each other. On the whole, both analyses show that traumatization is not necessarily associated with increased use of metaphors but could be clearly distinguished from more nuanced aspects of metaphor use. More specifically, both analyses indicate negative metaphors as a crucial indicator of trauma; they also reveal distinct but meaningfully coherent metaphor usage patterns for high- and low-scorers of SASRQ in terms of self- and other- references. In what follows, we will interpret these general patterns using representative linguistic examples.

First of all, both analyses highlight the positive and significant correlation between overall degrees of trauma and the use of negative metaphors. These results are unsurprising because traumatization is characterized by the experience of various negative emotions, such as anger, shame, and fear (Badour et al. 2015). This finding is consistent with previous research on general trauma language (e.g., Cohn, Mehl, and Pennebaker 2004; Halligan et al. 2003; Frewen et al. 2011). While previous research did not distinguish between literal and metaphor language, the present study indicates that highly traumatized people did not simply talk more about their negative feelings but were also more likely to use metaphorical expressions to provide more "granular" accounts of their feelings. This tendency could be observed from example (5), which was produced by an interviewee who scored 84 on SASRQ.

(5) 我自己甚至都可能会意识到我是不是**就像 (进入) 一个黑洞一样, 被负面情绪吸进去了**。

'Even I myself realized, if I was, **just like (in) a black hole, absorbed by negative emotions.**'

Example (5) provides a vivid image of how the speaker felt at the traumatic event. The experience of trauma, which is relatively abstract and elusive, is interpreted as the speaker's physical reactions to a strong external force or a powerful object. The speaker being overwhelmed by depressed feelings is compared to herself being physically "absorbed into a black hole". A similarly pessimistic attitude could also be identified in examples (1) and (3) discussed in the previous section. Compared with general emotion terms such as "sad" or "despair", such expressions contain more specific and concrete details about the negative feelings.

Another pattern of interest is high scorers' preference for self-related metaphors. Speakers' SASRQ scores were significantly correlated with SELF AND SELF ($r=.339$, $p=.021$) and self-reference ($r=.311$, $p=.036$), which means high scorers were more likely to use metaphors in the reflection of their current state of being. While SELF AND SELF metaphors capture the incongruence between different facets of emotions and thoughts, self-referential metaphors focus more on the identity and characteristics of the self as an integral whole. Traumatization was also positively and significantly related to metaphors from the observer perspective ($r=.334$, $p=.023$), which presupposes the self as a default component of metaphorization. This means people with higher degrees of trauma were more likely to use metaphors when reflecting on their connections with others, life, and the broader social context. The correlation between trauma and the self-related variables is illustrated using the following examples, produced by two interviewees who scored above average:

(6) 我仿佛**身体里面有两个小人, 然后一个小人喊着说**:"你要冷静的看一看这边啊, 你看一看这些民主社会"之类的, **另外一边就在说**:"你是在这读一年书而已, 可是这一年已经被损失了这么多"。

'It feels like **there are two little guys in my body, and one is shouting**: "you should be calm and see what happened here, you should see the democratic society" and the like. Then **the one on the other side says**: "you are just doing a master here for only one year, just in the one year you have lost so much".'

(7) 因为会觉得自己是无辜的, 自己**是受了无妄之灾的**。

'Because I think I am innocent, I am **a victim of an unexpected disaster**.'

Example (6) is a SELF AND SELF metaphor depicting the inner conflict experienced by the speaker. The self, usually perceived as an integral whole under non-traumatic conditions, is now split into two little guys who hold diametrically opposing opinions. One represents the interviewee's rational thinking as a mature social being, and the other expresses her concerns over her life and studies as an emotional being. The expression is also an instance of metaphors from the observer perspective. Instead of explaining the confusion and struggles she experienced in mind, the speaker adopts an external vantage point and describes how she felt as both the experiencer of the process and a witness who is watching herself from the outside. With a similar focus on the self, example (7), as a self-referential metaphor, shows how the traumatized self as a whole is perceived with a metaphorical identity, i.e., a "victim of an unexpected disaster".

The increase of self-related metaphors in high scorers' language might be explained by the altered sense of self as a result of trauma exposure (Tedeschi and Calhoun 1995). Quite a few expressions convey a sense of discontinuity between the self and the surroundings, which is a natural consequence of trauma exposure. According to Muldoon et al. (2019: 333), such expressions represent the speaker's attempts to "integrate and re-evaluate one's self in the light of the traumatic event". This tendency also provides linguistic evidence for the claim that trauma victims tend to perceive tighter connections between the traumatic experience and themselves and view the trauma as a central part of their self-identity (Berntsen, Willert, and Rubin 2003).

By contrast, the regression model draws upon high scorers' attenuated attention toward others and personal situations, which appears to be a natural consequence of maintaining a self-centered perspective. Compared with high scorers, those traumatized to a lesser extent were more inclined to metaphorize about OTHERS and PERSONAL SITUATIONS in a relatively rational and non-involved way. Example (8) is illustrative:

(8) 学校毕竟是个挺**净土**的一个地方, 之前愤怒也是因为你怎么**把手伸到学校这块地方来了**。

'The university is, after all, like **a pure land**. The reason why I felt angry is because how can you **lay hands on this place**.'

This expression was produced by an interviewee who got only 2 points on SASRQ. The university, which is supposed to stay clear from political activities, is compared to a "pure land", and the protesters entering and occupying the campus are conceptualized as "laying their hands on this place". Although both metaphor vehicle terms describe the speaker's understanding of the traumatic event, neither taps into her emotional feelings or even mentions the existence of the self.

The low degree of self-involvement observed among low-scores is consistent with the findings of Kross et al. (2014) and Kaplow et al. (2018), which suggest that the preference for the third-person observer perspective over first-person representations is associated with less distress, less maladaptive post-trauma processing, and greater psychological distance in introspection. The other-focused tendency among low-scorers is markedly different from the self-centeredness of high-scorers, as indicated by correlation analysis. However, the contrast could be discerned only when the two analyses are performed in juxtaposition. While previous research mostly adopted single statistical methods, the present study shows how methods with contrasting theoretical underpinnings could be combined to explore different facets of the same issue.

Different from previous studies that focused solely on trauma victims' linguistic expressions, the subject-level analysis took measurable psychological states into consideration and explored the dynamic interactions between metaphor use and the subjective experience of trauma. Results show that overall degrees of traumatization could be distinguished from several nuanced aspects of metaphorical language, confirming the possibility of metaphors to resonate with objectively measurable aspects of emotion. The meaningful convergence of statistical patterns offers valuable insights for the empirical study of trauma metaphors and mental health communication in general. The findings also reveal the combinatorial advantage of using complementary statistical methods, emphasizing the need to advocate methodological pluralism in future research.

5 Conclusion

The present study demonstrates the application of quantitative methods to the study of trauma metaphors. Taken together, the metaphor-level and subject-level analyses contribute to a more comprehensive understanding of trauma and its dynamic interactions with metaphor use, establishing measurable psychological states as an important factor in explaining metaphor variation. On the practical level, the study showcases the real-world complexities underlying trauma metaphors. It also underlines the value of metaphors in distinguishing between different degrees of trauma. Although the findings are not sufficient to serve diagnostic purposes, they could still be used as convenient referential points at the pre-diagnostic stage or adapted to develop new diagnostic tools.

On the methodological level, we have shown how quantitative research methods could capture metaphor usage patterns that are invisible to purely qualitative analysis. In the subject-level analysis, in particular, we illustrated the idea of methodological pluralism, demonstrating how statistical methods with different theoretical underpinnings could be juxtaposed to generate complementary insights into the interplay between metaphor and traumatization. The analysis also highlighted the underestimated value of psychometric variables in extending the scope of traditional metaphor analysis and uncovering therapeutically relevant metaphor usage patterns.

The present study is limited in several aspects. The first is the non-randomized nature of the sample. Due to logistic reasons, the sampling was restricted to a population of homogeneous demographic features, and the findings might be influenced by potential confirmation bias. For example, people who had concerns about begetting physical abuse for commenting on the social unrest were unlikely to sign up for the study. Therefore, whether the findings could be generalized to the whole trauma population remains to be tested. The proportion of females and males was also not balanced, making it difficult to compare across genders. Future research could replicate the methods used in this study on a larger traumatic population to further explore the relationship between traumatization and metaphor use and the potential influence of trauma type, language, and cultural background. Secondly, due to the lack of research on trauma metaphors, variables examined in this study were mostly selected based on previous findings of general trauma language. To identify attributes that are directly pertinent to trauma metaphors, bottom-up analyses of emergent metaphorical themes are required. Thirdly, this study only focused on the association between metaphors and overall degrees of trauma. Since traumatic feelings could be further categorized into various clinical symptoms, such as dissociation and re-experiencing (American Psychiatric Association, 2013), it would also be interesting to explore metaphor usage patterns at the symptom level. Lastly, while this study only considers the immediate effects of the traumatic event, a longitudinal study of metaphor use would also be an intriguing perspective for future research.

References

American Psychiatric Association. 2013. *Diagnostic and statistical manual of mental disorders* (5th edn). Washington, DC: Author.

Badour, Christal L., Heidi S. Resnick & Dean G. Kilpatrick. 2017. Associations Between Specific Negative Emotions and DSM-5 PTSD Among a National Sample of Interpersonal Trauma Survivors. *Journal of Interpersonal Violence* 32(11). 1620–1641.

Batten, Sonja V., Victoria M. Follette, Mandra L. Rasmussen Hall & Kathleen M. Palm. 2002. Physical and psychological effects of written disclosure among sexual abuse survivors. *Behavior Therapy* 33(1). 107–122.

Berntsen, Dorthe, Morten Willert & David C. Rubin. 2003. Splintered memories or vivid landmarks? Qualities and organization of traumatic memories with and without PTSD. *Applied Cognitive Psychology* 17(6). 675–693.

Blenkiron, Paul. 2005. Stories and analogies in cognitive behaviour therapy: A clinical review. *Behavioural and Cognitive Psychotherapy* 33(1). 45–59.

Bolognesi, Marianna, Roosmaryn Pilgram & Romy van den Heerik. 2016. Reliability in content analysis: The case of semantic feature norms classification. *Behavior Research Methods* 49(6). 1984–2001.

Borbely, Antal F. 1998. A psychoanalytic concept of metaphor. *The International Journal of Psychoanalysis* 79(5). 923–936.

Bowdle, Brian F. & Gentner, Dedre. (2005). The career of metaphor. *Psychological Review* 112(1). 193–216.

Cameron, L. (2003). *Metaphor in educational discourse*. London: Continuum.

Cameron, Lynne. 2007. Patterns of metaphor use in reconciliation talk. *Discourse Society* 18(2). 197–222.

Cameron, Lynne. 2010. What is metaphor and why does it matter? In Lynne Cameron & Robert Maslen (eds.). *Metaphor analysis: Research practice in applied linguistics, social sciences and the humanities*. 3–25. London, UK: Equinox Pub.

Cameron, Lynne & Robert Maslen. 2010. *Metaphor analysis: Research practice in applied linguistics, social sciences and the humanities*. London, UK: Equinox Pub.

Cardeña, Etzel, Cheryl Koopman, Catherine Classen, Lynn C. Waelde & David Spiegel. 2000. Psychometric properties of the Stanford Acute Stress Reaction Questionnaire (SASRQ): A valid and reliable measure of acute stress. *Journal of Trauma Stress* 13(4). 719–734.

Citron, Francesca M. M. & Adele E. Goldberg. 2014. Metaphorical sentences are more emotionally engaging than their literal counterparts. *Journal of Cognitive Neuroscience* 26(11). 2585–2595.

Citron, Francesca M. M., Cristina Cacciari, Jakob Funcke, Chun-Ting Hsu & Arthur M. Jacobs. 2019. Idiomatic Expressions Evoke Stronger Emotional Responses in the Brain than Literal Sentences. *Neuropsychologia* 131. 233–48.

Cohn, Michael A., Matthias. R. Mehl & James. W. Pennebaker. 2004. Linguistic markers of psychological change surrounding September 11, 2001. *Psychological Science* 15(10). 687–693.

Costa, Adriana & Gerard Steen. 2014. Metaphor as a window on talk about trauma and post traumatic growth. *Scripta* 18(34). 283–299.

Ehlers, Anke, & David M. Clark. 2000. A cognitive model of post-traumatic stress disorder. *Behaviour Research and Therapy* 38(4). 319–345.

Fainsilber, Lynn & Andrew Ortony. 1987. Metaphorical uses of language in the expression of emotions. *Metaphor and Symbolic Activity* 2(4). 239–250.

Foa, Edna B. 1995 *The Posttraumatic Diagnostic Scale (PDS) manual*. Minneapolis, MN: National Computer Systems.

Foley, Patrick S. 2015. The metaphors they carry: Exploring how veterans use metaphor to describe experiences of PTSD. *Journal of Poetry Therapy* 28(2). 129–146.

Frewen, Paul A., David J. A. Dozois, Richard W. J. Neufeld, Maria Densmore, Todd K. Stevens & Ruth A. Lanius. 2011. Self-referential processing in women with PTSD: Affective and neural response. *Psychological Trauma: Theory, Research, Practice, and Policy* 3(4). 318–328.

Friedberg, Robert D. & Laura H. Wilt. 2010. Metaphors and stories in cognitive behavioral therapy with children. *Journal of Rational-Emotive & Cognitive-Behavior Therapy* 28(2). 100–113.

Gelo, Omar Carlo Gioacchino & Erhard Mergenthaler. 2012. Unconventional metaphors and emotional-cognitive regulation in a metacognitive interpersonal therapy. *Psychotherapy Research* 22(2). 159–175.

Halligan, Sarah L., Tanja Michael, David M. Clark & Anke Ehlers. 2003. Post-traumatic Stress Disorder following assault: The role of cognitive processing, trauma memory, and appraisals. *Journal of Consulting and Clinical Psychology* 71(3). 419–431.

Horst, Paul. 1941. The role of predictor variables which are independent of the criterion. *Social Science Research Council* 48(4). 431–436.

Hou, Cailan. (2009). 成人自评 [Self-assessment for adults]. In Jia Fujun and Hou Cailan. (eds), 心理应激与创伤评估手册 *[The Handbook of Psychological Stress and Trauma Measurement]*, 29–33. Beijing: People's Medical Publishing House.

Jaeger, Jeff, Katie M. Lindblom, Kelly Parker-Guilbert & Lori A. Zoellner. 2014. Trauma narratives: It's what you say, not how you say it. *Psychological Trauma: Theory, Research, Practice, and Policy* 6(5). 473–481.

Kaplow, Julie B., Britney M. Wardecker, Christopher M. Layne, Ethan Kross, Amanda Burnside, Robin S. Edelstein & Alan R. Prossin. 2018. Out of the mouths of babes: Links between linguistic structure of loss narratives and psychosocial functioning in parentally bereaved children. *Journal of Trauma Stress* 31(3). 342–351.

Kenny, Lucy M. & Richard A. Bryant. 2007. Keeping memories at an arm's length: Vantage point of trauma memories. *Behavior Research and Therapy* 45(8). 1915–1920.

Kopp, R. R. (1995). *Metaphor Therapy: Using Client-Generated Metaphors in Psychotherapy*. Brunnel/Mazel.

Kopp, Richard R. & Daniel Eckstein. 2004. Using early memory metaphors and client-generated metaphors in Adlerian therapy. *Journal of Individual Psychology* 60(2). 163–174.

Kopp, Richard R. & Michael Jay Craw. 1998. Metaphoric language, metaphoric cognition, and cognitive therapy. *Psychotherapy* 35(3). 306–311.

Kövecses, Zoltán. 2010. *Metaphor: A practical introduction*. New York: Oxford University Press.

Krippendorff, Klaus. 2004. *Content analysis: An introduction to its methodology*, 2nd edn. Thousand Oaks, California: Sage Publications.

Kross, Ethan, Ayduk Ozlem & Mischel Walter. 2005. When asking "why" does not hurt: Distinguishing rumination from reflective processing of negative emotions. *Psychological Science* 16(9). 709–715.

Kross, Ethan, Emma Bruehlman-Senecal, Jiyoung Park, Aleah Burson, Adrienne Dougherty, Holly Shablack, Ryan Bremner, Jason Moser & Ozlem Ayduk. 2014. Self-talk as a regulatory mechanism: How you do it matters. *Journal of Personality and Social Psychology* 106(2). 304–324.

Lakoff, George. 1992. Multiple selves: The metaphorical models of the self inherent in our conceptual system. Paper presented at The Conceptual Self in Context, Emory University, Atlanta (GA).

Lakoff, George & Mark Johnson. 1980. *Metaphors we live by*. Chicago: University of Chicago Press.

Lakoff, George & Mark Johnson. 1999. *Philosophy in the flesh: The embodied mind and its challenge to western thought*. New York: Basic Books.

Littlemore, Jeanette & Sarah Turner. 2020. Metaphors in communication about pregnancy loss. *Metaphor and the Social World* 10(1).45–75.

McIsaac, Heather K. & Eric Eich. 2004. Vantage point in traumatic memory. *Psychological Science* 15(4). 248–253.

McMullen, Linda M. 1985. Methods for studying the use of novel figurative language in psychotherapy. *Psychotherapy: Theory, Research, Practice, Training* 22(3). 610–619.

McMullen, Linda M. 1989. Use of Figurative Language in Successful and Unsuccessful Cases of Psychotherapy: Three Comparisons. *Metaphor and Symbolic Activity* 4(4). 203–225.

Meili, Iara. 2018. *Metaphors of post-traumatic growth and resilience in cultural-clinical psychology*. Zurich, Switzerland: University of Zurich Doctoral Dissertation.

Metcalfe, Janet & Walter Mischel. 1999. A hot/cool-system analysis of delay of gratification: Dynamics of willpower. *Psychological Review* 106(1). 3–19.

Mooren, Nora, Julie Krans, Gérard Näring & Agnes van Minnen. 2019. Vantage perspective in analogue trauma memories: An experimental study. *Cognition and Emotion* 33(6). 1261–1270.

Moser, Karin S. 2000. Metaphor analysis in psychology: Method, theory, and fields of application. *Forum: Qualitative Social Research* 1 (2). https://www.qualitative-research.net/index.php/fqs/article/view/1090 (accessed 25 Oct, 2021).

Moser, Karin S. 2007. Metaphors as symbolic environment of the self: How self-knowledge is expressed verbally. *Current Research in Social Psychology* 12. 151–178.

Muldoon, Orla T., S. Alexander Haslam, Catherine Haslam, Tegan Cruwys, Michelle Kearns & Jolanda Jetten. 2019. The social psychology of responses to trauma: Social identity pathways associated with divergent traumatic responses. *European Review of Social Psychology* 30(1). 311–348.

Ni, Michael Y., Yao Xiaoxin I, Leung Kathy S. M., Yau Cynthia, Leung Candi M. C., Lun Phyllis, Flores Francis P., Chang Wing Chung, Cowling Benjamin J., & Leung Gabriel M. 2020. Depression and post-traumatic stress during major social unrest in Hong Kong: A 10-year prospective cohort study. *The Lancet (British Edition)* 395(10220). 273–284.

Nigro, Georgia & Ulric Neisser. 1983. Point of view in personal memories. *Cognitive Psychology* 15(4). 467–482.

O'Kearney, Richard & Kelly Perrott. 2006. Trauma narratives in post-traumatic stress disorder: A review. *Journal of Trauma Stress* 19(1). 81–93.

Rasmussen, Brian & Lynne Angus. 1996. Metaphor in psychodynamic psychotherapy with borderline and non-borderline clients: A qualitative analysis. *Psychotherapy* 33(4). 521–530.

Rechsteiner, Karin, Andreas Maercker, Eva Heim & Iara Meili. 2020. Metaphors for trauma: A cross-cultural qualitative comparison in Brazil, India, Poland, and Switzerland. *Journal of Trauma Stress* 33(5). 643–653.

Robinson, John A. & Karen L. Swanson. 1993. Field and observer modes of remembering. *Memory* 1(3). 169–184.

Semino, Elena. 2008. *Metaphor in discourse*. Cambridge & New York: Cambridge University Press.

Semino, Elena. 2011. Metaphor, creativity, and the experience of pain across genres. In Joan Swann, Rob Pope & Ronald Carter (eds.), *Creativity in language and literature: The state of the art*, 83–102. Basingstoke & New York: Palgrave Macmillan.

Sims, Peter A. 2003. Working with metaphor. *American Journal of Psychotherapy* 57(4). 528–536.

Steen, Gerard J., Aletta G. Dorst, J. Berenike Herrmann, Anna Kaal, Tina Krennmayr & Trijntje Pasma. 2010. *Method for linguistic metaphor identification: From MIP to MIPVU*. Amsterdam: John Benjamins Publishing Company.

Stott, Richard, Warren Mansell, Paul Salkovskis, Anna Lavender, & Sam Cartwright-Hatton. 2010. *The Oxford guide to metaphors in CBT: Building cognitive bridges*. Oxford & New York: Oxford University Press.

Tay, Dennis. 2014. Metaphor theory for counseling professionals. In Jeanette Littlemore & John R. Taylor (eds.), *The Bloomsbury companion to cognitive linguistics*, 352–367. London & New York: Bloomsbury Academic.

Tay, Dennis. 2017. Quantitative metaphor usage patterns in Chinese psychotherapy talk. *Communication & Medicine* 14(1). 51–69.

Tay, Dennis. 2020. Affective Engagement in Metaphorical versus Literal Communication Styles in Counseling. *Discourse Processes* 57(4). 360–375.

Tay, Dennis & Jennifer Jordan. 2015. Metaphor and the notion of control in trauma talk. *Text & Talk* 35(4). 553–573.

Tedeschi, Richard & Lawrence G. Calhoun. 1995. *Trauma and transformation: Growing in the aftermath of suffering*. Thousand Oaks: SAGE Publications.

Wallace-Hadrill, Sophie M. A. & Sunjeev K. Kamboj. 2016. The impact of perspective change as a cognitive reappraisal strategy on affect: A systematic review. *Frontiers in Psychology* 7. 1715–1715.

Wardecker, Britney M., Robin S. Edelstein, Jodi A. Quas, Ingrid M. Cordón & Gail S. Goodman. 2017. Emotion language in trauma narratives is associated with better psychological adjustment among survivors of childhood sexual abuse. *Journal of Language and Social Psychology* 36(6). 628–653.

Williams, Alishia D. & Michelle L. Moulds. 2007. Cognitive avoidance of intrusive memories: Recall vantage perspective and associations with depression. *Behavior Research and Therapy* 45(6). 1141–1153.

Wilson, Johnson P. & Jacob D. Lindy. 2013. *Trauma, Culture and Metaphor: Pathways of Transformation and Integration*. New York: Routledge.

Witztum, Eliezer, Onno van der Hart & Barbara Friedman. 1988. The use of metaphors in psychotherapy. *Journal of Contemporary Psychotherapy* 18(4).

Jane Dilkes
Prospecting for metaphors in a large text corpus: Combining unsupervised and supervised machine learning approaches

1 Introduction

This chapter discusses some methods used to identify metaphor automatically in a large text corpus. It is taken from a wider ongoing investigation into the language style that surrounds metaphor use in online communities, and what that might say about the relationship between metaphor use and state of mind (Dilkes, 2022).

Metaphor is a figure of speech in which a target concept is described in terms of source concepts, such that existing understandings of a source concept may be available to shape understandings of the target concept. The focus in the current investigation is on metaphor themes, where a theme is "an abstraction from the metaphorical statements in which it does or might occur. A metaphor theme is available for repeated use, adaptation and modification by a variety of speakers or thinkers on any number of specific occasions" (Black 1977:438).

The data for the wider investigation this chapter relates to consists of all the posts made by participants on two internet fora, each of which is analysed separately. For the first forum investigated it has been found that the language style of a post differs significantly depending on whether or not typical community metaphors are present in that post, with use of those metaphors co-occurring with language of a style that has been associated with better mental health (Tausczik and Pennebaker 2010).

Identifying metaphor automatically in text is recognised as a challenging problem that is essential for a number of applied Natural Language Processing tasks, including machine translation; opinion mining; and information retrieval (Shutova 2015). In the area of metaphor research also there is a pressing need for "greater precision in reliably identifying conceptual metaphors from the systematic analysis of language patterns" (Gibbs 2017:265). But although there is much current interest in this issue, it remains an unsolved task (Veale, Shutova, and Klebanov 2016). A summary of the Association for Computational Linguistics (ACL) 2020 metaphor detection shared task notes that over the last decade approaches to automatic metaphor detection have explored features

---

Jane Dilkes, University of Birmingham, e-mail: jdilkes@pm.me

https://doi.org/10.1515/9783110687279-009

based on "concreteness and imageability, semantic classification using WordNet, FrameNet, VerbNet, SUMO ontology, property norms, and distributional semantic models, syntactic dependency patterns, sensorial and vision-based features" (Leong et al. 2020:1). But it has been suggested that hand-constructed resources such as WordNet do not have the density and diversity of connections needed to support realistic automatic interpretation of metaphor (Veale, Shutova, and Klebanov 2016:75). More recently focus has switched to the use of deep learning models, with more than half the entries for the ACL 2020 metaphor detection task using BERT (Bidirectional Encoder Representations from Transformers), a transformer-based deep learning model trained on unlabelled text, which considers left and right contexts simultaneously, across all layers (Devlin et al. 2019).

In order to remain open to what metaphor is present in the diverse, naturally-occurring data under consideration here – to undertake a corpus-driven rather than a corpus-based investigation (Deignan 2005) – this investigation uses unsupervised and supervised machine learning to prospect for metaphor themes in the data, and the language used to express them. Techniques explored in this chapter include k-means clustering, dimensionality reduction, topic modelling, word vector similarity, graph-based ranking, and finally supervised learning draws on all the insights gained through unsupervised methods to predict the presence of identified metaphor themes for individual records (forum posts) in the data.

2 About machine learning

"Machine learning is about extracting knowledge from data" (Müller and Guido 2017:1). While in classical programming humans write specific program rules to process data based on what is already known, a machine learning system in comparison is not explicitly programmed – it is trained to look for statistical structure, usually in large and complex datasets for which mathematical statistics are not practical (Chollet 2018:5).

Supervised learning is the passing of labelled inputs (data plus answers) to a machine learning algorithm. That algorithm then works to produce a set of rules that will allow the prediction of outputs (answers) from unlabelled input data (Chollet 2018:5). Unsupervised learning consists of all machine learning for which it is not already known what "answers" are sought (Müller and Guido 2017:133). Unsupervised transformations of unlabelled data create new representations of that data that may provide new insights, which may support analysis using other methods.

2.1 Machine learning in the current study

In the current study unsupervised learning techniques are used to explore what metaphor themes are present in the data, and what language is used to express those metaphors. That new knowledge is then used to label the data for supply to a supervised deep learning algorithm to produce a model with which to classify new data, which provides further new insights into the data. The Python programming language is used to implement machine learning. Python is commonly used for machine learning and has a wide range of relevant open source libraries, and an active, exploratory, and collaborative community.

2.2 Summary

Machine learning is a type of statistical learning that is well suited to the large and diverse internet forum data used in the current investigation. In this chapter unsupervised learning methods are used to explore the data for metaphor themes, then supervised learning builds on that new knowledge to predict the presence or absence of community metaphor themes in individual forum posts.

In the next section the internet forum data used in this chapter is described, alongside a rationale for limiting that data based on the number of posts that participants have made for initial analyses to locate community metaphor.

3 Data used

3.1 Data source

The naturally occurring text data used here consists of 260,239 posts from the internet forum of a UK cancer charity, a forum for people living with cancer, from the start of the forum in June 2008 to the end of May 2020. The posts were collected using the Scrapy Python web scraping framework; the forum administrators were happy to allow this public data to be collected for this research. Posts by participants officially associated with the forum (moderators and health care professionals) were excluded from the data. Anonymous posts were also excluded because some of the processing is based on number of posts made, which the composite "anonymous" participant distorts. Each post is stored as a separate record in a single data file.

3.2 Selecting data based on the number of posts made

The focus of the ongoing wider investigation is the triangular relationship between metaphor use, community, and state of mind. The Scattertext Python library, "a tool for visualizing linguistic variation between document categories" (Kessler 2017:1), is used in the current section to compare data based on the number of posts made by participants – between groups of participants that are more, or less, established within the community.

The categories used for this broad-brush exploratory comparison are participants who have made more than 1,000 posts, compared with participants who have made fewer than 20 posts, with 20 selected as a balance between considering participants who have been relatively active on and involved with the forum (around half the participants have only ever made one post, for example), while still having made a relatively small number of posts. Running Scattertext on the top 500 terms for these two groups shows that the newer forum participants use more literal and specific language that focuses on their current personal physical lived experience, while established forum participants use more figurative language. Terms that are potentially metaphoric in this context are italicised in the results summaries below.

3.2.1 Top terms for participants with a post count >1,000

Tokens welcome, hubby, ok, bouts, we're, *journey*, forum, hold, feelings, *ring*, psa, number, double
Phrases 2 bouts, bouts of breast cancer, *cancer journey*, warm welcome, *boxing gloves*

3.2.2 Top terms for participants with a post count < 20

Tokens i'm, neck, tumour, bowel, blood, removed, stomach, ultrasound, ct, biopsy, ok
Phrases 5 weeks, 3 weeks, 6 weeks, blood test, left side, right side, left breast

The group of participants who have made more than 1,000 posts made 24 uses of the potentially metaphoric term *journey* per 25,000 terms, and 94 uses per 1,000 posts. In comparison, the group of participants who have made fewer than 20 posts made four uses of *journey* per 25,000 terms, and 16 uses per 1,000 posts.

In order to make the majority of terms legible for the following static screenshot of the interactive Scattertext visualisation (Figure 8.1), just the 100 top terms are included. In Figure 8.1 "each axis corresponds to the rank frequency a term occurs in a category of documents" (Kessler 2017:1).

In the upper-left corner are terms frequently used by participants with more than 1,000 posts but infrequently or never used by participants with fewer than 20 posts. In the bottom-right corner are terms frequently used by participants with fewer than 20 posts, terms that are infrequently or never used by participants with more than 1,000 posts.

Amongst these top 100 terms from the data as a whole, *journey*, underlined in the diagram, is used an average amount by the group who have made more than 1,000 posts, but is used infrequently by the group who have made fewer than 20 posts. Even though just one potentially metaphoric term *journey* is present in this more limited visualisation, it can still be seen from the diagram that the language of each group has a very different focus. The presence of *journey* also shows that (i) it is the most dominant potential metaphor in this corpus, and (ii) it is relatively dense in the corpus given its appearance in this analysis of the top 100 corpus terms.

Since the purpose of the first part of the current investigation is to identify typical metaphor themes of this community, the data used for the initial exploratory analyses excludes participants who have made fewer than 20 posts, whose language understandably has an overwhelmingly literal focus.

3.3 Summary

The data used in the current study consists of all posts from an internet forum for people who are living with cancer. Since it has been shown that participants who have made fewer than 20 posts tend to use more literal language, the initial exploratory analyses to find community metaphor themes use data from participants who have made 20 or more posts.

3.3.1 Outline of the rest of the chapter

In sections 4 – 9 I describe the method used to identify metaphors in the data, which involves the use of unsupervised and supervised machine learning to identify dominant metaphor themes, and the linguistic instantiations of those themes. I begin in Section 4 by discussing the use of text data in machine learning. Then in sections 5 to 6, I explain how I combine term frequency control

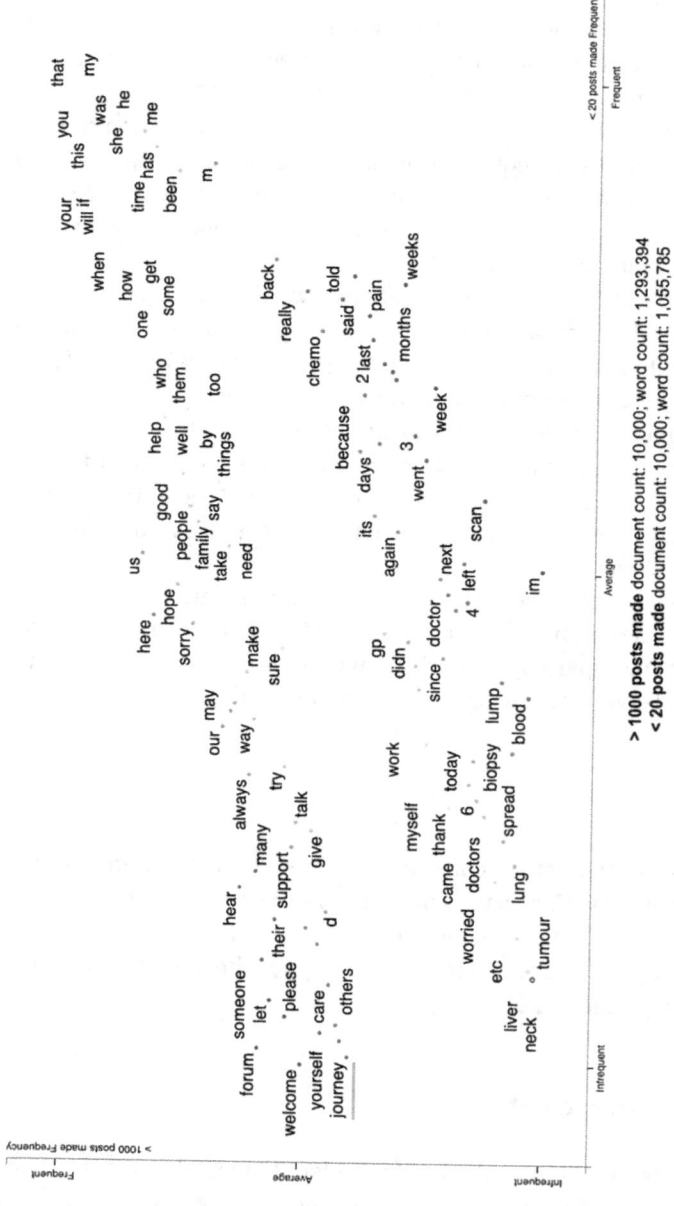

Figure 8.1: 100 top terms for participants with >1,000 posts (top) and participants with < 20 posts (bottom).

with dimensionality reduction, including a more in-depth topic modelling investigation, to identify the dominant metaphor themes in the data.

Having identified the metaphor themes, in sections 7 and 8 I consider two procedures to identify the ways in which those metaphor themes are represented linguistically in the data. The first procedure (using word vectors) allows the identification of a wider range of potentially metaphoric language, whereas the second method (graph-based ranking) is used to consider the true metaphoricity of the potentially metaphoric terms identified. Finally, in section 9, the information obtained through unsupervised learning methods informs the training of a supervised learning algorithm. A model is produced to identify metaphors automatically in the data. This also provides insights into the language style that surrounds metaphor use in this context, which may be related to the functions that those metaphors perform.

The next section addresses the processing of the text data for analysis, and the selection of the lexical item of focus.

4 Processing the text data

This section addresses some of the pre-processing that is required in order to be able to use machine learning with text data.

4.1 Natural language processing (NLP)

In the current investigation the text data is processed using the spaCy Natural Language Processing (NLP) Python library (Honnibal and Montani 2020). Using statistical language models to process text according to its context, the spaCy parser is accurate and quick (Honnibal and Montani 2020a). Its English part of speech tagger uses the OntoNotes5 version of the Penn Treebank tag set. In addition, tags (more fine-grained than POS tags) are mapped to the Universal Dependencies v2 POS tag set (Honnibal and Montani 2020b). As well as being highly accurate and consistent, automatic tokenization and tagging can avoid disagreements over the manual identification of lexical units prior to the identification of metaphor (Veale, Shutova, and Klebanov 2016).

4.2 Lexical unit of focus

Although every token in a text may be used for an investigation, for some analyses it is more productive to focus on a subset of tokens, or to focus on a different lexical unit. In the current metaphor-focused investigation, since many metaphors take the form of a multi-word expression rather than a single word (Deignan 2010) (Cameron and Maslen 2010), as well as being considered as individual tokens text is also organised into n-grams, noun chunks, and sentences, for analysis. The lexical units described in the table 8.1 below are used in the current investigation.

Table 8.1: Lexical units used in the current investigation.

Lexical unit	Description
token	Individual tokens are identified here using the spaCy tokenizer. Since spaCy can identify parts of speech, it can be used to select only the nouns present in the data, for example, or the lemmas of those nouns.
n-gram	For some investigations n-grams are sought, where n-grams are the collocations (common phrases) of a specified length of the lexical terms of focus. For example, bigrams are collocations of two lexical terms; trigrams are collocations of three lexical terms. In the current study n-grams are processed using the Gensim Python library *Phraser*, which automatically detects n-gram collocations from a stream of sentences.
noun chunk	SpaCy is used to generate noun chunks from the data, where a noun chunk is a base noun phrase – a flat phrase that has a noun as its head. "You can think of noun chunks as a noun plus the words describing the noun" (Honnibal and Montani 2020b).
sentence	For a later concordance analysis, the spaCy tokenizer is used to extract sentences from the text.

4.3 Focusing on nouns in order to find metaphoric language

Nouns refer to things that have spatial dimensions. Because of this nouns may make any unconventional (potentially metaphoric) reference more accessible: they may be the most recognizable and vivid of metaphors (Goatly, 2011). The Metaphor Identification Procedure (Pragglejaz, 2007) similarly notes that it is generally easiest to assign a basic sense to nouns, making the understanding of metaphoric nouns as metaphoric more accessible compared to metaphor based on other parts of speech. And since noun-based metaphor has more potential to activate other sensory metaphoric associations, according to the dynamic view it is potentially more likely to activate metaphorical thinking (Müller, 2008).

Goatly (2011) suggests the following hierarchy of force of metaphor source terms:
- nouns (most active)
- verbs and adjectives (less active)
- adverbs and prepositions (least active).

As this study is part of a wider investigation into the measurable psychological impact of metaphor use, the focus is on finding metaphors for which the source term is a noun.

4.4 Vectorization

Some of the machine learning methods investigated in the current study work with numeric tensors, not text. So, once the lexical items of focus (terms) are extracted from the text data, for example all the noun lemmas, those terms are vectorized.

Vectorization is the process of turning a collection of text documents into numerical feature vectors called a *Bag of Words* representation, where "words" represents the lexical unit of focus. After vectorization, the text documents are described by occurrences of the terms contained in them, while the relative position of those terms in the document is ignored. That loss of information about relative position is why generating n-grams or noun chunks prior to vectorization can be more revealing of information about the text for some analyses, since n-grams and noun chunks retain some information about word order.

The vectorization process, as well as creating the vector of numerical features representing the terms in the text data, also creates a dictionary detailing which text term is associated with which numerical feature. So, when the analysis requiring numerical tensors has been run, the output can be converted to text for display and interpretation. In the current study the scikit-learn Python library (Pedregosa et al. 2011) *CountVectorizer* is used to vectorize text.

4.5 Term frequency control

The max_df (the maximum documents in which a term may appear) and min_df (the minimum documents in which a term may appear) parameters supplied to the *CountVectorizer* facilitate a finely grained exploration of the data (table 8.2), and changing the value of these parameters can radically change the output. If a float is supplied in the range 0.0 to 1.0 this refers to the proportion of documents. If an integer is supplied, this refers to the number of documents.

Table 8.2: Max_df and min_df definitions.

Parameter	Description
max_df	ignore terms that appear in more than this proportion or number of documents
min_df	ignore terms that appear in fewer than this proportion or number of documents

4.5.1 Controlling term frequency to look for metaphors

In setting the max_df value, the diversity of the data is considered. In terms of the current study, if data from just one forum participant is used, the settings chosen for a particular investigative purpose are likely to be different to those chosen when the very diverse data from all forum participants is considered together. In looking for metaphors, the max_df value might be set higher if just one participant is being investigated because that one participant is more likely to use the same metaphoric language frequently. The choice of max_df value is also influenced by the lexical unit of focus. For example, since n-grams are more complex and specific than are noun lemmas, each n-gram is likely to be rarer in the data than are many of the noun lemmas.

Exploring the data with different term frequency settings can be a productive way of understanding the density of metaphor in a particular context. Since the current investigative focus is on finding metaphor themes that are particularly representative of this language community, and not creative metaphors, the min_df is set above 1, so that terms are only considered that are present in more than one document in the corpus.

4.5.2 Comparison with keyness

The corpus linguistics technique of calculating the *keyness* of terms compares their frequency in the corpus of focus against their frequency in a reference corpus of general language use, with differences between the two corpora checked for statistical significance. Keyness is used to explore what a corpus is "about". But other lexical sets may be present in the low-frequency vocabulary of the focus corpus that do not obviously seem to be relevant to the "aboutness" of the corpus and may therefore be missed by the focus on keyness. It is these groupings in low-frequency vocabulary that suggest metaphorical activity (Phillip 2010). Term frequency control can be used to locate those other meaningful terms within a corpus that do not have keyness.

4.5.3 Using k-means clustering to consider the effectiveness of term frequency control for finding metaphors

Clustering is the partitioning of data into groups, called clusters, consisting of data points that typically occur together. K-means is a simple and commonly used unsupervised algorithm to locate cluster centres by which to group data based on similarity. The number of clusters to search for must be supplied to the algorithm and running the algorithm to find various numbers of clusters is another way of exploring the structure of the data.

The simplicity of k-means clustering can also be a weakness: since each cluster is defined by its centre it is inevitably a simple shape, with each cluster having approximately the same diameter (Müller and Guido 2017). In k-means clustering, a random distribution of cluster centres is made, then the following two-step process is run until the assignment of data points to clusters no longer changes:
1. A data point is assigned to its nearest cluster centre
2. Each cluster centre is calculated as the mean of each data point assigned to it

K-means clustering was applied here using the scikit-learn Python library *Kmeans* algorithm to find three clusters and output the top 25 terms from each cluster. The data for this investigation consists of noun lemmas, from which bigrams and trigrams were formed. For the condition in which term frequency is controlled, max_df was set to 0.1, and min_df to 2.

In the output for which term frequency was not controlled, in the first table below, there are no potentially metaphoric terms in any of the clusters. In comparison, in the output for which term frequency was controlled to focus the data on less common terms, the second table below, the potentially metaphoric token *journey* is present in cluster two. Because there is less repetition of common terms between the clusters for which term frequency was controlled, they are also easier to make sense of as separate concepts. Cluster one is perhaps about hospital appointments to discuss results; cluster two appears to be about support from various sources; cluster three may also be about diagnostic results, but with a slightly different focus to cluster one.

Table 8.3: Top 25 terms from 3 k-means clusters when term frequency was not controlled.

Cluster	Term frequency not controlled
1	time mum day dad thing cancer year life way people family week lot month one friend pain treatment chemo husband bit feeling support care hospital
2	cancer year treatment time people thing day chemo breast week way life mum diagnosis lot dad family month stage surgery friend one husband doctor forum
3	cancer time thing day treatment week year chemo people way lot mum dad life result family bit one pain gp care month luck husband friend

Table 8.4: Top 25 terms from 3 k-means clusters when term frequency was controlled.

Cluster	Term frequency controlled
1	result luck doctor gp bit breast hospital pain surgery appointment today thank problem stage nurse scan question post test lump symptom diagnosis radiotherapy advice tomorrow
2	friend support husband forum care other feeling help heart site *journey* diagnosis situation post loss memory child pain advice place hug word love thought moment
3	news result luck thank scan today diagnosis care appointment post forum bit friend thought support husband consultant other finger test breast touch hope hug stage

4.6 Summary

In order to be used with methods that accept only numeric tensors, text must first be processed so that the lexical items of focus (for example tokens, or noun lemmas, or noun chunks) are extracted from it. Those lexical items are then represented as a numerical tensor (vectorized), with the vectorization process also providing a method for screening terms based on their frequency in the corpus, which allows a finely controlled focus on those rarer terms that may be more likely to be metaphoric.

The next section investigates dimensionality reduction in conjunction with term frequency control for finding potentially metaphoric language in the data.

5 Dimensionality reduction

Dimensionality reduction is commonly used for reducing data to two or three dimensions in order to plot it, or "to provide a lower-dimensional representation of documents that reflects concepts instead of raw terms" (Crain et al. 2012). In the current section three dimensionality reduction methods are explored: principal component analysis, factor analysis, and latent dirichlet allocation. The data consists of noun lemmas, from which bigrams and trigrams are formed. For each method, the 25 top terms are output from the three top components found. For each of these analyses the scikit-learn Python library is used to vectorize the text data, with a max_df setting of 0.1 and a min_df setting of 2, and to perform the relevant dimensionality reduction. For this investigation *variable* represents a lexical item, for example noun lemma, or trigrammed noun lemmas.

5.1 Principal component analysis

In principal component analysis (PCA) a multivariate dataset is decomposed into a set of successive orthogonal components that explain the maximum amount of its variance (scikit-learn.org 2020). In this way the least important components can be dropped from the data while the most valuable parts of all the original variables are retained (Müller and Guido 2017). The PCA process works as follows:
1. find the direction in the data along which the features of that data (variables) are most correlated with each other
2. find the direction in the data that contains the most information while being most orthogonal to the previous component
3. repeat step 2

Although only three components are output in this investigation, it can be seen from the PCA results table below that each component is relatively meaningful. Component 1 is perhaps about hospital appointments; component 2 could be about the wider support context, including the internet forum, and includes the potentially metaphoric *journey* token; component 3, which also includes the *journey* token, is perhaps about the emotionally challenging situation of waiting for test results.

Table 8.5: PCA results.

Component	Top 25 terms found in three components
1	result appointment test breast gp lump scan surgery biopsy doctor consultant luck hospital news symptom lymph_node radiotherapy oncologist stage surgeon ct_scan wait waiting mastectomy nurse
2	forum support husband diagnosis result other site advice help question experience information post appointment situation news nurse test touch gp breast chat *journey* type place
3	result news heart hug memory feeling love *journey* today thought scan daughter post word child son test moment hand finger tomorrow waiting tear world emotion

5.2 Factor analysis

"Factor analysis uses frequency counts of linguistic features to identify sets of features that co-occur in texts" (Biber 1988:63). In factor analysis a large number of variables is reduced to a smaller number of factors, each of which combines multiple variables based on the correlations between them. Factor analysis can produce similar components to PCA, but has the advantage that it is not constrained by the same requirement that all components must be orthogonal to each other (scikit-learn.org 2020).

It can be seen from the factor analysis results table below that as with PCA, the three factors can be interpreted in a meaningful way, with factors 1 and 3 containing the potentially metaphoric *journey* token. The first component is perhaps about feelings and family; the second about physical problems associated with living with cancer; and the third about the experience of breast cancer more specifically.

5.3 Latent dirichlet allocation

Latent dirichlet allocation (LDA) is a probabilistic model for findings groups of words that frequently appear together (scikit-learn.org 2020), which works well

Table 8.6: Factor analysis results.

Factor	Top 25 terms found in three factors
1	heart feeling memory support grief loss child love husband parent help hug daughter other word emotion thought *journey* son forum situation mother world death comfort
2	pain bit today night hair side_effect body food bed radiotherapy cycle heart memory morning op hour head weight lymph_node couple tablet yesterday session end drug
3	breast mastectomy heart *journey* feeling lump hug diagnosis memory result stage head lung grade o_k lymph_node emotion shock tear lass test butt boob hand thought

for the forum data used in this investigation in which each post is a separate document.

As with the results for PCA and factor analysis above, the three LDA topics can be interpreted in a meaningful way, and topic 1 contains the *journey* token. The first topic is perhaps about feelings and family; the second is perhaps about medical appointments; the third topic could relate to support, including specifically the internet forum.

Table 8.7: LDA results.

Topic	Top 25 terms found in three topics
1	friend feeling thank heart word thought hug love daughter child bit pain wife memory *journey* husband moment loss today work son hand parent world story
2	luck result gp surgery appointment doctor breast hospital scan symptom test radiotherapy lump consultant oncologist stage biopsy op problem tomorrow body finger lymph_node tumour mastectomy
3	forum news care support post site diagnosis other advice help question nurse experience husband touch hope situation thread chat place lung wish information decision while

5.4 Summary

Dimensionality reduction methods in conjunction with term frequency control were found to be productive in finding meaningful themes or concepts in the data. There are similarities between the concepts found via each method, and also differences: each provides more insight into the data. In addition, the potentially metaphoric term *journey* is present in two of the three components for both principal component analysis and factor analysis, and one of the three components for latent dirichlet allocation, suggesting that this could be the primary metaphor theme in use in this data.

In the next section latent dirichlet allocation is used again in a larger-scale more in-depth investigation.

6 Topic modelling with latent dirichlet allocation

"Often, when people talk about topic modelling, they refer to one particular decomposition method called latent dirichlet allocation" (Müller and Guido 2017:350). In topic modelling, terms frequently used together in documents are organised into "topics", where it is up to the investigator to determine what a topic might be about, and if it can be said to be about anything. Running this more in-depth topic modelling on this data is a way of exploring further:
- what metaphor themes are present in the data
- what language is used to express the metaphor themes in this context
- what metaphoric language typically occurs together, or is used to address similar concerns
- the dominant concerns of the forum

6.1 Determining the optimal number of topics

In topic modelling, the coherence value indicates how likely it is that the terms in a topic do occur together in any particular document. The optimal number of topics for a set of data can be estimated, or selected via a processing loop that calculates the coherence value of a model with a particular number of topics: the model used is the one with the greatest coherence value. For the LDA models in the current section, the number of topics to use is calculated using the Gensim Python library *CoherenceModel* topic coherence pipeline, which is based on Röder, Both, and Hinneburg (2015). For this investigation, the Gensim Python library *ldamallet* LDA model is used.

6.2 Visualisation of the LDA output

PyLDAvis, an interactive visualisation of the LDA model output (Sievert and Shirley 2014), is used to explore the topics found by the model. In the visualisation:
- pale bars represent a term's frequency across the entire corpus
- darker bars represent the frequency of a term in a given topic
- The λ slider is used to adjust the term rankings – small values of λ (near 0) highlight potentially rare, and exclusive, terms for the selected topic; large values of λ (near 1) highlight frequent, but not necessarily exclusive, terms for the selected topic
- the areas of the circles represent that topic's overall prevalence
- the centres of the circles represent the distance between topics (Sievert and Shirley 2014)

6.3 LDA topic modelling output

6.3.1 Noun lemmas, trigrams, max_df=0.1, min_df=2

In this analysis only noun lemmas were included, and bigrams and trigrams were formed from them. The *CountVectorizer* was run with a max_df setting of 0.1, and a min_df setting of 2. The topics in this LDA output each have a clear focus, and this is reflected in the 0.63 coherence value. Twenty-five topics were found, of which topic 18 (Figure 8.2) appears to be a metaphor-related topic.

All topic terms that are potentially metaphoric in this context are underlined in the image, and are also listed below in descending order of prevalence in the data as a whole:
(1) journey
(2) step
(3) eye (look cancer in the eye)
(4) ring (boxing ring)
(5) path
(6) attack
(7) road
(8) ride
(9) rollercoaster
(10) glove (boxing glove)
(11) boxing
(12) star

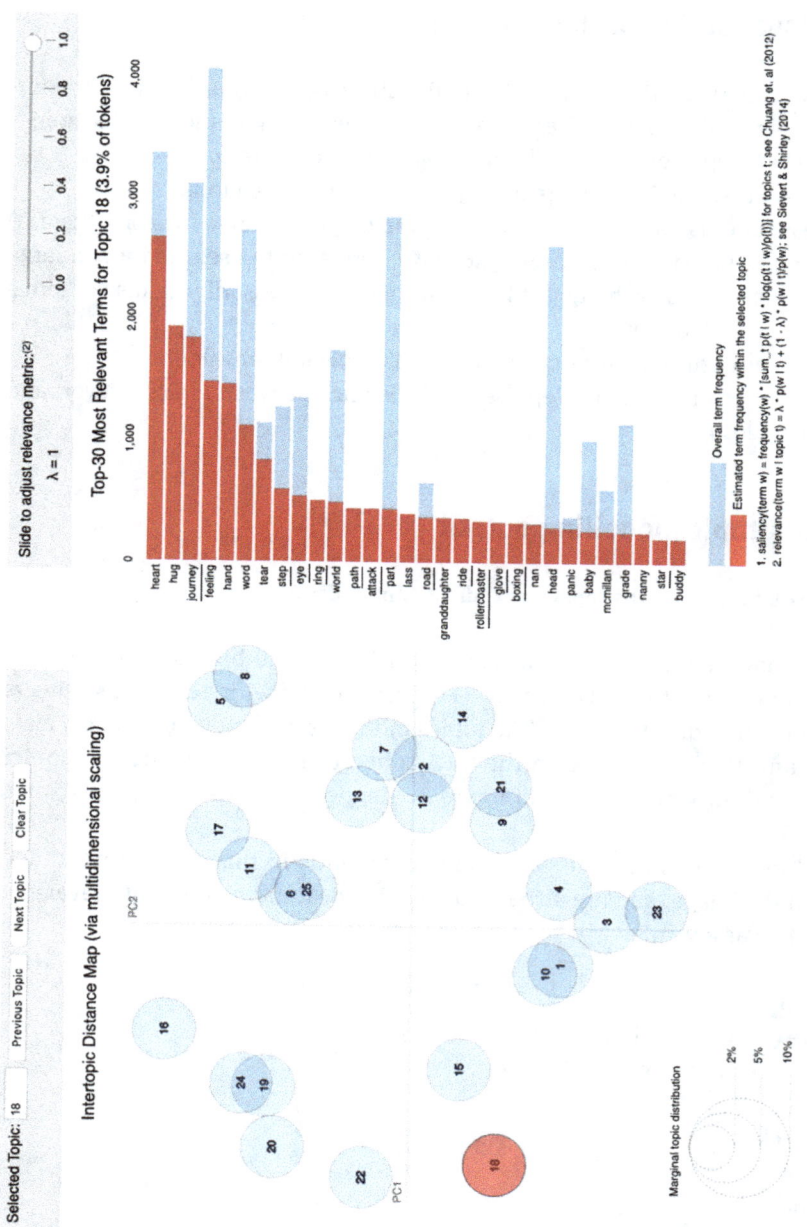

Figure 8.2: LDA a metaphor-related topic.

That all of these potentially metaphoric terms are found together in a single topic supports the understanding of them as potentially metaphoric, as well as demonstrating that they are typically used together, or to address similar concerns. Three potential metaphor themes are present here: journey, fight, and personification (look cancer in the eye). However, a fight token is not present in this topic.

For comparison, a non-metaphoric topic from the same LDA output (Figure 8.3) consists of the following terms relating to food and eating, listed in order of prevalence in the data as a whole:

food, weight, body, water, stuff, diet, drink, plenty, meal, tea, level, stone, idea, taste, energy, amount, coffee, appetite, cream, fluid, change, oil, couple, cake, fruit, milk, cup, glass, load, chocolate

6.3.2 All parts of speech, trigrams, max_df=0.1, min_df=2

For the analysis in this section, all parts of speech were included, and bigrams and trigrams were formed from them. The *CountVectorizer* was again run with a max_df setting of 0.1, and a min_df setting of 2. The coherence value for this output is 0.53, and there are 25 topics, of which topic 14 (Figure 8.4) appears to be a metaphor-related topic.

All terms that are potentially metaphoric in this context are underlined in the image and are also listed below it in descending order of prevalence in the data as a whole.

(1) journey
(2) kick
(3) path
(4) rollercoaster
(5) brake
(6) butt
(7) boxing glove
(8) cancer butt

It is useful to see the n-gram *boxing glove* confirm the previous interpretation of *glove* as related to *boxing*. The potentially metaphoric verb *kick* is also present, which, alongside *butt* and *cancer butt* represents the metaphorical concept *kicking cancer's butt*. But as anticipated, the majority of this metaphoric language is based on nouns, which will continue to be the focus of the current investigation.

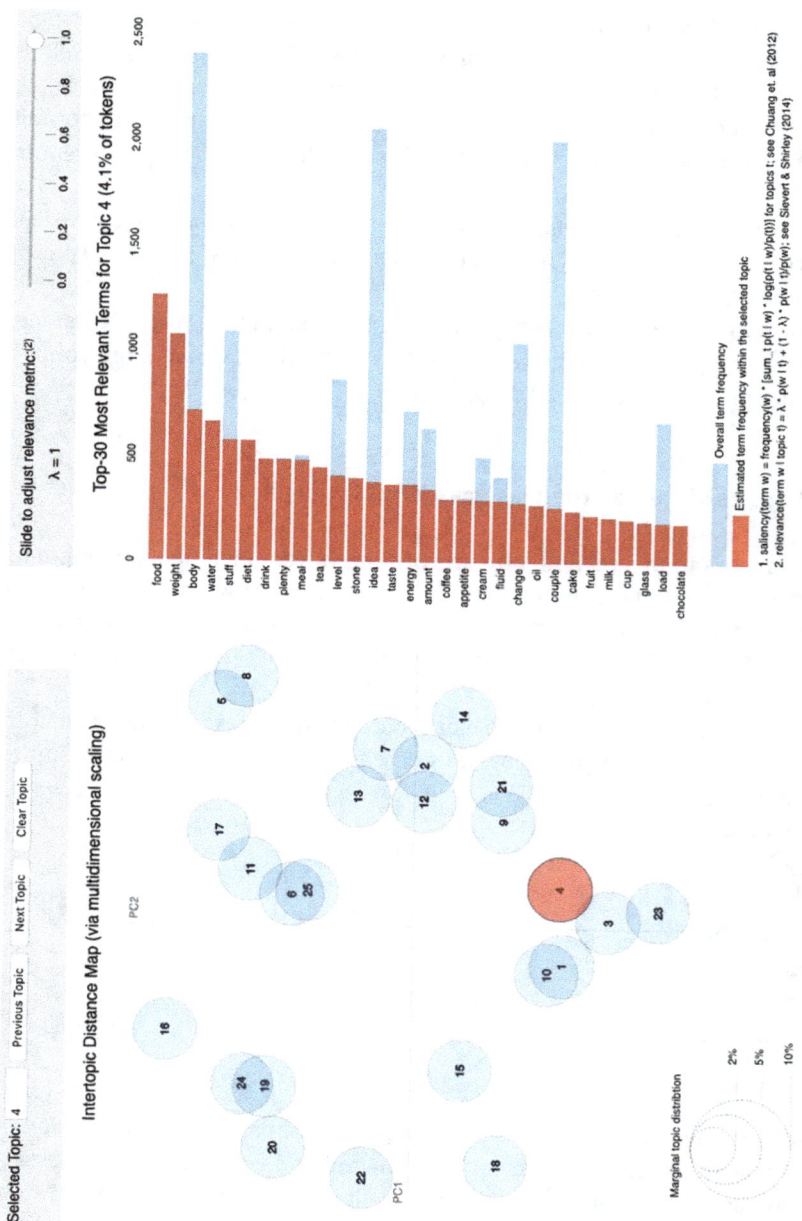

Figure 8.3: LDA non-metaphoric food-related topic.

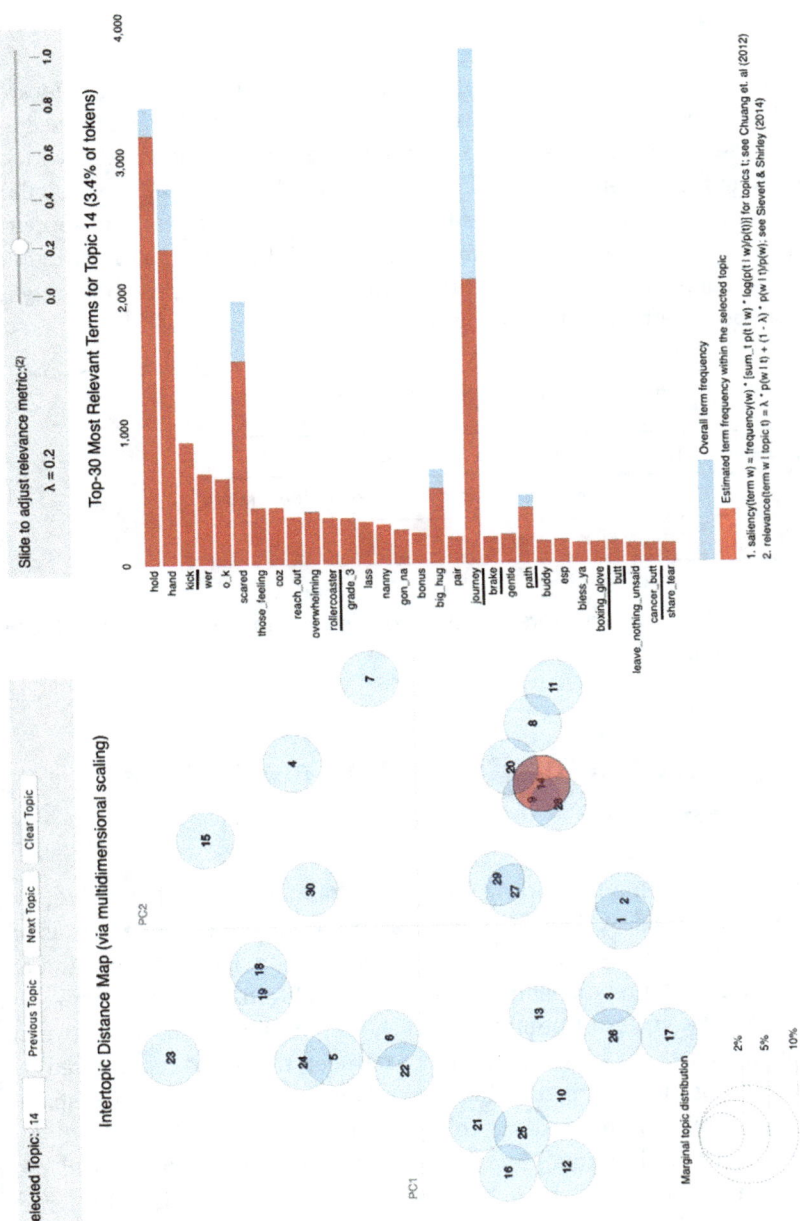

Figure 8.4: LDA metaphor-related topic.

6.4 Summary

Topic modelling was used in conjunction with term frequency control to locate the dominant potential metaphor themes in the data, and the language used to express those themes in this context. This method also demonstrates which metaphoric language tends to occur together in the data, or to address similar concerns. The potentially metaphoric language found so far appears to support two main themes, which are summarised in the following table. Although the second theme has been referred to in the table as "fight", the token *fight* has not yet been found as a way of invoking this theme.

Table 8.8: Potential metaphor themes found via topic modelling.

Metaphor theme	Terms used to express the theme
journey	journey, step, path, rollercoaster, road, ride, brake
"fight"	attack, kick, boxing, glove

In the next section word vectors are used to explore language related to these potentially metaphoric terms.

7 Using word vectors to explore metaphoric language

The word2vec algorithm created by a research team at Google (Mikolov et al. 2013) uses a neural network to learn word associations from a large corpus of text. The model can be used to find potential near synonyms for words, and to better understand the relationships between words. Word2vec represents each distinct word as a vector of numbers such that the cosine similarity between the vectors indicates the semantic similarity between the words represented by those vectors. For the investigation in this section, word vectors from the spaCy *en_core_web_lg* model are used to explore what terms are most similar to the potentially metaphoric terms already found in the data, to understand the wider meaning of and relationship between those terms, and to look for terms that do similar work: since the language model is based on common usage, similarly used common metaphoric terms should have semantic similarity even where their literal meaning is not similar. The term *fight* is also included, because although it has not yet been found in the data, a potential "fight" metaphor theme has been found. Including the *fight* term in this analysis may provide some insight into its relevance within this data.

In order to plot the word vectors, principal component analysis (section 5.1) was used to reduce the vector for each included term to two dimensions.

7.1 Vector plots

In the following vector plots, tokens already found to have potential metaphoric significance within this data are written in bold and uppercase so that they can be found more easily. To constrain the output to focus on tokens most similar to the potentially metaphoric terms already found, the spaCy word vector similarity method was used.

7.1.1 nouns with > 0.55 similarity to any of the existing metaphoric tokens

The following vector plot (Figure 8.5) shows all nouns in the data that have a similarity > 0.55 with any of the potentially metaphoric terms already found.

Although the plot is still somewhat dense with overlapping terms, most of them can be read, and it is helpful to see a visual representation of their semantic proximity. This provides information about the work of different terms in invoking metaphor. Some of the potentially metaphoric terms are located close together in the plot, suggesting that they perform a similar function. The terms most similar to the established potentially metaphoric terms are listed in the results table below.

7.1.2 nouns, verbs, and adjectives with >0.55 similarity to journey token

As a more focused example, in the following vector plot (Figure 8.6) all nouns, verbs, and adjectives have been included that have >0.55 similarity to the *journey* token only. These terms also could form part of an investigation into new potentially metaphoric language.

7.2 Using vector norms to find dissimilar concepts in a text

A vector norm is the L2 norm of a token's vector (the square root of the sum of the values squared); it represents the vector as a single value (Honnibal and Montani 2020). It is fundamental to metaphoric language that dissimilar concepts

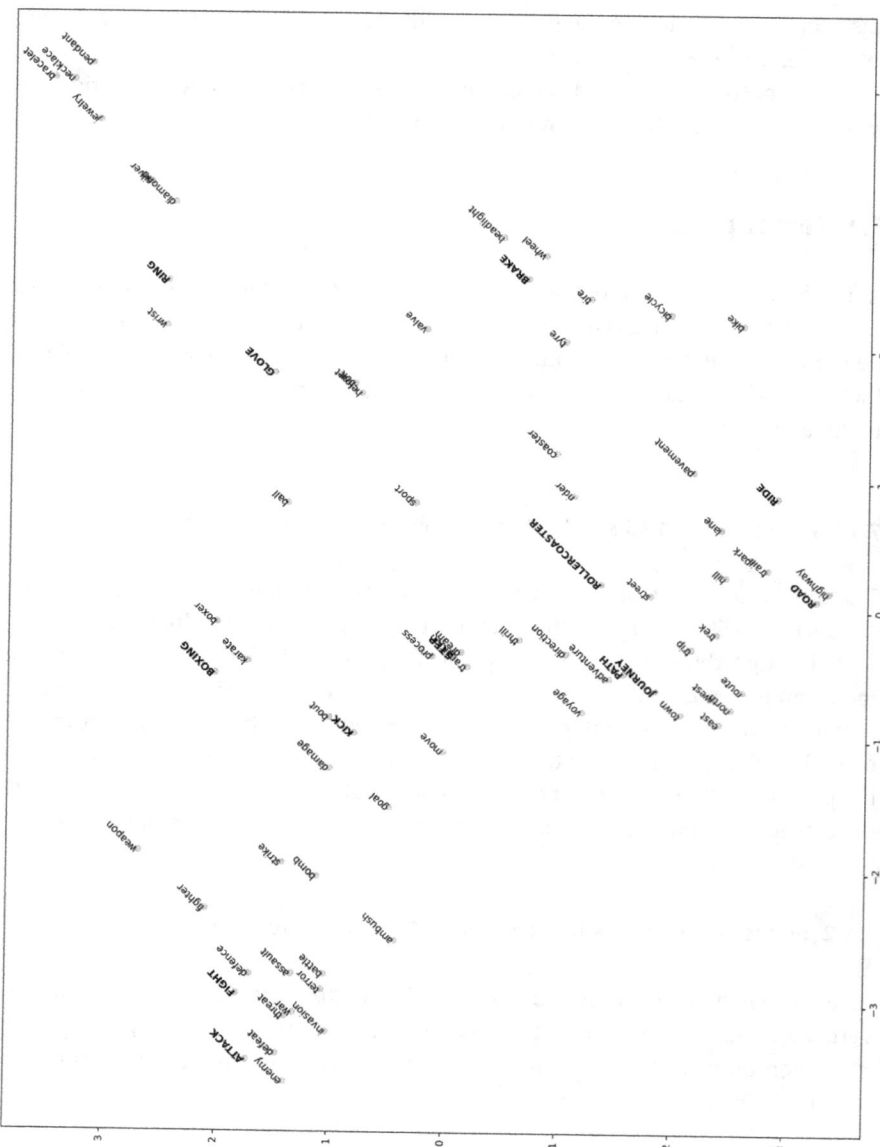

Figure 8.5: Vector plot of terms found to have potential metaphoric significance plus other similar nouns.

Table 8.9: Terms most similar to the established metaphoric terms.

Potentially metaphoric terms	Similarly used nouns from the vector plot
journey	town, adventure, voyage
step	process, transition
path	
rollercoaster	direction, thrill
road	highway, trail
ride	
brake	
fight, attack	defence, assault, threat, battle, terror, war, invasion, defeat, enemy
kick, boxing	boxer, karate, damage
glove	
ring	

are used together, with a more concrete source concept typically being used to frame an understanding of a more abstract target concept. Vector norms can be used to highlight when dissimilar concepts are used together, for example by calculating the distance between the vector norms of two tokens or calculating the standard deviation of vector norms in a text.

In the following example (table 8.10), which uses all the posts from one forum participant, the standard deviation of the vector norms for all nouns in each post was calculated. The following post containing metaphoric language was found to have the highest standard deviation of vector norms ($\sigma=1.455$). The included tokens are listed below the post text, along with their vector norm. Note that proportionally dominant use of the word *cancer* in this post in conjunction with the other nouns increases the standard deviation, while community metaphoric language, which is only present here in verb form, is not included in the calculation.

Table 8.11 lists the tokens from this post that have been included in the calculation of the standard deviation of vector norms:

Of all posts from the same participant that contain terms already identified as potentially metaphoric, the vector norms of the nouns in the following in the post described in table 8.12 were found to have the lowest standard deviation ($\sigma=0.489$). This fairly long post has been truncated for privacy reasons, but all nouns included in the calculation are listed below the post.

Figure 8.6: Vector plot of nouns, verbs, and adjectives with > 0.55 similarity to journey.

Table 8.10: Post with highest standard deviation of vector norms of all nouns.

Post text
hay. that's amazing. you did good here's to kicking cancers butt all the way you rock.

Table 8.11: Vector norms for nouns included in calculation of standard deviation of vector norms.

Token	Vector norm
way	4.7604
good	5.2805
cancers	8.0736

Table 8.12: Post with lowest standard deviation of vector norms of all nouns.

Post text (truncated)
i know what you mean about the feeling of 'not real' . . . it's a bumpy ride but if you look around we're all on that same ride with you.

The following tokens were included in the calculation of the standard deviation of vector norms for this post:

token	vector norm	token	vector norm
given	4.9030	reach	5.5850
mean	4.9843	try	5.6073
others	4.9988	problem	5.7470
ones	5.0839	inspiration	5.8137
time	5.1279	downs	5.8171
give	5.1312	bit	5.8507
know	5.1606	help	5.8787
ups	5.1821	share	5.9220
hold	5.2284	days	5.9896

(continued)

token	vector norm	token	vector norm
talking	5.2475	jumping	6.0184
let	5.2976	advice	6.0325
look	5.3037	hug	6.3495
keep	5.3458	feeling	6.3642
holding	5.3478	_journey_	6.3805
talk	5.4693	_rollercoaster_	6.3836
lots	5.4869	ride	6.5781
day	5.5376	grade	6.6439

Although the metaphor source terms *journey* and *rollercoaster* are present in this post, their target is not made explicit: since the *cancer* token is not present, the dissimilarity that supports metaphoric interpretation is implicit rather than explicit, and this explains the relatively low standard deviation of vector norms for this metaphoric post. In addition, although the literal terms *journey* and *rollercoaster* are not very similar, their similar metaphorical use appears to be represented in their very similar vector norms, which are underlined in the table above.

This exemplifies an issue with a selectional preference violation approach to finding metaphor in text: "in the case of frequent conventional metaphors, no statistically significant violation can be detected in the data" (Veale, Shutova, and Klebanov 2016:90). At the same time, this issue supports the use of the similarity method (section 7.1) for finding additional metaphoric language relating to the community metaphor themes; it also supports inclusion of the relatively dissimilar literal concepts *journey* and *rollercoaster* in the same metaphor theme.

7.3 Summary

In this section word vectors were used to identify other nouns in the data that are used similarly to those terms already established as potentially metaphoric.

In the next section, a concordance analysis to check the metaphoricity of all of the potentially metaphoric terms in their context is combined with graph-based ranking to simultaneously explore the relative importance of concordance sentences.

8 Graph-based ranking

In this section concordance analysis is combined with graph-based ranking, to check the metaphoricity of a term within its sentence, and to rank the concordance sentences based on the combined rank of all nouns in that sentence.

It has been argued that the form of language reflects conceptual metaphorical meaning: that the conceptual metaphor CLOSENESS IS STRENGTH OF EFFECT influences understanding of literal closeness within forms in a sentence as reflecting the strength of the closeness of the relationship holding between those forms. For example:
1. They don't think it'll leave until tomorrow
2. They think it won't leave until tomorrow

Statement 1 is weaker, it is argued, because the negative *don't* in that statement is positioned further from *leave*, the item it negates, than is the negative *won't* in statement 2 (Lakoff and Johnson 2003:128–132).

In the previous analyses, apart from the establishment of n-grams, the order of terms in a document has not been considered. Graph-based ranking, a method that takes account of the position of a term within its sentence and its closeness to other terms, is used in the current section to rank concordance sentences based on the combined rank of their component nouns. In graph-based ranking a graph expresses the structure between variables. A graph in this context is made up of vertices, which are connected by edges. For the purposes of the current investigation the vertices are word lemmas, with the edges representing the relationships between them. In graph-based ranking:
- when one vertex links to another vertex, it increases the importance of that other vertex
- the importance of the linking vertex determines the importance of the links it creates

8.1 PageRank

Google PageRank (Brin and Page 1998) is a well-known example of a graph-based ranking algorithm, which uses collective knowledge of the web rather than only considering individual web pages. PageRank determines how important a web page is by counting the number and quality of links made to the page: it allows for connections to have a variable value, in that being linked to from a high-ranking page has more benefit in terms of rank than does being linked to from a lower-ranked page. The PageRank algorithm was so successful that it changed how the web is searched.

8.2 TextRank

Based on PageRank, TextRank is a graph-based ranking model for text, in which in addition to the use of local vertex-specific information, the importance of a particular vertex is determined by calculating global information recursively from the whole graph (Mihalcea and Taurau 2004). The TextRank method can be summarised as follows:
1. Identify the lexical units that best define the task at hand, then add the relevant terms as vertices in the graph
2. Identify relations that connect the terms, and use those relations to draw edges between vertices in the graph
3. Iterate the graph-based ranking algorithm until convergence
4. Sort vertices based on their final score, then use the values attached to each vertex for ranking/selection decisions (Mihalcea and Taurau 2004)

The PyTextRank Python library (Paco 2016) is used in the current section to calculate the TextRank of phrases and sentences extracted from the text. A short example first demonstrates the ranking process, then PyTextRank is applied to the main data.

8.3 Short example of graph-based ranking

The following excerpt (Post 8.2) from a randomly selected post is used in this example:

> Post 8.2 i had a little chuckle to myself when you described the problems with your medical compression suit. it was very brave of you to even try to wear the suit so soon after surgery.

The terms used in this example are the lemmas of all nouns, verbs, and adjectives. The rank is calculated for those lemmas, then those lemma ranks are used to calculate the rank of phrases extracted from the text. The lemmas included in this analysis are described in the table below in the order they appear in each sentence.

Table 8.13: Lemmas from example sentences used to calculate rank.

sentence	lemmas
1	had little chuckle describe problem medical compression suit
2	brave try wear suit surgery

8.3.1 Construct a lemma graph of the text

The first step in the ranking process is the construction of a lemma graph (Figure 8.7) in which vertices are connected to other vertices co-occurring within a window of a maximum of N words, with PyTextRank setting N=3. It is in this way that the order of vertices affects their rank, since vertices in the middle of a sentence are more likely to be connected to other vertices within that window of three vertices behind and ahead. For example, in the lemma graph (Figure 8.7) the lemmas *have*, *little* and *chuckle* are linked to each other since they appear within three words of each other in the first sentence. They are not linked to any other lemmas since all other lemmas are positioned more than three words away from them. The lemma *brave* is not linked to any other lemmas since in the original sentences it is positioned more than three words away from any other lemma. *Suit* is linked to *medical* and *compression* through its location in the first sentence, and to *wear* through its location in the second sentence.

8.3.2 Calculating the pagerank score for each vertex in the lemma graph

After the lemma graph has been constructed, the rank score for each vertex is set to 1, then the ranking algorithm is run for several iterations until it converges at a threshold of 0.0001 (Paco 2016). Table 8.14 shows the lemmas ranked in order.

8.3.3 Calculating the pagerank score for each noun chunk in the text

For each noun chunk (extracted using spaCy) a composite rank score was calculated based on the rank scores of its component ranked terms. It can be seen from table 8.15 that in this two sentence example the highest ranked noun chunk is *your medical compression suit*. And it is true that the two example sentences are about the addressee's medical compression suit.

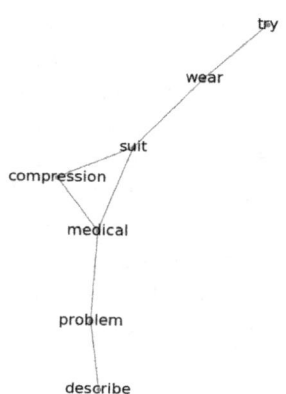

Figure 8.7: Lemma graph.

Table 8.14: Rank score for individual lemmas.

vertex/term	rank score	vertex/term	rank score
medical	0.149	compression	0.101
suit	0.149	describe	0.064
problem	0.113	try	0.064
wear	0.113	brave	0.016
little	0.108	surgery	0.016
chuckle	0.108		

Table 8.15: Noun chunks listed by rank score.

noun chunk	rank score	noun chunk	rank score
your medical compression suit	0.20	the problems	0.08
a little chuckle	0.12	surgery	0.06
the suit	0.10	it	0.00

8.4 Applying graph-based ranking to the main data

In the current section the graph-based ranking process is applied separately to all posts containing each separate potentially metaphoric noun from the list compiled previously. In the following analyses, because of the focus in the current study on metaphors expressed as nouns, only noun lemmas are added to the lemma graph: only nouns inform the ranking of a phrase. In addition, sentences, not noun chunks, are ranked based on the combined rank in all data analysed of their component nouns. Sentences are the focus here because noun chunks do not always provide enough context to determine whether a specific use of a term is metaphoric or not. In confirming whether a term is metaphoric in its context, the Macmillan online dictionary was used to check for more basic contemporary meanings of that term.

The output was limited to sentences containing the particular noun under investigation, and names and dates have been substituted with **. As well as ascertaining the actual metaphoricity of identified potentially metaphoric terms in this context, this analysis helps to build a picture of how they are used metaphorically in this context.

8.4.1 Ten top-ranked sentences containing journey

The ten top-ranked sentences containing *journey* as a noun, tabled below, demonstrate that use of *journey* in this context is typically metaphorical, referring to the experience of living with cancer. Sentence 7 contains the single literal use of *journey*.

Table 8.16: Ten top ranked sentences containing journey.

	Sentence	Rank
1.	my cousin's cancer journey ended yesterday	0.0299
2.	their cancer – your journey www.familiesfacingcancer.org	0.0287
3.	then the cancer journey started.	0.0279
4.	terminal cancer journey was tough.	0.0279
5.	no easy route this cancer journey.	0.0255
6.	his cancer journey lasted almost three years.	0.0252
7.	it is a nightmare journey to the cancer treatment centre via glasgow traffic.	0.0249
8.	this is your cancer journey . . .	0.0247
9.	cancer journeys are never the same.	0.0247
10.	our cancer journeys are all different.	0.0247

8.4.2 Ten top-ranked sentences containing rollercoaster

The ten top-ranked sentences containing *rollercoaster* are all metaphorical, referring to the experience of living with cancer, strongly indicating that it is correct to treat *rollercoaster* as metaphoric in this data. Where there is insufficient context to ascertain the metaphoricity of an extracted sentence, an additional extended concordance analysis was undertaken, with the extended results added in brackets.

Table 8.17: Ten top ranked sentences containing rollercoaster.

	Sentence	Rank
1.	lots of us in this cancer rollercoaster. . .	0.0261
2.	all aboard the cancer rollercoaster eh?	0.0234
3.	so many call this cancer journey a rollercoaster. . .	0.0226
4.	oh ***, welcome to the cancer rollercoaster.	0.0218
5.	you 've jumped on our cancer rollercoaster. . . .	0.0212
6.	much love and strength to everyone on the cancer rollercoaster.	0.0212

Table 8.17 (continued)

	Sentence	Rank
7.	when i 've heard people say cancer is a rollercoaster	0.0210
8.	its a rollercoaster (its a rollercoaster of emotions)	0.0205
9.	utter rollercoaster. (just gone through the utter rollercoaster of oesophageal cancer)	0.0205
10.	it 's quite some rollercoaster of feelings this breast cancer malarky.	0.0202

8.4.3 Ten top-ranked sentences containing fight

The use of *fight* is metaphorical in all but one of the ten top-ranked sentences including *fight* as a noun. Sentence 6 contains the single non-metaphorical use of *fight*. Although use of *fight* in this context is confirmed as predominantly metaphorical, the fact that in the topic modelling analysis *fight* was not found in the same topic as *journey*, for example, suggests that these two metaphors are not typically used together, and are not typically used to address the same concerns.

Table 8.18: Ten top-ranked sentences containing fight as a noun.

	Sentence	Rank
1.	wishing all cancer soldiers strength courage for their fight.	0.0259
2.	my mum lost the fight to lung cancer 6 months ago.	0.0254
3.	he lost his fight against bowel cancer.	0.0249
4.	mum lovely mum lost the fight to lung cancer 6 weeks ago.	0.0239
5.	my sister has only days left in her fight against breast cancer.	0.0235
6.	night baby baby missed fights and baths time.	0.0233
7.	my wife recently had a 12 year fight with recurrent bowel cancer.	0.0226
8.	*** lost her fight with this dreaded disease yesterday, liver / lung cancer.	0.0222
9.	my dad lost his fight with cancer on ***.	0.0219
10.	chemo is a fight!	0.0218

8.5 Findings for other potentially metaphoric terms

The same graph-based ranking analysis was run for the other potentially metaphoric terms collected in previous sections, with some results discussed below.

- *voyage* is used metaphorically unless it occurs in the phrase *bon voyage*. For example, *i have found it extremely therapeutic in my voyage to an unknown place*
- *highway* is predominantly used metaphorically, for example *the lymph system which is a bit like a super highway around the body for your immune system*; and *this is just a blip on life's highway*
- metaphoric use of *path* is mostly due to its particular metaphoric application within the UK health system
- *road* is predominantly used metaphorically, for example, *life can be a hard road to travel at times*
- *ride* is used metaphorically when used in conjunction with *rollercoaster*, or *bumpy*, for example *get back on that roller coaster and hold on tight and know its gonna be a bumpy old ride and ready for getting in the ring*
- *battle* is predominantly used metaphorically, and often in conjunction with *journey*. For example, *will understand all the emotions that go with the cancer journey / battle you may be on*; and *fighting the battle is part of a journey*
- use of *enemy* is split between metaphoric personification of cancer as an enemy, for example *you are a cruel wicked disease and you are a universal enemy*, and more literal use, for example *i wouldn't wish this on my worst enemy*
- *boxing* is predominantly used metaphorically, with very occasional reference to *boxing day* or *the real boxing ring*
- *glove* is used metaphorically where it is used with *boxing*
- *ring* is used metaphorically as *the ring* in terms of the fight with cancer, for example *i got my self some pink virtual boxing gloves and got in the ring with cancer*, and in terms of life as a fight, for example *getting back in the ring of life*. *ring* is not used metaphorically as a verb
- *war* is used metaphorically in terms of the *war on cancer*, but in the vast majority of cases *war* is used literally, for example *a 2nd world war veteran*

8.6 Dictionary of metaphoric terms

Based on the graph-based ranking analysis, the final dictionary of prominent metaphor themes in this data and the nouns used to invoke them is summarised in the following table.

Table 8.19: Metaphor themes and nouns used to invoke them.

Metaphor theme	Nouns used to express theme
journey	journey, rollercoaster, voyage, highway, road
fight	fight, battle, kick, ring

8.7 Summary

In order to ascertain the actual metaphoricity of potentially metaphoric terms collected from the data, a concordance analysis was combined with graph-based ranking, in which sentences containing a potentially metaphoric term were ranked according to the ranking of their component nouns in the extracted data as a whole. This gives more information about the relative importance of those sentences and the use of metaphoric terms within them than does running a concordance analysis without ranking.

In the next section the metaphor dictionary established here is used to label each forum post as containing or not containing the two dominant metaphor themes found in this data: *journey*, and *fight*. That labelled data is used to train a supervised learning model, which is then used to predict the presence or absence of the identified metaphor themes in a set of test data.

9 Using supervised learning to find metaphors

After the unsupervised learning investigations enough is now known about the language commonly used to invoke the dominant metaphor themes in this data to label (categorise) each post in the data according to whether either of those themes is or is not present in that post. Supervised learning can then be run on that labelled data, to produce a model to predict the category of each post in a set of unlabelled data.

In the current investigation the Keras deep learning Python library is used to set up a deep learning model, where deep means that successive layers of increasingly meaningful representations of the data are used, and the depth of a model represents the number of layers in that model (Chollet 2018). The data from all participants is used, and a random sample of 30,000 posts is split into equally sized sets of training, validation, and test data.

9.1 Labelling the data

For each post in the forum data, for each noun chunk in that post, if that noun chunk contains a noun whose lemma is in the metaphor dictionary, that post is labelled 1 (figure 8.8). Any posts that do not include any of the nouns from the metaphor dictionary are labelled 0 (figure 8.9).

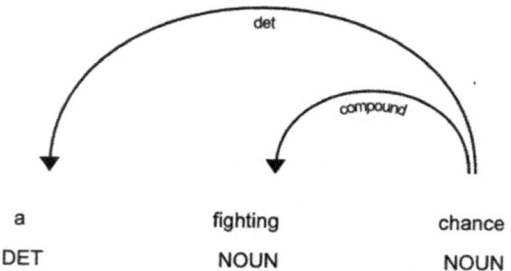

Figure 8.8: This noun chunk with fight as a noun is counted as a metaphor.

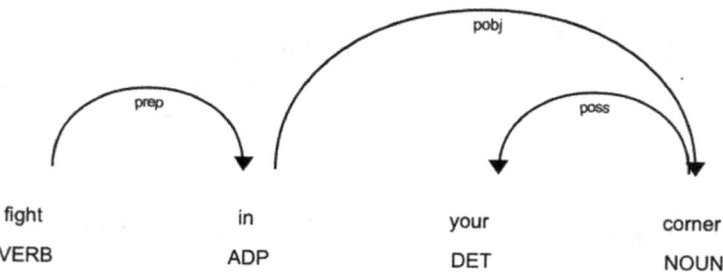

Figure 8.9: This noun chunk with fight as a verb is not counted as a metaphor.

9.2 Defining the supervised learning model

In supervised learning, text is typically processed by recurrent layers with feedback connections. For example, LSTM (long short-term memory) layers are recurrent neural network (RNN) layers that, unlike simple RNN layers, can carry information across many timesteps. Bidirectional LSTM layers are used in the current section to present the same information to the network in different ways, which can increase accuracy, and the memory of information across timesteps (Chollet 2018). A single dropout layer is introduced to prevent overfitting of the model to the training data, where a dropout layer randomly sets to 0 a specified proportion of input units, in this case 20%. The following description of the model used was output from Keras.

Table 8.20: Supervised learning model.

Layer (type)	Output	Shape			Param #
embedding_1	(Embedding)	(None	None	32)	320000
bidirectional_1	(Bidirection	(None	None	64)	16640
dropout_1	(Dropout)	(None	None	64)	0
bidirectional_2	(Bidirection	(None	64)		24832
dense_1	(Dense)	(None	1)		65

Because there are two prediction classes, the final (output) layer is a sigmoid layer, where "Sigmoid is equivalent to a 2-element Softmax, where the second element is assumed to be zero. The sigmoid function always returns a value between 0 and 1" (Keras 2020). To evaluate the model, the output is classified as 1 if the sigmoid output is > 0.5; otherwise it is classified as 0.

In the current investigation the supervised learning model was trained and validated over five epochs, then it was used to predict the label (category) of each post in the test data.

9.3 Evaluating the model

In machine learning, the F1 score, the standard performance measure for a model, takes into account the support (number of documents) for each condition. F1 is the weighted average of precision and recall, where precision is the number of true positives predicted divided by all positives predicted, and recall is the number of true positives predicted divided by the number of all positives. The *classification_report* from the scikit-learn Python library is used here to calculate the F1 score.

$$F1 \mid 2 * (precision * recall) / (precision + recall)$$

9.4 Predictions made by the model

9.4.1 Metaphoric noun retained in the data

When the metaphoric noun is retained in the text passed to the supervised algorithm, the accuracy of the model is very high, with a weighted average F1 score of 0.99. Each of the 10 posts classified as 1 (contains community metaphor) when labelled as 0 (does not contain community metaphor) contains a word from the metaphor dictionary, but not as a noun. For example, in the phrase *rollercoaster ride*, rollercoaster has been identified as an adjective; in the phrase *my mothers journey*, journey has been identified as a verb. The retained metaphoric nouns, which are the basis for the labelling of posts, provide a lot of information to the algorithm.

9.4.2 Metaphoric noun removed from the data

When the metaphoric noun is first removed from the text passed to the supervised algorithm, the algorithm must focus more on the wider difference in language style between posts labelled 1 and posts labelled 0. When the metaphoric noun was removed from the text, the model achieved a weighted average F1 score of 0.92; although this is lower than the 0.99 achieved in the previous analysis, it is still highly accurate. Thirty posts were predicted as 1 when labelled as 0, and 531 posts were predicted as 0 when labelled as 1. However, the purpose of this method is not just to obtain the highest accuracy score, but to investigate what the predictions of the model can tell us about the use of metaphor.

In the case where the metaphoric noun is first removed from the text passed to the supervised algorithm there is a clear difference in stance between a sample of posts predicted by the supervised learning model to contain one of the metaphor themes when labelled as not containing any of the themes, compared with a sample of posts predicted by the model to not contain any of the metaphor themes when labelled as containing at least one of the themes.

9.4.2.1 Posts predicted 1 when labelled 0
The following random sample of three of the posts wrongly predicted to contain one of the identified metaphor themes all contain other metaphor. The first contains the metaphor *i too am sailing in the same boat*; the second is an extended fight metaphor which however does not contain any of the nouns from the metaphor dictionary; and the third, described as an Apache Indian reading, also contains metaphor, for example *each of you will be the shelter for each other*.

Table 8.21: Post predicted to contain metaphor when labelled as not containing metaphor.

Post	Excerpt from post
1	how are you coping love. i wish i had some divine insight to give you. but i too am sailing in the same boat.
2	i choose to accept that the cancer has got there and the stage it at and now i am a cool-headed and strong "commander" in the war zone with my family by me for reinforcement against the big c enemy. i have read up on conventional approaches and explored the so-called lifestyle changes. i have tried to pinpoint what tactics could make a difference and will learn more i have no doubt to try to outwit the enemy. i have a plan i am armed with chemo drugs which is like going nuclear and i have my resilience tactics in place.
3	this is a non-religious reading from an unknown apache indian – it was the first one i came to and seems lovely. so hopefully you will think so too if not let me know. and i will look some more. apache blessing – author unknown. now you will feel no rain for each of you will be the shelter for each other. now you will feel no cold for each of you will be the warmth for the other. . . . . in this way you can ride out the storms when clouds hide the face of the sun. in your lives – remembering that even if you lose sight of it for a moment the. sun is still there. and if each of you takes responsibility for the quality of your. life together it will be marked by abundance and delight. i wish you both all the best of luck for the future. p.s. and if it is you doing the reading let me know. and i will re-arrange with a few our and us replacing the you. p p s we will want to see a photo on here. much love

9.4.2.2 Posts predicted 0 when labelled 1

A sample of the 531 posts wrongly predicted to not contain either of the identified metaphor themes in contrast, although they all contain a noun from the metaphor dictionary, are all focused on more literal detail, and on the writer's current experience of living with cancer. For example (Post 8.3):

> its just been a bit hard. i've not had any contact or support throughout this _journey_ so far. i've rang macmillan. but basically i've. muddled through. i think now i perhaps need a bit of help

9.5 Summary

After using unsupervised methods to gather and organise the dominant metaphor themes in this data and the language used to express them, supervised learning was used to (i) validate those prior methods on the basis of the accuracy of the supervised model they informed; (ii) reveal more metaphor from the data; and (iii) learn more about the language style surrounding metaphor use. The supervised models were highly accurate in predicting the presence of the metaphor themes in any post, and in addition they located metaphor not instantiated as the dominant themes, and highlighted a notable difference in language style between posts containing and not containing the metaphor themes.

10 Conclusion

In the current investigation machine learning techniques have been productive in finding dominant metaphor themes in the diverse text corpus of posts from an internet forum. Unsupervised learning techniques exposed previously unknown metaphoric themes and language. Supervised learning built on that new knowledge about metaphoric language, producing a model that is very accurate in predicting the category of a set of unlabelled test posts, which revealed more metaphor from the data, as well as providing more insights into the function of metaphor in this data (Dilkes, 2022).

In the ongoing wider investigation on which this chapter is based these machine learning techniques support a more finely grained comparison of language style between posts containing and not containing community metaphor themes, with significant differences in style found between those conditions. And further, in line with the primary hypothesis of the wider investigation, use of the community metaphor themes in a post has been found significantly to co-occur with language of a style that has been associated with better mental health (Tausczik and Pennebaker 2010).

References

Biber, Douglas. 1988. *Variation across speech and writing*. Cambridge: Cambridge University Press.
Black, Max. 1977. More about Metaphor. *Dialectica* 31(3/4). 431–457.
Brin, Sergei and Lawrence Page. 1998. The Anatomy of a Large-Scale Hypertextual Web Search Engine. *Computer Networks and ISDN Systems 30*(4). 107–117.
Cameron, Lynne and Robert Maslen. 2010. *Metaphor Analysis*. London: Equinox Publishing Ltd.
Cameron, Lynne, J. and Juurd, H. Stelma. 2004. Metaphor clusters in discourse. *Journal of Applied Linguistics* 1(2). 107–136.
Chollet, François. 2018. *Deep Learning with Python*. NY: Manning.
Crain, Stephen, P., Ke Zhou, Shuang-Hong Yang, and Hongyuan Zha. 2012. Dimensionality Reduction and Topic Modeling: From Latent Semantic Indexing to Latent Dirichlet Allocation and Beyond. In *Mining Text Data* Boston: Springer.

Deignan, Alice. 2005. *Metaphor and corpus linguistics*. Amsterdam: John Benjamins.
Deignan, Alice. 2010. Evaluative properties of metaphors. In *Researching and Applying Metaphor in the Real World*, 357–374 https://doi.org/10.1075/hcp.26. Amsterdam: John Benjamins.
Devlin, Jacob, Ming-Wei Chang, Kenton Lee, and Kristina Toutanova. 2019. BERT: Pre-training of deep bidirectional transformers for language understanding. *arXiv.org*. https://arxiv.org/abs/1810.04805 (accessed 30 November 2020).
Dilkes, J. (2022). *The social and psychological work of metaphor: A corpus linguistic investigation* [D_ph, University of Birmingham]. https://etheses.bham.ac.uk/id/eprint/12221/
Gibbs, Raymond, W. 2017. *Metaphor Wars*. Cambridge: Cambridge University Press.
Goatly, Andrew. 2011. *The language of metaphors*. 2nd ed. Abingdon: Routledge.
Honnibal, Matthew and Ines Montani. 2020. Industrial-Strength Natural Language Processing in Python. *spaCy*. https://spacy.io (accessed 30 November 2020).
Honnibal, Matthew and Ines Montani. 2020a. Facts & Figures. *spaCy*. https://spacy.io/usage/facts-figures (accessed 30 November 2020).
Honnibal, Matthew and Ines Montani. 2020b. Linguistic Features. *spaCy*. https://spacy.io/usage/linguistic-features (accessed 30 November 2020).
Keras. 2020. Layer activation functions. *Keras*. https://keras.io/api/layers/activations/ (accessed 7 December 2020).
Kessler, Jason S. 2017. Scattertext: A Browser-Based Tool for Visualizing how Corpora Differ. Paper presented at Proceedings of ACL 2017, System Demonstrations 85–90, Association for Computational Linguistics, Vancouver.
Lakoff, George, Jane Espenson, and Alan Schwartz. 1991. Master Metaphor List. http://araw.mede.uic.edu/~alansz/metaphor/METAPHORLIST.pdf (accessed 30 November 2021).
Lakoff, George and Mark Johnson. 2003. *Metaphors we live by*. Chicago: The University of Chicago Press.
Leong, Chee W., Beata B. Klebanov, Chris Hamill, Egon Stemle, Rutuja Ubale, and Xianyang Chen. 2020. A Report on the 2020 VUA and TOEFL Metaphor Detection Shared Task. Paper presented at ACL2020 18–29, Association for Computational Linguistics.
Müller, Cornelia. 2008. *Metaphors Dead and Alive, Sleeping and Waking*. Chicago: University of Chicago Press.
Müller, Andreas C. and Sarah Guido. 2017. *Introduction to machine learning with python*. 3rd ed. Sebastopol: O'Reilly.
Mihalcea, Rada and Paul Tarau. 2004. TextRank: Bringing Order into Texts. Paper presented at Proceedings of the 2004 Conference on Empirical Methods in Natural Language Processing 404–411, Association for Computational Linguistics, Barcelona.
Mikolov, Tomas, Kai Chen, Greg Corrado, and Jeffrey Dean. 2013. Efficient Estimation of Word Representations in Vector Space. *arXiv.org*. https://arxiv.org/abs/1301.3781 (accessed November 2020).
Paco, Nathan. 2016. PyTextRank, a Python implementation of TextRank for phrase extraction and summarization of text documents. *Derwen AI*. https://github.com/DerwenAI/pytextrank/ (accessed September 2020).
Pedregosa, Fabian, Ga̋el Varoquaux, Alexandre Gramfort, Vincent Michel, Bertrand Thirion, Olivier Grisel, Mathieu Blondel, Peter Prettenhofer, Ron Weiss, Vinent Dubourg, Jake Vanderplas, Alexandre Passos, David Cournapeau, and Matthieu Brucker. 2011. Scikit-learn: Machine learning in Python. *Journal of Machine Learning Research* 12. 2825–2830.

Phillip, Gill. 2010. Metaphorical keyness in specialised corpora. In Marina Bondi and Mike Scott (eds.), *Keyness in Texts*, 185–204 https://doi.org/10.1075/scl.41.13phi. Amsterdam: John Benjamins.

Pragglejaz. 2007. "MIP: A Method for Identifying Metaphorically Used Words in Discourse." Retrieved November 30, 2020 (https://www.lancaster.ac.uk/staff/eiaes/Pragglejaz_Group_2007.pdf).

Röder, Michael, Andreas Both, and Alexander Hinneburg. 2015. Exploring the Space of Topic Coherence Measures. Paper presented at WSDM '15: Proceedings of the Eighth ACM International Conference on Web Search and Data Mining 339–408, WSDM: Web Search and Data Mining, Shanghai.

scikit-learn.org. 2020. Decomposing signals in components (matrix factorization problems). https://scikit-learn.org/stable/modules/decomposition.html#decompositions (accessed 30 November 2020).

Semino, Elena, Zsofia Demjen, Andrew Hardie, Sheila A. Payne, and Paul E. Rayson. 2018. *Metaphor, Cancer and the End of Life*. Abingdon: Routledge.

Shutova, Ekaterina. 2015. Design and evaluation of metaphor processing systems. *Computational Linguistics* 41(4). 579–623 https://doi.org/10.1162/COLI_a_00233.

Sievert, Carson and Kenneth Shirley. 2014. LDAvis: A method for visualizing and interpreting topics. Paper presented at Proceedings of the workshop on Interactive Language Learning, Visualization, and Interfaces at the Association for Computational Linguistics 63-70 10.13140/2.1.1394.3043, Baltimore.

Tausczik, Yla and James Pennebaker. 2010. The Psychological meaning of words: LIWC and computerized text analysis methods. *Journal of Language and Social Psychology* 29(1). 25–54.

Veale, Tony, Ekaterina Shutova, and Beata, B. Klebanov. 2016. Metaphor: A computational perspective. *Synthesis Lectures on Human Language Technologies* 9(1). 1–160.

Jonathan Dunn
Cognitive linguistics meets computational linguistics: Construction grammar, dialectology, and linguistic diversity

1 Data-driven cognitive linguistics

Computational linguistics and cognitive linguistics come together when we use data-driven methods to conduct linguistic experiments on corpora. This chapter uses usage-based construction grammar to model geographic variation in language. The basic challenge is to show how grammatical structure emerges given exposure to usage and then how grammatical structures change given exposure to different sub-sets of usage. We first show how computational methods can be used to experiment with language learning by training a usage-based model of construction grammar. We then show how computational methods can be used to experiment with language variation by training a construction-based model of dialectology. To make these two experiments possible, we must also consider the validity of the corpora that we use for the experiments and how well they represent specific populations. Taken together, the work described here constitutes a computational theory of usage-based grammar that covers seven languages (English, French, German, Spanish, Portuguese, Russian, Arabic) and 79 distinct national dialects of these languages. Each part of the theory is an implemented computational model that can be evaluated using its predictions on held-out testing data.

How does a computational experiment work? The illustration in Figure 9.1 shows the three main components: First, language usage is represented using a corpus. Second, a computational model represents our linguistic theory. This means that all theories must be fully implemented. Third, we validate our theories using their predictions on held-out evaluation data. For example, in Section 3 we experiment with two variants of usage-based construction grammar, using the same data for training and testing across both theories. In this paradigm, whichever theory makes better predictions provides better generalizations.

The challenge for a computational experiment is that each component must be fully implemented. In other words, no part of the theory can be left under-specified. In this chapter we thus consider all aspects of this experiment in usage-based grammar, from data collection to language learning to language

---

Jonathan Dunn, University of Canterbury, e-mail: jonathan.dunn@canterbury.ac.nz

https://doi.org/10.1515/9783110687279-010

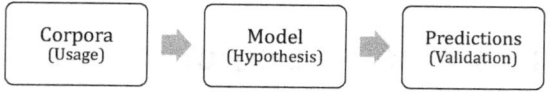

Figure 9.1: The Computational Paradigm.

variation. Our first question, in Section 2, is how to represent constructions in a computational manner. In other words, how do we define slot constraints? What are the relationships between slots? The important point here is that usage-based representations must be as unsupervised as possible, not relying on our own introspections to form syntactic generalizations. The basic idea is that the more we rely on introspection the less we rely on observed usage.

Our second question, in Section 3, is how to learn a grammar of constructions. In other words, construction grammar provides a rich framework for describing form-meaning mappings. But this rich framework creates an enormous number of *possible* constructions, most of which the learner is exposed to but does not actually learn. A usage-based theory of grammar must be able to balance memory (the ability to store frequent constructions) and computation (the ability to combine more abstract constructions on-the-fly). The important point here is that we can experiment with implementations of usage-based grammar that are not limited to just one narrow selection problem, like the dative vs. the ditransitive.

Our third question, in Section 4, is how to create corpora from purely digital sources like the web and social media. In other words, data-driven computational methods require massive amounts of data, so that interview-based or survey-based corpora are simply not sufficient. How do we create this kind of data? The section gives an overview of the 420 billion word *Corpus of Global Language Use* (Dunn 2020). While collections of language data of this size are what make computational methods possible, their scale requires different methods for using and validating the data.

Our fourth question, in Section 5, is how to evaluate digital corpora against local population demographics. In other words, how well do tweets, for example, represent actual language use by actual populations? We look at the relationship between data production, population size, and population demographics. Then, we use the difference-in-differences method to find out whether there is a significant presence of non-local populations in digital corpora. The important point in Sections 4 and 5 is that we are able to systematically evaluate digital corpora before we use them for linguistic experiments. Because we rely on corpora as representations of usage, it is essential to understand what populations these corpora represent.

Our fifth question, in Section 6, is how a construction grammar varies across national dialects of a language. In other words, we model geographic variation in the usage of constructions, assuming political boundaries as a constant. How is variation distributed across an entire construction grammar? What does geographic variation look like from the perspective of usage-based grammar? The important point here is that a computational approach to dialectology can make accurate predictions about which dialect a particular sample comes from, providing a measure of how well the model characterizes a particular dialect.

Thus, this paper provides an overview of one approach to computational cognitive linguistics, from language learning to language variation. The basic problem is to understand the relationship between exposure to usage and both (i) the emergence of grammatical structure and (ii) variation in grammatical structure. Each of these sections draws on a specific Python package used to implement the details in question.[1] Because visualization is important for understanding computational models, we also provide an interactive visualization for the geographic data.[2]

2 Representing constructions

This section reviews recent work on multi-lingual construction grammars (CxGs) that are learned directly from observed usage, as represented in a corpus (Dunn 2017, 2018a, 2019b, Dunn & Nini 2021; Dunn & Tayyar Madabushi 2021). The goal of the section is to show how we can approach the problem of using *unsupervised learning* to create a CxG. The term unsupervised learning refers to algorithms which do not start with ground-truth annotations. Such an approach is the culmination of usage-based hypotheses in linguistics, where constructions are based on the data and not filtered through introspections.

The Construction Grammar paradigm (CxG: Langacker 2008; Goldberg 2006) represents grammar using a hierarchical inventory of constraint-based *constructions*. In computational terms, a construction is a possibly non-continuous sequence in which each unit satisfies some combination of lexical, syntactic, and semantic constraints (e.g., Chang et al. 2012; Steels 2004, 2012, 2017). This section uses unsupervised methods to represent slot-constraints and their fillers.

---

[1] https://github.com/jonathandunn/.
[2] https://www.earthlings.io.

To understand why this is important, consider implementations of CxG such as Fluid Construction Grammar (FCG) and Embodied Construction Grammar (ECG) that require the manual specification of constraints using a knowledge representation framework like FrameNet (e.g., Laviola et al. 2017; Matos et al. 2017; van Trijp 2017; Ziem & Boas 2017; Dodge et al. 2017). While these approaches can provide high-quality representations of a few constructions, they cannot model the emergence of slot-constraints: their constraints are *defined* rather than *learned*. We instead follow work that models CxG from a usage-based perspective: first, generating potential constructions given a corpus (Wible & Tsao 2010; Forsberg et al. 2014); second, selecting the optimal set of constructions, where optimality is measured against a test corpus. This provides a model of how syntactic constraints are learned. The point is that there is a significant difference between a linguistic *annotation* of a construction and a linguistic *theory* of usage-based grammar.

Following previous work, constructions are represented as a sequence of slot-constraints, as in (1a). Slots are separated by dashes and constraints are defined by both type (Syntactic, Joint Semantic-Syntactic, Lexical) and filler (for example: *noun*, a part-of-speech or *animate*, a semantic domain).

(1a) [SYN:*noun* – SEM-SYN:*transfer*[V] – SEM-SYN:*animate*[N] – SYN:*noun*]
(1b) "He gave Bill coffee."
(1c) "He gave Bill trouble."
(1d) "Bill sent him letters."
(2a) [SYN:*noun* – LEX: "give" – SEM-SYN:*animate*[N] – LEX: "a hand"]
(2b) "Bill gave me a hand."

The construction in (1a) contains four slots: two with joint semantic-syntactic constraints and two with simple syntactic constraints. The examples in (1b) to (1d) are tokens of the construction in (1a). Lexical constraints, as in (2a), represent idiomatic sentences like (2b). These constructions are context-free because any sequence that satisfies the slot-constraints becomes a token or instance of that construction.

The difficulty of modelling slot-constraints is that constructions can overlap: multiple constructions in the grammar are allowed to represent a single phrase. For example, (2b) is actually a token of both (1a) and (2a). This makes identifying constructions more difficult because reaching the representation in (1a) does not rule out also reaching the representation in (2a). Both could be part of a single speaker's grammar.

	1	2	3	4
LEX	"he"	"mailed"	"George"	"a package"
SYN	**Noun**	Verb	**Noun**	Noun
SEM-SYN	ANIMATE[N]	**TRANSFER[V]**	PERSON[N]	**OBJECT[N]**

	1	2	3	4
LEX	"he"	"gave"	"George"	"a hand"
SYN	**Noun**	Verb	**Noun**	Noun
SEM-SYN	ANIMATE[N]	TRANSFER[V]	PERSON[N]	OBJECT[N]

Figure 9.2: Slot-Constraints as Transitions.

To illustrate the problem of construction parsing, we can view each slot as a node, with the beginning of a construction the root node (c.f., transition parsing for dependency grammars: Zhang and Nivre 2012; Goldberg et al. 2013). A construction's root can occur anywhere in a sentence. Each slot-constraint is a state, as visualized in Figure 9.2 with two forms of the ditransitive. There are four possible transitions: LEX, SYN, SEM-SYN, STOP. In the first example, the slot-constraints are generalized to any *transfer* verb and any *object* noun. In the second example, the verb and object slots require idiomatic lexical items. The problem is to find the sequence of slot-constraints that best represents the construction. From a usage-based perspective, the choice between these two representations is an empirical problem and cannot be resolved by introspection.

We first have to develop a pipeline for representing all the possible constraints shown in Figure 9.2. Such a pipeline provides our hypothesis space: any sequence of constraints that is observed in the training data is a potential construction. First, lexical constraints use word-forms separated at whitespace; no morphological analysis is included in the pipeline. The lexicon of allowed word-forms is drawn from a background corpus. An example of a lexical slot-constraint is given in (2a), where this particular construction requires the specific words "give" and "a hand", as in (2b).

Second, syntactic representations are drawn from the part-of-speech categories in the Universal POS tag set using the RDRPOS tagger (Petrov et al. 2012; Nguyen et al. 2016); this is a pre-defined syntactic ontology. An example of a syntactically-defined slot-constraint is given in (2a), in which any noun can fill the subject position.

Third, semantic constraints are defined using a domain dictionary in which each word-form is assigned to a cluster of word-forms. Clusters are based on word embeddings. First, a background corpus for each language is pos-tagged. No word sense disambiguation is used but word-forms are separated by syntactic category (i.e., *table_verb* is distinct from *table_noun*). A skip-gram embedding with 500 dimensions is trained for each language. Clusters are then formed by applying x-means to these embeddings (Pelleg and Moore 2000). These clusters are heterogenous syntactically. Each output cluster is further divided by syntactic category so that each semantic cluster only contains words from a single part-of-speech, allowing joint semantic-syntactic constraints.

Examples of construction representations that are learned in this unsupervised manner for shown in Table 9.1. At the top of each example is the construction itself, represented using slot-constraints. The idea is that any observed utterance which satisfies these constraints counts as a token of that construction. Below each representation, then, are tokens or examples that show which linguistic material represents that more abstract representation. There is a range of constructions here, from very abstract syntactic templates to item-specific phrases. This mixture of levels of abstraction is an important feature of usage-based construction grammar.

Table 9.1: Examples of Constructions and Their Tokens.

["very" – ADJ – NOUN] (a) *very strong link* (b) *very powerful tool* (c) *very favorable image* (d) *very good results*	*Partially-Idiomatic Adjective Phrase* The first example is a partially productive adjective phrase which is somewhat idiomatic because of the lexical constraint requiring "very".
[DET – ADJ – <335>] (a) *the vertical organization* (b) *a general consensus* (c) *the European Union>* (d) *the local resources*	*Semantically-Defined Noun Phrase* This example shows a noun phrase that is defined by semantic class; the number <335> refers to a group of nouns which we can see includes "organization" and "union".
["prepared" – "to" – VERB] (a) *prepared to accept* (b) *prepared to assist* (c) *prepared to support* (d) *prepared to act*	*Complex Verb Phrase* This shows a complex verb phrase that is lexically defined to contain "prepare" in addition to an infinitive verb phrase.
[NOUN – "funded" – <335>] (a) *EU funded project* (b) *state funded organization* (c) *ARPA funded consortium* (d) *EU funded research*	*Verb-Specific Semantically-Defined Object* This example shows a lexically-defined verb together with an object that is defined by semantic class; for simplicity, this is the same semantic class used above.

Table 9.1 (continued)

[NOUN – AUX – VERB – "below"] (a) *measures are described below* (b) *data is found below* (c) *documents are given below* (d) *framework is suggested below*	*Semantic Verb Phrase* This example shows a verb phrase that picks up a semantic class even though it contains only syntactic and lexical constraints; this illustrates the idea of competing slot-constraints.
["who" – AUX – VERB] (a) *who are involved* (b) *who are inconvenienced* (c) *who is paying* (d) *who had forgotten*	*Relative Clause* This example shows a relative clause, defined using a lexical constraint for "who"; there are no semantic constraints so that this is a highly abstract construction.
[ADJ – NOUN – "are" – VERB – "by"] (a) *nutritive requirements are covered by* (b) *alcoholic drinks are characterized by* (c) *veterinary registrations are completed by* (d) *internal policies are influenced by*	*Partial Passive Main Clause* This example shows a passive main clause, not complete in the sense that the passivized agent after "by" is not included in the construction representation itself.

This section has reviewed work on representing constructions from an unsupervised and usage-based perspective. Rather than use introspection to define slot constraints, we instead start by generating these potential constructions: *potential* because not every possible representation has been entrenched for any given speaker. The idea here is to capture exposure from corpus data: what potential constructions has the learner been exposed to? But this still leaves us with a problem: now we need to select some of the representations (as entrenched) and discard others (as not entrenched). The next section considers how we can model the selection or competition between constraints from a computational perspective.

3 A computational theory of usage-based grammar

Given a very large number of potential constructions like these, how do we model which specific ones best generalize the usage that we observe in a corpus? In other words, what is the relationship between exposure to potential constructions in a corpus and the emergence of grammatical structure? This section is where we implement a theory of usage-based grammar that faces the same challenge that language learners face: selecting which constructions to remember and use for generalization. This section draws on previous work that implements multiple hypotheses about usage-based grammar and compares them experimentally. For the sake of space, we focus on one particular theory, an algorithm that uses association values (specifically, the ΔP: Ellis 2007; Gries 2013; Dunn 2018b) to measure relationships between slots fillers. The basic idea is that representations with higher association values are more entrenched in the grammar.

An overview of our model of usage-based construction grammar is shown in Figure 9.3. The first step is to search through potential constructions, using ΔP as part of an algorithm to evaluate and discard poor representations. This creates a large but manageable pool of plausible constructions. The second step is to search through potential CxGs, where each potential CxG is a constructicon made up of constructions acquired in the first step. We use the Minimum Description Length paradigm (MDL: Rissanen 1978, 1986; Goldsmith 2001, 2006) to model usage-based grammar as part of this search. The MDL metric quantifies the trade-off between memory (operationalized as the encoding size of a grammar) and computation (operationalized as the encoding size of a test corpus given that grammar). In other words, any item-specific or idiomatic construction could be memorized, but that kind of storage comes at a cost. The final step is to evaluate the best grammars on held-out data. In this case, because we are working with large corpora, we retain five independent out-of-sample evaluation sets. This kind of design ensures that we do not over-fit a particular segment of a corpus.

Figure 9.3: Overview of Computational CxG Model.

3.1 Searching for constructions

The first part of the model, the association-based algorithm in Table 9.2, uses the total directional ΔP (a sum across all transitions) to evaluate potential sequences of constraints. To implement this idea, the search follows transitions from one slot-constraint to the next, proceeding left-to-right through the sentence. Any transition below a threshold ΔP stops that line of the search. This algorithm references local association values when choosing a transition from the current state. It also references global (i.e., construction-wide) association for selecting different paths, rather than using the frequency of specific templates (c.f., the frequency-based algorithm described in Dunn 2019b).

Table 9.2: Association-Based Selection Algorithm.

Variables
node = unit (i.e., word) in line
startingNode = start of potential construction
state = type of slot-constraint for node
path = route from root to successor states
[c] = list of immediate successor states
c_i, c_{i+1} = transition to successor constraint
candidateStack = plausible constructions
evaluate = maximize sum(ΔP for c_i, c_{i+1} in *path*)

Main Loop
for each possible *startingNode* in *line*:
RecursiveSearch(path = *startingNode*)
evaluate *candidateStack*

Recursive Function
RecursiveSearch(*path*):
for c_i, c_{i+1} in [c] from *path*:
if ΔP of c_i, c_{i+1} > *threshold*:
add c_i, c_{i+1} to *path*
RecursiveSearch(*path*)
else if *path* is long enough:
add to *candidateStack*

Any series of constraints identified by this search whose transitions exceed the ΔP threshold is added to the candidate stack. At the end of the search, this stack is scored using each candidate's total ΔP across all transitions. While primarily a transition-based parse, this approach thus incorporates some global evaluation methods (c.f., Nivre and McDonald 2008; Zhang and Clark 2008). A grid search for the best ΔP threshold per language is performed using independent test data (the corpora used for these experiments is described further in Sections 4 and 5).

This association-based algorithm is less influenced by the assumption that co-located slots govern one another's constraints. For example, in reference to

Figure 9.2, the slot filled by a *noun* in 3 and the slot filled by "a hand" in 4 have a local transition that is measured using the association between these two representations. Should we instead ignore the relationship between these two objects and focus on the relationship between each object and the verb slot? This algorithm tries to avoid specifying particular templates like this (i.e., a verb-centered frame) by using the global ΔP evaluation and the thread of associations to draw out these relationships.

But this raises an interesting empirical question: does the entrenchment of the ditransitive construction predict a higher association between the two object slots whether or not the verb itself is included? Is there a shared effect across all double-object constructions? A beam-search dependency parser could resolve this in a practical sense by simply evaluating more non-local relationships. But does CxG itself predict that such local relationships will be more entrenched because they are present within a single construction? This is the kind of question that becomes important when we develop a fully specified theory of construction grammar.

3.2 Searching for grammars

The second part of the algorithm uses Minimum Description Length and a tabu search to explore the space of possible CxGs. The process of searching over selected slot-constraints using a tabu search (Glover 1989, 1990) is adopted from previous work (Dunn 2018a). A tabu search is a meta-level heuristic search that evaluates a number of possible local moves for each turn and then makes the move which produces the best grammar. Importantly, a tabu search allows moves which make the grammar worse in the short-term (with a restricted set of tabu moves) so that the learner can climb out of local optima. Here, each state is a grammar that contains a specific set of constructions (i.e., a constructicon). The search works by taking a series of turns. During each turn, some constructions are *learned* (added to the constructicon) or *unlearned* (removed from the constructicon).

A grammar that provides better generalizations will allow the test corpus to be encoded using a smaller number of bits. The metric combines three encoding-based terms: L_1 (the cost of encoding the grammar), $L_2\{C\}$ (the cost of encoding pointers to constructions in the grammar), and $L_2\{R\}$ (the cost of encoding linguistic material that is not in the grammar and thus cannot be encoded using a pointer). A pointer here is a partial parse of an utterance that refers to a construction that is already contained in the grammar.

These terms represent the grammar, the data as described by the grammar, and the data that is not described by the grammar; note that both L_2 terms are combined below. In other words, $L_2(D|G)$ is the sum of both $L_2\{C\}$ and $L_2\{R\}$. D in this equation refers to the data set which is used to evaluate the model. The point is that the MDL metric is trying to minimize the combination of memory (L_1) and descriptive adequacy (L_2).

$$MDL = \min_G\{L_1(G) + L_2(D|G)\}$$

Encoding size, in turn, is based on probability: the encoding size of an item, X, is measured in bits, below, using the negative log of its probability. We describe how probabilities are estimated later in this section. The basic idea is that more probable constraints should have smaller encoding sizes. In other words, more entrenched items should be easier to retrieve.

$$L_C(X) = -log_2 P(X)$$

According to this model, a construction is only worth remembering if its contribution to decreasing the overall encoding size of the test corpus is smaller than its contribution to the encoding size of the grammar. This is important for CxGs because similar constructions overlap, describing the same sentences in the corpus. Each overlapping construction must be individually represented in the grammar, adding to the L_1 term: similar constructions must be encoded separately in L_1 but do not improve the encoding of L_2. For example, the two constructions in (1a) and (2a) describe the same utterance in (2b). Both of these constructions need to be encoded in the grammar, increasing L_1. But encoding only one of them would not increase the regret portion of L_2 because the utterance itself can still be encoded using a pointer to the construction that is in the grammar.

The encoding size of a grammar, L_1, is the sum of the encoding size of all constructions in that grammar. Each construction is a series of slot-constraints that must be satisfied for a linguistic utterance to be an instance of that construction. For each constraint, two items must be encoded: (i) the constraint type (lexical, semantic, syntactic) and (ii) the filler which defines that constraint.

The cost of (i) is fixed because each representation is considered equally probable: the grammar is not explicitly biased towards syntactic constraints. But the cost of (ii) depends on the type of representation: syntactic units come out of a much smaller inventory, so that any given part-of-speech is more probable and thus easier to encode. For example, if there are 14 parts-of-speech, then the probability of observing one of them is $1 \div 14 = 0.0714$ bits. On the other hand, because there are more lexical items, each word is less probable and thus more expensive to encode. For example, if there are 50k lexical items, then the probability is *1÷50,000 = 0.00002*. In this way, the grammar is allowed to employ item-specific slot-constraints, but doing so increases the encoding cost of the grammar. Here, a syntactic constraint contributes 3.8 bits but a lexical constraint contributes 15.6 bits. The total encoding size of a construction is the accumulated bits required to encode each slot-constraint, where N_R represents the number of representation types (here, 3) and T_R represents the number of possible slot-fillers for that type.

$$\sum_{i}^{N_{SLOTS}} -log_2\left(\frac{1}{N_{Ri}}\right) + -log_2\left(\frac{1}{T_R}\right)$$

The encoding size of the test corpus, L_2, contains two quantities: first, the cost of encoding pointers to constructions in the grammar; second, the cost of encoding on-the-fly any parts of the corpus that cannot be described by the grammar. The cost of encoding pointers is also based on probabilities, so that more probable or common constructions require fewer bits to encode. For example, a construction that occurs 100 times in a corpus of 500k words has a pointer encoding size of 12.28 bits, but a construction that occurs 1,000 times costs only 8.96 bits per use. In this way, the probability of potential constructions influences encoding size. The regret portion of the L_2 term is the cost of words which are not covered by constructions in the current grammar. Each of these is encoded on-the-fly (i.e., not remembered): the more unencoded words accumulate, the more each one costs.

There is a close relationship between MDL and Bayesian inference methods (c.f., Barak et al. 2017; Barak and Goldberg 2017; Goldwater et al. 2009). Information theory describes the relationship between the log probabilities of representations and their encoding size. But it does not estimate the probability of the grammar itself, which here is handled in two ways: First, there is a choice in CxG between different types of representation (LEX, SYN, SEM). This model does not enforce one type, but syntactic constraints are more likely because there are fewer categories. Second, pointers to constructions are assigned probabilities based on their observed frequency; this means that more likely constructions are cheaper to encode and implicitly favored by the model.

It is worth pausing at this point to think about what we have done here. Most linguistic theories are under-specified, in the sense that there are important details missing. What we have presented is a theory of usage-based construction grammar in which every necessary detail is made falsifiable and replicable. Our implementation of the MDL metric calculates the relationship between a given grammar and a given corpus. The data[3] and the code[4] for these experiments are both available for replication. This level of detail is required for a fully-specified linguistic theory. At the same time, the details of the model are subject to empirical evaluation and improvement. This cycle of rapid and direct empirical evaluation is what makes the computational paradigm so promising.

3.3 Evaluating grammars

At this point we turn to the evaluation of these usage-based grammars. We evaluate the association-based model that we have described here with an alternate frequency-based model (Dunn 2019b). The basic idea is that we evaluate these different hypotheses on the same test data, using the same representation pipeline, using the same implementation of the MDL metric. While we have not evaluated counter-factuals for every development decision made within the pipeline, both competing models rely on the same decisions. This gives us a measure of the relative quality of each hypothesis. The measure is relative in the sense that we can only compare implemented models.

MDL provides a single metric of a grammar's fit relative to a particular data set. This metric itself is dependent on each data set; we thus calculate a baseline encoding score that represents the encoding of the data set without a grammar and use this to derive a compression metric: MDL_{CxG}/MDL_{Base}. The lower this compression metric, the greater the generalizations provided by the CxG. Compression as used in MDL is similar to perplexity within language modelling.

The evaluation uses all seven languages in order to provide a cross-linguistic counter-factual: do the generalizations agree across languages? Additionally, we evaluate the theories against five independent sets of 10 million words for each language. Table 9.3 shows the average compression by model for each language across these five test sets. We also report the p-values for a paired t-test (paired by data set) to ensure that the difference in compression between theories is significant.

Lower compression scores reflect better generalizations; as shown in Table 9.3, the association-based model out-performs the frequency-based model for every language. In each case the difference between models is significant. The gap and the significance level, however, vary across languages. For Russian, there is a gap of 40.21% compression that is significant below the p = 0.0001 level. But for French and Portuguese that gap is only 2.76%

---

[3] https://publicdata.canterbury.ac.nz/Research/NZILBB/jonathandunn/CxG_Data_FixedSize/.
[4] https://github.com/jonathandunn/c2xg .

Table 9.3: Compression Rates by Language with Significance of Difference Between Models.

Language	Frequency	Association	P
Arabic	44.08%	*29.45%*	0.0001
German	52.49%	*18.69%*	0.0001
English	51.80%	*23.11%*	0.0001
French	43.28%	*40.52%*	0.0037
Portuguese	45.13%	*38.91%*	0.0137
Russian	54.14%	*13.93%*	0.0001
Spanish	60.34%	*26.36%*	0.0001

and 6.22%, with larger p-values to match. Association always provides a better model of the emergence of slot-constraints, but for French and Portuguese the two models are much closer together than for other languages.

What do these experiments tell us about usage-based construction grammar? First, it could have been the case that there is variation across languages and across data sets. In other words, maybe a frequency-based grammar best describes one language (i.e.,. English) but not another (i.e., German). Instead, we see a very robust result in which each of five independent evaluation sets for each of seven languages shows the same result. This scale of experimentation holds our theories to a high standard and gives us confidence that we are making generalizations about *language* rather than a simple description of one language's constructicon. Second, this gives us strong evidence that frequency alone is not sufficient for usage-based grammar: infrequent constructions can still be acquired. Thus, a theory of usage-based grammar that depends on frequency as its main descriptive mechanism is incorrect.

4 Working with digital language data

This section examines sources of demographic bias in gigaword corpora and how these biases can be corrected. This is important because computational experiments rely on large digital data sets. In other words, it is possible that although the scale and precision of these experiments is very robust, the findings do not reflect actual language use. The goal of this section is to justify the validity of these data sets as a source of linguistic experiments.

We are working with the *Corpus of Global Language Use* (CGLU: Dunn 2020), a collection of over 420 billion words across 295 languages and 189 countries. The goal of this corpus is to systematically gather comparable language samples from every country in the world. The expectation is that some languages (e.g., Swahili) will be found only in certain regions of the world. Other languages (e.g., English and French) will be found in all regions and, as a result of their geographic distribution, will participate more widely in different language mixing situations. Countries are grouped into sixteen larger geographic regions to simplify the analysis of language distribution. The distribution of the corpus across regions by number of words and by percentage of words is shown in Table 9.4. The corpus draws on web data and social media data, two different forms of digital language use. The inventory of regions is relatively straight-forward. It is

Table 9.4: Words Per Region.

Region	CGLU v.4.2		Twitter	
	Words	%	Words	%
Africa, North	1,223,532,000	0.29%	311,577,000	2.38%
Africa, Southern	26,868,000	0.01%	261,431,000	2.00%
Africa, Sub	5,938,870,000	1.39%	786,718,000	6.01%
America, Brazil	2,265,386,000	0.53%	291,254,000	2.23%
America, Central	8,877,634,000	2.08%	1,249,076,000	9.55%
America, North	51,921,657,000	12.15%	756,306,000	5.78%
America, South	22,441,384,000	5.25%	1,508,749,000	11.53%
Asia, Central	17,069,517,000	4.00%	311,615,000	2.38%
Asia, East	49,521,933,000	11.59%	579,847,000	4.43%
Asia, South	15,147,872,000	3.55%	937,978,000	7.17%
Asia, Southeast	21,386,781,000	5.01%	678,805,000	5.19%
Europe, East	65,413,609,000	15.31%	898,885,000	6.87%
Europe, Russia	15,363,644,000	3.60%	247,415,000	1.89%
Europe, West	143,748,386,000	33.65%	2,928,220,000	22.39%
Middle East	1,721,856,000	0.40%	800,238,000	6.12%
Oceania	1,743,571,000	0.41%	530,804,000	4.06%
TOTAL	423 billion	100%	13 billion	100%

worth noting, however, that Brazil and Russia are large enough and produce enough language data that they are separated from surrounding countries.

The number of words for a given region depends on more than simply the population of the region: (i) the number of sites indexed by the Common Crawl; (ii) the population's degree of access to internet technologies; (iii) data cleaning decisions for this project that are subject to future improvements (i.e., identifying words across different writing systems). Although the relationship between words in the corpus and individuals in the regions is imperfect, in the aggregate this data set can still be used to infer many things about language use around the world. The relationship between populations and digital language data is explored further in Section 5.

A computational approach to building digital corpora has three main steps, as shown in Figure 9.4 below: finding the data (i.e., crawling or using an API), cleaning the data (e.g., to remove duplicate text), and sorting the data by language (i.e., language identification). These steps are discussed in more detail elsewhere (Dunn 2020; Dunn and Adams 2020), but an overview is given here. A Python package is available for cleaning[5] and for language identification.[6] An interactive visualization for exploring the corpus is also available.[7]

Figure 9.4: Steps in Creating Digital Corpora.

This section presents the decisions made for processing the raw web data, as an example of what is required for working with this kind of data. Language samples are geo-located using country-specific top-level domains: we assume that a sample from a web-site under the ".ca" domain is from Canada. This approach does not assume that whoever produced that sample was born in Canada or represents a traditional Canadian dialect group. Some countries are not available because their top-level domains are used for non-geographic purposes (i.e., ".ai", ".fm", ".io", ".ly", ".ag", ".tv"). Domains that do not contain geographic information are also removed from consideration (e.g., ".com" sites). An important improvement in CGLU v.4.2 is the inclusion of geographic TLDs that are not in a Latin script; this significantly increases the amount of

---

5 https://github.com/jonathandunn/common_crawl_corpus .
6 https://github.com/jonathandunn/idNet .
7 https://www.earthlings.io .

data from languages like Hindi, Urdu, and Chinese that is collected. A complete list of TLDs is contained in the codebase. We evaluate the correspondence between this data and population demographics (in Section 5) as well as the linguistic similarity between geographic data drawn from different sources (in Section 6). The basic idea is that we can validate this kind of corpus by triangulating multiple sources to measure linguistic and demographic similarity. For example, if dialectal features in Twitter data correspond with dialectal features in traditional survey-based studies, this helps to validate the collection of Twitter data as a representation of local language use (Grieve et al. 2019).

The raw portions of the Common Crawl data set used to build the corpus are shown in Table 9.5, for the purpose of showing the scale of the task. The corpus uses every portion of the crawl from March 2014 to June 2019, totaling 147 billion web pages in total. No temporal divisions are included in the corpus because these dates represent the time of collection rather than the time of production: web data does not expire and there is a long-tail in which the same samples are observed multiple times across different periods. Deduplication can remove this long-tail but cannot add accurate time information.

Table 9.5: Common Crawl Raw Data Size.

Year	Period Represented (Months)	Pages
2014	March to December (8)	22.53 billion
2015	January to December (10)	17.98 billion
2016	January to December (9)	16.91 billion
2017	January to December (12)	37.28 billion
2018	January to December (12)	36.30 billion
2019	January to June (6)	16.05 billion
Total	64 months	147.05 billion

In isolation, web-crawled data provides a single observation of digital language use. Another common source of data is from Twitter (e.g., Grieve et al. 2019). We can use a baseline Twitter corpus as a point of comparison: does the Common Crawl agree with Twitter data? For example, recent work has shown that there is systematic agreement between geo-referenced corpora from the web and from Twitter across nine languages (Dunn 2021). In other words, the more precise geo-location of tweets enables us to confirm the less-precise geo-location of web data. We use a spatial search to collect Tweets from within a 50km radius of 10k cities taken from the GeoNames project.[8] This search method avoids biasing the selection of languages by relying on language-specific keywords or hashtags. The same deduplication and text cleaning methods are used as for the main web-crawled corpus. Because the language identification component only has reliable predictions for samples with at least 50 characters, a threshold of 50 characters is enforced after cleaning has taken place. The break-down of this cleaned comparison corpus by region is shown in Table 9.1 in Section 1; this represents two years of collection (July 2017 to July 2019).

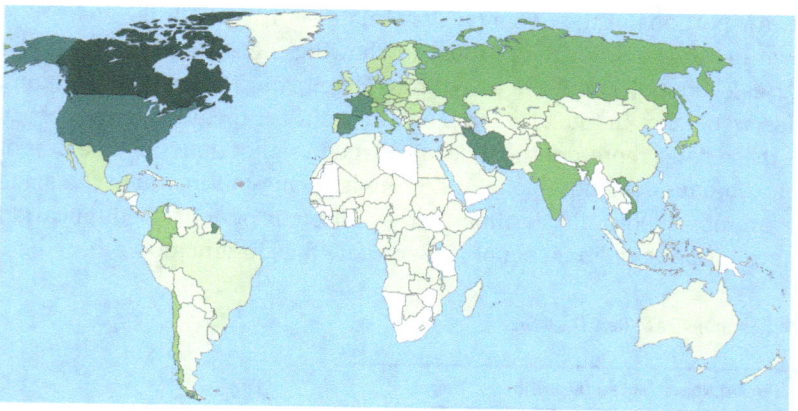

Figure 9.5: Map of Web Corpus.

The geographic distribution of the web corpus (by number of words per country) is shown in Figure 9.5; the distribution of the Twitter corpus is shown in Figure 9.6. The purpose of these maps is to provide a first pass at understanding *where* digital language data comes from. Why is this important? Recent work (Dunn and Adams 2019, 2020) has shown that a naïve corpus from these sources will over-represent North America and Western Europe. Thus, the danger is that our experiments are replicating the same geographic bias that is found in traditional dialectology studies (e.g., focusing on the US, the UK, France, etc.). Further, this work has shown that there is a significant linguistic difference between models trained on data from different countries, which means that geographic bias in our corpora could lead to bias in the experiments that we conduct using these corpora (c.f., Section 3). We examine this question further in the next section.

---

[8] https://www.geonames.org .

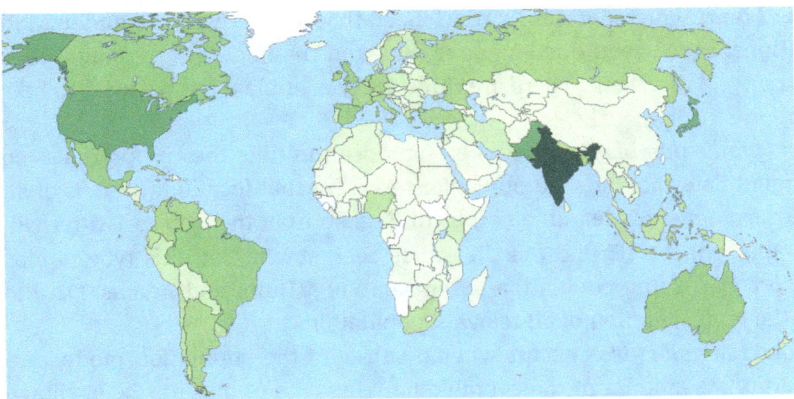

Figure 9.6: Map of Twitter Corpus.

The problem of language identification is often overlooked in linguistics, where language identity is taken as a given. First, what languages are distinct enough to require their own label? Second, how do we identify each language with sufficient accuracy? This corpus depends on *idNet*, a multi-layer perceptron model for language identification that covers 464 languages. Importantly, this model draws evaluation samples from over a dozen different registers. Previous work has focused on registers like Bible translations, which allow parallel data across many languages. But register variation within languages means that language use in a Bible translation may be significantly different than language use in other contexts. For our purposes, a rigorous held-out evaluation of *idNet* (Dunn 2020) shows that it is able to make highly accurate predictions about language labels across many registers.

5 Population demographics and digital language data

As soon as we try to use computational linguistics to tell us about *people* or *languages* we need to evaluate how well the data that we are using actually represents our object of study. The computational experiments in this chapter use digital corpora to study the role of exposure in language learning and language variation. But the data that we use to represent usage needs to be validated. In other words, the more we use digital corpora for scientific purposes, the more we need to control for *bias* in that data. In Section 6 we use digital corpora to represent geographic variation, so that it is essential to understand the relationship between this language data and the underlying communities we are trying to represent. There are three sources of bias that we need to take into account.

First, *production bias* occurs when one location (like the US) produces so much digital data that most corpora over-represent that location (Jurgens et al. 2017). For example, by default a corpus of English from the web or Twitter will mostly represent the US and the UK. It has been shown that this type of bias can be corrected using population-based sampling (Dunn and Adams 2020) to enforce the representation of all relevant populations.

Second, *sampling bias* occurs when a subset of the population produces a disproportionate amount of the overall data. This type of bias has been shown to be closely related to economic measures: more wealthy populations produce more digital language per capita (Dunn and Adams 2019). By default, a corpus will contain more samples representing wealthier members of the population. Thus, this is similar to production bias, but with a demographic rather than a geographic scope.

Third, *non-local bias* is the problem of over-representing those people *in* a place who are not *from* that place: tourists, aid workers, students, short-term visitors, etc. For example, in countries with low per-capita GDP (i.e., where local populations often lack internet access) digital language data is likely to represent outsiders like aid workers. On the other hand, in countries with large numbers of international tourists (e.g., New Zealand), data sets are likely to instead be contaminated with samples from these tourists.

Of these three sources of bias, non-local bias is the most difficult to uncover. We can identify production bias when the amount of data per country exceeds that country's share of the global population. In this sense, the ideal corpus of English would equally represent each country according to the number of English speakers in that country. Within a country, we can measure the amount of sampling bias by looking at how economic measures like GDP and rates of internet access correspond with the amount of data per person. Thus, we could use median income by zip code to ensure that the US is properly represented. But non-local bias is more challenging because we need to know which samples from a place like New Zealand come from those speakers who are only passing through for a short time. Such speakers would not be representative of New Zealand English as a dialect.

Only with widespread restrictions on international travel during the COVID-19 pandemic do we have access to a collection of digital language from which non-local populations are largely absent (Gössling et al. 2020; Hale et al. 2020). This section uses changes in linguistic diversity during these travel restrictions, against a historical baseline, to calibrate the collection of digital corpora. This is a part of the larger problem of estimating population characteristics from digital language data and removing the bias that could impact our use of computational experiments.

The first question is the degree to which the production of this data is driven by underlying populations (potential production bias) and by demographic factors like GDP (potential selection bias). These experiments are based on the Twitter portion of the data described above, because this data comes with more reliable temporal meta-data. We start, in Figure 9.7, by looking at the relationship between each country's population and share of the corpus. Each country is an observation that is represented by its average monthly data production and several demographic factors. Overall, there is a very significant correlation (Pearson) between population and the amount of data from each country (0.46). Thus, the number of people in a country is an important factor explaining how much data that country produces. While this is significant, however, it also means that there are many other factors that influence the geographic distribution of the data.

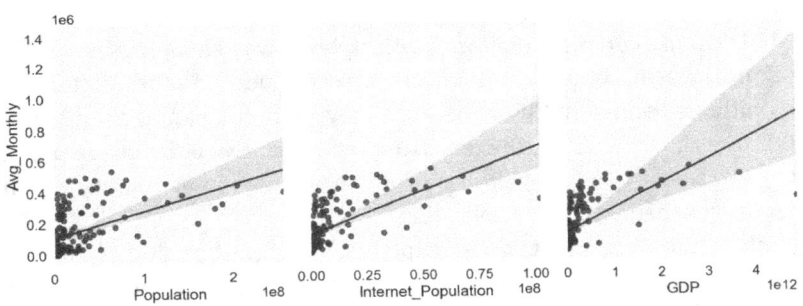

Figure 9.7: Demographic Factors and Digital Corpora.

To better understand the factors influencing the geographic distribution of the data, we work with three variables: *population*, the number of people in each country; *internet population*, the number of internet users in each country; and *GDP*, a measure of each country's economic output (United Nations 2011, 2017a, 2017b). Figure 9.7 shows three regression plots in which these variables (on the y axis) are compared with the average monthly data production per country (given in number of tweets per month on the x axis).

In each case, there is a close relationship between data production and demographics, with several extreme outliers. For *population*, the outliers are China and India. Both are highly populated countries with significantly lower than expected data production (especially China). Both countries have relatively low rates of internet access: 38% for China and 11% for India; this lowers the total population in each country. Thus, although the populations are quite large, most of the population is not able to produce digital language data. For the influence of GDP, the outliers are the US and China. For the US, in particular, the GDP is quite high: there seems to be a ceiling after which increased GDP is unlikely to influence digital behaviors. Further, that GDP is not evenly distributed across the entire population. For the influence of internet access, the outliers are again China and the US. With a few notable exceptions there is a relatively close relationship between data production and the demographic factors of each country.

With these three outliers removed (the US, China, India), there are very significant correlations between these three variables and the geographic distribution of the data: 0.46 (population), 0.61 (population with internet access), and 0.59 (GDP). This leaves some unexplained production factors. The most obvious missing factor here is social media platforms specific to given countries (e.g., Sina Weibo). These alternative platforms will siphon away enough users to distort the representation of a population given access only to other platforms. Further, Twitter is banned in China: because only some companies are allowed to use it through specific VPNs, the text is not representative of language use in China. Casual users of Twitter will use a VPN through another country which would distort this method of data collection.

Regardless, this shows that we can explain a significant portion of the geographic distribution of the data. This is important because we want to describe *populations* by observing *digital corpora*. If there is no relationship between the two in terms of distribution, it is difficult to make such inferences. What we have seen, however, is that there is a very significant relationship. What is the required threshold for establishing a relationship like this? We should think about this as a metric for evaluating digital corpora: data with a stronger relationship to demographic variables are more representative.

We measure linguistic diversity as a probability distribution over languages for each country. Given this probability distribution for each country, we compare countries using the Herfindahl-Hirschman Index (HHI). The HHI was developed in economics to measure market concentration: the more of a given industry is dominated by a small number of companies, the higher the HHI (Hirschman 1945). The measure is derived using the sum of the square of shares, in this case the share of each language in each country.

Table 9.6: Sample Language Distributions by Country.

	Israel	India	United States
HHI	0.207	0.356	0.852
Language #1	27.3%	50.8%	92.3%
Language #2	25.9%	30.8%	02.6%
Language #3	23.5%	03.4%	00.6%
Language #4	07.5%	02.5%	00.6%
Language #5	05.3%	01.4%	00.4%

Thus, the HHI is higher when the distribution is centered around just a few languages. For example, in Table 9.6 we focus on three countries that show a range of linguistic diversity: Israel, India, and the US. Israel has the lowest HHI (0.207). Looking at the share of the top five languages, we see roughly equal usage of three languages (in the 20s) followed by two significant minority languages. This lower HHI reflects the fact that a number of languages are being used together: no language has a monopoly. On the other extreme, the US has one of the highest values for HHI (0.852). There is one very dominant language (92%), one significant minority language (2.6%), and a number of very insignificant languages. English has a metaphoric monopoly on the linguistic landscape of the US. Global variation in linguistic diversity on Twitter is shown in Figure 9.8.

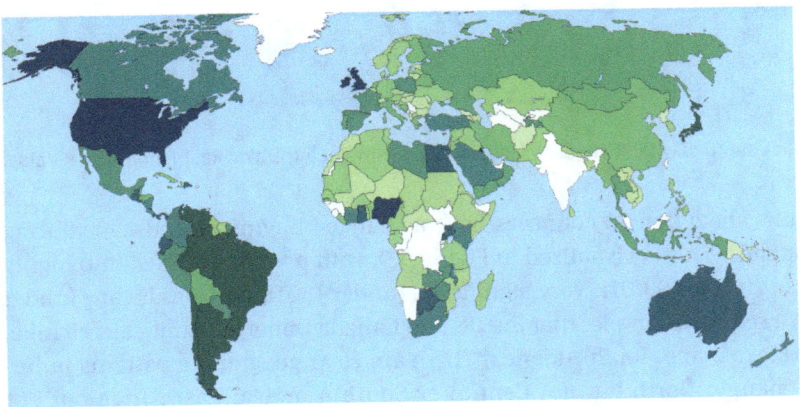

Figure 9.8: Map of Linguistic Diversity on Twitter, using the HHI.

The point of measuring linguistic diversity is to evaluate changes over time: to what degree do countries change during travel restrictions resulting from COVID-19? The point here is that, if Twitter is representing non-local populations, we should see a shift in diversity during travel restrictions. Models of this kind of bias can then be used to correct for that bias and make digital corpora align more closely with population demographics. We have a measure of diversity (the HHI) and data collected by month. The basic approach is to create two groups of samples: first, months during the pandemic (March through August, 2020); second, months not during the pandemic (March through August, 2019). These two groups are aligned by month so that seasonal fluctuations are taken into account (e.g., tourism high season in February for New Zealand and in July for Italy). Given these two groups of samples, we use a t-test for two independent samples to determine whether these groups are, in fact, different. If we reject the null hypothesis, it means that linguistic diversity during travel restrictions is significantly different than the seasonally-adjusted baseline.

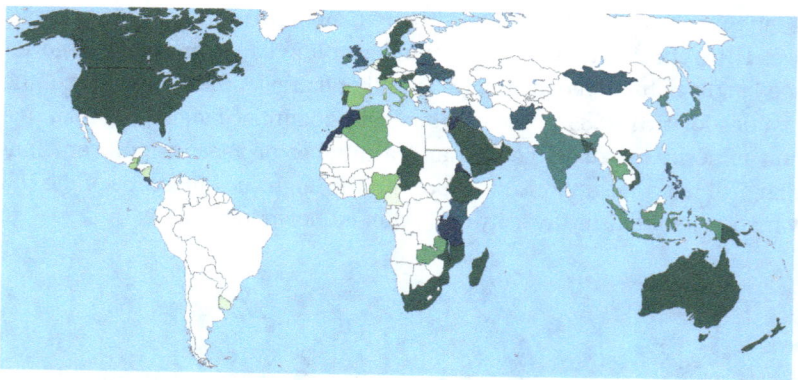

Figure 9.9: Countries with Changes to Linguistic Diversity During Travel Restrictions, By P-Value.

The results show that 70 countries have a changed linguistic landscape during the pandemic. This is visualized in Figure 9.9, with p-values classed into highly significant (under 0.001), very significant (under 0.01), and significant (under 0.05). We see, for example, that the US and Canada undergo significant change, but not Mexico and South America. There are clear geographic patterns in linguistic change: North but not Central or South America; East Africa but not West Africa; South/east Asia but not East Asia; Europe but not Russia.

These significant changes during international travel restrictions show that our measure (the HHI) and our data (tweets) offer a meaningful representation of underlying populations. If the data did not represent populations, we would not see the relationships examined above. There are no random fluctuations in the distribution of the data across countries or in the distribution of languages within countries (Dunn et al. 2020). At the same time, given a massive social change (i.e., the COVID-19 pandemic), the measure clearly identifies changes in the linguistic landscape. Thus, the measure is both precise (not disguised by noise) and accurate (observing change where we expect it). The key point is that the change in diversity during the COVID-19 period is identifiable against the background noise.

So far we have seen that there is a significant change in the linguistic diversity of many countries *during* the travel restrictions caused by COVID-19. But to what degree are these changes *related* to the travel restrictions themselves? For example, we could imagine a population that is changing over time which we just happen to observe in mid-change. It could be the case that a country has been becoming less diverse over the past decade because of fewer incoming immigrants; the approach taken so far in this paper would misinterpret such macro-trends to be a direct result of COVID-19.

We use a difference-in-differences method (Card and Krueger 1994) to correct for this. The basic idea behind a difference-in-differences approach is to conduct a *natural experiment* with a control group (here, data from 2018) and an effect group (here, data from 2020) differentiated by time. We have three months (July, August, September) that are shared across 2018, 2019, and 2020. So, using the same methods described above, we find out which countries have a significant change between 2019 and 2020. This is the period that takes place during travel restrictions. If travel restrictions influence linguistic diversity, we would expect such influence to take place during this period. We then find out if the countries which show a significant change in 2020 also show a significant change from 2018 to 2019. This provides a baseline: removing any country whose linguistic diversity was already in the process of changing.

Over this three-month period (July through September), 58 countries show a change in linguistic diversity during the pandemic. This is a smaller number than the main results reported above for two reasons: (i) the time span is shorter, giving less robust results and (ii) this particular time span came after some travel had resumed. Of these 58 countries that show a significant change in diversity, most (38) show no difference at all in the baseline period before the pandemic. Another eight show a much greater difference during the COVID-19 period (e.g., p-values of 0.03 vs 0.004 for baseline and COVID-19, respectively). This means that the pandemic has either created or has significantly contributed to 79.3% of the cases of changing linguistic diversity. The remaining 20.7% of changes, then, must have been created by macro-trends like immigration or changes in bilingual behaviour. The main conclusion from this difference-in-differences examination, however, is that most of these changes can be specifically connected to COVID-19.

The important point in this section has been that, like all sources of language data, digital corpora are subject to certain biases. In other words, there is not a perfect relationship between the data that our experiments are using and the populations that we want to study. As with all data, we need to systematically measure and remove this kind of bias in order to improve how well our experiments generalize across global populations. The study presented here is an example of what it means to validate this kind of data to take into account production bias, sampling bias, and non-local bias. Another approach, based on register variation, is to determine if digital language shows the same grammatical and lexical usage as non-digital language. Recent work has shown that traditional survey-based methods can be replicated using digital corpora (Grieve et al. 2019). Other recent work has triangulated different sources of digital corpora to show that they are closely related (Dunn 2021). This body of work is important for validating the corpora that our computational experiments depend on.

6 Global dialectology and computational construction grammar

So far we have seen how we can conduct computational experiments on theories of usage-based construction grammar. This section goes a step further and describes recent computational experiments on variation in construction grammars (Dunn 2018c, 2019a, 2019c). The goal is to show that a theory of usage-based grammar can also account for variation. In other words, a theory of grammar must be tested on its predictions for both language learning and language variation because these are essential aspects of language that any theory needs to describe. Here the difference between dialects is modelled as the preference for some constructions over others given a single umbrella-grammar. We experiment with the same association-based and frequency-based CxGs (c.f., Section 3), this time using their ability to make predictions about geographic variation. Thus, we previously evaluated these grammars and the theories they represent using internal measures like goodness-of-fit. Here we evaluate these grammars and the theories they represent using an external measure based on geographic variation: how well is each theory capable of capturing the difference between national dialects of a language?

Previous work on syntactic dialectology has depended on the idea that a grammar is an inventory of specific structures: the double-object construction versus the prepositional dative, for example. Under this view, there is no language-independent feature set for syntax in the way that there is for phonetics. But we can also view syntax from the perspective of a discovery-device grammar: in this case, our theory of grammar is not a specific description of a language like English but rather a function for mapping between observations of English and a lower-level grammatical description of English: $G=D(CORPUS)$. Thus, a discovery-device grammar (G) is an abstraction that represents what the grammatical description would be if we applied the learner (D) to a specific sample of the language (CORPUS). A discovery-device grammar allows us to generalize syntactic dialectology: we are looking for a model of syntactic variation, V, such that when applied to a grammar, $V(G)$, the model is able to predict regional variation in the grammar. But G is different for each language, so we generalize this to $V(D(CORPUS))$. In other words, we use an independent corpus for each language as input to a discovery-device grammar and then use the resulting grammar as a feature space for studying syntactic variation. This approach, then, produces an inventory of syntactic features for each language in a reproducible manner. From the perspective of cognitive linguistics, a usage-based grammar is ideally a discovery-device grammar. In other words, there is no individual grammar that is not driven by observed usage.

This section uses data-driven language mapping (c.f., Sections 4 and 5) to choose which languages in which countries need to be included as national dialects. The seven languages we consider account for 59.2% of the web-crawled corpus and 74.6% of the social media corpus. The corpora are regionalized to countries. Thus, the assumption is that any country which frequently produces data in a language has a national dialect of that language. For example, whether or not there is a distinct variety of New Zealand English depends entirely on how much English data is observed from New Zealand in these data sets. The models then have the task of determining how distinct New Zealand English is from other national dialects of English.

A Linear Support Vector Machine classifier is used to model dialects. This is a supervised method that observes a number of samples (i.e., vectors of construction frequencies representing samples from a given country) and estimates a function for mapping that vector into a hyperplane maximizing the separation between classes (i.e., national dialects). A Linear SVM is preferable to other linear classifiers with inspectable feature weights, such as Naïve Bayes, because it can better handle redundant representations. This is important because constructions vary in their level of abstraction so that a single utterance may have several constructions describing it, producing correlated features.

Constructions are quantified using their raw frequency; since all samples are the same size, this is relative frequency. Thus, the grammar is turned into a vector that contains the frequency of each construction in each observed sample. Morphosyntactic dialectometry in this paradigm depends on the fact that speakers have a large number of grammatical structures available to them but can only choose a small sub-set of these structures in actual usage. Positive evidence for a speaker's preference is provided by each observed structure and negative evidence by each unobserved structure. In terms of cognitive sociolinguistics, an entire CxG can perform all of the functions that language is used for. Studying only a few constructions in isolation limits the functions that are represented. Thus, even if constructions are chosen because they have overlapping functions, this approach (i) may miss constructions that fulfil those same functions in other contexts or (ii) may miss some functions that are covered by those constructions in other contexts.

So long as the total choice space is relatively well covered (i.e., so long as the CxG has descriptive adequacy), the amount of negative evidence will be much higher than the amount of positive evidence. Corpus-based dialectology thus does not require the active elicitation of either specific variants or specific minimal pairs: given enough passively observed language use, the observed frequency of each structure (the input to the model) supports the estimation of each region's preferences for that structure against its competition (the output of the model).

True positives occur when the model assigns unseen samples to the correct dialect and false positives occur when the model incorrectly assigns a sample to a given dialect. The standard measures used to evaluate such an experiment are precision (the proportion of predictions for region X that actually belong to region X) and recall (the proportion of samples from region X that were correctly classified). The F-Measure reported here is the harmonic mean of these two measures averaged across all classes. The overall prediction accuracy across languages is shown in Table 9.7 (with the web corpus on the left and the Twitter corpus on the right). These scores are computed using cross-validation to protect against over-fitting. Within each data set, we compare the prediction accuracy using two different grammars: a frequency-based theory of CxG and an association-based theory of CxG. This is the same experimental comparison that we saw previously.

A classification-based approach has the goal of distinguishing between national dialects. We would expect, then, that the task of distinguishing between a small number of dialects is easier than distinguishing between a larger number of dialects. For example, there are only two dialects of German and Portuguese in the Twitter corpus. Models on the web corpus (left) have higher predictive

Table 9.7: F1 of Classification of Regional Varieties by Language and Grammar Type.

	Web Corpus		Twitter Corpus	
	Frequency CxG	Association CxG	Frequency CxG	Association CxG
Arabic	0.90	1.00	0.88	0.98
English	0.80	0.96	0.76	0.92
French	0.78	0.96	0.98	0.98
German	0.89	0.96	0.90	0.95
Portuguese	0.98	0.99	0.99	1.00
Russian	0.79	0.95	0.83	0.93
Spanish	0.78	0.95	0.82	0.94

accuracy than models on the Twitter corpus (right). This is true except in cases, such as Portuguese, where there is a wide difference in the number of national varieties represented (for Portuguese, two vs. four). For reasons of data availability, only English and Spanish have strictly aligned varieties; in both of these languages, the grammars perform better on the web corpus than the Twitter corpus, although the gap is wider for English than for Spanish.

What does the F-Measure tell us about models of syntactic variation? First, the measure is a combination of precision and recall that reflects the predictive accuracy while taking potentially imbalanced classes into account: how many held-out samples can be correctly assigned to their actual region-of-origin? On the one hand, this is a more rigorous evaluation than simply finding a significant difference in a syntactic feature across varieties within a single-fold experimental design: not only is there a difference in the usage of a specific feature, but we can use the features in the aggregate to characterize the difference between national dialects. On the other hand, it is possible that a classifier is over-fitting the training data so that the final model inflates the difference between varieties. For example, let's assume that there is a construction that is used somewhat frequently in Pakistan English but is never used in other varieties. In this case, the classifier could achieve a very high prediction accuracy while only a single construction is actually in variation. Before we interpret these models further, we evaluate whether this sort of confound is taking place.

If a classification model depends on a small number of highly predictive features, thus creating a confound for dialectology, the predictive accuracy of that model will fall abruptly as such features are removed (Koppel et al. 2007). Within authorship verification, *unmasking* is used to evaluate the robustness of

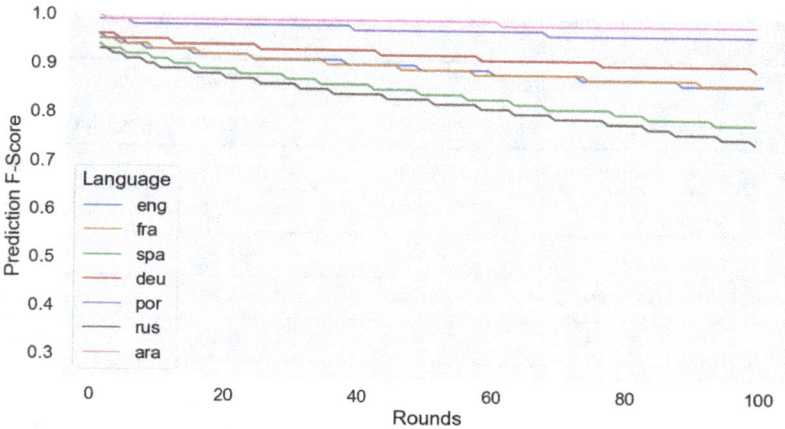

Figure 9.10: Unmasking on Web Corpus.

a text classifier: First, a linear classifier is used to separate documents; here, a Linear SVM is used to classify national dialects of a language. Second, for each round of classification, the features that are most predictive are removed: here, the highest positive and negative features for each national variety are pruned from the model. Third, the classifier is retrained without these features and the change in predictive accuracy is measured: here, unmasking is run for 100 iterations using the association-based grammar as features, as shown in Figure 9.10 (with the web-based corpus). For example, this removes 28 constructions from the model of English each iteration (two for each national dialect), for a total of approximately 2,800 features removed. The figures show the F-Measure for each iteration. On the left-hand side, this represents the performance of the models with all features are present; on the right-hand side, this represents the performance of the models after many features have been removed. This provides a measure of the degree to which these models are subject to a few highly predictive features.

There is a relationship between the rate of decline and the number of national dialects included in the model. What we see, however, is that the performance is not showing the steep decline that we would expect if these results were an artifact. The purpose of this evaluation is to show that a classification approach to dialectology is not subject to the confound of a small number of highly predictive features.

The point of this section has been to extend our theory of usage-based grammar to geographic variation. The work discussed here shows that the same computational grammars learned in Sections 2 and 3 can be used to identify dialect membership on held-out testing data with a high degree of accuracy. In other words, we are evaluating predictions not only about what constructions are learned but also which constructions are favored by each national dialect. This is significant because the scale of these experiments covers seven languages and dozens of national dialects, so that our theory of usage-based grammar is tested in many different contexts. A rigorous experimental paradigm shows, again, that an association-based grammar makes better predictions than a frequency-based grammar, across all languages and data sets. These models do not depend on a few highly predictive constructions. This set of experiments is important as yet another piece of evidence that we can use to test our linguistic theories: a fully specified theory of usage-based grammar that covers both language learning and language variation.

7 Computational cognitive linguistics

This paper has presented work that shows how a computational model of usage-based grammar provides a fully replicable and falsifiable theory that can be evaluated against corpora. Our experiments show that association is more important than frequency for learning generalizations. What makes this work important is its scale: these findings are robust on out-of-sample experiments across seven languages. One potential weakness in the computational paradigm is the kind of language data that we are forced to rely on (written digital texts). We know, however, that all sources of data are subject to bias; Sections 4 and 5 have worked to measure and correct for the bias present in digital corpora. The result is a robust and fully-specified (i.e., falsifiable) theory of usage-based grammar that extends from language learning to language change.

What does this line of work mean for cognitive linguistics? First, it is clear that this theory of usage-based grammar looks somewhat different from existing theories (Langacker 2008; Goldberg 2006). The main difference is that a fully falsifiable linguistic theory must be expressed with much greater mathematical precision. Every concept must be defined in a computable manner, rather than using human intuition and metaphoric terminology. Second, the level of abstraction here is significantly higher than in traditional linguistic argumentation. In other words, specific constructions like the dative or the ditransitive are not, themselves, directly specified or enumerated. This theory of usage-based grammar is by necessity a discovery-device grammar, in the sense that any given grammar (i.e., description of a language) exists only in relationship to the corpus that it is describing. Thus, the theory in fact covers all languages and all dialects, although here it is evaluated on only seven languages.

This is the beginning and not the final formulation of computational cognitive linguistics. There are many remaining weaknesses and many missing components. These can be addressed by continued rigorous empirical evaluation. For example, there have also been computational theories of metaphor that implement and evaluate predictions about metaphor in the same way that this paper has worked with construction grammar (Dunn 2013a, 2013b, 2013c, 2014a, 2014b, 2015a, 2015b). However, there is currently no overlap between a computational theory of construction grammar and a computational theory of metaphor, an obvious area for future research. After all, constructions are form-meaning mappings which interact with metaphor (Sullivan 2013). A better theory of computational cognitive linguistics would make predictions about (1) the entrenchment of constructions, (2) geographic variation in construction usage, and (3) where and how metaphors can be expressed in specific constructions. But the underlying idea is the same: to formalize linguistic theory as a computational model and evaluate the theory's predictions on held-out testing data.

References

Barak, Libby & Adele Goldberg. 2017. Modeling the Partial Productivity of Constructions. In *Proceedings of the Spring Symposium on Computational Construction Grammar and Natural Language Understanding*. Association for the Advancement of Artificial Intelligence. 131–138.

Barak, Libby, Adele Goldberg & Suzanne Stevenson. 2017. Comparing Computational Cognitive Models of Generalization in a Language Acquisition Task. In *Proceedings of the Conference on Empirical Methods in Natural Language Processing*. Association for Computational Linguistics. 96–106.

Card, David & Alan Krueger. 1994. Minimum Wages and Employment: A case study of the fast-food industry in New Jersey and Pennsylvania. *American Economic Review*, 84.

Chang, Nancy, Joachim De Beule & Vanessa Micelli. 2012. Computational construction grammar: Comparing ECG and FCG. In Steels, L. (ed.), *Computational Issues in Fluid Construction Grammar*. Berlin: Springer. 259–288.

Dodge, Ellen, Sean Trott, Luca Gilardi & Elise Stickles. 2017. Grammar Scaling: Leveraging FrameNet Data to Increase Embodied Construction Grammar Coverage. In *Proceedings of the Spring Symposium on Computational Construction Grammar and Natural Language Understanding*. Association for the Advancement of Artificial Intelligence. 154–162.

Dunn, Jonathan. 2013a. How Linguistic Structure Influences and Helps To Predict Metaphoric Meaning. *Cognitive Linguistics*, 24(1): 33–66. doi: 10.1515/cog-2013-0002

Dunn, Jonathan. 2013b. Evaluating the Premises and Results of Four Metaphor Identification Systems. In *Proceedings of the Conference on Intelligent Text Processing and Computational Linguistics, Vol. 1*. Heidelberg: Springer. 471–486. doi: 10.1007/978-3-642-37247-6_38

Dunn, Jonathan. 2013c. What Metaphor Identification Systems Can Tell Us About Metaphor-in-Language. In *Proceedings of the First Workshop on Metaphor in Natural Language Processing*. Association for Computational Linguistics. 1–10.

Dunn, Jonathan. 2014a. Measuring Metaphoricity. In *Proceedings of the Annual Meeting of the Association for Computational Linguistics*. Association for Computational Linguistics. 745–751. doi: 10.3115/v1/P14-2121

Dunn, Jonathan. 2014b. Multi-Dimensional Abstractness in Cross-Domain Mappings. In *Proceedings of the Second Workshop on Metaphor in Natural Language Processing*. Association for Computational Linguistics. 27–32. doi: 10.3115/v1/W14-2304

Dunn, Jonathan. 2015a. Modeling Abstractness and Metaphoricity. *Metaphor & Symbol, 30*(4): 259–289. doi: 10.1080/10926488.2015.1074801

Dunn, Jonathan. 2015b. Three Types of Metaphoric Utterances That Can Synthesize Theories of Metaphor. *Metaphor & Symbol, 30*(1): 1–23. doi: 10.1080/10926488.2015.980694

Dunn, Jonathan. 2017. Computational Learning of Construction Grammars. *Language and Cognition, 9*(2): 254–292. doi: 10.1017/langcog.2016.7

Dunn, Jonathan. 2018a. Modeling the Complexity and Descriptive Adequacy of Construction Grammars. In *Proceedings of the Society for Computation in Linguistics*. Association for Computational Linguistics. 81–90. doi: 10.7275/R59P2ZTB

Dunn, Jonathan. 2018b. Multi-Unit Directional Measures of Association: Moving Beyond Pairs of Words. *International Journal of Corpus Linguistics, 23*(2): 183–215. doi: 10.1075/ijcl.16098.dun

Dunn, Jonathan. 2018c. Finding Variants for Construction-Based Dialectometry: A Corpus-Based Approach to Regional CxGs. *Cognitive Linguistics, 29*(2): 275–311. doi: 10.1515/cog-2017-0029

Dunn, Jonathan. 2019a. Modeling Global Syntactic Variation in English Using Dialect Classification. In *Proceedings of the Sixth Workshop on NLP for Similar Languages, Varieties and Dialects*. Association for Computational Linguistics. doi: 10.18653/v1/W19-1405

Dunn, Jonathan. 2019b. Frequency vs. Association for Constraint Selection in Usage-Based Construction Grammar. In *Proceedings of the Workshop on Cognitive Modeling and Computational Linguistics*. Association for Computational Linguistics. doi: 10.18653/v1/W19-2913

Dunn, Jonathan. 2019c. Global Syntactic Variation in Seven Languages: Towards a Computational Dialectology. In *Frontiers in Artificial Intelligence*, 2. doi: 10.3389/frai.2019.00015

Dunn, Jonathan. 2020. Mapping Languages: The Corpus of Global Language Use. *Language Resources and Evaluation*. doi: 10.1007/s10579-020-09489-2

Dunn, Jonathan. 2021. Representations of Language Varieties Are Reliable Given Corpus Similarity Measures. In *Proceedings of the Eighth Workshop on NLP for Similar Languages, Varieties, and Dialects*. Association for Computational Linguistics. 28–38.

Dunn, Jonathan & Benjamin Adams. 2019. Mapping Languages and Demographics with Georeferenced Corpora. In *Proceedings of Geocomputation 2019*. doi: 10.17608/k6.auckland.9869252.v2

Dunn, Jonathan & Benjamin Adams. 2020. Geographically-Balanced Gigaword Corpora for 50 Language Varieties. In *Proceedings of the Language Resources and Evaluation Conference*. European Language Resources Association. 2528–2536.

Dunn, Jonathan & Andrea Nini. 2021. Production vs Perception: The Role of Individuality in Usage-Based Grammar Induction. In *Proceedings of the Workshop on Cognitive Modeling and Computational Linguistics*. Association for Computational Linguistics. 149–159.

Dunn, Jonathan & Harish Tayyar Madabushi. 2021. Learned Construction Grammars Converge Across Registers Given Increased Exposure. In *Proceedings of the Conference on Computational Natural Language Learning*. Association for Computational Linguistics. 268–278.

Dunn, Jonathan, Tom Coupe & Benjamin Adams. 2020. Measuring Linguistic Diversity During COVID-19. *Proceedings of the Workshop on NLP and Computational Social Science*. Association for Computational Linguistics. 1–10. doi: 10.18653/v1/P17

Ellis, Nick. 2007. Language Acquisition as Rational Contingency Learning. *Applied Linguistics*, 27(1): 1–24.

Forsberg, Markus, Richard Johansson, Linnéa Bäckström, Lars Borin, Ben Lyngfelt, Joel Olofsson & Julia Prentice. 2014. From Construction Candidates to Constructicon Entries: An experiment using semi-automatic methods for identifying constructions in corpora. *Constructions and Frames*, 6(1): 114–135.

Glover, Fred. 1989. Tabu Search, Part 1. *ORSA Journal on Computing*, 1(3): 190–206.

Glover. Fred. 1990. Tabu Search, Part 2. *ORSA Journal on Computing*, 2(1): 4–32.

Goldberg, Adele. 2006. *Constructions at Work The Nature of Generalization in Language*. Oxford: Oxford University Press.

Goldberg, Yoav, Kai Zhao & Liang Huang. 2013. Efficient Implementations of Beam-Search Incremental Parsers. In *Proceedings of the Annual Meeting of the Association for Computational Linguistics*. Association for Computational Linguistics. 628–633.

Goldsmith, John. 2001. Unsupervised Learning of the Morphology of a Natural Language. *Computational Linguistics*, 27(2): 153–198.

Goldsmith, John. 2006. An Algorithm for the Unsupervised Learning of Morphology. *Natural Language Engineering*, 12(4): 353–371.

Goldwater, Sharon, Thomas Griffiths & Mark Johnson. 2009. A Bayesian framework for word segmentation: Exploring the effects of context. *Cognition*, 112(1):21–54.

Gössling, Stefan, Daniel Scott & C. Michael Hall. 2020. Pandemics, tourism and global change: A rapid assessment of COVID-19. *Journal of Sustainable Tourism*, 1–20.

Gries, Stefan Th. 2013. 50-something years of work on collocations: What is or should be next. *International Journal of Corpus Linguistics*, 18(1): 137–165.

Grieve, Jack, Chris Montgomery, Andrea Nini, Akira Murakami & Diansheng Guo. 2019. Mapping lexical dialect variation in British English using Twitter. *Frontiers in Artificial Intelligence*, 2:11.

Hale, Thomas, Anna Petherick, Toby Phillips & Samuel Webster. 2020. Variation in government responses to COVID-19. *Blavatnik School of Government: Working Paper*, 31.

Hirschman, Albert. 1945. *National power and the structure of foreign trade*. University of California Press.

Jurgens, David, Yulia Tsvetkov & Dan Jurafsky. 2017. Incorporating Dialectal Variability for Socially Equitable Language Identification. In *Proceedings of the Annual Meeting of the Association for Computational Linguistics*. 51–57. Association for Computational Linguistics.

Koppel, Moshe, Jonathan Schler & Elisheva Bonchek-Dokow. 2007. Measuring differentiability: Unmasking pseudonymous authors. *Journal of Machine Learning Research*, *8*: 1261–1276.

Langacker, Ronald. 2008. *Cognitive Grammar: A Basic Introduction*. Oxford: Oxford University Press.

Laviola, Adrieli, Ludmila Lage, Nalália Marção, Tatiane Tavares, Vânia Almeida, Ely Matos & Tiago Torrent. 2017. The Brazilian Portuguese Constructicon: Modeling Constructional Inheritance, Frame Evocation and Constraints in FrameNet Brasil. In *Proceedings of the Spring Symposium on Computational Construction Grammar and Natural Language Understanding*. Association for the Advancement of Artificial Intelligence. 193–196.

Matos, Ely, Tiago Torrent, Vânia Almeida, Adrieli Laviola, Ludmila Lage, Nalália Marção & Tatiane Tavares. 2017. Constructional Analysis Using Constrained Spreading Activation in a FrameNet-Based Structured Connectionist Model. In *Proceedings of the Spring Symposium on Computational Construction Grammar and Natural Language Understanding*. Association for the Advancement of Artificial Intelligence. 222–229.

Nguyen, Dat Quoc, Dai Quoc Nguyen, Dang Duc Pham & Son Bao Pham. 2016. A Robust Transformation-Based Learning Approach Using Ripple Down Rules for Part-Of-Speech Tagging. *AI Communications*, *29*(3): 409–422.

Nivre, Joakim & Ryan McDonald. 2008. Integrating Graph-Based and Transition-Based Dependency Parsers. In *Proceedings of the Annual Meeting of the Association for Computational Linguistics*. 950–958. Association for Computational Linguistics.

Pelleg, Dau & Andrew Moore. 2000. X-means: Extending K-means with Efficient Estimation of the Number of Clusters. In *Proceedings of the Seventeenth International Conference on Machine Learning*. 727–734.

Petrov, Slav, Dipanjan Das & Ryan McDonald. 2012. A Universal Part-of-Speech Tagset. In *Proceedings of the Eighth International Conference on Language Resources and Evaluation*. European Association for Language Resources.

Rissanen, Jorma. 1978. Modeling by the Shortest Data Description. *Automatica*, *14*: 465–471.

Rissanen, Jorma. 1986. Stochastic Complexity and Modeling. *Annals of Statistics*, *14*: 1,080–1,100.

Steels, Luc. 2004. Constructivist development of grounded construction grammar. In *Proceedings of the Annual Meeting of the Association for Computational Linguistics*. Association for Computational Linguistics. 9–16.

Steels, Luc. 2012. Design methods for fluid construction grammar. In Steels, L. (ed), *Computational Issues in Fluid Construction Grammar*. Berlin: Springer. 3–36.

Steels, Luc. 2017. Requirements for Computational Construction Grammars. In *Proceedings of the Spring Symposium on Computational Construction Grammar and Natural Language Understanding*. Association for the Advancement of Artificial Intelligence. 251–257.

Sullivan, Karen. 2013. Frames and Constructions in Metaphoric Language. *Constructional Approaches to Language* 14. Amsterdam & Philadelphia: John Benjamins.

United Nations. 2011. *Economic and Social Statistics on the Countries and Territories of the World with Particular Reference to Children's Well-Being*. United Nations Children's Fund.

United Nations. 2017a. *National Accounts Estimates of Main Aggregates. Per Capita GDP at Current Prices in US Dollars*. United Nations Statistics Division.

United Nations. 2017b. *World Population Prospects: The 2017 Revision, DVD Edition*. United Nations Population Division.

van Trijp, Remi. 2017. A Computational Construction Grammar for English. In *Proceedings of Spring Symposium on Computational Construction Grammar and Natural Language Understanding*. Association for the Advancement of Artificial Intelligence. 266–273.

Wible, David & Nai-Lung Tsao. 2010. StringNet as a Computational Resource for Discovering and Investigating Linguistic Constructions. In *Proceedings of the Workshop on Extracting and Using Constructions in Computational Linguistics*: 25–31.

Zhang, Yue & Stephen Clark. 2008. A Tale of Two Parsers: Investigating and Combining Graph-based and Transition-based Dependency Parsing using Beam-search. In *Proceedings of the Conference on Empirical Methods in Natural Language Processing*. Association for Computational Linguistics. 562–571.

Zhang, Yue & Joakim Nivre. 2012. Analyzing the Effect of Global Learning and Beam-search on Transition-based Dependency Parsing. In *Proceedings of the International Conference on Computational Linguistics*. 1391–1400.

Ziem, Alexander & Hans Boas. 2017. Towards a Constructicon for German. In *Proceedings of the Spring Symposium on Computational Construction Grammar and Natural Language Understanding*. Association for the Advancement of Artificial Intelligence. 274–277.

Karlien Franco
What Cognitive Linguistics can learn from dialectology (and vice versa)

1 Introduction

Dialectology[1] is the field of linguistic research that concerns the study of dialects. Although a broad perspective on the concept of a dialect is often taken (e.g. Chambers & Trudgill 1980: 3), in this chapter a more limited interpretation is used. We consider what is often referred to as 'base dialects', which are prototypically characterized by geographical stratification. Bloomfield (1958 [1933]: 325), for instance, argues that "[e]very village, or, at most, every cluster of two or three villages, has its local peculiarities of speech."

The aim of this chapter is to showcase three case-studies that exemplify the advantage of a convergence between traditional dialectology, the field that investigates the geographical structure and social functioning of these dialects, and Cognitive Linguistics for both fields. We will specifically focus on lexical variation in dialectal data. First, we exemplify that dialect data is particularly suited for empirical research, a central tenet of CL since the "social turn" (e.g. Dabrowska & Divjak 2015: 6), because it is often systematically collected on a large scale and because it may reveal factors relevant for synchronic variation and diachronic change due its lectal stratification. In addition, the chapter will show that the concepts central to the framework of Cognitive Linguistics may explain geographical patterns that are found in dialect data. Specific focus will be on the concept of salience for lexical variation. Finally, while visual geographical mapping has always been central to dialectological research, this chapter relies on more recent visualization techniques throughout. This allows us to demonstrate how these novel techniques provide a picture of the structure found in dialect data that goes beyond the traditional dialectological analyses. Next to analysing the social and geographical structure in these data, these novel techniques offer insight into the lexicon at large.

After providing a brief overview of the dialectological tradition and of research on lexical variation in Cognitive Linguistics in §2, §3 describes the

---

1 In line with the definition of a dialect outlined in this paragraph, we use this term in a strict way, viz. referring to the study of the geographically stratified base dialects.

Karlien Franco, KU Leuven & FWO Vlaanderen, e-mail: karlien.franco@kuleuven.be

https://doi.org/10.1515/9783110687279-011

dialect data that will be used in the case studies. In §4 the first case-study is presented, which uses a quantitative technique (generalized additive modelling) whose interpretation relies heavily on the visualization of the results. With this technique, we showcase how the interaction between meaning and the spread of linguistic variants in terms of transmission and diffusion (cf. Labov 2007) explain aggregate-level patterns in the geographical spread of the dialect lexicon. Next, in §5, the principle of communicative need is considered, which has been re-gaining interest in computational approaches to linguistics recently (for a review, see Kemp et al. 2018). We integrate this view with a cognitive-linguistic approach to lexical variation and showcase some examples of its relevance in dialectological data. Finally, in §6, these case-studies are brought together in a discussion of the advantages of a further rapprochement between dialectology and Cognitive Linguistics.

2 Background

2.1 The dialectological tradition

Research into the geographical stratification of dialects gained ground in the wake of the neogrammarian search for exceptionless sound laws (Bloomfield 1958 [1933]: 321–345, Chambers & Trudgill 1980: 18–23). This gave way to an interest in the systematicity with which linguistic variants spread across geographical space, which resulted in the construction of a large number of dialect surveys and atlases, like the German surveys of Georg Wenker, which were later edited and published by Ferdinand Wrede, and the French dialect atlas project edited by Jules Gilliéron. However, relatively quickly, such dialectological enterprises showed that the spatial distribution of variants is highly heterogeneous. Although some general processes have been noticed, the search for complete regularity in the spread of sound laws was rapidly abandoned. For example, in 1927, Kloeke (cited in Bloomfield 1958 [1933]: §19.4) was the first to notice an example of the process of lexical diffusion ("every word has its own history"; ibid.: 328) in the pronunciation of the vowels in *muis* 'mouse' and *huis* 'house' in Dutch. The dialectal pronunciation of these vowels is geographically stratified: in the eastern periphery, the traditional Germanic pronunciation with [uː] is retained in both words, while in other locations, [y:] is used for both (in a third set of locations, in the centre of the language area, the present-day standard Dutch diphthong [œy:] occurs in both words, but this is a later development). However, additionally, in three relatively large regions towards the east of the language area, the pronunciation of both vowels differs: [muːs], [hyːs]. Kloeke argues that the use of [yː] spread from cultural centres in the west of the language area, first Flanders and later Holland, from the Middle Ages onwards. Towards the east of the language area, another group, the North Germanic Hanse, took up a culturally significant position, and they used the Germanic variant [uː]. Additionally, [yː] was considered the more elegant variant, which was even hypercorrectly used in words that do not generally have [yː] like [vyːt] for [vuːt] 'foot'. Crucially, the larger geographical expansion of the [yː] variant in the word *house* has been explained as a semantic frequency-related phenomenon: *house* probably occurs more, especially in formal speech, while the use of the word *mouse* is probably more limited to homely situations. Consequently, following from the confrontation with these types of non-exceptionless phonological developments, dialect geography became a field of research in its own right (Nerbonne & Kretzschmar 2003): it became the aim of the dialectologist to distinguish smaller dialect areas, characterized by a certain degree of linguistic uniformity, within a larger heterogeneous region.

The traditional method to distinguish dialect areas from each other relies on maps of the variants used in particular locations for a set of linguistic variables, like concepts or the pronunciation of particular words. These maps are then interpreted by the dialectologist, in order to identify possible isoglosses, borders for a single linguistic variable that distinguish areas where a particular variant is used from regions with a different variant (examples of such dialect maps in Dutch dialectology are, for example, presented in Blancquaert & Pée 1925–1982). If on a large number of maps, the same bundles of isoglosses can be found, they are interpreted as dialect borders. Recently, advances in dialectometry have automatized this process and made it more objective by taking into account quantitative measures of the linguistic distance between different locations (e.g. Goebl 1984, Hoppenbrouwers & Hoppenbrouwers 2001, Heeringa 2004, Wieling 2012). Alternatively, dialect areas have also been distinguished on the basis of subjective, perceptual distances of dialect speakers (Preston 1999, Weijnen 1946).

2.2 Meaning in Cognitive Linguistics and (dia-)lectal lexical variation

Geeraerts et al. (1994) examine the structure of lexical variation in the use of clothing terminology in Dutch. Crucially, it is the first study to systematically emphasize the importance of two distinctions. On the one hand, it shows that in order to obtain a full picture of the structure of lexical variation, semasiological research should be complemented with an onomasiological approach. The semasiological perspective examines the range of applications of a particular expression. Semasiology is, for this reason, often defined as research into the meaning of a particular item: given a particular word or expression, what are the referents to which the word applies? In the case of the Dutch word *monitor*, for instance, a semasiological analysis would reveal that it can refer both to a YOUTH LEADER, and to a COMPUTER SCREEN (Heylen et al. 2015). The onomasiological perspective, in contrast, investigates naming rather than meaning. An onomasiological approach, thus, starts from a particular (type of) concept and determines which names exist or can be used. For instance, an onomasiological analysis of the concept of English intensifiers would reveal that a large set of words can be used for this concept, including *very, really, so* and *pretty* (Tagliamonte 2008).

On the other hand, this study was the first to make the importance of the interaction between four different types of lexical variation for the structure of the lexicon explicit. First, it examines semasiological variation, the situation where a single lexical item can refer to more than one referent. For example, the lexical item *pants* can both be used to refer to a TWO-LEGGED TYPE OF OUTER GARMENT (IN GENERAL), but also to a more specific referent, viz. MEN'S UNDERWEAR. The second and third types of lexical variation that are distinguished concern two varieties of onomasiological variation: conceptual variation and formal variation. Conceptual variation concerns the situation where "a referent or type of referent may be named by means of various conceptually distinct lexical categories" (Geeraerts et al. 1994: 3–4). For example, to refer to a pair of BLUE JEANS, a language user can either choose to select a lexical item belonging to the concept BLUE JEANS and use a word like *jeans* or *blue jeans*, or (s)he can conceptualize the referent as a type of PANTS, a superordinate concept, and call the denotatum *trousers* or *pants*. In other words, conceptual variation concerns lexical construal phenomena. Formal variation, in contrast, occurs when a choice has to made between different synonymous expressions for a referent, belonging to the same conceptual category (Geeraerts 2016).[2] In the blue jeans example, this would involve determining the relative frequency of the terms *jeans* versus *blue jeans* or *trousers* versus *pants*. Finally, it shows how contextual variation can be at play both at the semasiological and onomasiological level. Contextual variation (also called speaker and situation related variation) is broadly defined: it includes

---

[2] In Geeraerts et al. (1994: 3–4), the distinction between formal variation and conceptual variation was defined less strictly, with formal variation concerning the case where a choice has to made between different synonymous expressions for a referent, regardless of whether they belong to the same conceptual category.

both the relatively stable lectal properties of the interlocutors involved (like their gender or their nationality), but also transient situation-related features, like the register of the speech event (Geeraerts, Kristiansen & Peirsman 2010: 8). For the (onomasiological) BLUE JEANS example, for instance, contextual variation may take the form of determining whether older people are more likely to refer to the concept as *blue jeans*.

Framed against this background, the findings of Geeraerts at al. (1994) show that prototypicality effects are pervasive in the lexicon. Prototype theory originated in psychological research on categorization (see Rosch 1978, 1987 [1974]), which showed that many categories, i.e. sets of objects that are considered to be equivalent, cannot realistically be described in terms of necessary-and-sufficient conditions. Instead, category membership is characterized by gradedness concerning the degree to which particular referents are typical for the category (non-equality), and by indeterminacy concerning category boundaries (non-discreteness). Traditionally, research in (extensions of) prototype theory takes a semasiological perspective: it concerns the range of applications of a particular expression. A classical example concerns the category of fruit. Non-equality shows up in the fact that an apple is a more prototypical type of fruit than a pineapple. Non-discreteness is exemplified by considering an olive: should, in folk classifications, olives, which are the edible seed-bearing parts of the olive tree, like apples are the edible seed-bearing parts of apple trees, be considered types of fruit?

Crucially, in Geeraerts et al. (1994), it was shown that prototypicality effects are also at play at the onomasiological level. Non-equality shows up in the fact that some concepts are more onomasiologically salient than others: the concept COFFEE, for instance, is more salient, i.e. psychologically more entrenched, than the concept BUBBLE TEA (a type of beverage that generally consists of a mixture of tea and milk, often with tapioca and other flavours added). Non-discreteness can show up in two ways (ibid.: 122): in the form of demarcation problems among semantic fields (e.g. where does the semantic field of vegetables end and that of fruits begin?) or in the form of fuzziness at the edges of concepts belonging to the same semantic field (e.g. in the semantic field of weather phenomena, where does the concept TO RAIN HEAVILY end and the concept TO STORM begin?).

The research paradigm was subsequently extended in several ways. Geeraerts, Grondelaers & Speelman (1999) provide a study of the diachronic lexical convergence and divergence between the two standard varieties of Dutch, Belgian and Netherlandic Dutch, and of the internal stratification of Belgian Dutch in terms of Colloquial Belgian Dutch. In this study, the notion of an onomasiological profile was introduced (it was further developed in Speelman, Grondelaers & Geeraerts 2003). The onomasiological profile of a concept can be considered as a way to comply with the notion of a linguistic variable and the principle of accountability in sociolinguistics (Labov 1969: 737), by taking into account *all* the different synonyms that can be used to refer to the same concept. Furthermore, the relative frequency of each variant is included in the calculation of the onomasiological profile to determine the degree to which the lexical items take up a strong position *vis-à-vis* alternatives for the concept. This allows for a quantification of the degree of homogeneity, or standardization, in the use of lexical variants for a particular concept.

More recently, some further advances have been made, especially on the methodological plane and situated against the background of Cognitive Sociolinguistics. This subfield combines the theoretical framework developed in Cognitive Linguistics with the tradition of variationist sociolinguistics of employing solid empirical methods to examine the socio-cultural position of a language user as a correlate of language variation and change. Thus, aside from (1) relying on the theoretical framework elaborated in Cognitive Linguistics in general, research in this prototypically structured paradigm is characterized by two other features (Kristiansen & Dirven 2008: 5–6). More specifically, it (2) explicitly includes the social dimensions of variation; and (3) uses solid empirical methods. In line with these views, recent studies on lexical variation are relying increasingly on the use of large-scale data and novel methods for the automatic analysis of the structure of variation (cf. Montes and Heylen, this volume).

3 Data

The data used in this chapter come from the digitized databases of the three large regional dictionaries of Dutch: the *Woordenboek van de Brabantse dialecten* 'Dictionary of the Brabantic Dialects' (WBD), the *Woordenboek van de Limburgse dialecten* 'Dictionary of the Limburgish Dialects' (WLD) and the *Woordenboek van de Vlaamse dialecten* 'Dictionary of the Flemish Dialects'. The databases are also available online at https://www.e-wvd.be/, https://e-wbd.nl/ and https://e-wld.nl/. The goal of these dictionaries is to make an inventory, as exhaustive as possible, of the lexicon in every situation in which the base dialects function as the means of communication (Weijnen, Goossens & Goossens 1983: 4). They are historical dictionaries in the sense that the dialect lexicon they describe is the early 20th century common lexical norm of a large part of the speech community (Kruijsen 1996). The data were in practice collected from the oldest generation of speakers in the second half of the 20th century. As a result, the dialect dictionaries not only serve a linguistic aim, viz.

systematically preserving the geographically stratified dialect lexicon, but they also provide a cultural and historical testimony of the everyday discourse practices of the dialect speakers in the early 20th century.

Geographically, the three dictionaries describe different dialect regions in the northern part of Belgium (Flanders) and in the Netherlands. Figure 10.1 shows the geography of the dialect regions relative to the rest of Belgium and the Netherlands. The WVD describes the dialects spoken in the west of Flanders, more specifically in the provinces West-Flanders and East-Flanders (not to be confused with the region Flanders, which spans the entire northern, Dutch-speaking part of Belgium). These dialects are called the Flemish dialects. The WBD comprises the province of North Brabant in the Netherlands and the provinces of Antwerp and Flemish Brabant (including the Brussels region) in Belgium. The data for the WLD come from the Netherlandic province of Limburg and the Belgian province of Limburg.

The largest part of the lexical items in the dictionaries are elicited by means of large-scale questionnaires sent out across the dialect area. Additionally, the dictionaries also use supplementary sources, like smaller-scale questionnaires or local dialect dictionaries. Because the data collected outside of the large dialect questionnaires may be less systematic in nature, the analyses below only include questionnaire data. The digitized version of the dictionaries that are used in this chapter are onomasiological in nature, organized per concept. They contain detailed information about the concept and semantic field, as well as on the location where a particular variant was recorded.

4 Aggregate-level patterns of the transmission and diffusion of loanwords

4.1 Transmission and diffusion

The concept of transmission entails an "unbroken sequence of native-language acquisition by children" (Labov 2007: 346). This type of generational change is the basis of family tree models of languages. According to Labov, transmission is the "normal type" of language change, through (sometimes imperfect) replication of the variable language of the older generation. However, it is a well-known fact that there is a second way in which languages can change, termed "diffusion" by Labov (2007). Specifically, through language contact, the structure of a language may change as well. This is the type of language change particularly

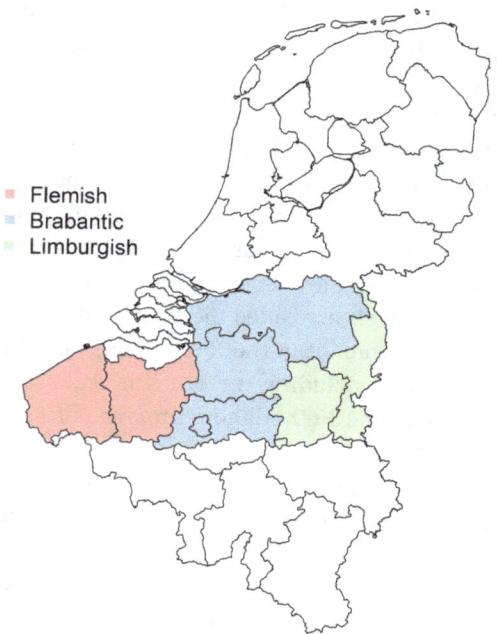

Figure 10.1: The Flemish, Brabantic and Limburgish dialect area.

exemplified by the wave model, as well as in gravity models of language change (Trudgill 1974).

However, the extent to which these processes are systematic in a language is unknown. Is every aspect of a language system equally likely to undergo transmission or diffusion? The first case-study (also see Franco et al. 2019a) will show that, at least in the lexicon, some domains are more prone to processes of transmission, whereas others are more prone to diffusion (for similar results on typological data, see Tadmor 2009). By framing patterns of transmission and diffusion of loanwords in a Cognitive Linguistics perspective where meaning plays a central role, the importance of language-external factors will be shown to variably affect the variation.

4.1 Case-study 1: Variation in loanword usage

The first case-study uses data from the WBD and WLD to inquire into the effect of meaning on the distribution of loanwords from Latin and French. Two semantic fields from the third part (general vocabulary) of these dictionaries were selected: clothing & personal hygiene and church & religion. In total, 416 church concepts and 328 clothing concepts were investigated in a total of 1440 locations. For each location, we calculated the ratio of French loanwords vis-à-vis other words per semantic field and the ratio of Latin loanwords vis-à-vis other words per semantic field, using the tags for loanwords status available in the dictionaries. Some examples are presented in Table 10.1.

Table 10.1: Example of French and Latin loanwords.

Source language	Society, school & education		Clothing & personal hygiene	
French	*medaille*	'scapular'	*bijou*	'jewel'
	voile	'headdress for girls during Holy Communion'	*winterpaletot*	'warm coat'
Latin	*crucifix*	'crucifix'	*stola*	'stole'
	monstrans	'monstrance'	*stool*	'bonnet of the "poffer"'

To analyze these data, Generalized Additive Models (GAMs) were used (Hastie & Tibshirani 1986, also see Zuur et al. 2009 and Wood 2017). These models can be considered an extension of Generalized Linear Models that allow for a combination of parametric and non-parametric relationships, which do not have to be specified a priori, between the response and the explanatory variables. Generalized Additive Models have become increasingly popular in dialectology for modelling spatial data (e.g. Wieling et al. 2011), as well as in other fields of linguistics (e.g. Tamminga et al. 2016, Tomaschek et al. 2018, Wieling 2018). In practice, for each source language, we start from the same model to compare the influence of the interaction between geography and semantic field on the ratio of non-native to native tokens. This model contains a smooth term for the interaction between longitude and latitude for each semantic field and a random intercept for location, as the total number of observations differs per location (although this factor does not reach significance in the model for the Latin variants).

Figure 10.2 shows the results of the mixed GAM for the French loanwords. The predicted surface for each semantic field is presented in a separate panel. In each panel, the Brabantic and Limburgish dialect areas are depicted, with province and country borders indicated in black. A continuous colour scale is plotted over this geographical area, with yellow hues indicating that the ratio of French to non-French tokens is high and red hues indicating that the amount of French tokens is lower. In areas where the predicted amount of French tokens is smaller than 0.03 (the lower bound of the continuous colour scale), the plots show no colour. It is important to note that stronger, darker colour hues (the reddish ones) indicate a smaller amount of borrowed lexical items. The numerical interpretation of the colour scheme is provided in the legend at the top left of each panel. The legends and colour schemes are kept stable for each map per source language to ensure comparability across semantic fields. The minimum and maximum values for the legend are based on the predicted values for the semantic field where French occurs the most, viz. clothing & personal hygiene. Additionally, the plots also show a number of green lines that run throughout the dialect areas. These lines can be interpreted as isoglosses.

The figure shows that the amount of French tokens is very high in the semantic field of clothing & personal hygiene on the right-hand side. The isoglosses on the map even seem to follow the state borders between Belgium and the Netherlands in the north of the province of Antwerp and the north and the east of Limburg in Belgium. In addition, the French words clearly show a process of diffusion in this field, with color hues decreasing nearly monotonously from south to north. In contrast, French tokens are less frequent in the field of church & religion on the left. The isoglosses, which do not show a large amount of smoothing in this field, seem to indicate that the larger the geographical distance from the city of Brussels in the southwest of the figure, where French has always held a strong position, the smaller the predicted amount of French.

Figure 10.3 shows the results for Latin loanwords. In these maps, the odds of encountering a Latin token equal to 0.01 is used as the lower bound for the color scale (in red hues). The upper bound is equal to the maximum of the predicted odds of encountering a Latin token in the field of church & religion, the field where Latin occurs the most (yellow hues). As this maximum is only 0.1, Latin loanwords are clearly less frequent overall than lexical borrowings from French.

The maps for the semantic field 'clothing & personal hygiene' (on the right) does not contain any color or isoglosses. This indicates that the predicted odds of encountering a Latin token in a location in these fields is even smaller than 0.01: the maximum predicted value for clothing concepts is 0.004 (in Deurne, province of Antwerp) and 0.002 for personality-related terms (in Vaals, Limburg).[3] The field of church & religion shows the largest amount of Latin tokens. This is probably due to the fact that many of the Latin names were introduced

---

[3] The numerical output of the GAMM also indicates that the smooth term for clothing & personality does not differ significantly from 0.

into Dutch as names for novel (catholic) concepts. Whether or not a lexical item is borrowed out of necessity (i.e. to avoid a lexical gap) or not, is a frequently mentioned factor that increases the borrowability of a lexeme (e.g. Onysko & Winter-Froemel 2011). As a result, this factor may serve as an explanation for the success of the Latin source language in this semantic field. In addition, very little geographical patterns are shown in this field. This confirms that these words were probably transmitted from generation to generation.

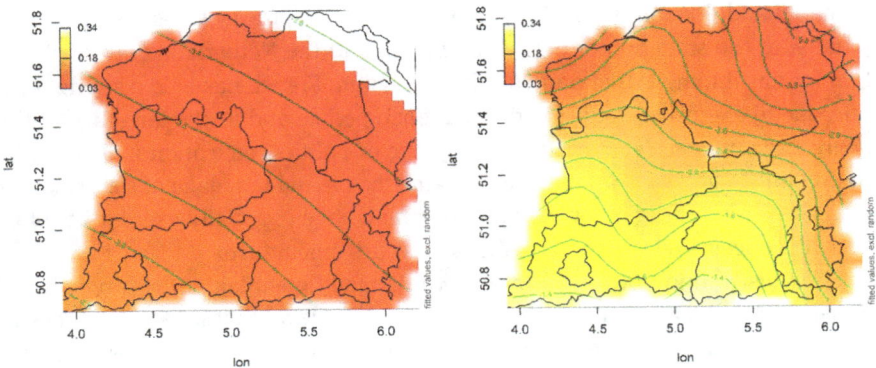

Figure 10.2: French loanwords (left: church & religion, right: clothing & personal hygiene).

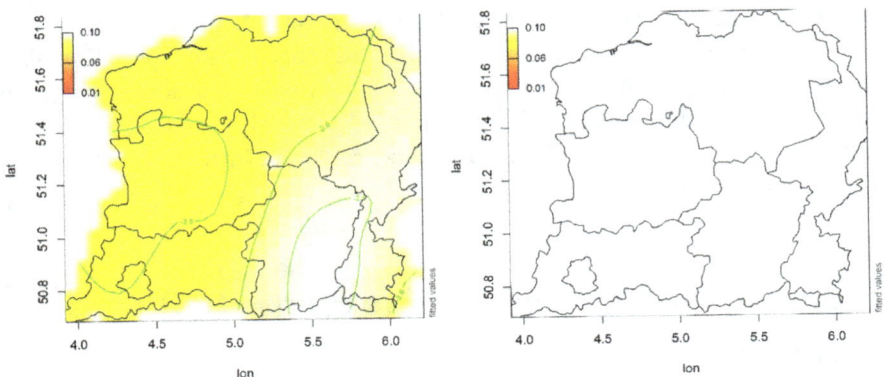

Figure 10.3: Latin loanwords (left: church & religion, right: clothing & personal hygiene).

Overall then, the first case study shows that a quantitative visualization technique can offer insight into the interaction between semantics and the aggregate spatial spread of linguistic variation. The distribution of the French loanwords in the Brabantic and Limburgish dialect area displays patterns of diffusion. In the field of church & religion, the proportion of French decreases as one moves further away from Brussels, where French is nowadays one of the official languages. In this city, French initially only served as the language of the nobility, but due to the fact that the French language was much more prestigious than the local Brabantic dialects, the number of people who used a variety of Dutch decayed over time, in favor of the French language (De Vriendt 2004: 20–29 and 91–94). In the field of clothing & personal hygiene, in contrast, the border with the Romance language area (in the south of both dialect areas) is probably more influential. In addition, on the map for clothing & hygiene, the isoglosses seem to run parallel to the state border between Belgium and the Netherlands. An explanation for this finding is that particularly in Belgium, French has held a strong position due to extensive contact with the French people and as the language of the *bourgeoisie*. It was also the official language of politics, education and administration until the 1930s, when Dutch became the official language of the region of Flanders. As a prestigious variety, French may have especially exerted its influence on concepts relating to someone's outward appearance.

The distribution of the Latin loanwords may be explained by a process of transmission, after initial language contact. In medieval times, Latin was mostly important as the language of the Catholic church although it also exerted its influence on Dutch for concepts relating to education, science, and for administration and government, as in many other European languages. Furthermore, words from Church Latin were borrowed for novel religious concepts when the people of the Low Countries were christened (Van der Sijs 2005: 124). Crucially, in comparison to French, the use of Latin is probably less prone to geographical variability, as Latin has predominantly been influential as a written, academic language that was transmitted through schooling. In sum, the analysis indicates that processes of transmission and diffusion are influenced by an interaction between semantic and geographical properties.

5 Communicative need and (experiential) salience

5.1 The principle of communicative need

The principle of communicative need or efficient communication has recently been gaining renewed attention in computational approaches to lexical-semantic research (e.g. Piantadosi et al. 2011, Mahowald et al. 2013, Karjus et al. 2020, and see Kemp et al. 2018 and Gibson et al. 2019 for overviews). This principle assumes a functional explanation for language diversity (e.g. Zipf 1949, Givón 1995, Haspelmath 1999) because "languages are under pressure to be simultaneously informative (so as to support effective communication) and simple (so as to minimize cognitive load)" (Kemp et al. 2018: 111). Recent studies have emphasized the fact that what may count as effective communication in one socio-cultural environment, may be inefficient in another one (e.g. Regier et al. 2016, Kemp et al. 2019). Thus, the principle combines two views that have played a role in the history of linguistic research: on the one hand, the need for a language user to be as informative as possible but no more informative than necessary (cf. Grice's maxim of quantity), and, on the other hand, the fact that the socio-cultural environment may interact with the structure of the lexicon.

Interpreted from a CL perspective where meaning takes a central position, three predictions can be made based on the principle. All three of these predictions give a central position to differences in salience. The following discussion will show that while the principle of communicative need has recently been regaining attention, its predictions are not novel to lexical semantics.

First, at the level of *semasiological variation*, the principle of communicative need would predict that language tends to avoid polysemous words. This principle of isomorphism (one form – one function) has a long tradition in functional approaches to linguistic research (e.g., Bolinger, 1977; Haiman, 1980). However, at the same time, it is well-known that polysemy is pervasive in language (Killgariff 1997). Nonetheless, the usefulness of polysemy phenomena has been explained in terms of efficiency against the background of a prototype-theoretical organization of language (Rosch 1978, Geeraerts 1997). More specifically, in such a view, the meaning of lexical items can be characterized in terms of core cases and flexible modulations on this core. The principle of isomorphism is compatible with this view if 'one function' is interpreted in a broad way, encompassing the entire conceptual core of the prototypical item (Geeraerts 1997: chapter 4).

Second, at the level of *conceptual onomasiological variation*, the principle of efficient communication predicts that semantic space will be categorized by language users in as much detail as necessary (to increase efficient communication), but not in more detail than necessary (to avoid excessive cognitive load). Thus, a hypothesis resulting from this prediction is that for semantic domains with a high degree of salience, or cultural relevance, in a particular community, a larger amount of lexicalized (sub-)concepts will be found than in semantic domains with a low degree of cultural relevance. Or, when different cultures are compared, a particular semantic domain will be categorized in more detail – as exemplified by the fact that more (sub-)concepts are lexicalized – in cultures where the domain is more salient for the language users.

While these hypotheses resemble the classical but controversial work on linguistic relativity (e.g. Boas 1911, Whorf 1964, and see Pullum 1989 for criticism), recent studies have found evidence that especially the second hypothesis holds. For example, Majid & Burenhult (2014) have shown that very few olfactory concepts are lexicalized by speakers of English. In contrast, speakers of Jahai, nomadic hunter-gatherers of the Malay Peninsula, can name and distinguish smell as easily as colour. In their community, smell also takes up a prominent place in everyday life and communication. In another paper, Regier et al. (2016) examine whether a single word used is for snow and ice, or if different words exist, across a variety of languages using data from several sources. They find that both in warmer and colder climates, languages are spoken where separate lexical items are used. However languages with only a single lexical item for both concepts only occur in warmer climates. Furthermore, similar observations were also formulated in early dialectological work. For example, in his seminal work on the dialects of Dutch, Weijnen (1966: 337) writes that some dialects of fisherman communities have a separate name for the eldest brother, whereas most other dialects do not make this distinction. He argues that the explanation for this organization of the lexicon is that the eldest brother needs to take up a caring position if the father drowns while fishing in these communities (a few other examples are mentioned in Goossens 1964 and in Weijnen 1966: 337).

Third, at the level of *formal onomasiological variation*, the principle of communicative need predicts that languages tend to avoid synonymy and homonymy and that this will be particularly prevalent for concepts with a high degree of salience for the language users. Of course, avoidance of homonymy and synonymy is a well-known characteristic of language for scholars in lexical semantics. A classic example is described in the research by Gilliéron & Roques, published in 1912, (cited in Geeraerts 2010: 62–63) on the Gascon dialects. In these dialects, regular sound change caused the Latin words for ROOSTER, *gallus*, and CAT, *cattus*, to merge as *gat*. Then, the word for ROOSTER was replaced by *azan* (the local variant of *faisan* 'pheasant'), *bigey* (probably related to *vicaire* 'curate') or *poule* (from Latin *pullus*). Crucially, the geographical region where two of these words (*azan* and *bigey*) are used, directly coincides with the isogloss that delineates the area where *gallus* and *cattus* would have merged due to the regular sound change (although the word *pullus* also occurs in some locations where the sound change would not have taken place). Interestingly, the explanation given for this onomasiological reorganization is the fact that the concepts of ROOSTER and CAT are relatively important in an agrarian society. Thus, perhaps these concepts were particularly likely to undergo rearrangement as a result of fear of homonymy due to their high degree of salience.

This prediction on the onomasiological level was tested on a larger scale in two case studies (case-studies 2 and 3) on the dialect databases described above (Franco & Geeraerts 2018, 2019). Crucially, in both studies, several measures were used which aim to quantify information that can be derived from visual analyses of dialect data and, more specifically, the fact that these data are by nature geographically stratified across a dialect area (another fruitful approach of research along these lines has been pursued under the heading of geostatistical dialectometry, e.g. Rumpf et al. 2009, 2010 and Pickl 2013). Moreover, the final case-study fully relies on visual analytics to interpret the results.

5.2 Case-study 2: Variation in plant names

In the second case-study, we examined the use of names for naturally occurring plants in the three dialect areas of the northern part of Belgium: the Flemish dialects in the west, the Brabantic dialects in the center and the Limburgish dialects in the east. Rather than concentrating on which names are used where, we examine lexical diversity in the names for plants, that is, the amount of variation that occurs for each plant. Following from the principle of communicative need, we would expect that plants that are more salient in the environment of the dialect speakers, will show less lexical diversity.

To operationalize the salience of plants for the dialect speakers, we made use of the digitized version of the standard reference work for the distribution of plants in the northern part of Belgium (Van Landuyt et al. 2006). This database contains two types of information. On the one hand, the database provides absolute numbers for the global frequency of a plant in the entire northern part of Belgium. On the other hand, it also has information about the frequency of each plant in the six ecological regions that are distinguished based on their ecological coherence in this region.[4] We use these figures to represent the local frequency of a plant. In the top panel of Figure 10.4, an example of a highly salient plant, the common aspen (Populus Termula), throughout the northern part of Belgium is shown (Van Landuyt et al. 2006: 688). At the bottom, the distribution of a plant that is only still found in particular ecological regions, the common cowslip (the Primula Veris), is visualized (Van Landuyt et al. 2006: 712).

---

4 In particular, the northern part of Belgium is, for the purposes of the database, divided up in squares of 1x1 km (so-called 'kilometer squares'). While not every kilometer square is investigated by the fieldworkers who provide the data for the database, the dataset contains information about the relative number of investigated kilometer squares in which the plant was found per ecological region.

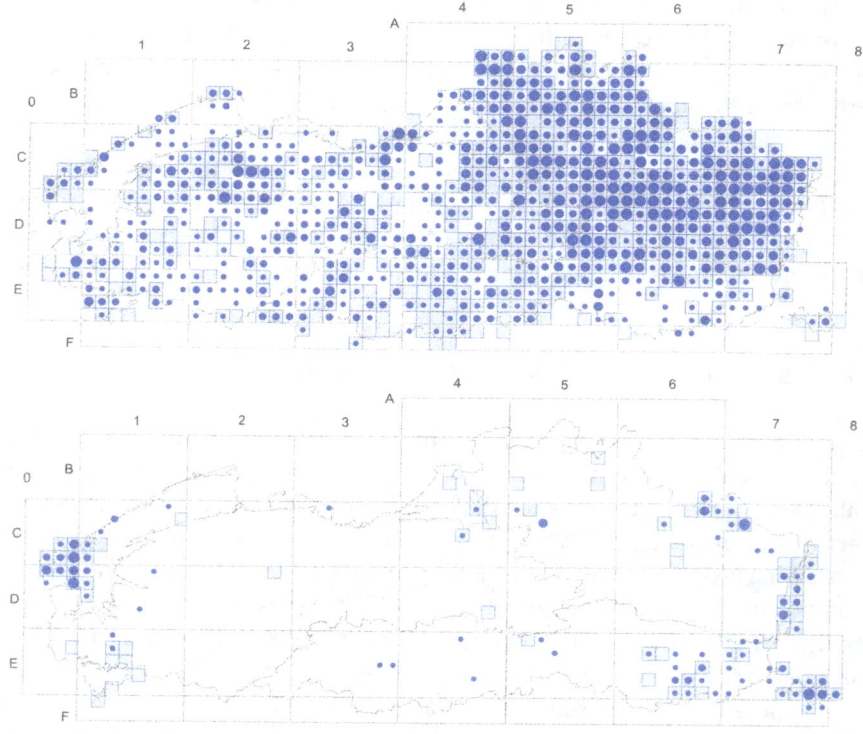

Figure 10.4: Top panel: geographical distribution of the common aspen (Populus tremula), a very frequent plant (Van Landuyt et al. 2006: 688). Bottom panel: geographical distribution of the common cowslip (Primula veris), a very infrequent plant (Van Landuyt et al. 2006: 712).

The magnitude of the dark blue dots is proportionate to the frequency of the plant in that location in the period 1972–2004. The pale blue squares reflect whether or not the plant was found in that location in the period 1939–1971.

As a next step, we used numeric measures to gauge the degree of lexical diversity per plant per region, which allowed us to conduct an aggregate-level analysis. More specifically, lexical diversity was operationalized in two ways. First, we calculated a variant of the type-token ratio (TTR) applied to the dictionary data: the number of dialectal variants (tokens) in a particular ecological region per plant, divided by the total number of unique dialect names (types) for the plant in the region. TTR ranges from 0 to 1 and it approaches 0 when a small number of types is available, given the number of tokens. It is equal to 1 when the number of types is equal to the number of tokens. In addition, we also examined the degree of internal uniformity in the names used for each plant in every region. Internal uniformity is a measure that was introduced in Geeraerts et al. (1999). It calculates the relative contribution of each lexical variant to the onomasiological profile of a plant. Internal uniformity ranges from 0 to 1 and takes a high values when one variant is very frequently used, which indicates that many language users share the same word to refer to a particular concept. It is closer to 0 when several variants occur with comparable frequencies, which shows that different language users have different words for a particular concept.

Using correlation analyses, we determined to which extent plant frequency and lexical diversity are related. In general, we found that a significant negative correlation (alpha = 0.05) exists between plant frequency and lexical diversity for all the dependent and independent variables (see Table 10.2). However, as the absolute values of the correlation coefficients are never larger than 0.261, the correlation between plant frequency and lexical diversity is not very strong. In addition, the results for TTR and internal uniformity contradict each other. While more frequent plants do occur with a smaller amount of different variants, given the number of data available (TTR), this does not necessarily ensure that one lexeme becomes the preferred lexeme over its competing synonyms throughout the ecological region (as evidenced by the negative correlation with internal uniformity). In other words: while for more frequent plants, the number of different variants decreases for the same amount of tokens, this does not mean that every language user chooses the same name in the same situation (i.e. ecological region). Geographical variation within an ecological region, for example, is not neutralized by the high natural frequency of a plant. In fact, if a plant has both a low value for TTR and for internal uniformity, this means that, while the plant does not have a large number of unique types given the number of available tokens, the number of records per lexeme per plant per region does not differ a lot and the tokens are distributed over the unique types in a relatively homogeneous way.

Overall then, this case-study exemplifies the benefit of using dialectological data to investigate a central question in lexical Cognitive Linguistics research: the importance of salience for language variation. Although a correlation between salience and diversity was found, this correlation is mitigated by lectal differences. In addition, it showcases a first of way of transforming dialectological information, which is typically presented on a map, into numbers that can be used in statistical analyses.

Table 10.2: Correlation between plant frequency and lexical diversity.

	Type-token ratio (TTR)	Internal uniformity
local relative frequency	−0.256 $p < 0.001$	−0.191 $p < 0.001$
global absolute frequency[5]	−0.261 $p < 0.001$	−0.156 $p < 0.001$

5.3 Case-study 3: Variation in names for foods and cooking concepts

In a final case-study, we used a visual technique to gauge the correlation between salience and lexical diversity (Franco & Geeraerts 2018). This case-study focused on the correlation between variation in the names for concepts relating to food and cooking and the salience of these concepts in the WBD (spoken in the center of the northern part of Belgium).[6]

Another difference with the previous case-study is the more elaborate operationalization of the lexical diversity of a concept, which was in the previous case-study operationalized as the type-token ratio and the measure of internal uniformity. However, these measures do not really take into account the fact that dialectal data is inherently geographically stratified. Thus, in this study, we operationalized lexical diversity with a composite measure, which we refer to as lexical geographical heterogeneity (also see Speelman & Geeraerts 2008, Geeraerts & Speelman 2010 and Franco et al. 2019b). This measure specifically accounts for the spatial distribution of linguistic data that would be visible from a dialect map.

As in the previous case-study, the lexical diversity variable considers the number of unique lexemes (i.e. types) per concept. However, in addition, it also reflects the fact that dialectal data are geographically stratified (geographic fragmentation). In dialectometry, several ways exist to gauge the spatial distribution of variants, e.g. by calculating (dis)agreement between locations (Séguy 1971), relative or weighted values of identity (Goebl 1984, 2010), Levenshtein

---

[5] Several measures of global frequency are available in the database, but because the results are the same across measures, we only report results for the absolute number of kilometer squares where a plant was found in the northern part of Belgium between 1972 and 2004 here.
[6] The dictionary also contains more general or evaluative concepts such as DINNER, HUNGRY and RAW but these are not considered in the analysis.

distance (e.g. Heeringa 2004, Wieling, Nerbonne & Baayen 2011), spatial autocorrelation (Grieve, Speelman & Geeraerts 2011), and Euclidian distance (e.g. Szmrecsanyi 2008). The variable we use does not rely on distance matrices between locations, but directly measures the overall distribution of linguistic variants for a particular concept. In practice, the operationalization of the degree of geographical fragmentation of a concept takes into account the average geographical distance between two locations with the same variant (dispersion) and the average geographical surface of a particular lexical item (range) per concept. Conceptually, the degree to which a particular concept shows dispersion concerns the degree to which, on average, the distribution of the lexical variants for the concept is characterized by the interference of other lexemes that are used for the same concept. A concept is highly dispersed if the lexical variants are scattered across geographical space in a heterogeneous way, without the formation of clear areas where a particular variant is used consistently, but rather with several variants used intermittently (an example can be found in Figure 10.5). Little dispersion occurs if homogeneous areas can be distinguished, as in Figure 10.6. Next to dispersion, geographical fragmentation is also influenced by the range (or surface) of a concept, because concepts for

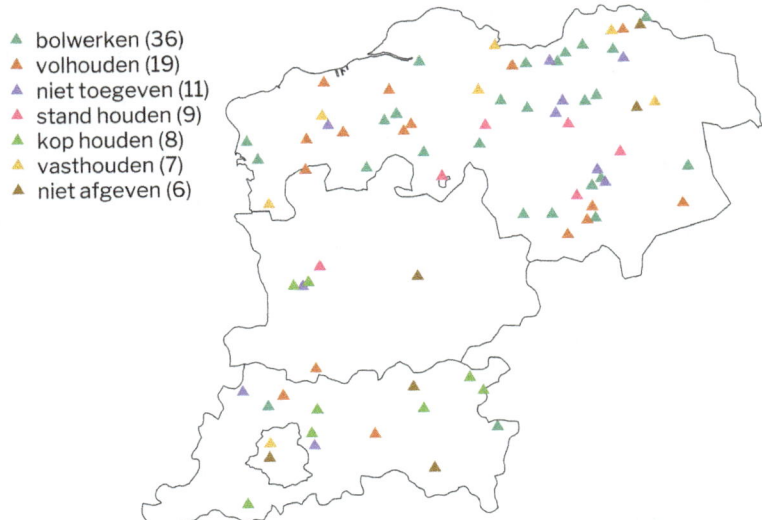

Figure 10.5: Geographical distribution of the lexical variants for IEMAND WEERSTAAN 'to resist someone' in the Brabantic data (only items that occur more than 5 times in the WBD are included; Franco et al. 2019b).

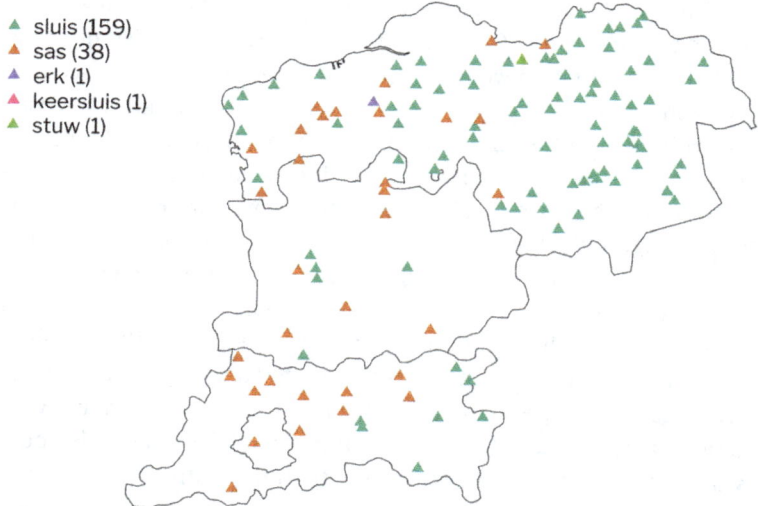

Figure 10.6: Geographical distribution of the lexical variants for SLUIS 'lock (in shipping)' in the Brabantic data (Franco et al. 2019b).

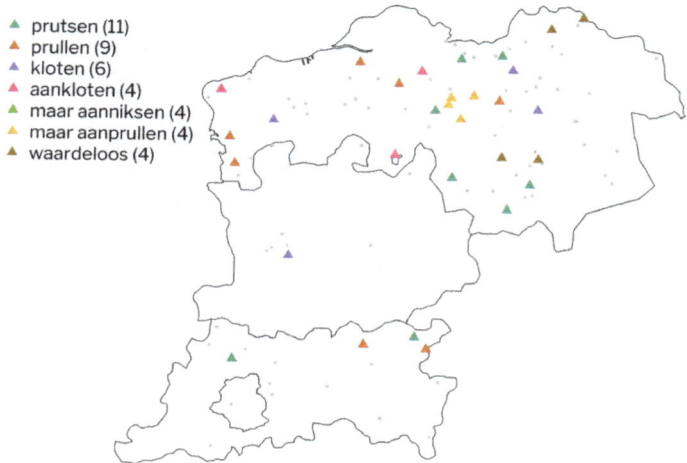

Figure 10.7: Geographical distribution of the lexical variants for NUTTELOZE ARBEID VERRICHTEN, NUTTELOOS WERK 'to mess about' in Brabant (Franco et al. 2019b). Only items that occur more than 3 times in the Brabantic data are plotted in colored symbols, but to show the total range of the concept, other locations for which data are available, are indicated in grey.

which the average surface covered by the variants is high, like in Figure 10.6, are spatially more homogenous than concepts with a lower geographical range. An example of a concept of the latter type is provided in Figure 10.7. To calculate the range per concept, we use the relationship between, on the one hand, the average geographical area spanned by the lexical items for the concept and, on the other hand, the total area where the concept occurs.

The composite variable, lexical geographical heterogeneity, is calculated by means of the following formula:

$$\text{lexical geographical heterogeneity} = \text{number of unique types} * \frac{\text{dispersion}}{\text{range}}$$

In the analysis, we use the natural logarithm of this variable, to account for its skewed distribution.

In this case-study as well, the aim was to test the prediction from the principle of efficient communication, that languages tend to avoid synonymy and homonymy and that this will be particularly prevalent for concepts with a high degree of salience for the language users. To determine the salience of the food and cooking concepts, we again use language-external data. Specifically, we rely on the frequency of each concept[7] on specialized recipe websites. These websites have the advantage that they aim to form a reflection of the type of foods consumed by the people consulting them (KVLV 2010: 3). The websites we used were those of *Ons Kookboek* (www.onskookboek.be), a highly popular cooking book in the northern part of Belgium, and *Dagelijkse Kost* (www.dagelijksekost.be), a popular cooking show that has been shown on the Flemish public network *Eén* daily since 2010.

There are two caveats that need to be mentioned with regard to the use of these websites. First, the recipes on both websites are published by producers from Belgium, but the dialect material also contains data from the province of North Brabant in the Netherlands. However, to as far as our knowledge, similar extra-linguistic systematic data from the Netherlands is not freely available. Second, both websites also contain dishes from today's culture, but the dialect material was collected in the second half of the 20th century (most of the data, 43%, for the semantic field food and cooking was collected in 1980). However, the fact that we only query the concepts available in the dictionary data alleviates this problem to some extent: products that have only recently been introduced and that have recently gained popularity will not have been presented in the dictionary. Furthermore, while the eating

---

[7] In practice, we searched the websites for the headword given in the dictionary, as well as any synonyms that occur in the standard variety of Dutch.

culture in Flanders has undergone changes since the second World War (Scholliers 1993), not many food products have disappeared. Instead, the Flemish kitchen has mostly become more diverse due to the increased industrialization and commercialization of the food industry.

To extract the frequency data from the recipe websites, we used site-restricted web searches on the Belgian version of Google (www.google.be). The validity of extracting data for linguistic research with this method has been shown by Grieve et al. (2013) en Asnaghi et al. (2014). In the analysis, we use the natural logarithm of the frequency information, to account for its skewed distribution. Because some concepts have a frequency of 0 on the cooking websites, which would cause their logarithmic transformation to be equal to negative infinity, we added a very small value (0.00001) to the absolute frequency of each concept before the logarithmic transformation.

Figure 10.8 shows the correlation between the log of the frequency of the concepts (on the x-axis) and the log of lexical diversity (on the y-axis). The Figure reveals two things. First, on the left-hand side of the Figure, quite a large number of

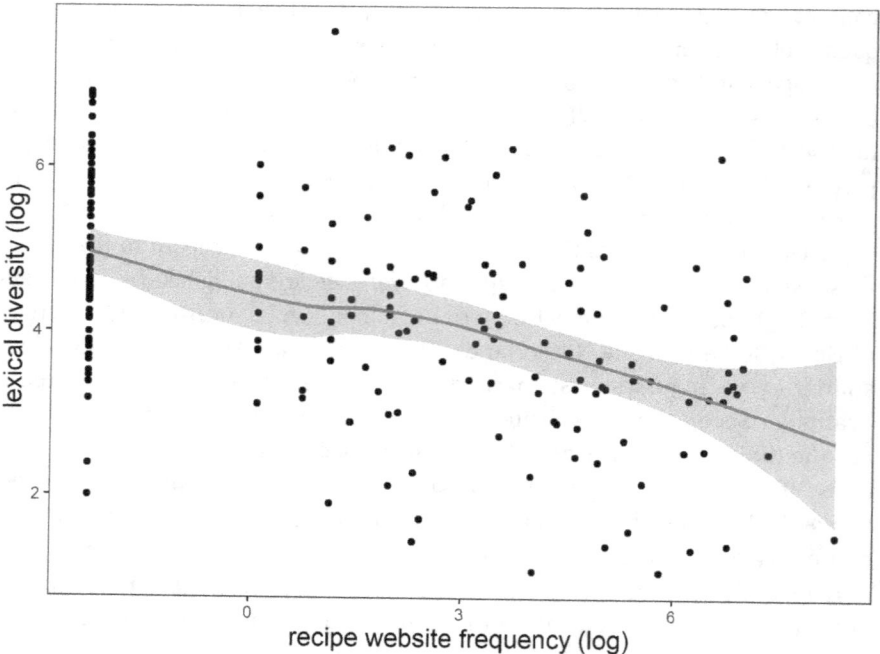

Figure 10.8: Scatterplot of recipe website frequency (log) and lexical diversity (log). The green line with error band shows a loess smooth.

concepts (N = 61) are shown that have a negative value on the x-axis (recipe website frequency). These are the concepts that have a frequency of 0 on the websites (which has become a negative value due to the logarithmic transformation). Second, the overall pattern confirms that a negative correlation can be found between cooking website frequency and lexical geographical fragmentation. This is also confirmed by the Spearman's correlation coefficient of -0.47 ($p < 0.001$).

As a next step, we investigate which concepts behave as expected given our hypothesis and which concepts do not. Figure 10.9 shows the same plot as Figure 10.8, but instead of point symbols, the concept names are plotted onto the plot area. In addition, the plot is divided into four quadrants, by plotting a dashed line at the average value of cooking website frequency on the x-axis and the average of lexical diversity on the y-axis.

From Figure 10.9, a number of conclusions can be drawn. First, the concepts in the first and fourth quadrant (top-left and bottom-right) are the concepts that confirm to the hypothesis the most. The concepts in the first quadrant have a high value for lexical diversity and a low cooking website frequency. In this quadrant, concepts like VLAAI MET REEPJES 'flan with strips of dough on top', DIKKE BOTERHAM 'thick slice of bread' and LENDENSTUK 'sirloin steak' are found. In the fourth quadrant, the concepts with the highest degree of salience and the lowest amount of lexical diversity are found. The concepts in this quadrant are mostly ingredients and basic preparations, such as SOEP 'soup', TIJM 'thyme', VENKEL 'fennel' and TAART 'pie'. Thus, for these concepts, we can conclude that the cooking website frequency measure does distinguish between concepts with a higher or lower degree of cultural relevance.

Second, it allows us to examine in more detail the concepts on the left-hand side of the Figure, with a negative value on the x-axis. It turns out that some of these concepts, like ROOMHOORN 'cream horn', GEROOKTE PANPALING 'smoked eel baked in a pan' and AARBEIENVLAAI 'strawberry flan', probably have a low frequency because their concept lemmas are rather descriptive or dialectal, without a clear single-word synonym in Standard Dutch. If these concepts do occur on the recipe websites, it is possible that the authors used a different description or a different multi-word expression or compound. A second group of negative value-concepts, such as NIKNAK 'a type of small biscuit, either in the form of letters, or with a piece of frozen sugar on top', BESCHUIT MET MUISJES 'rusk with aniseed comfits' and DROPWATER 'licorice water', are concepts related to folkloristic culture. *Niknakjes* are one of the typical kinds of candies that are eaten at Sinterklaas, the patron's saints day of Saint Nicholas, when children traditionally get gifts and candy. BESCHUIT MET MUISJES is another type of food-like candy that is eaten when a child is born in the Netherlands. DROPWATER is a type of drink that was created at home as a treat for children. It is also said to help for a cough.

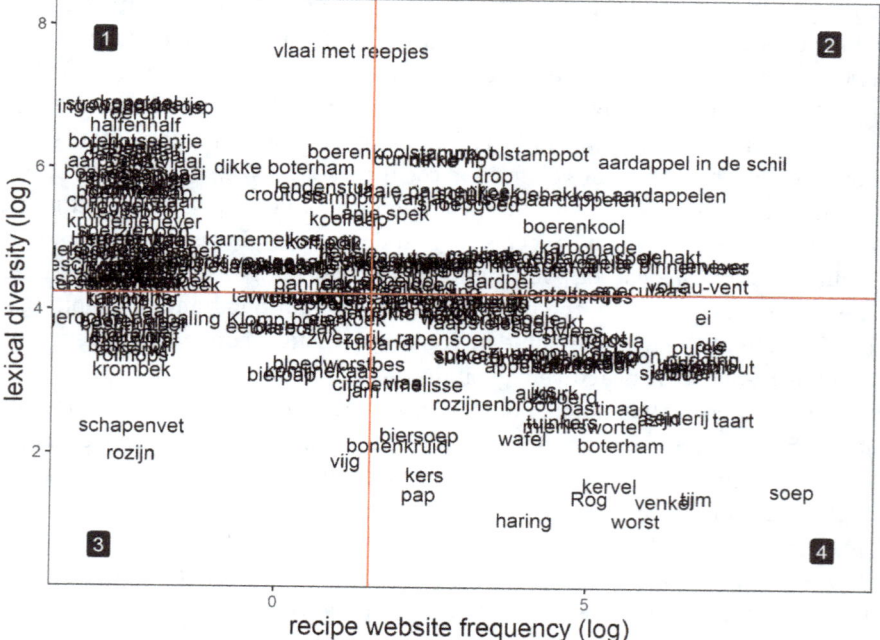

Figure 10.9: Scatterplot of recipe website frequency (log) and lexical diversity (log) with concept lemmas as plot symbols. Because many of the concepts in the dataset do not have a straightforward English translation, plotting translations makes the plot unreadable. Instead, an interactive version of this plot, which also shows English translations for the concepts is available in the supplementary materials.[8]

Third, in the second quadrant (top-right), the concepts with a relatively low value for lexical diversity but a high cooking website frequency are found. Inspecting the concepts contained in this quadrant reveals that there are quite a large number of preparations with potatoes such as AARDAPPEL IN DE SCHIL 'jacket potato', ZUURKOOLSTAMPPOT 'mashed potatoes with sauerkraut' en SCHIJFJES GEBAKKEN AARDAPPELEN 'slices of baked potatoes'. In addition, the second quadrant also contains a number of meat preparations. These two types of dishes reflect the traditional kitchen of the Low Countries, where potatoes and meat play a large role. Crucially, preparations of these dishes can, at least in the perception of the language users, show geographical patterns (e.g. there are dishes typically associated with particular cities like GENTSE WATERZOOI '(chicken) casserole from Ghent', or regions, like ASPERGES OP VLAAMSE WIJZE 'asparagus à la Flamand').

---

8 https://www.degruyter.com/document/isbn/9783110687156/html.

Perhaps these dishes contribute to local identity and, as a result, retain their local dialectal names. Furthermore, the quadrant also contains several types of candy such as DROP 'licorice', APPELBOL 'apple dumpling' and SPECULAAS 'spiced biscuit'. For these types of concepts, there are probably quite a number of children's words or jocular terms that increase their lexical diversity. For APPLE DUMPLING, for instance, the dictionary contains words like *kattenkop* (lit.: cat's head), *patoet* and *trollenbedol*.

Finally, in the third quadrant (bottom-left), relatively few concepts are found. One outlier in this quadrant is VIJG 'fig', a concept that is relatively infrequent on the cooking websites but that also shows little lexical geographical fragmentation. It is possible that the fig does not feature prominently on the recipe websites because it is mostly consumed as a snack rather than in the preparation of dishes. Another explanation for the low degree of lexical diversity in the concept FIG may be that the standard Dutch word, *vijg*, is relatively well-known for the dialect speakers because it also occurs with other meanings. According to the *Woordenboek der Nederlandsche Taal* 'Dictionary of the Dutch language', a large historical dictionary of Dutch, the word *vijg* is highly polysemous and often has a negative connotation in other meanings (e.g. as a jocular term for the droppings of donkeys and horses or as a term of abuse). In addition, it also occurs in a number of proverbs (e.g. *zo plat als een vijg* 'flat-chested (lit.: 'as flat as a fig')', *vijgen na Pasen* 'to be too late to be of any use (lit. 'figs after Easter')'). In short, the concept fig may show less variation than expected due to the influence of Standard Dutch, where the word *vijg* has a large range of usage contexts resulting in a high degree of entrenchment.

In this third and final case-study, we again analyzed whether more salient concepts show less lexical variation, a prediction based on the principle of efficient communication. Using dialectological data and visual analytics, we showcased that there is an inverse correlation between salience and lexical diversity, although many exceptions were found too (especially in quadrants 2 and 3).

5.4 Explaining the results

There may be three explanations for these divergent results. While the first explanation is of a practical nature, the second and third reason concern theory formation about the nature of salience and about the structure of the lexicon.

If an onomasiological perspective to the lexicon is taken and used to gauge frequency information, the data collected may be biased due to the fact that other synonyms than the ones that have been investigated, may occur in language. This problem was mentioned in particular for the concepts with descriptive or dialectal concept lemmas (such as GEROOKTE PANPALING 'smoked eel baked in a pan'). For these types of concepts, other descriptions may have been used by the recipe website editors. While a common solution for this problem is to investigate the complete onomasiological profile for a concept (Speelman et al. 2003), this solution is less straightforward when dialectal data or historical data is used (compare the problems with spelling variation when consulting historical corpora).

The second explanation for the results obtained is that they may simply be a result of the operationalization of the explanatory variable, salience, which was calculated as plant frequency in the northern part of Belgium and frequency on recipe websites. In essence, these measures gauge the experiential salience of the concepts under scrutiny (Geeraerts 2016, Franco & Geeraerts 2019), i.e. how often a language user comes into contact with a particular category in everyday life (e.g. by seeing it in their environment, or by buying it at the store or using it as an ingredient in cooking). In this sense, the measures rely on referential data, aimed at linking exemplars in the extra-linguistic world to linguistic knowledge (similar to Munsell charts in research on color coding, e.g. Kay et al. 2009, or the climate in a particular region, e.g. Regier et al. 2016). However, the salience of a concept is not solely influenced by how often language users encounter referents in their environment.

Instead, the salience of a concept is a multi-faceted phenomenon. For example, the low correlation coefficient for the plant names may be influenced by the fact that plants that are infrequent in a dialect area, may still have a high degree of salience due to folkloristic practices and beliefs. For example, the common club moss (Lycopodium clavatum), a poisonous plant that has become rare in the northern part of Belgium and that is categorized as 'endangered', may actually have a relatively high degree of salience due to its use since the Middle Ages in (homeopathic) medicinal preparations. An example of another dimension of salience can be found in the relatively low degree of variation in the names for the fig. This low degree was explained by the fact that the standard Dutch word *vijg*, which takes up a central position in the onomasiological profile for the concept, may be highly entrenched due to its many other meanings. Under this reasoning, the word itself would be highly entrenched due to its relatively high textual frequency and this semasiological entrenchment may then influence the (lack of) onomasiological variation.

The third explanation is that there are other factors that influence lexical diversity. More specifically, in previous studies, we showed that not only salience, but also other factors related to the prototypical structure of the lexicon affect lexical diversity (Franco et al. 2019b). One of these factors is also apparent in the third quadrant of the cooking terms. In this quadrant, next to meat and potato dishes, some candy concepts are located as well, such as DROP 'licorice', APPELBOL 'apple dumpling' and SPECULAAS 'spiced biscuit'. These types of concepts may have a high degree of lexical diversity, despite their relatively high degree of experiential salience, due to the fact that their positive connotations elicit expressivity in naming (e.g. through children's names). In standard languages as well, candy often gets creative and metaphorical names, such as Dutch *smoelentrekker* 'lit.: face puller', *bubble gum* or *bananarama*.

6 Concluding remarks and future perspectives

The focus of dialectology on distinguishing language areas does not necessarily coincide with the themes that play a central role in Cognitive Linguistics. Due to CL's commitment to studying language as a phenomenon that is firmly grounded in general cognitive capacities (Lakoff 1990), it has paid a lot of attention to how meaning is shaped and how this is reflected in the structure of language. Four characteristics of meaning are often mentioned: meaning is dynamic and flexible, perspectival, encyclopaedic and non-autonomous, and based on usage and experience (Geeraerts 2006). Therefore, the traditional focus has been on themes such as embodiment, polysemy, grammaticalization and construal phenomena, although the field has grown tremendously since the 1980s (see contributions in e.g. Geeraerts & Cuyckens 2007 and Dabrowska & Divjak 2015). However, there has only been limited convergence between Cognitive Linguistics and dialectology.

Nonetheless, there are several reasons why a convergence between the two fields may be beneficial for both. As exemplified in the first case-study, analyzing dialectological data may reveal factors that affect synchronic variation and diachronic change (also see the methods of comparative sociolinguistics, Tagliamonte 2012: 162–166). In this first case-study, a Cognitive Linguistics perspective to language was taken, where meaning has a central position. This view was then applied to research on classical concepts from sociolinguistics and language change (transmission and diffusion) using dialectological data. The aggregate quantitative visualization methodology that was used, analyzing a large set of concepts rather than a more limited set of linguistic variables, showed that processes of transmission and diffusion are influenced by the meaning that is expressed. Specifically, due to the socio-cultural background of a dialect community, some parts of the lexicon are more likely to be influenced by language contact.

These findings are relevant for Cognitive Linguistics because since the "social turn" (e.g. Dabrowska & Divjak 2015: 6), scholars have been increasingly integrating cognitive and social factors in their analysis of language. More specifically, in the last decades, many researchers have argued that Cognitive

Linguistics should incorporate lectal stratification, be it along a social, pragmatic, cultural or other axis (e.g. Geeraerts et al. 1994, Harder 2003, Croft 2009, Majid & Burenhult 2014, Dabrowksa 2015, Schmid 2016, as well as contributions in the field of Cognitive Sociolinguistics, e.g. Kristiansen & Dirven 2008, Geeraerts, Kristiansen & Peirsman 2010). Geeraerts (2005), for instance, shows that the need for this social or, more broadly, lectal dimension involves two aspects. First the usage-based nature of Cognitive Linguistics entails that the movement should take into account lectal variation for two reasons. On the one hand, any type of usage data is lectally stratified along some dimension (dialectal, sociolectal, ideolectal etc.). On the other hand, lectal differences reflect differences in meaning, in the sense that, for instance, *hammered* for the concept of BEING DRUNK is predominantly restricted to informal contexts, whereas *intoxicated* carries a more formal connotation. Dialectological data may offer a lot of insight into the importance of lectal differences due to its geographical structure.

Second, the social nature of language in turn implies that empirical methods should be used as language users cannot necessarily, on the basis of introspection, recall contextual variation due to the diasystemic nature of language. The nature of the dialectological datasets that have been collected in the last century fits in well with research projects that aim to examine the interaction between cognitive and lectal features, due to the fact that they consist of a large amount of naturalistic data that has been collected highly systematically (e.g. by distributing a questionnaire in many locations across a dialect area).

In addition, while the main aim of dialect geography has become to distinguish different varieties within a broader area, dialectologists have also offered explanations for the dialect areas that they find. Such explanations generally inquire into the ease of spatial diffusion of particular variants. They often focus on the importance of the interaction between geographical distance and language-external factors of a social or political nature, like mobility, population size, different types of language learning or the presence of a language border (Weinreich, Labov & Herzog 1968: 153–155, Chambers & Trudgill 1980: 196–204, Labov 2007, Britain 2011). Furthermore, differences between the structure of local communities or between the salience of local practices may cause variation within a particular domain of related concepts (also see Chambers & Trudgill 1980: 120–123), like in Weijnen's (1966: 337) work on the fisherman communities of Dutch (see 5.1).

As a result, findings from dialectology resemble some of the views that have gained a lot of popularity in contemporary linguistics. One example is the fact that frequency phenomena were already argued to play a role in Kloeke's work on lexical diffusion. However, traditional dialectology is generally a relatively theory-free approach to linguistics (Britain 2013, Watt 2018). In more recent approaches to dialectology, including in the closely related field of sociolinguistics, more attention has been paid to integrating dialect-geographical data with linguistic theory (e.g. Weinreich, Labov & Herzog 1968, Labov 1994–2010, Anderwald & Szmrecsanyi 2009, De Vogelaer & Seiler 2012), but dialectological work in CL is still relatively rare (exceptions include Swanenberg 2000, Berthele 2003, Speelman & Geeraerts 2008, Szelid & Geeraerts 2008, Geeraerts & Speelman 2010, Szmrecsanyi 2010, Grieve, Speelman & Geeraerts 2011, Franco et al. 2019a, b). Thus, an elaborate model of language and meaning may help to bring together the dialectological findings that have been obtained in the past.

This point was particularly emphasized in the second and third case-studies, which inquired into the effect of experiential salience on lexical diversity in dialect data. After re-interpreting the principle of communicative need from a CL perspective on lexical variation, one of its predictions for onomasiological research was put to the test on dialectological data. The case-studies confirm that the principle may explain the degree of lexical (geographical) diversity in dialect data to a large extent: concepts that are more salient for language users are more likely to be prone to synonymy avoidance. However, in both case-studies, exceptions were found as well, which shows that lexical variation is a multifaceted phenomenon and that speaker and situation related variables may play a role as well.

Turning to the main point of this chapter, with the case-studies outlined above we have tried to show that a convergence between the two field is beneficial for both. On the one hand, finding rapprochement with dialectology is useful for Cognitive Linguistics, because using dialectological data to examine research questions that are central to the study of languages has its own benefits. As De Vogelaer & Seiler (2012: 2) put it: "As compared to most cross-linguistic and diachronic data, dialect data are unusually high in resolution." More specifically, dialectological data have the benefit of not only showcasing temporal, but also spatial processes of language change. In addition, the availability of large-scale dialectological datasets offers an ideal site for the empirical study of language. Furthermore, ideas that take up a central role in dialectology may also provide novel insight into the structure of the linguistic system.

On the other hand, what does Cognitive Linguistics have to offer to dialectology? As already mentioned above, dialectology is often considered a relatively theory-free field of study. Although many of the explanations offered in this paper, were already discussed by dialectologists in the 20th century, they were sometimes examined as isolated, almost coincidental linguistic observations. The Cognitive Linguistics paradigms two benefits that may be useful for dialectology. First, its view on the lexicon and on meaning may offer an updated view on dialectological findings that were often grounded in a structuralist way of thinking (cf. fear of polysemy and homonymy/synonymy). In addition, the emphasis of Cognitive Linguistics on the use of naturalistic data (especially since the social turn), as well as the empirical approach that is employed, have resulted in a better understanding and availability of visual and statistical analysis techniques. By using these techniques, the extent to which classic dialectological findings influence processes of language variation and change may be examined in a systematic way.

References

Anderwald, Lieselotte & Benedikt Szmrecsanyi. 2009. Corpus linguistics and dialectology. In Anke Lüdeling & Merja Kytö (eds.), *Corpus linguistics. An international handbook*, 1126–1139. Berlin & New York: Mouton de Gruyter.

Asnaghi, Costanza, Dirk Speelman & Dirk Geeraerts. 2014. Geographical patterns of formality variation in written Standard California English. *Literary and Linguistic Computing 31*(2). 244–263.

Berthele, Raphael. 2003. The typology of motion and posture verbs: A variationist account. In: Bernd Kortmann (ed.), *Dialectology meets typology: Dialect grammar from a cross-linguistic perspective*, 93–126. Berlin & New York: De Gruyter Mouton.

Blancquaert, Edgar & Willem Pée (eds.). 1925–1982. *Reeks Nederlandse dialectatlassen (RND) [series of Dutch dialect atlases.]*. 16 volumes. Antwerp & Malle.

Bloomfield, Leonard. 1958 [1933]. *Language* (6th edition). London: George Allen & Unwin.

Boas, Franz. 1911. Introduction. In Franz Boas (ed.), *Handbook of American Indian Languages. Part 1*, 1–83. Washington: Government Printing Office.

Bolinger, Dwight. 1977. *Meaning and Form*. London/New York: Longman.

Britain, David. 2011. The heterogeneous homogenisation of dialects in England. *Taal & Tongval 63*(1). 43–60.

Britain, David. 2013 Space, diffusion and mobility. In J.K. Chambers & Natalie Schilling, *The handbook of language variation and change*, 471–500. Chichester: Wiley-Blackwell.

Chambers, J.K. & Peter Trudgill. 1980. *Dialectology*. Cambridge: Cambridge University Press.

Croft, William. 2009. Toward a social cognitive linguistics. In Vyvyan. Evans & Stéphanie Pourcel (eds.), *New Directions in Cognitive Linguistics*, 395–420. Amsterdam & Philadelphia: John Benjamins.

Dabrowska, Ewa. 2015. Individual differences in grammatical knowledge. In Ewa Dabrowska & Dagmar Divjak, *Handbook of Cognitive Linguistics*, 650–668. Berlin & Boston: De Gruyter Mouton.

Dabrowska, Ewa & Dagmar Divjak. 2015 *Handbook of Cognitive Linguistics*. Berlin & Boston: De Gruyter Mouton.

De Vogelaer, Gunther & Guido Seiler. 2012. The dialect laboratory: Introductory remarks. In Gunther De Vogelaer & Guido Seiler (eds.), *The dialect laboratory: Dialects as a testing ground for theories of language change*, 1–32. Amsterdam & Philadelphia: John Benjamins Publishing.

De Vriendt, Séra. 2004. *Brussel [Brussels]*. Tielt: Lannoo.

Franco, Karlien & Dirk Geeraerts. 2018. Om op te eten. Variatie in de lexicale diversiteit van voeding en voedselwaren [for eating. Variation in the lexical diversity of food]. In Timothy

Colleman, Johan De Caluwe, Veronique De Tier, Anne-Sophie Ghyselen, Liesbet Triest, Roxane Vandenberghe and Ulrike Vogl (eds.), *Woorden om te bewaren: Huldeboek voor Jacques Van Keymeulen [words to keep: Festschrift for Jacques Van Keymeulen]*, 219–232. Gent: Skribis.

Franco, Karlien & Dirk Geeraerts. 2019. Botany meets lexicology: The relationship between experiential salience and lexical diversity. In Janice Fon (ed.), *Dimensions of Diffusion and Diversity*, 113–146. Berlin: De Gruyter Mouton.

Franco, Karlien, Dirk Geeraerts, Dirk Speelman & Roeland Van Hout. 2019a. Maps, meanings and loanwords: The interaction of geography and semantics in lexical borrowing. *Journal of Linguistic Geography* 7(1). 14–32.

Franco Karlien, Dirk Geeraerts, Dirk Speelman & Roeland van Hout. 2019b. Concept characteristics and variation in lexical diversity in two Dutch dialect areas. *Cognitive Linguistics* 30(1). 205–242.

Geeraerts, Dirk. 1997. *Diachronic prototype semantics: A contribution to historical lexicology.* Oxford: Clarendon.

Geeraerts, Dirk. 2005. Lectal variation and empirical data in Cognitive Linguistics. In Francisco Ruiz de Mendoza Ibáñez & Sandra Peña Cervel (eds.), *Cognitive Linguistics. Internal dynamics and interdisciplinary interactions*, 163–189. Berlin & New York: Mouton de Gruyter.

Geeraerts, Dirk. 2006. *Cognitive Linguistics: Basic readings.* Berlin: De Gruyter Mouton.

Geeraerts, Dirk. 2010. *Theories of lexical semantics.* Oxford: Oxford University Press.

Geeraerts, Dirk. 2016. Entrenchment as onomasiological salience. In Hans-Jörg Schmid (ed.). *Entrenchment and the psychology of language learning. How we reorganize and adapt linguistic knowledge*, 153–174. Berlin & Boston: De Gruyter Mouton.

Geeraerts, Dirk & Hubert Cuyckens. 2007. *The Oxford handbook of Cognitive Linguistics.* Oxford: Oxford University Press.

Geeraerts, Dirk & Dirk Speelman. 2010. Heterodox concept features and onomasiological heterogeneity in dialects. In Dirk Geeraerts, Gitte Kristiansen & Yves Peirsman (eds.), *Advances in Cognitive Sociolinguistics*, 23–39. Berlin: De Gruyter Mouton.

Geeraerts, Dirk, Stefan Grondelaers & Peter Bakema. 1994. *The Structure of lexical variation: Meaning, naming, and context.* Berlin: De Gruyter Mouton.

Geeraerts, Dirk, Stefan Grondelaers & Dirk Speelman. 1999. *Convergentie en divergentie in de Nederlandse woordenschat: Een onderzoek naar kleding- en voetbaltermen [convergence and divergence in the Dutch lexicon. A study into clothing and soccer terminology].* Amsterdam: Meertens Institute.

Geeraerts, Dirk, Gitte Kristiansen & Yves Peirsman. 2010. *Advances in Cognitive Sociolinguistics.* Berlin: De Gruyter Mouton.

Gibson, Edward, Richard Futrell, Steven T. Piantadosi, Isabelle Dautriche, Kyle Mahowald, Leon Bergen, Roger Levy. 2019. How efficiency shapes human language. *Trends in Cognitive Sciences* 23(5). 389–407.

Givón, T. 1995. *Functionalism and Grammar.* Amsterdam & Philadelphia: John Benjamins.

Goebl, Hans. 1984. *Dialektometrische Studien. Anhand Italoromanischer, Rätoromanischer und Galloromanischer Sprachmaterialien aus AIS und ALF.* Tübingen: Niemeyer.

Goebl, Hans. 2010. Dialectology and quantitative mapping. In Alfred Lameli, Roland Kehrein & Stefan Rabanus, *Language and space. An international handbook of linguistic variation. Volume 2: Language mapping*, 433–457, 2201–2212. Berlin: De Gruyter Mouton.

Goossens, Jan. 1964. Enkel- en veeltoepasselijkheid van betekenaars op de taalkaart [single and multiple applicability of signifiers on the language map]. In *Taalgeografie en semantiek. Lezingen gehouden voor de dialectencommissie der Koninklijke Nederlandse Academie van Wetenschappen op 27 december 1962 door dr. J. Goossens en dr. Jan van Bakel* [language geography and semantics. Lectures held for the dialect committee of the Royal Dutch Academy of Sciences on 27 December 1962 by dr. J. Goossens and dr. Jan van Bakel], 3–27. Amsterdam: Noord-Hollandse uitgevers maatschappij.

Grieve, Jack, Dirk Speelman & Dirk Geeraerts. 2011. A statistical method for the identification and aggregation of regional linguistic variation. *Language Variation and Change* 23(2). 193–221.

Grieve, Jack, Costanza Asnaghi & Tom Ruette. 2013. Site-restricted web searches for data collection in regional dialectology. *American Speech* 88. 413–440.

Haiman, John. 1980. The iconicity of grammar: Isomorphism and motivation. *Language* 56(3). 515–540.

Harder, Peter. 2003. The status of linguistic facts: Rethinking the relation between cognition, social institution and utterance from a functional point of view. *Mind & Language* 18(1). 52–76.

Haspelmath, Martin. 1999. Optimality and diachronic adaptation. *Zeitschrift für Sprachwissenschaft* 18(2). 180–205.

Hastie, Trevor & Robert Tibshirani. 1986. Generalized additive models. *Statistical Science* 1(3). 297–318.

Heeringa, Wilbert. 2004. *Measuring dialect pronunciation differences using levenshtein distance*. Nijmegen: Radboud University doctoral dissertation.

Heylen, Kris, Thomas Wielfaert, Dirk Speelman & Dirk Geeraerts. 2015. Monitoring polysemy: Word space models as a tool for large-scale lexical semantic analysis. *Lingua* 157. 153–172.

Hoppenbrouwers, Cor & Geer Hoppenbrouwers. 2001. *De indeling van de Nederlandse streektalen: Dialecten van 156 steden en dorpen geklasseerd volgens de FFM*. Assen: Van Gorcum.

Karjus, Andres, Richard A. Blythe, Simon Kirby & Kenny Smith. 2020. Communicative need modulates competition in language change. *arXiv*, 2006.09277. Available at: https://arxiv.org/abs/2006.09277.

Kay, Paul, Brent Berlin, Luisa Maffi, William R. Merrifield & Richard S Cook. 2009. *The World Color Survey*. Stanford: CSLI.

Kemp, Charles, Yang Xu & Terry Regier. 2018. Semantic typology and efficient communication. *Annual Review of Linguistics* 4. 109–128.

Kemp, Charles, Alice Gaby & Terry Regier. 2019. Season naming and the local environment. In Ashok K. Goel, Colleen M. Seifert & Christian Freksa (eds.), *Proceedings of the 41st Annual Conference of the Cognitive Science Society*, 539–545. Montreal: Cognitive Science Society.

Kilgarriff, Adam. 1997. I don't believe in word senses. *Computers and the Humanities* 31(2). 91–113.

Kristiansen, Gitte & René Dirven. 2008. *Cognitive Sociolinguistics*. Berlin & New York: De Gruyter Mouton.

Kristiansen, Gitte, Karlien Franco, Stefano de Pascale, Laura Rosseel & Weiwei Zhang (eds.). 2021. *Cognitive Sociolinguistics revisited*. Berlin & Boston: De Gruyter.

Kruijsen, Joep. 1996. De Nijmeegse dialectlexicografische projecten [The dialect-lexicographical projects of Nijmegen]. *Trefwoord 11*. 93–107.
KVLV. 2010. *Ons Kookboek* [our cook book]. s.l.: KVLV.
Labov, William. 1969. Contraction, deletion and inherent variability of the English copula. *Language* 45(4). 715–762.
Labov, William. 2007. Transmission and diffusion. *Language* 83(2). 344–387.
Labov, William. 1994–2010. *Principles of linguistic change. Vol. 1: Internal factors. Vol. 2: Social factors. Vol. 3: Cognitive and cultural factors.* Oxford & Chichester: Wiley-Blackwell.
Lakoff, George. 1990. The invariance hypothesis. *Cognitive Linguistics* 1(1). 39–74.
Mahowald, Kyle, Evelina Fedorenko, Steven T. Piantadosi & Edward Gibson. 2013. Info/information theory: Speakers choose shorter words in predictive contexts. *Cognition* 126(2). 313–318.
Majid, Asifa & Niclas Burenhult. 2014. Odors are expressible in language, as long as you speak the right language. *Cognition* 130(2). 266–270.
Nerbonne, John & William Kretzschmar. 2003. Introducing computational techniques in dialectometry. *Computers and the Humanities* 37(3). 245–255.
Onysko, Alexander & Esme Winter-Froemel. 2011. Necessary loans – luxury loans? Exploring the pragmatic dimension of borrowing. *Journal of Pragmatics* 43(6). 1550–1567.
Piantadosi, Steven T., Harry Tily & Edward Gibson. 2011. Word lengths are optimized for efficient communication. *PNAS* 108(9). 3526–3529.
Pickl, Simon. 2013. Lexical meaning and spatial distribution. Evidence from geostatistical dialectometry. *Literary and Linguistic Computing* 28(1). 63–81.
Preston, Dennis R. 1999. Introduction. In Dennis R. Preston, *Handbook of perceptual dialectology*. Volume 1, xxiii–xl. Amsterdam: Benjamins.
Pullum, Geoffrey K. 1989. The great Eskimo vocabulary hoax. *Natural Language and Linguistic Theory*. 275–281.
Regier, Terry, Alexandra Carstensen & Charles Kemp. 2016. Languages support efficient communication about the environment: Words for snow revisited. *PLoS ONE* 11(4). e0151138.
Rosch, Eleanor. 1978. Principles of categorization. In Eleanor Rosch & Barbara B. Lloyd (eds.), *Cognition and categorization*, 27–48. New York: Wiley.
Rosch, Eleanor. 1987. Linguistic relativity. *ETC: A Review of General Semantics* 44(3). 254–279.
Rumpf, Jonas, Simon Pickl, Stephan Elspass, Werner König & Volker Schmidt. 2009. Structural analysis of dialect maps using methods from spatial statistics. *Zeitschrift für Dialektologie und Linguistik* 76(3). 280–308.
Rumpf, Jonas, Simon Pickl, Stephan Elspass, Werner König & Volker Schmidt. 2010. Quantification and statistical analysis of structural similarities in dialectological area-class maps. *Dialectologia Et Geolinguistica* 18. 73–100.
Schmid, Hans-Jörg. 2016. Why Cognitive Linguistics must embrace the social and pragmatic dimensions of language and how it could do so more seriously. *Cognitive Linguistics* 27(4). 543–557.
Scholliers, Peter. 1993. *Arm en rijk aan tafel: Tweehonderd jaar eetcultuur in België*. Berchem: EPO.
Séguy, Jean. 1971. La relation entre la distance spatiale et la distance lexicale. *Revue de Linguistique Romane* 35. 335–357.

Speelman, Dirk & Dirk Geeraerts. 2008. The role of concept characteristics in lexical dialectometry. *International Journal of Humanities and Arts Computing* 2(1–2). 221–242.

Speelman, Dirk, Stefan Grondelaers & Dirk Geeraerts. 2003. Profile-based linguistic uniformity as a generic method for comparing language varieties. *Computers and the Humanities* 37(3). 317–37.

Swanenberg, Jos. 2000. *Lexicale variatie cognitief-semantisch benaderd: Over het benoemen van vogels in Zuid-Nederlandse dialecten*. Nijmegen: Radboud University doctoral dissertation.

Szelid, Veronika & Dirk Geeraerts. 2008. Usage-based dialectology. Emotion concepts in the Southern Csango dialect. *Annual Review of Cognitive Linguistics* 6. 23–49.

Szmrecsanyi, Benedikt. 2008. Corpus-based dialectometry: Aggregate morphosyntactic variability in British English dialects. *International Journal of Humanities and Arts Computing* 2(1–2). 279–296.

Szmrecsanyi, Benedikt. 2010. The English genitive alternation in a cognitive sociolinguistics perspective. In Dirk Geeraerts, Gitte Kristiansen & Yves Peirsman, *Advances in Cognitive Sociolinguistics*, 141–166. Berlin: De Gruyter Mouton.

Tadmor, Uri. 2009. Loanwords in the world's languages: Findings and results. In Martin Haspelmath & Uri Tadmor. *Loanwords in the World's Languages*, 55–75. Berlin & Boston: De Gruyter Mouton.

Tagliamonte, Sali A. 2008. So different and pretty cool! Recycling intensifiers in Toronto, Canada. *English Language and Linguistics* 12(2). 361–394.

Tagliamonte, Sali A. 2012. *Variationist Sociolinguistics. Change, Observation, Interpretation*. Chichester: Wiley-Blackwell.

Tamminga, Meredith, Christopher Ahern & Aaron Ecay. 2016. Generalized Additive Mixed Models for intraspeaker variation. *Linguistics Vanguard* 2(s1). 000010151520160030.

Tomaschek, Fabian, Benjamin V. Tucker, Matteo Fasiolo & R. Harald Baayen. 2018. Practice makes perfect: The consequences of lexical proficiency for articulation. *Linguistics Vanguard* 4(s2). 20170018.

Trudgill, Peter. 1974. Linguistic change and diffusion: Description and explanation in sociolinguistic dialect geography. *Language in Society* 3(2). 215–246.

Van der Sijs, Nicoline. 2005. *Groot Leenwoordenboek [large loanword dictionary]*. Utrecht: Van Dale Lexicografie.

Van Landuyt, Wouter, Ivan Hoste, Leo Vanhecke, Paul Van den Bremt, Ward Vercruysse & Dirk De Beer. 2006. *Atlas van de Flora van Vlaanderen en het Brussels Gewest [atlas of the flora in Flanders and Brussels]*. Brussels: Research Institute for Nature and Forest, National Botanic Garden of Belgium & Flo.Wer.

Watt, Dominic. 2018. Section 1 – Theory. Introduction. In Charles Boberg, John Nerbonne & Dominic Watt, *The Handbook of Dialectology*, 17–21. Hoboken & New Jersey: Wiley Blackwell.

Weinreich, Uriel, William Labov & Marvin L. Herzog. 1968. A theory of language change. In Winfred P. Lehmann & Yakov Malkiel, *Directions for historical linguistics. A symposium*, 97–195. Austin & London: University of Texas Press.

Weijnen, Antonius. 1946. De grenzen tussen de Oost-Noord-Brabantse dialecten onderling [the mutual border between the East-North Brabantic dialects]. In *Oost-Noord-Brabantse dialectproblemen. Lezingen gehouden voor de dialectencommissie der Koninklijke Nederlandse Akademie van Wetenschappen op 12 april 1944.* [East-North Brabantic dialect problems. Lectures held for the dialect committee of the Royal Dutch Academy of

Sciences on 12 April 1944], 1–17. Amsterdam: Noord-Hollandsche Uitgeverij Maatschappij.

Weijnen, Antonius. 1966. *Nederlandse Dialectkunde [Dutch dialectology]*. Assen: Van Gorcum.

Weijnen, Antonius, Jan Goossens & P. Goossens. 1983. Inleiding. In Antonius Weijnen, Jan Goossens. & P. Goossens (eds.), *Woordenboek van de Limburgse dialecten: Inleiding & I. Agrarische terminologie, Aflevering 1: Akker- en weidegrond [dictionary of the Limburgish dialects: Introduction & I. Agrarian terminology. Volume 1: Field and meadow]*, 1–77. Assen: Van Gorcum.

Whorf, Benjamin L. 1964. Science and linguistics. In John B. Carroll (ed.), *Language, thought, and reality: Selected writings of Benjamin Lee Whorf*, 207–219. Cambridge: MIT Press.

Wieling, Martijn. 2012. *A quantitative approach to social and geographical dialect variation*. Groningen: University of Groningen doctoral dissertation.

Wieling, Martijn. 2018. Analyzing dynamic phonetic data using generalized additive mixed modeling: A tutorial focusing on articulatory differences between L1 and L2 speakers of English. *Journal of Phonetics 70*. 86–116.

Wieling, Martijn, John Nerbonne & R. Harald Baayen. 2011. Quantitative social dialectology: Explaining linguistic variation geographically and socially. *PLoS ONE 6*(9). E23613.

Wood, Simon. 2017. *Generalized additive models. An introduction with R (2nd edition)*. Boca Raton: Taylor & Francis.

Zuur, Alain F., Elena N. Ieno, Neil J. Walker, Anatoly A. Saveliev & Graham M. Smith. 2009. *Mixed effects models and extensions in ecology with R*. New York: Springer.

Zipf, George K. 1949. *Human behavior and the principle of least effort. An introduction to human ecology*. Cambridge: Addison-Wesley Press.

Index

Advertising 169, 172, 173, 178, 180, 191, 192
Autocorrelation 50, 52–57, 60, 61, 67, 327

Bootstrapping 67, 83, 89, 90, 95
Bottom-up designs 6

Causatives
– Analytic causatives 138, 140
– Lexical causatives 138
– Morphological causatives 138
Cluster analysis 15, 35, 37–39 See also Clustering 1, 37, 105, 108, 230, 239
See also Clustering Analysis 112
Computational experiment 273, 286, 291, 293, 298
Context features 107, 109–111, 114
Conditional inference tree 137, 141, 149, 150, 151, 153, 154, 156, 158, 160, 161, 162
Construction 5, 7–9, 109, 110, 137–141, 146, 149, 153, 155, 158, 160–163, 186–187, 259, 273–284, 286, 298–300, 302, 303–304, 310
Corpora
– Digital corpora 274, 288, 291, 293, 294, 296, 298, 303
– Geo-referenced corpora 289

Data analytics 1–9, 13, 14, 50, 51, 62, 129, 160, 163, 173, 178, 179, 182, 191, 192
Dialectology 9, 33, 273, 275, 290, 298–302, 309–311, 317, 335–337
Diffusion 9, 310, 315, 316, 318–320, 335, 336
Domain knowledge 1, 20, 25, 34

Emergence 275, 276, 279, 286
Explicatures 180, 186, 187
Exposure 84, 87, 221, 273, 275, 279, 291

Forecasting 50, 57, 59, 63, 68, 69 See also Prediction
Factor analysis
– Confirmatory factor analysis 79, 88
– Exploratory factor analysis 15, 35, 36, 37, 38

Goodness-of-fit indices 81, 91–93, 96

Implicatures 180, 186, 187
(In)direct causation hypothesis 139–141, 161, 162
Interactions 25, 27, 149, 151, 155, 156, 162, 175, 180, 181, 186, 190, 198, 222
Introspection 4, 13, 141, 199, 222, 274, 277, 279, 336

Lectal variation 8, 138–141, 151, 162, 163, 336
Lexical diversity 323–326, 330–333, 335, 337
Lexical semantics 5, 103, 104, 107, 109, 112, 114, 129, 321, 322
Lexical variation 9, 309, 310, 311, 312, 314, 333, 337
Language and linguistics
– Cognitive sociolinguistics 300, 314, 336
– Corpus linguistics 19, 29, 30, 35, 37, 40, 239
– Dutch 6, 8, 9, 103, 105, 106, 112, 127–129, 139–141, 161, 163, 310, 311–315, 319, 320, 322, 331, 333–336
– Mandarin Chinese (Mainland China, Taiwan, Singapore) 6, 212
– Language style 9, 229, 235, 268, 270
– Linguistic diversity 292, 294, 295, 296, 297

Machine learning
– Supervised 9, 230, 231, 233, 235, 265–270, 275, 299
– Unsupervised 9, 230, 231, 233, 235, 239, 265, 269, 270, 274, 278, 279
MCA 179, 182, 183, 185
Metaphor
– Metaphor analysis 198, 223
– Metaphor identification 9, 175, 201, 203, 208, 236
– Metaphor usage patterns 199, 210, 219, 223
– Personification metaphors 8, 170, 171, 173, 174, 176, 177, 182–189, 191
Models
– ARIMA models 7, 59, 62

- Linear models 9, 15, 21, 22, 24, 25, 27–29, 33, 39, 40, 317
- Linear mixed effect / multilevel models 21, 30
- Gaussian mixture model 35, 37
- Generalized additive models 9, 21, 33, 317
- Generalized linear models 9, 21, 27, 28, 29, 31, 33
- Vector space models 7, 104, 105, 107, 109, 114, 115, 116, 127, 129

Methods
- Box-Jenkins method 7, 50
- Empirical methods 5, 314, 336
- Introspective methods 5
- Tree-based methods 8, 137, 149, 150, 151, 163

Modification indices 82, 97, 98, 99
Multimodal 1, 170, 173, 175, 178–180

Natural Language Processing 3, 9, 229, 235

Onomasiological 104, 128, 140, 312–315, 321–323, 325, 333, 334, 337

Polysemy 7, 8, 103, 107, 129, 321, 335, 337
Prediction 23, 24, 52, 62, 63, 65–69, 150, 153, 156, 160, 230, 267, 268, 273–275, 290, 291, 298, 300, 301, 303, 304, 321, 323, 329, 333, 337 See also Forecasting
Principle of No Synonymy 139
Product types
- Experience products 174, 183, 184, 188, 191
- Search products 174, 182–184, 188, 189, 191

Psychological trauma 8, 197
Psychometric data 8, 199, 200, 201
Psychotherapy 7, 50, 56, 57, 64, 67, 69, 71, 199, 204, 214

Random effect 30, 31, 33 See also Models, Linear mixed effect.
Random forest 8, 15, 39, 40, 137, 141, 144, 149–151, 153, 156, 160, 162
Replication crisis 14–16, 20
Reproducible research 14, 15, 17 See Reproducibility 7, 15, 17, 18

Regression
- Logistic regression 8, 15, 21, 28, 29, 31, 33, 137, 139, 141, 149, 151, 153, 156, 158, 160, 162, 163
- Multinomial logistic regression 28, 137, 141, 151, 153, 156, 158, 160, 162
- Multiple regression 21, 24, 28, 29, 31, 77, 82, 100, 200, 209, 217–219
- Poisson regression 15, 21, 28, 29, 31, 33

Salience 104, 180, 212, 309, 321–323, 325, 326, 329, 331, 333–335, 337
SASRQ 199, 202, 209, 219–221
Significance tests 19, 20, 29, 31, 33, 89
Slot-constraint 275, 276, 277, 278, 281, 282, 283, 284, 286
spaCy 235, 250, 251, 259
Statistical thinking 2
Subject-level analysis 200, 209, 217, 222, 223

Time series. 7, 33, 49, 50, 54, 55, 59, 61, 62, 66, 67, 69, 71 See also Models, ARIMA models
Token-based 105
Training and validation 63
Transmission 9, 310, 315, 316, 320, 335
Trauma 8, 197–202, 204, 205, 207–209, 211, 214, 216–223

Usage-based
- Usage-based grammar 273–276, 280, 285, 286, 298, 303, 304

Validity
- Convergent validity 80, 81, 87, 92
- Discriminant validity 80–82, 91–93
Variables
- Endogenous variables 79
- Latent variables 33, 77, 78, 79, 80, 86, 89, 91, 94, 98, 100
- Observed variables 77, 80
Vectorization 237, 240
Visual analytics 8, 103, 107, 112, 114, 115, 129

www.ingramcontent.com/pod-product-compliance
Lightning Source LLC
Chambersburg PA
CBHW070749230426
43665CB00017B/2305